OHIO VALLEY RACE TYPES.

OHIO VALLEY GENEALOGIES

RELATING CHIEFLY TO FAMILIES IN HARRISON, BELMONT
AND JEFFERSON COUNTIES, OHIO, AND WASHING-
TON, WESTMORELAND, AND FAYETTE
COUNTIES, PENNSYLVANIA

BY

CHARLES A. HANNA

Originally published: New York, 1900
Reprinted: Genealogical Publishing Co., Inc.
1001 N. Calvert St., Baltimore, Md. 21202
1968, 1972, 1989, 1998
Library of Congress Catalogue Card Number 68-18633
International Standard Book Number 0-8063-0167-8
Made in the United States of America

OHIO VALLEY GENEALOGIES

INTRODUCTION

There is, perhaps, no one subject taught in our schools and institutions of learning to-day on which more misinformation has been imparted to the students than that of American history; and probably there is no part of that subject concerning which American people are more in ignorance than the part relating to their own racial origin.

Good Americans, generally, approved of the spirit of Mark Twain's rejoinder to Max O'Rell, when, in the course of a recent international exchange of compliments between the French and the Missouri humorists, the latter, to the charge that the average American did not usually know the name of his own grandfather, allowed that such might be the truth; but thought that Brother Jonathan was more apt to be sure of the name of his own father than were some others. The oft-repeated story of the observation made by a successful American gentleman traveling in Europe, who, when shown by an English lord the pictures of the latter's illustrious ancestors for some hundreds of years back, admitted that he had nothing of the kind at his home in America, because he was an illustrious ancestor himself,—is a characteristic illustration of the spirit in which, until quite recently, matters of race and family history have generally been regarded by the busy American workers of the present day.

Nevertheless, there is one class of our fellow citizens which has never been negligent in preserving the traditions and histories of their fathers; and never backward in letting America and the world at large know all about their merits and accomplishments. These are the people of New England—a people who, from the time of their first settlement in America, have preserved written records of most of their communities, and of almost every member living in and making a part of those communities; so that, as a consequence, there are few persons of New England descent living in the United States to-day, but who can find pages and volumes of history and eulogy in print as perpetual monuments to the virtues of one or several of their more or less remote progenitors.

Another and much more important consequence of this habit of committing to writing the history of men and communities in New England, is, that nearly all of our so-called histories of America have been written by New England men, are based chiefly upon New England records and examples, and have necessarily had to pass over in silence, or in a cursory way, the history of these other portions of our country and our citizens, of whom none of these written records have been preserved.

It is not strange, therefore, that in most of our schools to-day and, I venture to say, in the public schools of eastern Ohio, American history is taught chiefly from books written by New England men, or their descendants; is viewed in these books from the conventional New England stand-point; and is based largely upon New England traditions, prejudices, and, in some cases, misrepresentations.

The chief misrepresentation to which attention may be called at this time, is the one so repeatedly made in certain of the newspapers and reviews, and by certain orators, and after-dinner speakers, that all the progress made by America since it was first colonized, and all the glorious history of which Americans are so proud, has been made because its people are of the Anglo-Saxon race, and in their progress are only continuing in the new world what their English forefathers had begun in the old.

Now, as a matter of fact, no such thing is the case. And while there should be no just praise withheld from the descendants of Englishmen for what their forefathers have done for America, it would be as great a wrong to them if we were to say that they had done nothing whatever, as it is to other Americans, of non-English origin, for the descendants of Englishmen to claim that the English have done it all.

How can these claims that the great men of American history are of exclusively English origin be considered in face of the fact that, of Washington's hundred generals, more or less, not half of them were of English blood; or, that of the great generals of the civil war on both sides, but little more than one-third were of English extraction; or, that of our twenty-four presidents, less than half the number have been of that stock; or, that of our great editors, three-fourths have been non-English in origin; or, that of our great judges, less than half have been English; or, that of American inventors of world-wide fame, about three out of every four have been of another race than English; or, that of the great leaders in the National congress, not half of them have been English by descent; or, that in our population to-day, nearly one-half are of other races than English. Yet these facts are all capable of ready demonstration, and can be verified by any one who will take the trouble to consult any standard biographical and statistical dictionary.

In the State of Ohio, for instance, if the English are to have the sole credit for all the good that has come to America, what would become of the fame of Arthur St. Clair, of Jeremiah Morrow, of Allen Trimble, of Duncan McArthur, of Joseph Vance, of Wilson Shannon, of Mordecai Bartley, of Reuben Wood, of Rutherford B. Hayes, of Seabury Ford, of William Medill, of James E. Campbell, of Thomas L. Young, of Joseph B. Foraker, of Charles Foster, of William McKinley, and of some few others who have been governors of the State? Or, of Presidents Grant, Hayes, Garfield, and McKinley? Or, of certain supreme court judges, such as Jacob Burnet, John McLean, Joseph R. Swan, John C. Wright, Thomas W. Bartley, W. B. Caldwell, William Kennon, Hocking H. Hunter, George W. McIlvaine, W. J. Gilmore, Rufus P. Ranney, Josiah Scott, John Clark, W. W. Johnson, and John H. Doyle? Or, of certain well-known journalists, such as Whitelaw Reid, W. L. Brown, John A. Cockerill, Joseph Medill, Samuel Medary, W. W. Armstrong, the Farans and McLeans, and Richard Smith? Or, of Bishop Simpson, of John A. Bingham, and of Salmon P. Chase? Or, of William Dean Howells and of John Q. A. Ward? Or, of Generals U. S. Grant, Phil Sheridan, Quincy A. Gilmore, James B. Steadman, Irvin McDowell, John Beatty, O. M. Mitchell, James B. McPherson, Henry W. Lawton, and the fighting families of the McCooks?

No, the truth of the matter is, that a vast proportion of American people, sometimes classed by the historians as British, have had their hard-earned laurels transferred to the brows of the so-called Anglo-Saxons, or English; and very much of the honor and glory which are so frequently claimed for the English in this country, really belong to the people of another, and a distinctly different race.

These people are the Scotch-Irish, as they have come to be called, who have done vastly more in the settlement and development of the central and southern portions of our country than the English, and yet a people who have been too busy making history to spare the time to write it; and one whose early annals, for this reason, have been, until recent years, so far neglected as to be well-nigh forgotten. This is the race to which belong, with the exception of those of Howells, Garfield, and Sheridan, probably all of the names given above; and to that and the German race, also, belong, it is safe to say, at least seventy-five per cent. of the sturdy farmers and substantial citizens of eastern Ohio.

It is needless to ask in addition, therefore, what would become of the fair name and fame of the Buckeye State, if the English were the only people who have made America what it is to-day.

Nevertheless, the Scotch-Irish communities and people of the Central States, as a rule, have few traditions or remembered history back of the time when settlements were first begun there, in the early years of the present century. These people know in a general way that their respective fathers or grandfathers came from the East—from Pennsylvania usually—and in most cases from the territory originally included in the counties of Washington, Westmoreland, Cumberland, York, or Chester. The majority of them know that they are of Scotch-Irish descent; without understanding clearly what that term, in its American sense, signifies, some having the impression that it means the descendants of a married couple, of whom one parent is Scotch, and the other Irish. It may be that this feeling of belonging to a mixed nationality deters them from making any inquiries as to what are the real sources of the Scotch-Irish blood.

If the facts are ascertained, however, they will find that they have a race history than which no other nation or people can boast one more proud, whether it be English or German, Roman or Castillian. The Scotch-Irish are not, nor have they ever been, of Irish blood—using the latter word in its racial sense; but are purely Scottish. Their emigrant ancestors in this country, to whom the name was first applied, were people of unmixed Scotch descent, who came to America from their Scottish communities in the North of Ireland; and all the glorious history and ancestral traditions of their Scottish forefathers belong to their descendants in the United States to-day, just as much as the history and ancestral traditions of the English belong to people of early New England stock.

And, truly, it is a noble heritage, and one that will not suffer a whit by comparison with that of the English. It begins in the time of Agricola, the Roman general, who, when he had conquered all the present territory of England, and carried his victorious banners north to the Grampian hills in Scotland, found there a foe who could effectually hinder his further advance, and cause him for the first time to acknowledge that here was at last an unknown and unconquerable race beyond his own conquered ULTIMA THULE. It continues in the plundering forays and invasions of the Scots and Picts, who carried their dreaded arms from one end of the island to the other, unchecked; and, later, in the piratical incursions of the Vikings, who came westward from their safe retreats within the Norwegian fiords, to fight, to plunder, to destroy, and eventually to settle, among the sea-girt islands and peninsulas of western Scotland. Its dark and bloody deeds are instanced by the tragic history of Macbeth; and its bright and chivalrous actions are shown by incidents like that of the Battle of Otterburn, so spiritedly set forth in the glowing pages of Froissart, who says of it, that "of all the battles that have been described in my history, great and small, this was the best fought, and the most severe." Scotland's early glory came in the days of William Wallace and Robert Bruce, when its independence was won from the English by the sword; and continued through the two centuries following, because kept fresh by the blood of opposing Scots and English shed on more than two hundred battlefields. Its high ideal of freedom was realized first in the days of Knox and of Melville, when those men bid defiance to tyrants, and dared declare that rulers were amenable to law, and could be punished by law; and was again vindicated in the days of their successors, the Scots clergy, who, "when the light grew dim, and flickered on the altar, . . . trimmed the lamp, and fed the sacred flame," and kept alive for themselves, for their children, and for all mankind, the precious heritage of human liberty.

The Scotsman is of composite race. The forefathers of three-fourths of the Scotch-Irish in the United States lived in the western Lowlands of Scotland, and their blood was of various strains, blended into what finally became that of the Scottish race. The basis of the race was the Romanized Briton (and from this line the Lowland Scot gets his Celtic blood, and not from Ireland), with more or less marked departures, occasioned by intermarriages, first with the Picts and Scots, then with the Angles, the Danes, and the Norsemen. From the last-named stock comes most of the Teutonic blood of the western Scot; while the Angles occupied and largely peopled the east coast. After the eleventh century, the Normans came into Scotland in large numbers, and occupied much of the land; so that many families can claim Norman descent. Long before the seventeenth century, when the emigration to Ireland began, the various race groups had become fused into one composite whole, having the attributes of the Celt, the Norse, the Angle, and the Norman; thus typifying many centuries ago the identical race which we are beginning to recognize here as the American—a combination of the Teuton and the Celt. Let us hope the type may include all the virtues of both without the defects of either.

The real history of the forefathers of that part of the American people who live in eastern Ohio, therefore—with a few individual exceptions—is not to be found in the pages of the historians and writers of England; but of those of Scotland. Their lives and spirits have been not unworthily portrayed by the wizard hand of Scott, and their joys and sorrows have been divinely sung in the inspired notes of Burns. And it is in the heart-touching stories of MacLaren, and Barrie, and Stevenson, that we find the true prototypes and the doubles of ourselves and our friends in Ohio.

The history of Scotland as a country, and of Scottish men and institutions, however, is as a sealed book to ninety-nine out of every hundred students in most of our high-schools and colleges; and it is partly because of the entire absence of any information to the contrary in the ordinary historical text-books, that the erroneous impression has gained ground in so many places outside of New England, that our American colonies and American institutions are almost entirely of English origin.

Now, to bring the matter nearer home to the readers of this sketch, let us take a few of the family names that are so well known in the Ohio Valley, and see how many of them are English, and how many are Scotch.

In 1898, Mr. Orville Dewey contributed some interesting articles to the Cadiz Republican, giving an account of the early history of his own family, and from this we learn that the Deweys came from Connecticut. They were English, although there were many of the early Scotch-Irish who settled in New England. The Hollingsworths were originally Pennsylvania Quakers, tracing back through the North of Ireland to England. The Browns were also English; likewise, the Scotts, Arnolds, Laceys, Hearns, Woods, and others. But the early representatives of nearly all of these families having intermarried with the eastern Ohio Scotch-Irish, their descendants living there to-day are more Scotch than English. Other originally English families from the North of Ireland may be mentioned, of whom were the Hammonds, the Phillipses, and the Haverfields; but their forefathers lived and intermarried amongst the Scotch for so long a time before coming to America that their descendants in Harrison county to-day can hardly be said to retain more than a trace of the English blood, or traits, or anything else English but the names.

The Cunningham family originated in the district of Cunningham, in Ayrshire; as did likewise the Carrick and Kyle families in the other two districts of that county.

Other Ayrshire family names represented in eastern Ohio are those of Aiken, Alexander, Allison, Anderson, Barclay, Blair, Boggs, Boyd, Caldwell, Cannon, Clark, Cochran, Collins, Coulter, Crawford, Culbertson, Dunlap, Ervin, Ferguson, Fullerton, Fulton, Hamilton, Hunter, Jackson, Jamison, Kennedy, Logan, McCready, Mitchell, Montgomery, Moore, Morrison, Patton, Porter, Rankin, Rea, Richey, Rogers, Simpson, Thompson, Vance, Wallace, Watson, Welch, Wiley, Wilson, and a great many more besides.

The McFaddens are first mentioned in history in connection with their residence on the Island of Mull, off the coast of and belonging to Argyleshire. Nearly all the "Macs" living in Ohio, it may be safely said, are of Scottish descent, and usually Celtic or Highland Scots. The prefix "Mac" (meaning "son of"), is of Celtic origin, and in early times it was rarely found in connection with the names of the Lowland clans, except in the cases of McCulloch and McClellan, and a few other ancient Galloway families. Later in Scotland's history, however, the "Macs" were carried pretty much all over the country, and into Northern Ireland, as the clans continued to migrate and to intermarry with the Lowlanders. The name, McConnell, is corrupted from McDonald, or McDonnell, at one time the largest and most powerful of the Highland clans.

From the counties of Wigtonshire and Kirkcudbrightshire (once forming the ancient principality of Galloway, and from whence come the Galloway cattle,) besides the McCullochs and the McClellans, come also the Agnews, Boyles', Douglasses, Carnahans, Carsons, Glendennings, Gordons, Hannas, Herrons, Kerrs, McCreas, McBrides, McMaths, Mc-Mychens, McMillans, Maxwells, Ramseys, Stewarts, and others.

James Hogg, the "Ettrick Shepherd," and poet, was from Selkirkshire, and the name also occurs in Perthshire.

From Fifeshire come the Bealls, the Hendersons, and also some of the Gillespie families.

From Dumbartonshire, just north of Glasgow, come the Calhouns and the Macfarlands.

From Elginshire come the Birnies.

From Inverness, in the Highlands, come the McBeans, McKinleys, and Finlays, (all septs of the once powerful Clan Chattan, of whom the chiefs were McIntoshes and McPhersons); also the Davidsons and Grants.

From Lanarkshire, the Biggars.

From Forfarshire, the Lyons and the Ogilvies.

From Stirlingshire, the Buchanans, Forsythes, and Pattersons.

From Edinburghshire, the Craigs, Kerrs, Gilmores, Ramseys, and Waddells.

From Sutherland, in the northern Highlands, the McKays, McCoys, McKees, etc., many of whom are also found in Galloway.

From Dumfriesshire, south of Glasgow, the Carothers', Elliotts, Dicksons (and, possibly, also the Dickersons), the Johnstons, and the Kirkpatricks.

From Caithness, the most northern county of Scotland, the McRaes (and, possibly, also the Raes, Reas, or Rays, although many of this name lived in Galloway and Ayrshire).

From Renfrewshire, the Knoxes.

Nearly all the Scotch who settled in the North of Ireland at the time of the first plantation of Ulster (1606 to 1625), came from the western Lowland counties of Scotland, lying on the opposite coast and less than thirty miles distant from county Down. The greater part of them came from Ayrshire and Galloway, and those two districts in Scotland were the nesting-places of the early Scottish ancestors of the majority of the people living in the Ohio Valley to-day. The scene of Scott's " Guy Mannering " is laid in Wigtonshire (the western half of Galloway), as is also that of much of S. R. Crockett's " Galloway Herd." All readers of Burns, and of Stevenson's "Master of Ballantrae," are familiar with Ayrshire. The places and people of these districts are also well known to those who have read of the persecutions and sufferings of the early Scottish Covenanters.

The story of the Scottish emigration to Ulster may be outlined in a few paragraphs. It begins near the close of the year 1602, when Con Mc-Neale O'Neale, of Castlereagh, got into serious trouble, by reason of not having his wine-casks full at the time when he had invited some of his relatives to have a "wee drop" with him. Con ruled the Upper Clannaboye, the north half of County Down; and happened to be holding high state in

his halls of Castlereagh with his brothers, and cousins, and relatives of
near degree.   They were all "proper" men—to use a Celtic term of re-
spect—and quite naturally drank Con's cellar dry; whereupon he despatched retainers to Belfast, two miles distant, for a fresh supply of wine.
There his servants had a quarrel with certain soldiers of Queen Elizabeth, who were stationed at Belfast Castle, and they came back to their
master without the "drink."   This naturally roused Con to fury, and he
threatened dire vengeance on his clansmen if they did not return to the
fight, punish the English, and recover the wine.   The second encounter
proved more serious than the first; an English soldier was killed, and
the Irish Government took the matter up.   Con was charged with "levy-
ing war against the Queen," and thrown into the Castle as a prisoner,
from whence he seemed likely to escape only by the loss of his head.   In
this extremity, Con's wife appealed for help to Hugh Montgomery, Laird
of Braidstane, in Ayrshire, whose home lay on the Scottish coast, across
the Irish channel.   Montgomery, for a "consideration," agreed to help
Con to escape; and to that purpose immediately sent his relative, Thomas
Montgomery of Blackston, who was the owner of a trading-sloop, to Car-
rickfergus Castle.   Arriving there, the canny Thomas, without loss of
time, proceeded to make love to the keeper's daughter; and to such good
effect, that having been admitted to the Castle, he contrived to get the
prison-guard to drink a very large quantity of what was possibly some
of the same wine over which the fight had arisen.   Con was then furnished with a rope, by which he let himself out of a window, found
Thomas Montgomery's sloop waiting for him in the Lough, and was
across to Braidstane and safety within a few hours.   Here, Con
entered into an agreement with Hugh Montgomery, by which he agreed
to cede to him half his lands in Clannaboye (the proportion afterwards
being increased to two-thirds), on condition that the latter should pro-
cure him a free pardon from King James for all his offences, and get Con
admitted to the King's presence, and allowed to kiss the King's hand.
Through the assistance of Mr. James Hamilton, an influential courtier,
this pardon was later obtained, and Con admitted to His Majesty's presence; and two-thirds of Con's estates were in due time confirmed to Hamilton (who also required a "consideration") and Montgomery by the
Crown.
     As soon as the patents were issued by the Irish Council, Con's benefi-
ciaries crossed into Scotland again, to call upon their whole kith and kin

to aid them in the plantation of their estates, it having been a condition imposed by the King, in confirming the grant, that the lands were to be "planted" with English and Scottish colonists; and to be granted only to those of English and Scottish blood, "and not to any of the mere Irish." To Hamilton fell the western portion of North Down, to Montgomery, the eastern; and both seem to have added to their estates, as Con O'Neale was forced to sell the third which he had reserved for himself. Both were Ayrshire men, and both from the northern division of the county. Hamilton was of the Hamilton family of Dunlop; and Montgomery was from near Beith. The former founded the towns of Bangor and Killyleagh, and raised churches in each of the six parishes embraced in his estate—Bangor, Killinchy, Holywood, Ballyhalbert, Dundonald, and Killyleagh. Montgomery's estate embraced the country around Newton and Donaghadee known as the Great Ards. He belonged to a family having numerous connections throughout North Ayrshire and Renfrewshire, and to them he turned for assistance. His principal supporters were his kinsmen, Thomas Montgomery. his brother-in-law, John Shaw, son of the laird of Wester Greenock, and Colonel David Boyd, of the noble house of Kilmarnock. With their help he seems to have persuaded many others of high and low degree to join in trying their fortunes in Ireland, among them being the Montgomeries, Calderwoods, Agnews, Adairs, Cunninghams, Shaws, Muirs, Maxwells, Boyles, Harvies, and many others with good west-country surnames.

The success of this settlement made by Hamilton and Montgomery was immediate; for four years after the foundation of the colony—in 1610—Montgomery alone was able to bring before "the King's mustermaster a thousand able fighting men to serve, when out of them a militia should be raised." Four years after this time, in a letter written from North Down by the Earl of Abercorn to John Murray, King James's secretary of state, he says, in referring to the same colonists: "They have above 2,000 habile Scottis men well armit heir, rady for his Majestie's service as thai sall be commandit." This muster of 2,000 men able to bear arms, represented an emigration of at least 10,000 persons.

Meantime, across the river Lagan, in county Antrim, a plantation had been made by Sir Arthur Chichester, then Lord Deputy of Ireland. This, though not at first peculiarly Scottish, was soon to become so. In 1603, Chichester obtained a grant of the Castle of Belfast. and around this fortress a village soon sprang up. The Commissioners' Survey, taken in the year 1611, reports that "the town of Belfast is plotted out in a good forme, wherein are many famelyes of English, Scotch, and some Manksmen already inhabitinge, and ane inn with very good lodging." The Settlement Commissioners passed along the north shore of Belfast Lough, finding everywhere houses springing up, and in every part of the Lord Deputy's lands, "many English famelies, some Scottes, and dyvers cyvill Irish planted." While South Antrim was thus "planted," mainly by English settlers, the northern half of the county was opened up for settlement, without the violent transference of land from Irish to Briton, which was carried out in other parts of Ulster. The northeast corner of Ireland had been long held by the MacDonnells (the Highland pronunciation of this name is MacConnell), a clan which also peopled the island of Jura, and Cantyre on the mainland of Scotland. The chief of these Scoto-Irishmen, Randall MacDonnell, after the Earl of Tyrone's rebellion, resolved to throw in his lot with the Government, and turn loyal subject. This he did, and as reward received a grant of the northern half of county Antrim, from Larne to Portrush, and the honor of knighthood. He set himself to the improvement of his lands, letting out to the natives on the coast, and also to the Scottish settlers, such arable portions of his lands as had been depopulated by the war, for terms varying from twenty-one to 301 years. These leases seem to have been largely taken advantage of by the Scottish settlers, who allowed the natives to keep the "Glynnes," or Glens, and themselves took possession of the rich land along the river Bann, from Lough Neagh to the town of Coleraine, near its mouth. Thus, in time, county Antrim, from north to south, became nearly as Scottish as the portion of county Down lying north of the Mourne mountains.

The plantations in counties Down and Antrim, however, were limited in scope in comparison with the "Great Plantation in Ulster," for which James I.'s reign will be forever remembered in Ireland.

About the year 1607, O'Neill, Earl of Tyrone, and MacDonnell, Earl of Tyrconnel, with a number of the lesser Irish chiefs, having rebelled against the King and been proclaimed traitors, their lands were confiscated by the Crown; and all of northern Ireland—Londonderry, Donegal, Tyrone, Cavan, Armagh, and Fermanagh—passed into the hands of the King.

The plan adopted by James for the colonization of these six "escheated" counties, was to take possession of the finest portions of this great tract of country (amounting in all to nearly four millions of acres); to divide it into small estates, none larger than two thousand acres; and to grant these to men of known wealth and substance. Those who accepted grants were bound to live on their lands themselves, to bring with them English and Scottish settlers, and to build for themselves and for their tenants fortified places for defence, houses to live in, and churches in which to worship. The native Irish were assigned to the poorer lands and less accessible districts; while the allotments to the English and Scots were kept together, so that they might form communities, and not mix or intermarry with the Irish. The purpose was not only to transfer the ownership of the land from Irish to Briton, but to introduce a British population in place of an Irish one.

James seems to have seen that the parts of Scotland nearest Ireland, and which had most intercourse with it, were most likely to yield proper colonists. He resolved, therefore, to enlist the assistance of the great families of the southwest, trusting that their feudal power would enable them to bring with them bodies of colonists. Thus, grants were made to Ludovick Stewart, Duke of Lennox, who had great power in Dumbarton-shire; to James Hamilton, Earl of Abercorn, and his brothers, who represented the power of the Hamiltons in Renfrewshire. North Ayrshire had been already largely drawn on by Hamilton and Montgomery, but one of the sons of Lord Kilmarnock, Sir Thomas Boyd, received a grant; while from South Ayrshire came the Cunninghams and Crawfords, and Andrew Stewart (Lord Ochiltree) and his son. But it was on Galloway men that the greatest grants were bestowed. Almost all the great houses of the time are represented—Sir Robert MacLellan, Laird Bomby, as he is called, who afterwards became Lord Kirkcudbright; John Murray of Broughton, one of the secretaries of state; Vans (Vance) of Barnbarroch; Sir Patrick McKie of Laerg; Dunbar of Mochrum; one of the Stewarts of Garlies, from whom Newtown Stewart takes its name. With the recipient of 2,000 acres, the agreement was that he was to bring "forty-eight able men of the age of eighteen or upwards, being born in England or the inward [i. e., southern] parts of Scotland." The progress of the colonies in the different counties is very accurately described in a series of reports by Government inspectors, at various periods between the years 1610 to 1620, and in the letters of Chichester himself, which are to be found in the Calendar of State Papers for Ireland, and in the Carew Papers (both published by the British Government).

The most interesting of these reports are those regarding "under-takers" (as the grantees were called), who took possession in the year 1610, made up their minds to remain and to thrive in Ulster, and who founded families whose names were afterwards to be well known in Ireland. In Donegal, on Lough Swilly, will be found on the map the names of two villages, Manor Cunningham and Newtown Cunningham. The men who introduced so Scottish a name into so Irish a county are thus noticed in the report of 1611: "Sir James Cunningham, Knight, Laird Glangarnoth, 2,000 acres, took possession, but returned into Scotland. Three families of British residents preparing to build . . . John Cunningham of Cranfield, 1,000 acres, resident with one family of British . . . Cuthbert Cunningham, 1,000 acres, resident with two families of British; built an Irish house of coples, and prepared materials to re-edify the Castle of Coole-McEtreen." In county Tyrone, "The Earl of Abercorn, chief undertaker in the precinct in the county of Tyrone, has taken possession, resident with lady and family, and built for the present near the town of Strabane some large timber houses . . . His followers and tenants have since May last built twenty-eight houses of fair coples, and before May by his tenants, who are all Scottish men, the number of thirty-two houses of like goodness." "The Lo. Uchelrie [Lord Ochiltree] 3,000 acres in the county of Tyrone, being stayed by contrary winds in Scotland, arrived in Ireland at the time of our being in Armagh, upon our return home, accompanied with thirty-two followers, gent. of sort, a minister, some tenants, freeholders, and artificers."

In 1618, the Irish Government instructed Captain Nicholas Pynnar to inspect every allotment in the six "escheated" counties, and to report on each one, whether held by "natives" or "foreign planters." Pynnar's report (published in the Irish State Papers), presents a very exact picture of what had been done by the settlers in the counties inspected—Londonderry, Donegal, Tyrone, Armagh, Cavan, and Fermanagh. He states that, " there are upon occasion 8,000 men of British birth and descent for defence, though a fourth part of the lands is not fully inhabited." Of these, fully three-fourths must have been Scots; and if there be added the great colonies in Down and Antrim, there must have been an immigration from Scotland of between 30,000 and 40,000 in these ten years.

The only county in which the Scottish settlers failed to take firm root was Fermanagh, for there, in 1618, when Pynnar reported, a large number of the Scottish proportions had been sold, and were held by Englishmen. The result is seen in the small number of Presbyterians in comparison to Episcopalians to be found at the present day in county Fermanagh.

The most exact account of the emigration to Ulster is contained in a book of travels in Scotland and Ireland, by Sir William Brereton, of Cheshire, England. He states that he came to Irvine, in Ayrshire, on July 1st, 1635, and was hospitably entertained by Mr. James Blair, and that his host informed him that "above ten thousand persons have within two years last past left this country wherein they lived, which was betwixt Aberdine and Enuerness [Inverness], and are gone for Ireland; they have come by one hundred in company through this town, and three hundred have gone hence together, shipped for Ireland at one tide. None of them can give a reason why they leave the country; only some of them who make a better use of God's hand upon them have acknowledged to mine host in these words, 'that it was a just judgment of God to spew them out of the land for their unthankfulness.' One of them I met withal and discoursed with at large, who could give no good reason, but pretended the landlords increasing their rents; but their swarming in Ireland is so much taken notice of and disliked, as that the Deputy has sent out a warrant to stay the landing of any of these Scotch that come without a certification."

The closing sentence of the foregoing extract gives us a brief and characteristic description of Scottish motives and methods in the colonization and settlement of a new country, that may well be applied to every one of their successive migrations, or "swarmings," from that day to this. It was the spirit of unrest, the thirst for adventure, and, chiefly, the desire to better their worldly condition, that led them into the Land of Promise in that day, and at numerous periods since. They came without regard to the jealous forebodings of the governing few, already on the ground, who feared they themselves would be outnumbered by the strangers; they likewise paid no regard to the official restrictions by which the rulers of Ireland at that time, and the Councils of American colonies a century later, sought to prevent their entry.

The emigration from Ireland to America of the grandchildren and great-grandchildren of these Scottish colonists of the sixteenth century began soon after 1700; and for more than three-quarters of a century afterwards, Ulster poured into America a continuous stream, sometimes reaching the dimensions of a flood, of people of Scottish birth or descent. In 1718, several hundred of them came together from the Valley of the Bann, south of the town of Coleraine, in county Londonderry, landing at Boston. Here, they were not permitted by the Puritans to remain, but were obliged to go out to the frontiers, forming colonies along the coast of Maine, at Londonderry, in New Hampshire, and at Worcester, in Massachusetts. In the latter place, they built a church, and contemplated having Presbyterian services, after the manner of their fathers; but the bigoted Puritans, then in the majority, tore down the building in the night; forced them to abandon the project, and taxed them to support their own State Church. Many of these settlers were thus obliged to move further out towards the frontier, where they founded the towns of Pelham and Coleraine, in Massachusetts.

A great many Scotch and Scotch-Irish also emigrated to New York, to New Jersey, and to Maryland, Virginia, and the Carolinas. But it was to Pennsylvania, the Quaker Colony, that the great bulk of the Ulster migration came. They began to reach there before 1710; and before 1720, thousands had come into the colony by way of Newcastle, Del. (then included in Pennsylvania). At first, they generally settled near the disputed Maryland boundary line. Before 1730, they had occupied much of the lower lands in the townships of East and West Nottingham, Cecil county, Maryland, and Mill Creek and White Clay Creek in Newcastle county, Delaware. In Pennsylvania they settled in the townships of London Britain, New London, Londonderry, London Grove, East and West Nottingham, Upper and Lower Oxford, East and West Fallowfield, Sadsbury, East and West Caln, and the newer townships between, in Chester county; Little Britain, Colerain, Bart, Sadsbury, Salisbury, Drumore, Martic, and Donegal in Lancaster county; and Derry, Paxtang, and Hanover, in Dauphin county. They had also gone into Bucks county in large numbers, settling in Warwick and Warminster townships, along Neshaminy creek; and in Northampton county, in Allen and Hanover townships.

James Logan, then secretary of the province, and himself a Scotch-Irish Quaker, writing of them to the Penns in 1724, states that they had generally taken up the southern lands (towards the Maryland line), and as they rarely approached him with proposals of purchase, he calls them "bold and indigent strangers, saying as their excuse, when challenged for titles, that we had solicited for colonists and they had come accordingly." They were, however, understood to be a tolerated class, exempt from quit-rents by an ordinance of 1720, in consideration of their being a frontier people, and forming a cordon of defence about the non-fighting Quakers. They thus served to protect them, if need be—and the necessity often arose—from the murderous incursions of the Indians, and from Maryland and Virginia invaders who claimed part of the land as within the bounds of their own colonies.

In 1729, Logan expresses himself as pleased to find that Parliament is about to take measures to prevent the too free emigration from Ulster to America. "It looks," he writes, "as if Ireland is to send all its inhabitants hither, for last week not less than six ships arrived, and every day, two or three arrive also. The common fear is that if they thus continue to come they will make themselves proprietors of the Province. It is strange that they thus crowd where they are not wanted. . . The Indians themselves are alarmed at the swarms of strangers, and we are afraid of a breach between them—for the [Scotch-] Irish are very rough to them." In 1730, he writes and complains of the Irish as having in an "audacious and disorderly manner" possessed themselves about that time of the whole of Conestoga Manor, a tract of about 15,000 acres, which had been reserved by the Penns for themselves, as it contained some of the best land in the Province. In taking this land by force, he says, they alleged that "it was against the laws of God and nature, that so much land should be idle while so many Christians wanted it to labor on, and to raise their bread." This same spirit on the part of the Scotch-Irish led them in after years (1745-50) to settle in the Tuscarora and Path Valleys, where their cabins were burned by the provincial authorities, and later (1763-8), along Redstone creek in what is now Fayette county, where they were warned off by the Quaker Assembly, "under pain of death;" and later still (1779 and 1784-7) along and near Short creek, in what is now the territory of Jefferson, Belmont, and Harrison counties, Ohio, where they were repeatedly driven off by United States troops, their cabins burned, and their improvements destroyed; but to which localities they as persistently returned and rebuilt, and remained on the land, improving it, until the Territory was thrown open for settlement.

In another letter written by Logan, about the same time (1730), he says: "I must own, from my own experience in the land-office, that the settlement of five families from Ireland gives me more trouble than fifty of any other people. Before we were broke in upon, ancient Friends and first settlers lived happily; but now the case is quite altered."

Logan's successor, Richard Peters, had a somewhat similar experience with the Scotch-Irish emigrants of his day. In a letter written by him in 1743, he states that he went to the Manor of Maske, to warn off and dispossess the squatter settlers. This was another choice tract of upwards of 40,000 acres, located in the wilderness by the Penns as a reservation, lying on both sides of Marsh creek, then in Lancaster, now in Adams county, being the site of Gettysburg, and including the bottom lands southward to the Maryland line. On that occasion, the people who were settled there, to the number of about seventy, assembled and forbade Penn's surveyors to proceed. On the latter persisting, the settlers broke the surveyors' chain, and compelled them to retire. Peters had with him at the time a sheriff and a magistrate; and many of the settlers were afterwards indicted; but a compromise was effected, by which the squatters were permitted to lease and purchase the Penn titles for a comparatively insignificant consideration; and they were left in possession.

The reasons for the emigration of the Scotch from Ulster to America are in part the same as those given to Brereton by the emigrant from Scotland to Ireland in 1635, which are noted above. But there was another and more cogent reason in addition. In Ireland, notwithstanding the fact that they had saved that country to Protestantism and to the Crown in the revolution of 1688, the Scots were grievously and unjustly discriminated against in the matter of their religion, which was, of course, generally of the Presbyterian form. These discriminations took the form of certain enactments by the Bishop's party in the Irish Parliament (which was then entirely ruled by the ecclesiastics of the Episcopal or State Church). These enactments deprived Presbyterians of the right to hold office in Ireland, required them to pay tithes in support of the Episcopal clergy, prohibited marriages from being performed by any but a Bishop-ordained priest, either of the Roman or Episcopal Church; and annulled marriages theretofore performed by Presbyterian ministers, declaring illegitimate the children of such marriages. Adding to these the economic causes arising from a discriminating tariff levied against Irish woollens and linens, in favor of the English manufacturers, and the raising of rents by the landlords, to whom a great majority of the Ulster Scotch-Irish were but tenants, and we have a sufficient explanation of the reasons for the exodus which took place from Ireland to America during the eighteenth century. Archbishop Boulter, Primate of Ireland, writing to the Bishop of London in 1728 concerning the emigration to America, says:

Dublin, March 13, 1728.

My Lord—As we have had reports here that the Irish gentlemen in London would have the great burthen of tithes thought one of the chief grievances that occasion such numbers of the people of the north going to America, I have for some time designed to write to your lordship on that subject.

But a memorial lately delivered in here by the Dissenting ministers of this place, containing the causes of this desertion, as represented to them by the letters of their brethren in the north, (which memorial we have lately sent over to my lord lieutenant), mentioning the oppression of the ecclesiastical courts about tithes as one of their great grievances. I found myself under a necessity of troubling your lordship on this occasion with a true state of that affair, and of desiring your lordship to discourse with the ministry about it.

The gentlemen of this country have, ever since I came hither, been talking to others, and persuading their tenants, who complained of the excessiveness of their rents, that it was not the paying too much rent, but too much tithes that impoverished them; and the notion soon took among the Scotch Presbyterians, as a great part of the Protestants in the north are, who it may easily be supposed do not pay tithes with great cheerfulness. And indeed I make no doubt but the landlords in England might with great ease raise a cry amongst their tenants of the great oppression they lay under by paying tithes.

What the gentlemen want to be at is, that they may go on raising their rents, and that the clergy should still receive their old payments for their tithes. But as things have happened otherwise, and they are very angry with the clergy, without considering that it could not happen otherwise than it has, since if a clergyman saw a farm raised in its rent, e. g., from 10 to 20 l. per annum, he might be sure his tithe was certainly worth double what he formerly took for it. Not that I believe the clergy have made a proportionable advancement in their composition for their tithes to what the gentlemen have made in their rents. And yet it is upon this rise of the value of the tithes that they would persuade the people to throw their distress.

In a conference I had with the Dissenting ministers here some weeks ago, they mentioned the raising the value of the tithes beyond what had been formerly paid, that a proof that the people were oppressed in the article of tithes. To which I told them, that the value of tithes did not prove any oppression, except it were proved that that value was greater than they were really worth, and that even then, the farmer had his remedy by letting the clergy take it in kind.

And there is the less in this argument, because the fact is, that about the years 1694 and 1695, the lands here were almost waste and unsettled, and the clergy in the last distress for tenants for their tithes, when great numbers of them were glad to let their tithes at a very low value, and that during incumbency, for few would take them on other terms; and as the country has since settled and improved, as those incumbents have dropped off, the tithe of those parties has been considerably advanced without the least oppression, but I believe your lordship will think not without some grumbling. The same, no doubt, has happened where there have been careless or needy incumbents, and others of a different character that have succeeded them.

I need not mention to your lordship that I have been forced to talk to several here, that if a landlord takes too great a portion of the profits of a farm for his share by way of rent (as the tithe will light on the tenant's share), the tenant will be impoverished; but then it is not the tithe but the increased rent that undoes the farmer. And indeed, in this country, where I fear the tenant hardly ever has more than one-third of the profit he makes of his farm for his share, and too often but a fourth or perhaps a fifth part, as the tenant's share is charged with the tithe, his case is no doubt hard, but it is plain from what side the hardship arises.

Another thing they complain of in their memorial is, the trouble that has been given them about their marriages and their school-masters. As to this I told them, that for some time they had not been molested about their marriages; and that as to their school-masters, I was sure they had met with very little trouble on that head, since I had never heard any such grievance so much as mentioned till I saw it in their memorial.

Another matter complained of is, the sacramental test, in relation to which I told them the laws were the same in England.

As for other grievances they mention, such as raising the rents unreasonably, the oppression of justices of the peace, seneschals, and other officers in the country, as they are of no ways of an ecclesiastical nature, I shall not trouble your lordship with an account of them, but must desire your lordship to talk with the ministry on the subject I have now wrote about, and endeavor to prevent their being prepossessed with an unjust opinion of the clergy, or being disposed, if any attempt should be made from hence, to suffer us to be stript of our just rights.

The spirit of emigration—fostered no doubt by the accounts sent home by their countrymen who had preceded them—seized these people to such an extent that it threatened almost a total depopulation. Such multitudes of husbandmen, laborers, and manufacturers flocked to the other side of the Atlantic, that the landlords began to be alarmed, and to present ways and means for preventing the growing evil. Scarce a ship sailed for the colonies that was not crowded with men, women, and children. It is stated by Proud, in his history of Pennsylvania, that by the year 1729, six thousand Scotch-Irish had come to that colony, and that before the middle of the century, nearly twelve thousand arrived annually for several years. In September, 1736, alone, one thousand families sailed from Belfast, on account of the difficulty of renewing their leases.

The first extensive emigration took place from about the year 1718 to the middle of the century. A second emigration occurred from about 1771 to 1773, although there was a continuous current westward between these two periods.

The cause of this second emigration was somewhat similar to the first. It is well known that a greater portion of the lands in Ireland are owned by a comparatively small number of proprietors, who rent them to the farming classes on long leases. In 1771, the leases on the estate of the Marquis of Donegal having expired, the rents were so largely advanced that many of the tenants could not comply with the demands, and were deprived of the farms they had occupied. This roused a spirit of resentment to the oppression of the large landed proprietors, and an immediate and extensive emigration to America was the result. From 1771 to 1773, there sailed from the ports in the north of Ireland, nearly one hundred vessels, carrying upwards of 25,000 passengers, nearly all of whom were Presbyterians. This was shortly before the breaking out of the Revolutionary War, and, as has been often remarked, these people, leaving the old world in such a temper, became a powerful contribution to the cause of liberty, and to the Independence of the colonies.

The Scotch-Irish emigrants landed principally at Newcastle and Philadelphia, and thence found their way northward and westward into the eastern and middle counties of Pennsylvania. From thence, one stream followed the Cumberland and Virginia valleys into Virginia and North and South Carolina, and from these colonies, passed on into and settled Tennessee and Kentucky. Another powerful body went into western Pennsylvania, and settling on the head waters of the Ohio, became famous, both in civil and ecclesiastical history.

The Pennsylvania Scotch-Irish began to settle west of the Blue Ridge mountains before 1750, where up to that time the Indians held undisputed sway. Fear of an Indian outbreak led the Penns in that year to send the justices of Cumberland county over the mountains into the Tuscarora, Aughwick, and Path Valleys, where the settlers were dispossessed, their cabins burned, and their bonds taken that they should return to the older settlements. Some of them did return for a brief period, but soon went back, while others hid themselves away in the woods, and after the justices had departed, built themselves new cabins, and continued to improve their "claims." Before 1760, small settlements were made by members of this hardy and adventurous race around the the military posts of Forts Bedford, Redstone, and Ligonier; and in 1768,

Rev. John Steel and others were sent by the Provincial authorities to warn off the settlers at Redstone (in Fayette county) and Turkey Foot (in Somerset county). In 1769, however, the land having been ceded by the Indians, all of southwestern Pennsylvania was thrown open to settlement, and within the next ten years more than 25,000 people were living in the territory now comprising the counties of Westmoreland, Allegheny, Fayette, and Washington. In 1790, the population of these four counties amounted to upwards of 63,000, Washington county alone containing nearly 24,000 inhabitants.

THE FRIENDS, OR QUAKERS.

The founder of the society of Friends was George Fox, who was born at Drayton in the Clay, in Liecestershire, England, in July, 1624. His father was a Puritan weaver, and the son, originally intended for the church, was apprenticed to a shoemaker and dealer in wool. "In 1643," he says, "I left my relations, and broke off all familiarity with young or old." For the next few years, he was in spiritual darkness, and groped after the light. He dates the beginning of his Society from Liecestershire, in 1644. The course of Quakerism was at first toward the north of England. It appeared in Warwickshire in 1645; in Nottinghamshire in 1646; in Derby in 1647; in the adjacent counties in 1648, 1649, and 1650. It reached Yorkshire in 1651; Lancaster and Westmoreland, 1652; Cumberland, Durham, and Northumberland, 1653; London, and most other parts of England, Scotland, and Ireland, in 1654. In 1655, Friends went beyond sea, "where truth also sprung up," and in 1656 "it broke forth in America, and many other places." (Fox's Journal, II., 442.)

The Society of Friends was not organized by the establishment of meetings to inspect the affairs of the church until some years after Fox began preaching, and then a prominent part of the business of these meetings was to aid those Friends who were in prison, for persecution followed hard upon their increase in numbers. In 1661, 500 were in prison in London alone; there were 4,000 in jail in all England; and the Act of Indulgence liberated 1,200 Quakers in 1673. But Quakerism flourished under persecution. They showed a firmness which has been seen nowhere else in the annals of religious history. Other Dissenters might temporize, plot against the Government, or hold meetings in secret; the Quakers, never. They scorned these things. They received the brutal violence of the Government in meekness; they met openly, and in defiance of its orders; they wearied it by their very persistence. Nevertheless, the simplicity, the earnestness, the devotion, and the practical nature of this system of theology, when contrasted with the dry husk of Episcopacy, and the jangling creeds of the Dissenters, won them adherents by the thousands. They came mostly from the lower ranks of society, but from all sects.

Quakerism is distinctively the creed of the seventeenth century. Seekers were in revolt against the established order. It gave these seekers what they were looking for. In theology, it was un-Puritan; but in cultus, modes, and forms, it was more than Puritan. The Quaker was the Puritan of the Puritans. He was an extremist, and this brought him into conflict with the established order. He believed that Quakerism was primitive Christianity revived. He recognized no distinction between the clergy and the laity; he refused to swear, for Christ had said, swear not at all; he refused to fight, for the religion of Christ is a religion of love, not of war; he would pay no tithes, for Christ had said, ye have freely received, freely give; he called no man master, for he thought the terms, Rabbi, Your Holiness, and Right Reverend connoted the same idea. He rejected the dogmas of water baptism and the Puritan Sabbath, and in addition to these, claimed that inspiration is not limited to the writers of the Old and New Testaments, but is the gift of Jehovah to all men who will accept it, and to interpret the Scriptures, men must be guided by the Spirit that guided its authors. Here was the cardinal doctrine of their creed, and the point where they differed radically from other Dissenters. Add to this the doctrine of the Inner Light, the heavenly guide given directly to inform or illuminate the individual conscience, and we have the corner-stones of their system.

In July, 1656, Ann Austin and Mary Fisher, the vanguard of a Quaker army, appeared in Boston from Barbadoes. They were the first Quakers to arrive in America. They were imprisoned and shipped back. In October of the same year, a law was passed, which provided a fine for the shipmaster who knowingly brought in Quakers, and obliged him to carry them out again. The Quaker was to be whipped, and committed to the house of correction. Any person importing books, "or writings concerning their devilish opinions," or defending their "heretical opinions," was to be fined, and, for the third offense, banished. Nor was any person to revile the magistrates and ministry, "as is usual with the

Quakers." The law of October, 1657, imposed a fine for entertaining a Quaker. If a Quaker returned after being sent away once, he was to lose one ear; if he returned the second time, the other ear; and the third offense was punished by boring the tongue. The law of October, 1658, banished both resident and foreign Quakers, under pain of death. In Massachusetts, Quakers had their ears cut off; they were branded; they were tied to the cart-tail and whipped through the streets; women were shamefully exposed to public gaze; and in 1659-60, three men and one woman were hanged on Boston Common. Such was the welcome of the first Quakers to American soil.

Pennsylvania, the Quaker Colony, was founded by William Penn, in 1681, under a patent granted by Charles II. on March 4th of that year. The first colony left England in August, 1681, in three ships, the John and Sarah, from London, the Amity, from London, and the Factor, from Bristol. The John and Sarah is said to have landed first: the Amity was carried by a gale to the West Indies; and the Factor, having proceeded up the Delaware as far as the present town of Chester, was, on December 11th, frozen up in the channel, and its passengers obliged to pass the winter there. William Penn had sent his cousin, Captain William Markham, with the colonists, as deputy governor, and did not emigrate himself until the month of August, 1682, when he embarked on the Welcome. After a passage of some two months, during which smallpox broke out among the emigrants, and carried off one-third of their number, Penn and his fellow colonists landed at Newcastle, Del., on October 27th. Of the history of Penn's colony, and of the Quaker government during the next ninety-three years, and until it was finally overthrown in 1776 by the Revolutionary Scotch-Irish, it is not necessary here to speak. Much of this is familiar history to every school-boy. But the influence of the Quakers in the settlement and growth of the states south of Pennsylvania, has never been sufficiently recognized; and as it was from these states that most of the Quaker emigrants to Harrison and adjoining counties came, it will be appropriate to inquire into the history of the Quaker in the South. "They appeared in Virginia," says Dr. Stephen B. Weeks (from whose work on Southern Quakers and Slavery much of this sketch is condensed), "soon after their organization; they were in the Carolinas almost with the first settlers; they were considerable in number and substance; they were well-behaved and law-abiding; they maintained friendly relations with the Indians; they were industrious and frugal; they were zealous missionaries; and through their earnest and faithful preaching became, toward the close of the seventeenth century, the largest and only organized body of Dissenters in these colonies.

"They have always been zealous supporters of religious freedom. They bore witness to their faith under bodily persecution in Virginia; under disfranchisement and tithes in the Carolinas and Georgia. By reason of their organization and numbers, they were bold and aggressive in North Carolina, in the struggle against the Established Church. They took the lead in this struggle for religious freedom in the first half of the eighteenth century, as the Presbyterians did in the latter half. They continued an important element in the life of these states until about 1800, when their protest against slavery took the form of migration. They left their old homes in the South by thousands, and removed to the free Northwest, particularly Ohio and Indiana. These emigrants composed the middle and lower ranks of society, who had few or no slaves, and who could not come into economic competition with slavery. They were accompanied by many who were not Quakers, but who were driven to emigration by the same economic cause, and so great was this emigration that in 1850, one-third of the population of Indiana is said to have been made up of native North Carolinians and their children.

"Soon after 1800, Quakers disappeared entirely from the political and religious life of South Carolina and Georgia. They now number only a few hundred in Virginia. They are now relatively less important in North Carolina than in colonial days, but are still an important factor in the making of that state."

Under the Ordinance of 1787, passed by Congress for the government of the Northwest Territory, neither slavery nor involuntary servitude, except for crime, was to be allowed in any part of this territory; and with a legal guarantee in the organic law of the territory, it became a fit home for men who found themselves driven to migration by the institution of slavery in the South.

When we come to study these Quaker migrations in detail, there is little to differentiate those of one state from those of another. They went in substantially the same way, but owing to difference in location, pursued different routes. At first, North Carolina Quakers went very largely to Tennessee, while Virginia Quakers, being nearer, went directly to Ohio. In this way, Virginia Quakers took possession of Ohio, while North Carolina Quakers pressed on to Indiana.

The first settlers going West, after the opening of the Northwest

Territory to settlement, stopped naturally in Ohio. As there were then no Friends' meetings in that territory, Quaker emigrants left their certificates at Redstone (in Fayette county) and Westland (in Washington county), Pennsylvania. The first certificate to Westland meeting is dated June 24, 1785. Most of the certificates to Westland and Redstone came from Virginia meetings. The migrations of Carolina Friends to this part of the West were few, until after the establishment of the Ohio meetings. After 1785, certificates from Virginia monthly meetings to Redstone and Westland became numerous; about half of them represent families, some of them being young couples who turned to the West for their fortunes. Those Friends who took certificates to Redstone and Westland were but the advance guard of the western migration which set in about the year 1800. They continued to go to these meetings for a year or two longer; thus South River sent twelve to Westland in 1801, and the southern Goose Creek sent fifteen in 1801 and 1802, of which thirteen were families, besides a considerable number sent before the beginning of the present century. Meetings were soon established within the Northwest Territory, and then Westland soon disappears as a stopping-place. Thus, in 1802, we find certificates from South River to "Concord Monthly Meeting, Northwest Territory;" but this name almost immediately gives place to "Concord Monthly Meeting, State of Ohio," and the migrations at once become very numerous. Mr. Williams' very full account of the emigration of his own family from North Carolina to Concord settlement (in Colerain township, Belmont county) may be found in his magazine, the " American Pioneer," vol. ii. During the first ten years of the century, most of the emigrants from Virginia went from Crooked Run, Hopewell, South River, and the two Goose Creek Monthly Meetings; during the second decade they went from Hopewell, South River, and the southern Goose Creek Monthly Meetings. The migration from the northern Goose Creek and Hopewell became active again about 1825, and continued so until 1836. The meetings in Virginia which belonged to Baltimore Yearly Meeting were the first to send out settlers, for they were nearer the western country, and had less to hold them in the way of local associations. From 1812-16, there was a considerable migration from the lower meetings of the Virginia Yearly Meeting. Of the meetings belonging to this Yearly Meeting, South River furnished the greater number of emigrants. From this meeting there went eighty-six families, and forty-three single persons, their removal covering the forty years from 1801 to 1840. In the same way, migrations from the southern Goose Creek began with the century, were to Westland first, and then to Ohio. These removals sapped the life of the Meeting, and it was laid down in 1814. In 1811, the movement began among all the lower meetings. Emigrants from Virginia went largely to Ohio. Those who took certificates to the Indiana meetings belong to the later period.

The first migration from North Carolina to the West was made directly over the Allegheny mountains, by the adventurers who laid the foundations of Tennessee. The first considerable movement of Friends from North Carolina to the Northwest was made from the Contentnea Quarter. It was emphatic and sweeping in its character. It was literally a migration. A letter written from Concord, Belmont county, Ohio, (the Quaker settlement a few miles southeast of New Athens), by Borden Stanton, one of the leaders of this migration, to Friends at Wrightsborough, Ga., who were also thinking of going West, and who did so at a later date, has fortunately been preserved. It reveals to us the motives, the troubles, and the trials of these modern pilgrims to an unknown land. It is dated 25th of 5th month, 1802, and reads as follows:

Dear Friends—Having understood by William Patten and William Hogan, from your parts, that a number among you have had some thoughts and turnings of mind respecting a removal to this country; and . . . as it has been the lot of a number of us to undertake the work a little before you, I thought a true statement (for your information) of some of our strugglings and reasonings concerning the propriety of our moving . . .

I may begin thus, and say, that for several years Friends had some distant view of moving out of that oppressive part of the land, but did not know where, until the year 1799, when we had an aceptable visit from some traveling Friends of the western part of Pennsylvania. They thought proper to propose to Friends for consideration, whether it would not be agreeable to best wisdom for us unitedly to remove northwest to the Ohio river,—to a place where there were no slaves held, being a free country. This proposal made a deep impression on our minds . . .

Nevertheless, although we had had a prospect of something of the kind, it was at first very crossing to my natural inclination; being well settled as to the outward. So I strove against the thoughts of moving for some time . . . as it seemed likely to break up our Monthly Meeting, which I had reason to believe was set up in the wisdom of Truth. Thus, I was concerned many times to weigh the matter as in the balance of the sanctuary; till at length, I considered that there was no prospect of our number being increased by convincement, on account of the oppression that abounded in that land . . .

Under a view of these things, I was made sensible, beyond doubting, that it was in the ordering of wisdom for us to remove; and that the Lord was opening a way for our enlargement, if found worthy. Friends generally feeling something of the same, there were three of them who went to view the country, and one worthy public Friend. They traveled on till they came to this part of the western country, where they were stopped in their minds, believing it was the place for Friends to settle. So they returned back, and informed us of the same in a solemn meeting; in which dear Joseph Dew, the public Friend, intimated that he saw the seed of God sown in abundance, which extended far northwestward. This information, in the way it was delivered to us, much tendered our spirits, and strengthened us in the belief that it was right. So we undertook the work, and found the Lord to be a present helper in every needful time, as he was sought unto; yea, to be as "a pillar of cloud by day and the pillar of fire by night;" and thus we were led safely along until we arrived here.

The story of their departure from their old homes can be given substantially in their own words (records of Contentnea Quarterly Meeting):

It appears by a copy of the minutes of a monthy meeting on Trent river, in Jones county, N. C. held in the ninth and tenth months, 1799, that the weighty subject of the members thereof being about to remove unitedly to the territory northwestward of the Ohio river, was and had been before that time deliberately under their consideration. And the same proposal was solemnly laid before their Quarterly Meeting, held at Contentnea on the ninth of the tenth month; which, on weighing the matter and its circumstances, concluded to leave said Friends at their liberty to proceed therein, as way might be opened for them; yet the subject was continued till their next Quarter. And they having (before the said Monthly Meeting ceased) agreed that certificates be signed therein for the members, to convey their rights respectively to the Monthly Meeting nearest to the place of their intended settlement, showing them to be members whilst they resided there; such certificates for each other mutually were signed in their last Monthly Meeting, held at Trent aforesaid, in the first month, 1800; which was then solemnly and finally adjourned and concluded, and their privilege of holding it, together with the records of it, were delivered up to their Quarterly Meeting, held the 18th of the same month, 1800.

They stopped first at the settlements of Friends on the Monongahela river, in Fayette and Washington counties, Penna., to prepare for their new settlement over the Ohio. They brought their certificates with them, laid their circumstances, with extracts from the minutes of their former monthly and quarterly meetings in Carolina, before Redstone Quarterly meeting, and received the advice and assistance of Friends there.

Thus they proceeded, and made their settlement in the year 1800; and were remarkably favored with an opportunity to be accommodated with a quantity of valuable land at the place which was chosen for their settlement by the Friends who went to view the country, before the office was opened for granting lands in that territory.

Borden Stanton continues (Friends' Miscellany, XII., 216-223):

The first of us moved west of the Ohio in the ninth month, 1800; and none of us had a house at our command, to meet in, to worship the Almighty Being. So we met in the woods, until houses were built, which was but a short time. In less than one year, Friends so increased that two preparative meetings were settled; and in last twelfth month a monthly meeting, called Concord, also was opened, which is now large. Another preparative meeting is requested, and, also, another first and week-day meeting. Four are already granted in the territory, and three meeting-houses are built. Way appears to be opening for another Monthly Meeting; and, I think, a Quarterly Meeting. . . .

I may say that as to the outward [i. e., worldly possessions], we have been sufficiently provided for, though in a new country. Friends are settling fast, and seem, I hope, likely to do well.

This seems to have been the first considerable migration from North Carolina to the West. It seems also to have been the only case on record where a whole meeting went in a body. But it was not the only case of removal from Contentnea Quarter. Removals from this Quarter either to the West, or to upper meetings of the same Quarter, continued until Carteret, Beaufort, Hyde, Craven, and Jones counties were depopulated of Quakers, and the meetings there laid down. Friends in these counties now reported to Core Sound Monthly Meeting, in Carteret county. Migration from Core Sound began in 1799, when Horton Howard, secretary of the monthly meeting, took a certificate to Westland. Josiah Bundy and Joseph Bishop also removed to Westland that year. In 1802, ten parties asked for certificates; no destination was given, but we are justified in assuming that it was Westland or Concord. In 1802-04, the movement was to Concord, Northwest Territory. There was then no more emigration from there until 1831. Migrations began from Contentnea Monthly Meeting in 1800. Between 1800 and 1815, we find thirty-six certificates issued. Two were to Redstone, one to Indiana, and all the rest to Ohio, most of them to Concord.

In the following list, an attempt has been made to give the names of those families which were the leaders in the westward migration, or which furnished the most recruits to it, from the various monthly meetings in the East. The names of the meetings to which the particular families went have also been given, with an approximation of the date:

Hopewell Monthly Meeting, Va., sent to Concord (1803-05), members of the families of Lupton, Piggot, Jenkins, Pickering, Miller, Ellis, Steer, Bevin; to various other monthly meetings in Ohio (1804-   ): McPherson, George, Walter, Wickersham, White, Walton, Wilson, Allen, Adams, Branson, Cope, Crampton, Faucett, Hackney, Janney, Lloyd, Little, Lupton, Pickering, Steer, Smith, Swayne, Townsend, Taylor.

Fairfax Monthly Meeting, Va.—To Short Creek, Harrison county (1803-22): Lacy, Ball, Hague, Rattekir, Wood, Schuley; to other Ohio meetings (1807-44): Wright, Richardson, Connard, Wilkinson, Wood, Swayne, Janney, John, Myers, Wilson.

Goose Creek (northern) Monthly Meeting, Va.—To Concord (1805 08): Evans, Pancoast, Sinclair, Spencer, Gregg, White, Whiteacre, Can by, Dillon, Smith; to other meetings, nearly all in Ohio (1820-54): Tal bott, Buchanan, Rose, Hampton, Hughes, Nichols, Bradfield, Trehern, Mead, Wilson, Birdsall, Brown, Shoemaker, Taylor; to Salem, Colum biana county (1806-07): Craig, Smith, Canby, Janney, Gilbert.

Crooked Run Monthly Meeting, Va.—To Concord (1803-06): Fau cett, Pickering, Wright, Lupton, Piggott, Holloway, Branson, Como Smith, Wright, Sharp.

Goose Creek (southern) Monthly Meeting, Va.—To Concord (1802- 06): McPherson, Bond, Coffee, Broomhall, Pidgeon.

South River Monthly Meeting, Va.—To Concord (1802-05): Pid geon, Gregg, Bloxom, Wildman; to Salem, (1805-07): Stanton, Carle, Macy, Gurrell, Fisher; to other meetings, mostly in Ohio: Redder, Mil liner, Holloway, Fisher, Ferrell, Early, Moorman, Stratton, Johnson, Preston, Burgess, Ballard, Terrell, Lea, Cox, Cadwalader, Butler, Mor gan, Bailey, Lynch.

Cedar Creek Monthly Meeting, Va.—To Salem (1812-23): Stanley, Blackburn; to Short Creek (1813-41): Moorman, Terrell, Maddox, Har grave, Creek.

White Oak Swamp Monthly Meeting, Va.—To Ohio meetings, not specified (1811-36): Ratcliff, Crew, Ladd, Harrison, Bates, Hockaday, Hargrave, Terrill, Andrews, Binford, Johnson, Ricks. Most of these went to Short Creek.

Western Branch Monthly Meeting, Va.—To Concord (1805-33) Bond, Morlan, Curl, Johnson, Anthony, Lewis, Larow, Moorland, Perdue Howell, Powell, Butler, Stanton, James, Draper, Ricks, Chapel, Hunnicutt, Trotter, Lawrence.

Mount Pleasant Monthly Meeting, Va.—To Concord (1805): Vimon, Davis, Bundy, Woods; to other Ohio meetings (1804-24): Thomas, Lundy, Bond, Ballard, Sumner, Beek, Pierce, Stalker, Scooly, Green, Gray, Williams, Robinson, Pierson, Wildman, Ward, Johnson, Pike, Lewis, Cary, Hunt, Anthony, Hiatt, Betts, Bundy, Jones, Chew, Davis.

Piney Grove Monthly Meeting, S. C.—To Ohio meetings (1805-12): Stafford, Mendenhall, Beauchamp, Thomas, Marine, Moorman, Harris, Morris, Lingagar, Almond.

Piney Woods Monthly Meeting, N. C.—To Ohio (1806-28): Goodwin, Smith, Harrel, Bamb, Elliott, Thornton, Bogue, Moore, Newby.

Rich Square Monthly Meeting, N. C.—To Short Creek (1805-11): Patterson, Maremoon (or Moreman), Taylor; to other Ohio meetings (1805-12): Patterson, Maremoon, Hicks, Crew, Reams.

Contentnea Monthly Meeting, N. C.—To Concord (1802-05): Hall, Edgerton, Outland, Doudna, Albertson, Dodd, Bailey, Morris; to other meetings in Ohio (1805-34): Copeland, Bundy, Collier, Cox, Price, Hollowell, Hobson, Spivy, Thomas, Peele, Hall, Jinnett.

Bush River Monthly Meeting, S. C.—To Ohio meetings, not specified (1805-   ): Galbreath, Marmaduke, Mendenhall.

Wrightsborough Monthly Meeting, Ga.—To Ohio meetings, not specified: Butler, Hollingsworth, Moore, Jay, Pearson, Killey, Henderson, Williams, Brooks.

Gravelly Run Monthly Meeting, Va.—To meetings chiefly in Ohio (1822-30): Butler, Thomas, Peebles, Binford, Wrenn, Johnson, Hunnicutt, Sems, Watkins.

Core Sound Monthly Meeting, N. C.—To Concord (1802-04): Harris, Thomas, Scott, Williams, Mace.

Cane Creek Monthly Meeting, N. C.—To Ohio meetings, not specified (1805-09): Stanton, Haydock, Cox, Hadly, Baker, Clark, Hussey, Hasket, Moffit, Hale, Ratcliff.

New Garden Monthly Meeting, N. C.—To Ohio meetings, not specified (1803-31): Hines, Hodgson, Perkins, Starbuck, Williams, Thornburgh, Flanner, Macy, Bunker, Low, Brown, McMuir, James, Jenkins, Russell, Knight, Swain, Blizzard, Jessop, Coffin, Hunt.

Springfield Monthly Meeting, N. C.—To Ohio meetings, not speci-

fied (1803-32): Pidgeon, Reece, Newby, Kersey, Bundy, Tomlinson, Mendenhall, Wright, Kellum, Beard, Harlan, Millikan, Spears, Spencer, Hog-
gatt.

Deep River Monthly Meeting, N. C.—To Ohio meetings, not specified (1811-37): Pike, Pegg, Cook, Jones, Stafford, Hubbard.

Many of the first comers to Concord and Short Creek, Ohio, emigrating before those meetings were definitely established, left their certificates with the nearest meetings in Pennsylvania, being those of Westland,
in Washington county, and Redstone, in Fayette county. The following
families came to one or both of these places: From Hopewell, Va.
(1786-1803): Faulkner, Perviance, Townsend, Sidwell, Berry, Mills,
Blackburn, Branson, Hodge, Lewis, Brock, White, Bailey, Smith, Roberts,
Wells, Morris, Finch, Antrim. From Fairfax, Va. (1785-1833): Smith,
Stokes, Wharton, Davis, Hough, Ward, Mitchner, Plumber, Shine. From
Crooked Run, Va. (1787-1803): Cadwalader, Reyley, Hank, Russel, Berry,
Wright, Hunt, Richards, Mullen, Updegraff, Lupton,Wood, Evans,Cleaver,
Yarnell, Painter, Dillhorn, Taylor, Holloway, Penrose, Miller. From
Goose Creek (southern), Va. (1801-03): Oliphant, Erwin, Lewis, Morlan,
Richards, Whitaker, Pidgeon, Schooley, Wright, Parsons, Sinclair. From
South River, Va. (1801-02): James, Hanna, Baugham, Harris, Holloway,
Terrell, Stratton, Ferrall, Carle, Via, Tellus. From Core Sound, N. C.
(1799-1802): Howard, Bundy, Bishop, Dew, Ward, Mace, Stanton, Will-
iams. From Contentnea, S. C. (1800): Thomas Arnold. From Mt. Pleas-
ant, Va. (1802): Bradford. From Bush River, S. C. (1802-03): Pugh,
Jay, Kelly, O'Neal, Mills, Peaty, Horner, Wright.

The locations of the various monthly meetings named in the foregoing list are as follows:

Bush River.—Newberry county, S. C., eight miles northwest from
Newberry.

Cane Creek.—Alamance county, N. C., fourteen miles south from
Graham.

Cedar Creek.—Hanover county, Va.

Contentnea.—Wayne county, N. C., fifteen miles north from Golds-
boro.

Core Sound—Carteret county, N. C., six miles north from Beaufort.

Crooked Run.—Warren county, Va., nine miles south from Winchester.

Deep River.—Guilford county, N. C., twelve miles southwest from
Greensboro.

Fairfax.—Loudoun county, Va., seven miles west of north from Leesburg.

Goose Creek (northern).—Lincoln, Loudoun county, Va.

Goose Creek (southern).—Bedford county, Va., ten miles southeast from Bedford City.

Gravelly Run.—Dinwiddie county, Va., about four miles east from Dinwiddie.

Hopewell.—Frederick county, Va., six miles north from Winchester.

Mount Pleasant.—Frederick county, Va., nine miles southwest from Winchester.

New Garden.—Guilford county, N. C.

Piney Grove—Marlborough county, S. C., nine miles north from Bennettsville.

Piney Woods.—Davidson county, N. C., twelve miles north of east from Lexington.

Rich Square.—Northampton county, N. C.

South River.—Campbell county, Va., near Lynchburg (?).

Springfield.——Guilford county, N. C., near High Point.

Western Branch.—Isle of Wight county, Va., seven miles, nearly southeast from Isle of Wight Court House.

White Oak Swamp.—Henrico county, Va.

Wrightsborough.—McDuffie county, Ga., thirty-six miles northwest from Augusta.

THE GERMANS.

Though more than twenty-five thousand names of German immigrants are recorded in the Pennsylvania Archives from 1725 to 1775, few of those are recorded who arrived in Pennsylvania prior to 1700. In volume seventeen of the Archives, Second Series, may be found the names of all who took the oath of allegiance between 1727 and 1775, comprising about thirty thousand names, with the names of the vessels in which they came to America, ports from which they sailed, and dates of departure. Probably four-fifths of the Germans living in Harrison county to-day can find the names and dates of arrival of their emigrant ancestors in that volume.

In 1683, some Germans arrived in Pennsylvania, and commenced a settlement at what is now Germantown. Among these, were Pastorious, Hartsfelder, Schietz, Spehagel, Vandewall, Uberfeld, Strauss, Lorentz, Tellner, and others. About the year 1684 or 1685, a land company was formed at Frankfort-on-the-Main, which bought 25,000 acres from William Penn. Those who left their Fatherland from 1700 to 1720, the Palatines, so-called, because they came principally from the Palatinate States, along the Rhine, whither many had been forced to flee from their homes in France, and other parts of Europe, endured many privations before they reached the Western Continent.

In 1708 and 1709, upwards of 10,000, many of them very poor, arrived in England, and were there for some time, in a starving, miserable condition, lodged in warehouses, with no subsistence beyond what they got by begging on the streets; until some sort of provision was made for them by Queen Anne. In 1709, 3,000 of them were sent to Ireland, but of this number many returned to England, on account of insufficient provision having been made for them by the Royal Commissary. In the summer of 1710, several thousand of these Palatinates, who had been maintained at the Queen's expense in England (and for sometime afterwards in America), were shipped to New York; and of these, many came to Pennsylvania. Among these German emigrants were Mennonites, Dunkards, German Reformed, and Lutherans. Their number was so great, that James Logan, Secretary of the Province of Pennsylvania, wrote in 1717, "We have, of late, a great number of Palatines poured in upon us without any recommendation or notice, which gives the country some uneasiness, for foreigners do not so well among us as our own English people."

Those who arrived between 1700 and 1720, settled in the lower parts of Montgomery, Bucks, Berks, and Lancaster counties. In 1719, Jonathan Dickinson wrote, "We are daily expecting ships from London, which bring over Palatines, in number about six or seven thousand. We had a parcel who came out about five years ago, who purchased land about sixty miles west of Philadelphia [the Pequea settlement, in Lancaster county], and prove quiet and industrious. Some few came from Ireland lately, and more are expected thence."

From 1720 to 1730, several thousand landed at Philadelphia, and others came by land, from the province of New York. The latter settled in Tulpehocken, having left New York because they had been ill-treated by the authorities of that province. The influx now became so great as to cause some alarm. It was feared by some that the numbers from Germany, at the rate they were coming in during the last three years of this decade, would soon produce a German colony here, and perhaps such a one as Britain once received from Saxon-land, in the fifth century. Jonathan Dickinson went so far as to state, that it was apprehended Sir William Keith, a former governor, with two of his friends, had sinister projects of forming an independent province in the West, towards the Ohio, to be peopled by his friends among the Palatines. In 1727, six vessels arrived at Philadelphia with Germans; three in 1728; three in 1729; and three in 1730.

From 1730 to 1740, about sixty-five vessels, filled with Germans, arrived at Philadelphia, bringing with them ministers and schoolmasters to instruct their children. A large number of these remained in Philadelphia; others removed seventy to eighty miles from that city—some settling in Lebanon county, and others west of the Susquehanna, in York county.

From 1740 to 1755, upwards of one hundred vessels arrived with Germans; in some of them, though small ships, there were from 500 to 600 passengers. In the summer and fall of 1749, not less than twenty vessels, with German passengers to the number of twelve thousand, arrived.

At first, the immigration of Germans into Pennsylvania was confined to the Sectaries, the Quietists, and the other religious denominations, who, on account of their extremity in doctrines and practice, found it difficult to get along with their more conservative Protestant brethren. The Labadists, for instance, were followed by the Mennonites, who took up much land, and formed many communities in the counties of York, Lancaster, and Adams; by the Seventh Day Baptists, the followers of Spener, who established their monastery at Ephrata; by the Voltists, and the Cocceians; and by the hundred other sects of the day. But after these Sectaries came the Deluge. The Germans had found out that there was a land of peace on the other side of the Atlantic; and they knew by sad experience that their own country was a land of war. A man was deprived, practically, not only of the enjoyment of his own religion; but he was also robbed incessantly of the fruits of his labor. This was a state of things which he naturally rebelled against, and emigration afforded him the only relief.

The religious fanaticism of Louis XIV., which so long desolated the low countries, and which, when he revoked the edict of Nantes, deprived that monarch of his best and most thrifty subjects, broke in upon the Palatine in the shape of one of the most desolating wars of which there is any record in history. Turrenne, Saxe, Vendome, Villars, Villeroy, Taillard, Marsin, Berwick, Noailles, and Luxembourg, each in his turn, helped to desolate the Palatine, and to contribute immigrants to the colonies. The homeless and ravished peoples of Germany sought and found homes in the new land of peace and plenty. At one time the immigration of German Palatines into Pennsylvania and Maryland was in excess of all other immigration. Many hundreds thus came into Maryland, many thousands into Pennsylvania. They came chiefly from the harried Palatinate, but also from Alsace, Suabia, Saxony, and Switzerland. There were Wittenbergers, and people from Darmstadt, Nassau, Hesse, Eisenberg, Franconia, Hamburg, Mannheim—all classed as "Palatines."

In 1790, there were nearly 145,000 Germans in Pennsylvania, the total population then not exceeding 435,000. These included the Sectaries above referred to, the Dunkards, and the Hessian soldiers, who had been taken prisoners by Washington's army, and preferred not to be exchanged after the Revolution. A great proportion of this latter class settled in Somerset county, Pennsylvania, from whence many have come into Harrison county. These German subsidiary troops were bought in Brunswick, Hanau, Anspach, Waldeck, Hesse-Cassel, Hesse-Darmstadt, Brandenberg, etc., in large numbers. They cost George III. the sum of $8,-100,000, and 11,000 of them died, or perished in battle. The other immigrants were German Calvinists, Moravians, Schwenkenfelders, Omishites, Dunkards, Mennonites, and Separatists (or Seventh Day Baptists).

Up to about 1760, the Germans in Maryland were supplied from these plentiful sources, by way of Pennsylvania. A good many Palatines came in by direct consignment to Chesapeake Bay, but the great majority of the Germans drifted down from York and Lancaster counties, Pennsylvania, and occupied the land along Antietam creek, and about Hagerstown and Frederick in Maryland, and the lower Shenandoah Valley in Virginia.

THE VIRGINIANS.

The first settlers of the Virginia Panhandle were mainly of the Cavalier class, many of them coming from the northern and eastern counties east of the mountains, and a few from the Virginia valley, the latter usually being of Scotch-Irish descent. In later years, when the Scotch-Irish occupied Washington county, many of them crossed the line and settled in Ohio (now Brooke) county, Virginia, in the vicinity of Wellsburg. Some of the early settlers in Harrison county were from that section; and not a few were of the old tide-water, horse-racing, gambling, and cock-fighting class, which before the middle of the century, formed the aristocracy and much of the middle-class population of Virginia. Dr.

Joseph Doddridge, although himself born in Bedford county, **Penna.**, belonged to this latter class, his father, originally from Maryland, having settled near West Middletown, in Washington county, about 1773. The son became first a Methodist, and later, an Episcopalian clergyman, and settled at Wellsburg, where he died in 1826. Two years before his death, he wrote a book, called "Notes on the Settlement and Indian Wars of the Western Parts of Virginia and Pennsylvania, from 1763 to 1783," which contains the best written account we have of the early customs, habits of life, and occupations of those pioneers, many of whom were the forefathers of Harrison county citizens of the present day. In reading Doddridge's account, it must be borne in mind that he wrote of two very different classes of settlers, that class amongst which he spent his life being for the most part of the cavalier type—the jolly, rollicking, careless, lawless, and often shiftless character so long associated with the development of the slave-holding South. The other class was the Scotch-Irish —sometimes erroneously called the Puritans of the South, sober-minded, God-fearing, Psalm-singing Presbyterians, for the most part, whose only relaxation after a week of hard toil in the forest or field was to ride or walk from one to fifteen miles to meeting of a Sabbath, there to listen to a series of dry theological dissertations, lasting from morning until night, with but a brief intermission for lunch. Some unfriendly and untruthful writers about the Scotch-Irish, have sought to apply Doddridge's description of the least law-abiding of his fellow pioneers as a general condemnation of this race; maliciously misrepresenting the facts as to the class about whom the description was written. A direct testimonial as to the character of the two classes, given by an eye-witness more than a century ago, has but recently come to light, being an extract from the Diary of Rev. David McClure, published in 1899. David McClure was the first Presbyterian minister to labor in the settlements west of the Alleghenies, having come out as a missionary in 1772, traveled among the Indians of Ohio as far west as Coshocton, and ministered to the scattered settlers of Western Pennsylvania for a period of six months or more. Under date of December 17, 1772, Mr. McClure writes:

Attended a marriage, where the guests were all Virginians. It was a scene of wild and confused merriment. The log-house, which was large, was filled. They were dancing to the music of a fiddle. They took little or no notice of me, on my entrance. After setting awhile at the fire, I arose and desired the music and dancing to cease, and requested the bride and bridegroom to come forward. They came snickering and very merry. I desired the company, who still appeared to be mirthful and noisy, to attend with becoming seriousness, the solemnity.

As soon as the ceremony was over, the music struck up, and the dancing was renewed. While I sat wondering at their wild merriment, the lady of a Mr. Stevenson sent her husband to me, with her compliments, requesting me to dance a minuet with her. My declining the honor, on the principle that I was unacquainted with it, was scarcely accepted. He still politely urged, until I totally refused. After supper, I rode about three miles, to the house of a friend.

The manners of the people of Virginia, who have removed into these parts [Fayette county, Penn.], are different from those of the Presbyterians and Germans. They are much addicted to drinking parties, gambling, horse-race, and fighting. They are hospitable and prodigal. Several of them have run through their property in the old settlements, and have sought an asylum in this wilderness.

Doddridge states that the first settlements along the Monongahela were commenced in 1772. In 1773, they extended to the Ohio. The first settlers came mostly from Maryland and Virginia, and generally traveled by way of Braddock's route. Some from Pennsylvania came by the military road, passing through Bedford and Ligonier. Their removals were generally on horses with pack-saddles. Settlement entitled the settler to 400 acres of land, free. Their claims were usually located by means of the tomahawk, with which they blazed the trees marking their boundary lines. Hence, such claims came to be called "Tomahawk Rights." They usually chose ground in a hollow or depression, for their houses and barns; so that whatever came to the house might come down hill.

Generally, the male members of the prospective settler's family came over the mountains in the spring, and after clearing a plot of ground, planting a small patch of corn, and sometimes erecting a rough log cabin, they went back for their families, and brought them out in the fall. They depended much upon lean venison, wild turkeys, and the flesh of the bear at times, for food. They awaited with much anxiety for the first growth of the potatoes, pumpkins, corn, etc., and when the young corn came, it was made a time of jubilee, and the green ears were roasted for a feast. When the corn hardened and was gathered in the fall, it was customary to provide meal for the family Johnny-cake ("journey-cake," it was then called) by grating the ears on a tin-grater.

The original settlers were usually their own mechanics, and each man made everything needed by himself, that could not be conveniently brought along from the older settlements. The hominy-block and hand-mills were found in most of their houses. The block was hollowed out at the top by burning, and the play of the pestle ground the corn. Sometimes a sixteen-foot sweep was used to lessen the toil, in pounding corn into meal for mush or cakes. The hand-mill was another and a better contrivance, made of two circular stones, the under being the bed-stone, and the upper, the runner. These were enclosed in a wide hoop, or band, having a spout to discharge the meal. The "runner" was moved by a long staff, or pole, passing through an upright fixed in the stone. Such mills are still used in the Holy Land, as they were in the time of Christ.

Their water-mills were tub-mills, readily made, and at small expense. This mill consisted of an upright shaft, at the lower end of which a water-wheel, four or five feet in diameter was attached, the upper end of the shaft passing through the bed-stone, and carrying the runner, secured to its top. Sifters were used in lieu of bolting cloths, made of deer-skin parchment, stretched over a hoop, and pierced with small holes, by means of a hot wire.

The material for their clothing, aside from deer-skins, was spun by the women of the household. Almost every pioneer woman could weave linsey-woolsey cloth, and make the family clothing. Every family tanned its own leather. The tan-vat was a large trough, sunk in the ground; bark was shaved and pounded; wood-ashes were used in lieu of lime, for removing the hair; bear's grease, hog's lard, and tallow served for dressing the leather, instead of fish-oil; the currying was done with a drawing-knife; the blacking made of hog's lard and soot. Most families contained their own tailors and shoemakers. Those who could not make shoes, easily learned to make shoe-packs, which were made, like moccasins, of a single piece of leather, fitted to and removed from the foot by means of a cord gathering. In cold weather, these moccasins were stuffed with dried grass, deer's hair, or dried leaves, to keep the feet warm. Plows were made of wood; harrows, with wooden teeth; and cooper-ware of staves.

Fights were of frequent occurrence among the younger male members of the community; and the method of fighting was very dangerous to the participants. Although no weapons were used, fists, teeth, and feet were employed at will; and the favorite mode of disabling an antagonist was to gouge out one of his eyes.

The furniture for the tables, for several years after the settlement of the country, consisted of a few pewter dishes, plates, and spoons, but chiefly of wooden bowls, trenchers, and noggins. If these last were scarce, gourds and hard-shelled squashes made up the deficiency. The iron pots, knives, and forks, were brought from east of the mountains, with the salt and iron, on pack-horses. For a long time after the first settlement of the country, the inhabitants married young. There was no distinction of rank, and very little of fortune; on this account, first love usually resulted in marriage; and a family establishment cost but a little labor, and nothing more. Marriages were celebrated at the house of the bride, and the announcement of a prospective wedding created a general sensation; it was looked upon by young and old as an occasion for frolic, feasting, and fun; and was more efficacious in gathering a crowd of people together than even a log-rolling, house-raising, or hunting expedition. The groom usually started early from his father's house so as to reach the home of the bride by noon, the hour generally set for the ceremony—as it was always followed by a bountiful dinner. The assembled company were all pioneers, and there being no store, tailor, or dress-maker within a hundred miles of the trans-Allegheny settlements, they all came dressed in home-made garments. The men wore shoe-packs or moccasins, leather breeches, usually made of buck-skin, linsey hunting shirts, and leggins. The women dressed in linsey petticoats, and linsey or linen bed-gowns, coarse shoes, stockings, kerchiefs, and buckskin gloves, if any. The horses were caparisoned with old saddles, old bridles or halters, and pack-saddles, with a bag or blanket thrown over them; a rope or cord formed the usual girth. The wedding procession, on such occasions, marched in double file, where the horse-paths permitted—for they had no roads. Such paths were sometimes barred by fallen trees, and sometimes barred with mischief aforethought, by interlocking grapevines and saplings, to intercept the progress of the procession. Sometimes a party of neighbors would wait in ambush, and when the procession came up, fire a blank charge from their rifles, which covered the party with clouds of smoke, created surprise and shrieks amongst the ladies, and chivalrous bluster on the part of their escorts. As the procession neared the house of the bride, it sometimes occurred that two or more young men would start for the domicile on horseback, full tilt, to win the bottle of whiskey, which it was previously understood would be hung out from the entrance to the cabin as a prize for the first arrival. The start of the race was announced by an Indian-like yell; and the more the route was encumbered by fallen logs, brush, and muddy hollows, the better opportunity it gave the rival swains to show their horsemanship. The bottle gained, the winner returned to the party, first handing it to the groom, and thence it went from one rider to another, in the manner of a loving cup, each taking a draught, the ladies included.

For the wedding dinner, the table, made of a large slab of timber, hewn out with a broad ax and set on four sticks, was spread with beef, pork, fowl, and sometimes deer and bear steak. Sometimes, there were a few old pewter dishes and plates, but the majority of the guests ate from wooden bowls and trenchers. A few pewter spoons were generally to be seen, but the most of them were made of horn. If knives were scarce, the men used their scalping-knives, or hunting knives, which they always carried in the belts of their hunting-shirts.

After dinner was over, dancing commenced, and it usually lasted until the following morning. The figures danced were reels, quadrilles, and jigs. The dance always commenced with a quadrille, which was followed by a jig; none were allowed to steal away for sleep and if the girls became tired, they were expected (as chairs were very scarce) to sit upon the knees of the gentlemen.

About nine or ten o'clock at night, some of the young ladies would steal away with the bride, and see her safely tucked in bed. The bridal chamber was frequently a loft or attic, above the dancers, to which access was gained by climbing a ladder, and such a chamber was floored with clap-boards, lying loose, and without nails. Some of the young men, in the meantime, would lead away the groom, and send him up the ladder to join his bride; followed later in the evening by refreshments, of which the chief constituent was a huge flash of whiskey, called by the frolickers, "Black Betty."

These entertainments sometimes lasted for several days, none desisting until the party was thoroughly fagged out. If any of the bride's neighbors felt themselves slighted by not being bidden to the festivities, it sometimes occurred that they would show their resentment by cutting off the manes, foretops, and even tails of the horses belonging to the wedding-party.

OHIO VALLEY GENEALOGIES *

JOHN ADAMS, a native of Ireland, settled in Short Creek township, Harrison county, Ohio, about 1805, where he d. 1812; m. ———, d. 1846; had issue: 1. William; 2. James; 3. Samuel, b. Dec. 1, 1809; m. (1st) 1842, Sarah Chambers, d. February 7, 1851, daughter of David Chambers, of Green township; m. (2d) April 2, 1857, Mary Clark, daughter of James Clark, of Athens township (had issue by first wife: i. Joshua, b. August 2, 1842; ii. Rachel, b. September 3, 1844; iii. John, b. December 11, 1850; d. April 27, 1882; had issue by second wife: iv. Clark, m. November 26, 1884, Dora Copeland, daughter of Henry Copeland, of Green township; v. Sarah-Elizabeth); 4. Hannah; 5. Joshua; 6. John.

JOHN ADAMS, a native of Pennsylvania, b. November 13, 1774; settled in Freeport township, Harrison county, Ohio, about 1807, where he d. 1835; m. May 2, 1799, Rachel Asher; b. in Pennsylvania May 16, 1776; d. August 25, 1851; had issue:

I. Rebecca, b. February 29, 1800. II. Elizabeth, b. April 16, 1801. III. Rachel, b. December 18, 1803. IV. Samuel, b. January 16, 1806, in Erie county, Penn.; came with his parents to Ohio; settled in Moorefield township, Harrison county, 1828, where he d. November 17, 1880; m. January 24, 1828, Elizabeth Johnson, d. May 19, 1883, daughter of William and Nancy Stalson Johnson, early settlers in Moorefield township; had issue: 1. John, b. January 17, 1831, in Moorefield township; m. January 13, 1853, Mary E. Swearingen, b. December 30, 1835, daughter of John and Nancy Pumphrey Swearingen, natives of Virginia (had issue: i. Henry-T.; ii. Annie-E.; iii. Albert-D.; settled in Chicago, Ill.; iv. W.-S.; v. Emma-V.; vi. Sadie; vii. Mary-E.); 2. Rachel-A., m. ——— Romans; 3. Mary, m. ——— Johnson; settled in Washington, Davis county, Ind.; 4. William; 5. Samuel, d. young; 6. Rebecca, m. J. Moore. V. John, b. June 20, 1808. VI. Julia-A., b. December 13, 1811. VII. Anthony, b. October 4, 1815.

THOMAS ADAMS, b. in Pennsylvania, about 1790; removed to Cadiz township, Harrison county, Ohio, 1815; settled in Nottingham township, in 1846, where he d. 1855; m. Charity Blair, a native of Ohio, b. 1792, d. 1866, daughter of John Blair; had issue: 1. John, d. in infancy; 2. Maria-Rogers; 3. Percival, b. September 10, 1820, in Cadiz township; m. March 27, 1845, Mary J. Downs, b. August 26, 1822, daughter of Richard and Elizabeth McKinney Downs (the former b. 1797, in Carroll county, Ohio; the latter b. January 22, 1797, in Lancaster county, Penn.); (had issue: i. John-F., b. March 20, 1846; ii. Albert-B., b. May 23.

---

* In the family records given in the following pages, the names of the children of the first one of th family to settle in the Ohio Valley are usually preceded by roman capital numerals (I., II., III., IV. etc.) : the names of the grandchildren, by arabic numerals (1, 2, 3, 4, etc.) : and the names of the great grandchildren by roman lower-case numerals (i., ii., iii., iv., etc.).

1849; iii. Eliza-J., b. March 14, 1851, d. November 14, 1887; iv. Richard-M., b. August 27, 1853; v. Thomas-P., b. December 3, 1857; vi. James-B., b. July 12, 1860; vii. Margaret-B., b. December 13, 1865); 4. James, d. in Nottingham township, October 8, 1888; 5. Matthew, settled in Cadiz; 6. Albert, settled in Missouri; 7. Isabelle, m. Thomas Rogers, settled in Crawford county, Ohio; 8. William, settled in Cadiz; 9. John, settled in Uhrichsville, Tuscarawas county, Ohio; 10. Sarah-E.

WILLIAM ADAMS, a native of Pennsylvania, of Scotch-Irish descent, m. Mary ———, b. in Pennsylvania; settled in Archer township, Harrison county, Ohio, 1819; had issue, among others: 1. Samuel, b. January 20, 1808; d. June 13, 1874, in Archer township; m. 1833, Jane C. Stewart, b. in Pennsylvania, daughter of James Stewart, a native of Ireland who settled in Philadelphia July 4, 1811, thence removing to Washington county, Penn. (had issue, among others: 1. Samuel-W., b. November 18, 1839, m. Flora J. Gray, daughter of Samuel and Eliza Gray, residents of Findlay).

WILLIAM ADAMS, b. September 5, 1799, in Fayette county, Penn.; resided in Short Creek township, Harrison county, Ohio, until 1880; thence removed to Freeport township; d. January 8, 1881; m. in Pennsylvania, Elizabeth Clark, d. December 10, 1869, daughter of Joshua Clark; had issue: 1. David, settled in Short Creek township; m. (1st) November 10, 1855, Lucinda Marsh, of Iowa, d. December 9, 1865; m. (2d) March 14, 1867, Mary Ann Moore (had issue by second wife: i. ———, d. in infancy; ii. William-Moore; iii. Robert-C.).

JAMES AIKEN, a native of Ireland, emigrated to America and settled, about 1803, near Hickory, in Washington county, Penn.; had issue: 1. James, b. 1802, in Ireland; came to Washington county, Penn., with his parents; removed in 1826, to Jefferson, German township, Harrison county, Ohio, and in 1870 to Jewett, Rumley township, where he d. 1885; m. in Jefferson, 1829, Jane Scott, b. 1806 in Washington county, Penn., d. 1867, daughter of Josiah Scott (had issue: i. Elizabeth; ii. John, a minister, settled in Wayne county, Ind.; iii. Martha; iv. Jane, m.

John Roberts; v. Annie, m. James Dennis, settled at Wellsville, Ohio; vi. Robert, settled in Amsterdam, Jefferson county, Ohio; vii. James, b. June 19, 1840; m. March 11, 1865, Maria Mikesell, daughter of Joseph and Magdalene Hoobler Mikesell; viii. Samuel-B.; ix. Josiah; x. Alexander, served in the Civil War; xi. Benjamin; xii. George); 2. John, settled in Chester county, Penn.; 3. William, settled in Baltimore, Md.; 4. Alexander, settled in Pittsburg, Penn.; 5. David, settled in Washington, D. C.; 6. Margaret, m. ——— Agnew, settled in Washington county, Penn.

JOHN ALEXANDER, a native of County Antrim, Ireland, emigrated to America and, about 1826, settled in Pennsylvania; two years later removed to Freeport township, Harrison county, Ohio, where he d. June, 1869; m. in Ireland Mary Allen; d. 1838; had issue: 1. Eleanor; 2. Thomas; 3. Jesse; 4. Mary-Ann; 5. John, settled in Kansas; 6. James, b. March 8, 1829; m. May 27, 1852, Margaret Forsythe, daughter of Matthew Forsythe, of Freeport (had issue: i. Matthew, settled in Freeport township; ii. November 20, 1888, Nancy Harbison; ii. Mary; iii. John; iv. Maggie-E.); 7. Hannah-J.; 8. Elizabeth, settled in Kansas.

JAMES ALLEN, a native of Maryland, d. 1792; m. Rebecca Miller; had issue, among others: I. Reuben, b. in Maryland, 1783; removed in 1812 to Cadiz township, Harrison county, Ohio, where he d. July 8, 1875; m. 1812, Johanna McMillan, d. 1869, daughter of John McMillan, a resident of Harrison county; had issue: 1. Isaac, b. September 16, 1813; m. 1841, Sarah Barrett, daughter of David Barrett, of Cadiz township (had issue: i. Reuben; ii. Rebecca-J., m. R. M. Black; iii. Albert; iv. Winifred); 2. Rebecca; 3. Esther; 4. Amos; 5. Mary-Jane; 6. Ruthann; 7. Johanna; 8. James.

JAMES ALLISON, a native of Ireland, b. 1790; d. at Hopedale, Ohio, 1881; emigrated to America and first settled in Philadelphia, Penn., about 1805; removed to Pittsburg, Penn., and thence to Cadiz, Harrison county, Ohio, where he resided until about 1818; removing thence to Stark county, where he resided until about 1825; m. in Cadiz, Margaret Hervey, d. 1837; daughter of

William and Margaret· Hervey; had issue: 1. Margaret, m. John Galoraith; 2. John-Rea; 3. David, b. in Stark county, Ohio, April 20, 1820; m. (1st) 1854, Mary Crouch, d. 1865, daughter of Levi Crouch, who settled in Green township before 1817, where he d. 1862; m. (2d) 1867, Martha-E. Smith, daughter of Joel Smith (had issue: i. Henry-F.; ii. Willard-R.; iii. Howard-Smith); 4. Henry; 5. Sarah; 6. James, d. 1859; 7. Mary-Jane, m. John Hammond; settled in Athens township, Harrison county; 8. Joseph; 9. Elizabeth, m. Daniel Eaton; settled in Jefferson county, Ohio; 10. Isabella, d. 1830.

SAMUEL AMSPOKER, see Family of Henry Ferguson.

ROBERT ANDERSON, b. in Ireland, 1753; d. September 2, 1838, in Claysville, Washington county, Penn.; emigrated to America and first settled in Maryland about 1780, where he remained until 1786, and then removed to Washington county, Penn.; m. 1781, in Maryland, Margaret Johnson, b. in Ireland, 1760; d. September 13, 1827; had issue:

I. Samuel, b. 1783, in Maryland; d. February 22, 1866; removed to the Stillwater Valley, in Stock township, Harrison county, Ohio, about 1838, locating seven miles west from Cadiz; m. 1813, Catherine Forbes, daughter of John Forbes, of Scotch-Irish ancestry; had issue: 1. Robert, b. in Claysville, Penn., October 11, 1815; came with his father to Harrison county, in 1838; located in North township; m. July 1, 1840, Esther McCollough, a native of Archer township, of Scotch descent (had issue: i. Sarah-A., b. May 23, 1842; m. Thomas McDivitt; ii. William-B., b. in Stock township, Dec. 29, 1843; served in the Civil War; m. Sept. 6, 1870, Mary Buchanan, b. near Jewett, Ohio, Dec. 19, 1845; of Scotch-Irish descent, daughter of Joseph and Elizabeth Hines Buchanan; iii. Samuel-L., b. in Harrison county, January 22, 1846; iv. Isabel-J., b. in Harrison county, January 12, 1848; m. S. J. Rippeth, who d. Dec. 19, 1883; v. Joseph-M., b. in Carroll county, Feb. 20, 1850; a Presbyterian minister; settled in Cincinnati: vi. Mary-E., b. in Carroll county, March 5, 1852; m. Thomas Brough; vii. Thomas-H., b. in Carroll county, August 28, 1854; viii. Martha-F., b. in Carroll

county, December 30, 1856, d. Feb. 17, 1888; m. Thomas Whittaker; ix. John-E., b. August 15, 1862; d. March 25, 1864); 2. John; 3. James; 4. Samuel; 5. Hugh; 6. William; 7. Jane; 8. Thomas. II. Richard, b. in Maryland; III. John, b. in Washington county, Penn., as were also his younger brothers and sisters; IV. William; V. Robert; VI. Mary; VII. Hugh; VIII. James; IX. Jane; X. Margaret; XI. Thomas; XII. ——, d. in infancy.

WILLIAM ARBAUGH, a native of Maryland, of German descent, and a soldier of the Revolution, had issue: I. Jacob; II. Daniel; III. Rachel; IV. Margaret; V. John, b. in Maryland, where he m. Rosanna Wentz, a native of that State; removed to Rumley township, Harrison county, Ohio, about 1820; had issue: 1. Sarah; 2. Margaret; 3. Lavina; 4. Lydia; 5. John; 6. James; 7. Adam; 8. Levi, b. October 28, 1825; m. (1st) December 23, 1858, Elizabeth Reid, d. 1885; daughter of Hugh and Margaret Fulton Reid, pioneers of Archer township, Harrison county; m. (2d) April, 1889, Louisa Hilbert, of Defiance, Ohio.

JONATHAN ARNOLD, of Welsh descent, removed probably from Virginia to Luzerne township, Fayette county, Penn., before 1786, there settling " at a place called the West Bend of the Monongahela River, six or seven miles above Redstone Old Fort (now Brownsville); " d. 1799 (before July 5th); m. Sarah Scott; had issue: I. Jonathan; II. Benjamin, d. about 1804; m. Comfort (or Mary) Cullum (her father of Scotch-English descent; her mother, Dutch), b. about 1758; d. in Archer township, Harrison county, Ohio, 1856, having removed there with her children from Fayette county about 1810; had issue: 1. Rezin, b. in Luzerne township, Fayette county, Penn., Feb. 25, 1786; d. at Manhattan, Kan., Nov. 23, 1858; served in the War of 1812; m. (1st), Dec. 24, 1821, Anna Arrison, b. July, 1794; d. Feb. 16, 1823; m. (2d) at Cadiz, Dec. 9, 1824, Maria Eleanor Robertson, b. Aug. 25, 1802; d. Nov. 15, 1869; daughter of Robert and Beulah Stanley Robertson (the latter descended from George Maris, a Quaker preacher who emigrated to Pennsylvania in 1683; the former, son of John and Eleanor Dick Robertson); (had issue: i. Josephine-A., b. Sept. 30, 1825; m. J. H. Brouse; ii. Marion, b. April 25, 1827; m. Mary O. Borden; iii. William-Stanley, b. March 16, 1829; d. at Los Angeles, Cal., Sept. 7, 1870; m. Katharine Davidson; iv. Maria-Louisa, b. May 3, 1831; m. Dr. S. Whitehouse; v. Laura-Anna, b. June 19, 1833; m. D. W. Lane; vi. Benton, b. March 7, 1835; vii. Amanda-Tingley, b. March 18, 1837; viii. Robert-Robertson, b. in Morgan county, Ohio, Feb. 15, 1839; d. March 5, 1863; ix. John-Hanna, b. July 18, 1841; d. Nov. 7, 1862; x. James-D., b. May 5, 1844; d. Jan. 8, 1891; xi. Charles-Robertson, b. Aug. 15, 1846); 2. Jonathan; 3. James; 4. Comfort, m. Jonathan West, (see West Family); 5. Aneka (Axie), m. James Mehollin; 6. Sophia, m. 1815, Nathan Ross, of Richland; 7. Frances, m. 1819, Charles Conaway; 8. William, b. 1798; d. at Cadiz, 1874; m. May 17, 1831, Jane C. Hoyt, b. 1806; d. 1872; daughter of Jesse and Sarah Hoyt, natives of New York (descendants of Simon Hoyt, who emigrated from England to Massachusetts about 1638); (had issue: i. John, d. in Kansas, 1855, while serving as a Government Surveyor; ii. Mary-A., m. John W. Simmons; iii. Sarah, d. in Washington, Guernsey county, Ohio, 1869; m. James Knox, of Cadiz; iv. Jesse, settled in Washington, D. C.; v. William-H., m. (1st) 1866, Lydia Hunter, d. Feb. 28, 1886, daughter of Judge Joseph R. Hunter, of Cadiz; m. (2d) Caroline Thompson, daughter of James Thompson, of Cadiz township; vi. George, settled at Columbus, Ohio; vii. Jane, settled at Portland, Oregon). III. Levi. IV. William. V. Jemima, m. Rezin (?) Virgin. VI. Rachel, m. William (?) Hammond. VII. Hannah. VIII. Sarah.

GAVIN ARTHURS, see Family of Jonathan West.

THOMAS ATKINSON, d. in Amwell (now Franklin) township, Washington county, Penn., June-September, 1784, leaving children: Mercy, m. —— Ellet; Eleanor, m. Charles (?) Cracraft; Elizabeth, m. —— Ellet; Jean, m. —— Sargent; William; George; Thomas; and (probably) John. George Atkinson, probably the son of Thomas Atkinson first named above, died in Brooke county, West Virginia, 1824, leaving children: Thomas, Mary, Margaret, Eleanor, Sarah, Martha, Ruth,

and Elizabeth. Of these: George, b. May 1, 1778; d. Aug. 27, 1854; m. Sarah Snodgrass, b. Dec. 1, 1786; d. Dec. 23, 1854; had issue: 1. Mary, b. Oct. 7, 1812; m. David Hilbert; 2. Elizabeth, b. Dec. 12, 1813; m. 1833, James Roberts; 3. Elenora, b. March 5, 1816; m. James Ross; 4. Samuel, b. Nov. 30, 1817; d. Oct. 30, 1821; 5. Rebecca, b. Oct. 17, 1818; d. March 17, 1860; m. Andrew Finley Ross, son of Reynolds and Martha Finley Ross, of Westmoreland county, Penn.; 6. George-S., b. Nov. 14, 1819; m. Matilda Simeral, b. Dec. 25, 1818; daughter of James and Mary Ann Vincent Simeral (had issue: i. James-S., b. Aug. 8, 1845; d. March 11, 1895; ii. Frank-H., b. Oct. 12, 1847; m. Mary Bell Shauf; iii. Charles-D., b. Jan. 24, 1851; d. June 18, 1885; iv. Anna-Amanda, b. Nov. 5, 1853; d. Nov. 16, 1855; v. Emma-Caroline, b. Nov. 5, 1853; d. Sept. 24, 1855); 7. Sarah, b. March 1, 1823; m. Levi J. Kennard; 8. Francis, b. June 28, 1825; d. April 11, 1854; m. Eliza Bostwick; 9. Leann, b. Feb. 1, 1827; d. Oct. 1, 1840.

SAMUEL AULD, see Family of Archibald Stewart.

JOHN BAKER (son of John Baker), b. in Pennsylvania, 1777; came with his parents to Green township, Harrison county, Ohio, in 1802; d. Feb. 12, 1847; m. Margaret Buchanan; d. 1829; had issue: 1. Delilah, d. in infancy; 2. John; 3. George; 4. Elizabeth; 5. Rezin, b. November 10, 1810; d. May 26, 1876; m. February 13, 1835, Sarah Thompson, daughter of Thomas Thompson, of Cadiz township (had issue: i. John-L., b. November 20, 1836; ii. Thomas-J., b. January 9, 1838; iii. Weston, b. November 17, 1841; iv. ——, d. aged twenty-two months; v. Elijah-W., b. January 4, 1847); 6. Samuel; 7. William, d. in infancy.

DAVID BARCLAY, b. May 18, 1790, in county Derry, Ireland; emigrated to Baltimore, Md., in 1826, thence removed to Pittsburg, Penn., where he remained two years, and came to Nottingham township, Harrison county, Ohio, where he d. April 9, 1876; m. in Ireland, September 26, 1822, Elizabeth Kissick, b. in County Derry, March 17, 1801; d. January 9, 1871; had issue: 1. James, b. in Ireland; 2. William, b. in Ireland; 3. Barbara, m. —— Love; 4. Eleanor, m. —— McAdams; 5. David;

settled in Allegheny County, Penn.; 6. John; 7. Joseph, b. September 3, 1846, in Nottingham township, where he settled; m. April 30, 1872, Sarah Scott, b. December 28, 1846, in Athens township, Harrison county, daughter of Thomas and Sarah Hogg Scott; 7. Elizabeth, b. Feb. 18, 1841; m. Joseph M. Easter, b. 1841; d. 1871; son of James and Sarah Mehollin Easter; 8. Ann, m. —— Lee; settled in Jefferson county, Ohio; 9. Jane, d. in childhood.

ARTHUR BARRETT, a native of West Virginia, b. 1743; removed to Harrison county, Ohio, in 1803, settling on Brushy Fork Creek, in Cadiz township, where he d. 1828; had issue: I. Nancy. II. Susan. III. Hannah. IV. Rachel. V. Sarah. VI. Thomas, d. Sept.-Dec., 1849; m. Alaneda ——; had issue: 1. Thomas; 2. Warden; 3. Arthur; 4. Esther, m. —— Wilson; 5. Emma, m. —— Spurrier; 6. Belinda, m. —— Cadwalader; 7. Anna, m. —— Miller; 8. Rachel, m. —— Sears. VII. Arthur, b. in Virginia, 1780; came to Ohio with his father; settled in Cadiz township, where he d. 1845; m. (1st) Mary Huff, d. 1814; daughter of William Huff, a famous Indian scout and fighter, who was a pioneer in Ohio; m. (2d) Elizabeth Wolf, d. 1887; had issue by first wife: 1. Meredith; 2. Lewis; 3. William-H., b. June 10, 1812; m. May 25, 1837, Eliza V. Betz, of Jefferson county, Ohio, b. 1817, daughter of William and Elizabeth Betz (had issue: i. Meredith-Mc.; ii. Marion-B.; iii. Brice-W., a Methodist Episcopal minister, d. 1866, in Mount Union, Ohio; iv. Mary-E., m. Henry Haverfield; v. Margaret-E., m. William Birney; vi. Emma-E., m. Samuel Crawford; vii. William-F.; settled at Martin's Ferry, Ohio; viii. Flora-M.); 4. Mary; had issue by second wife: 5. Louisa; 6. Aeneas; 7. John; 8. David. VIII. David. IX. Aeneas. X. Isaac, d. before Aug. 21, 1858; m. Hannah ——; had issue: 1. Erasmus, m. —— Keesey; 2. Arthur; 3. Hiram; 4. Mary-Ann, m. —— White; 5. Tabitha, m. —— Ford.

CONRAD BARRICKLOW, b. in New Jersey, where his emigrant ancestor, a native of Holland, had settled before 1671, emigrating with a brother, who located on Long Island; d. in Franklin township, Fayette county, Penn., 1802,

where he had settled about 1790; served in the Revolutionary War; m. Sarah Farrington; had issue: I. Henry, b. 1771; d. April 27, 1851; m. about 1802, Meriba Oglevee, b. 1773; d. May 15, 1848; removed to Harrison county about 1809; had issue, among others: 1. John, b. in Fayette county, Penn., Oct. 18, 1803; d. July 21, 1875; m. (1st) 1836, Rachel Watson, b. 1819; d. 1839; daughter of Robert S. and Rachel Wilson Watson; m. (2d), 1853, Ann Johnston, d. 1875; daughter of Nicholas Johnston (had issue by first wife: i. Henry, b. March 2, 1837; d. Feb. 28, 1873; served in the Civil War; m. 1869, Rebecca J. McFadden, daughter of Samuel McFadden; ii. Robert-Watson, b. March 6, 1839; m. Aug. 20, 1867, Isabella Alice Moore, daughter of John Moore, of Cadiz); 2. Sarah; 3. Joseph, b. in Fayette county, Penn.; d. April 13, 1875; m. 1846, Phœbe Bartow, b. May 21, 1813 (had issue: i. Henry-S., b. Dec. 10, 1847; m. Oct. 11, 1883, Elizabeth B. Haverfield, d. Sept. 13, 1884, daughter of James and Elizabeth Haverfield; ii. Maribah-Anne, b. April 22, 1849; iii. Joseph-E., b. July 1, 1855; m. Oct. 10, 1883, Mary L. Walker, daughter of Isaac and Angeline Walker); 4. Anna; 5. Henry; 6. Julia; 7. Conrad; 8. Farrington, b. in Athens township, June 6, 1817. II. Daniel. III. John. IV. Farrington. V. Anne ("Nancy"), b. 1778; d. Oct. 16, 1845; m. 1790, Joseph Oglevee, a native of Cecil county, Maryland, who had settled in Franklin township, Fayette county, Penn., about 1788-89; b. 1760; d. Sept. 14, 1835; had issue: 1. Jesse, b. 1804; d. Jan. 26, 1876; m. 1826, Elizabeth Galley, b. 1807; d. 1858; daughter of Philip Galley (had issue, eight children, of whom: i. Joseph, b. June 2, 1827; m. 1850, Rebecca Stoner; ii. John; iii. Philip); 2. John; 3. Farrington.

William Hoese von Barkeloo and his brother, Harman Jansen von Barkeloo, with his wife and two children, landed in New York, where Harman died before 1671. William m. Elizabeth Jane Cloessen in 1666, and d. in 1683. His son, Direk, m. Jamelia (or Janetjie) Van Arsdale, Sept. 17, 1709, and settled at Freehold, Monmouth county, N. J. Conrad, b. Dec. 4, 1680; d. 1714; settled at Raritan, and m. a daughter of Jacob Loes, of Monmouth county. Their son, Conrad, removed to Bucks county, and was the ancestor of the Barkalows there. The family came from Borkelo, in Zutphen, Province of Guilderland, Holland. The name is variously spelled in America, Barkalow, Barcalow, Baricklo, Barricklow, Borcelo, etc.

FREDERICK BARRICKLOW, son of Henry, b. Dec. 3, 1794; d. May 1, 1858; m., 1826, Nancy Dugan, b. 1800; d. Oct. 17, 1881; daughter of John and Catherine McClelland Dugan, of Fayette county, Penn.; removed to Harrison county in 1832; had issue: 1. John-D., b. Nov. 6, 1828; m. Mary Dunlap, daughter of Adam and Martha Thompson Dunlap; served in the Civil War; 2. Henry, b. March 10, 1829; m., October, 1878, Mary Henderson, of Jefferson county, Ohio; 3. Alexander; 4. Margaret-A.; 5. George-W., b. Aug. 7, 1837; m. 1869, Ruth Emily Gregg, daughter of Presley and Sarah Gregg, of Indiana.

JAMES BEALL, b. 1778; d. Dec. 29, 1834; removed from Washington (?) county, Penn., to Wheeling township, Belmont county, Ohio; m. Jane Baird, b. 1783; d. Nov. 11, 1883; had issue: 1. John, m. (1st) Mary A. Hield, b. 1817; d. March 2, 1842; m. (2d) Agnes T. Vincent, daughter of Thomas C. and Jane McCurdy Vincent, of Green township (had issue by first wife: i. Amanda-M., m. James Paul; ii. William-R., m. Laura Clark; had issue by second wife: iii. Jane-C., m. Wesley B. Hearn; iv. Mary-Q., m. Jesse W. Grimes; v. Thomas; vi. Ida-F., vii. Laura-A.; viii. Emma-A., m. Henry H. McFadden; ix. Anna, m. R. N. Dodds, and settled at Springfield, Ill.; x. John-A., a physician, m. Ocena Billinghurst; settled at Detroit, Mich.); 2. Isabel; 3. James, m. Sarah Jamison; 4. Eleanor, m. John McDowell; 5. William, b. 1822; d. Oct. 4, 1856; m. Mary Culbertson, b. 1823; d. May 15, 1889; 6. Jane, m. George McKibbon; 7. Mary-A., b. Dec. 19, 1807; d. May 30, 1834; m. George McKibbon; 8. Josiah, m. Martha Anderson.

JAMES P. BEALL, a native of Pennsylvania, removed before 1826 to Nottingham township, Harrison county, Ohio, where he resided until 1857; thence settled in Crawford county, Ohio, where he d. February 24, 1869; m. (1st) ———; m. (2d) Minerva Huff, d. January 14, 1875, daughter of William Huff (whose sons William, Reuben, Jackson, and Johnson Huff were Indian

scouts in eastern Ohio, Jackson being killed by the Indians); had issue by first wife: 1. Jane, settled in Crawford county; 2. Zenas; had issue by second wife: 3. Elizabeth; 4. Cassandra; 5. Colmore-C., b. June 5, 1826, in Nottingham township; d. March 15, 1880; m. January 24, 1850, Hannah Rogers, b. in Nottingham township, August 19, 1830, daughter of Barrett and Nancy Carson Rogers, natives of Ohio; 6. James-P.; 7. Cyrus; 8. John (Cyrus and John served in the Civil War, dying in the service); 9. Rebecca; 10. Susan; 11. Minerva; 12. Zephaniah.

SAMPSON BEATTY, a native of Ireland, b. 1786; d. November 27, 1849, in Archer township, Harrison county, where he had settled in 1826; m. April 20, 1826, Rachel Johnson, d. June 25, 1850, daughter of Samuel Johnson, a resident of Pennsylvania; had issue, among others: 1. Arthur, b. January 25, 1827, in Archer township; m. March 27, 1851, Susan McDivitt, daughter of Samuel McDivitt, of Stock township, Harrison county; 2. John served in the Civil War; d. 1862, in Knoxville, Tenn.; 3. Jeremiah, served in the Civil War.

STEWART BEEBE, whose paternal ancestor came from England to Massachusetts about 1623, d. at Wilbraham, Hampden county, Mass., 1825; m. Huldah ———; d. 1803; had issue, among others:

I. Walter-Butler, b. at Wilbraham, Mass., 1785-86; d. at Cadiz, Jan. 24, 1836; m. Nancy Maholm, b. 1779-80; d. Oct. 13, 1856; daughter of Samuel and Jane Maholm, of Cadiz; had issue: 1. Walter-Butler, m. 1841, Maria Bayless Welch, b. 1812; d. Aug. 10, 1891; daughter of Rezin and Eliza Bayless Welch, of Cadiz (had issue: i. Eliza-Bayless, m. E. Z. Hays; ii. Nancy-Jeanette, m. John A. Norris, and settled at Columbus; iii. Stuart; settled at Columbus); 2. Stewart, removed to Iowa; 3. James, removed to Coshocton, Ohio (had issue, among others: i. James; ii. Stacy).

II. Rhoda, b. in Hampden county, Mass., June 19, 1792; d. at Cadiz, March, 1876; m. 1819, William Shotwell, son of Hugh and Rosetta Arrison Shotwell (see Shotwell Family).

EDWARD BETHEL, a native of Virginia, removed in 1813 from Loudoun county, that State, to Flushing township, Belmont county, Ohio; had issue:

I. Simpson, a native of Loudoun county, Va.; removed to Athens township, Harrison county, Ohio, about 1810, wnere he died; m. in Virginia, Nancy Holloway; d. in Harrison county; had issue: 1. John, b. June 29, 1806, in Loudoun county, Va.; removed with his parents to Athens township, Harrison county, where he d. April 4, 1887; m. in Harrison county, Elizabeth Oglevee, a native of that county, b. 1804; d. December 5, 1881; daughter of John and Agnes Passmore Oglevee (had issue: i. Simpson, b. Dec. 29, 1828, in Athens township; m. September 23, 1858, Frances Clemens, d. October 26, 1884, daughter of James Clemens, a resident of Athens township; ii. Agnes, m. John Price; iii. John-H.; iv. Sarah-Jane, m. Monroe Dunn; v. Mary-E., m. Samuel Dunlap; vi. Caroline, m. Samuel Compher; vii. Hiram; viii. Isaac-H., b. in Athens township; ix. Elizabeth, m. W. J. Dunlap); 2. Mary; 3. James; 4. Caroline; 5. Hiram. II. James, b. in Virginia about 1795; m. Mary Brock; had issue: 1. Edward; 2. Benjamin; 3. Alfred, m. Margaret McCall (had issue: i. John-A.; ii. James-O., b. December 19, 1848; removed to Moorefield township, Harrison county, 1869; m. June 30, 1870, Nancy M. Slater, b. October 1, 1846, daughter of James Wells and Margaret Dunlap Slater; iii. Jesse-B.; iv. Franklin; v. Mary; vi. Jane; vii. ——, d. in infancy; viii. ——, d. in infancy); 4. Abner; 5. Marion; 6. James-S., settled in Belmont county; 7. Sarah; 8. Lucinda, settled in Kansas; 9. Elizabeth-A.; 10. Mary, b. April 25, 1826; m. August 18, 1844, Joseph Lafferty. b. October 26, 1819, in Virginia; d. March 29, 1886, in Moorefield township. son of Samuel and Margaret Figley Lafferty (had issue: i. ——, d. in infancy; ii. ——, d. in infancy; iii. James; iv. Elizabeth; v. Mary-E.; vi. Sarah-E.; vii. Laura-L.; viii. George-F.); 11. Mary; 12. Eliza-J.; 13. Quintery. III. Anne-Katherine. IV. William V. Henry, had issue, among others: 1. Broudus. b. in Loudoun county, Va.; removed from Belmont county to Harrison county; d. March 17, 1870; m. June 14, 1827, Sarah Smith, d. November 28, 1876, daughter of William Smith (had issue: i. James; ii. Anna; iii. Mary-E.; iv. Henry-Matthess; settled in Moorefield township; v. William-S., b. September 3, 1834; settled in Freeport township,

Harrison county, where he m. October 19, 1858, Phebe Ann Price, d. December 11, 1890, daughter of Reynolds K. and Mary Michnor Price, residents of Harrison county; vi. Louis-B.; vii. Sarah-E., m. W. C. Smith; viii. Barnett; ix. David-R., settled in Freeport; x. Ruth-Ann; xi. Celinda, m. —— Niblock). VI. Thompson. VII. John-Thornton, b. in Virginia, February 11, 1802; removed about 1834 from Belmont county to Harrison county, and settled four miles from Freeport, in Freeport township, Harrison county, where he d. March 1, 1877; m. September 14, 1824, Mary Jackson Billingsby, a native of Virginia; d. August 15, 1870; had issue: 1. Lorinda; 2. Vitura; 3. Celestine; 4. Melinda; 5. Ruth; 6. George-W., b. February 21, 1833, in Belmont county; removed to Harrison county with his parents; settled in Freeport, Harrison county. VIII. Elizabeth.

JOHN. HUGH. ROBERT, and WILLIAM BINGHAM (Hugh and Robert, at least, brothers, and thought to be the sons of Richard Bingham, of Scottish descent), emigrated to America between 1736 and 1760, and before 1774 settled in the Manor of Maske, now Cumberland, Liberty, and Hamiltonban townships in Adams (formerly York) county, Penn.; John Bingham died there Dec. 18, 1739, aged twenty-six years; William Bingham's name appears on a petition from the settlers in Cumberland township in 1755; the names of Hugh and Robert Bingham appear on the tax-list of Hamiltonban township for 1767 (the earliest one now extant), together with the names of Samuel and Thomas Bingham, in the same year. It is possible that John or William Bingham, first named above, may have been the father of Samuel, Thomas, Hugh, and Robert, the last three of whom, at least, were brothers; cf these:

A. Samuel, may have been a brother to Hugh. Robert. and Thomas above; or, possibly, the son of Hugh above (see IV. below).

B. Thomas, see below.

C. Robert. probably the same who died in Hamiltonban township, November-December, 1798, and who had issue: 1. Samuel; 2. Abraham; 3. Eve; the executors mentioned in his will were William Bingham, James Agnew, and

Barnabas McSherry; the name of Catharine Bingham appears as witness to will of Barnabas McSherry in 1823.

D. Hugh, d. in Hamiltonban township, September-October, 1777; m. Martha Armor, daughter of Thomas (?) and ―― McKinley Armor, and probably sister or aunt to Thomas Armor, an active Revolutionary patriot, who died in Yorktown, Penn., February-March, 1785 (he mentions in his will " cousins " Robert and Thomas Bingham); had issue:

I. Samuel; settled in Metal township, Franklin county, Penn., where he d. September, 1801; m. Mary ――; had issue: 1. Elizabeth; 2. Jean; 3. Mary; 4. Catharine, m. ―― Anderson; 5. John, possibly the same who d. in Green township, Franklin county, Penn., August, 1818 (leaving a wife, Hannah, and children: i. Elizabeth; ii. Eleanor, m. ―― Furrey; iii. David; iv. John; v. James; vi. Samuel); 6. Hugh, m. his cousin, Jean Bingham, daughter of Hugh (IV. below); 7. Samuel; 8. Thomas.

II. William, b. 1748; d. Feb. 2, 1816; m. (probably) Ann ――, b. 1760; d. April 9, 1838; had issue: 1. James; 2. Thomas; 3. Hugh; 4. Charles-W., served as an officer in the War of 1812; m. Margaret Agnew of Emmitsburg, Md. (had issue: i. Sophia; ii. William; iii. Agnew; iv. Albert; v. Martha; vi. Margaret, m. 1866, Samuel McFarland, of Smith township, Washington county, b. June 11, 1812; d. June 29, 1829; vii. James, a physician, settled at Clinton, Allegheny county; viii. Emma, m. Dr. W. V. Riddle; ix. Mary; x. Charles-Carroll); 5. John; 6. Armor; 7. Anna-Eliza; 8. William.

III. Robert, possibly the Robert who d. in 1798, whose will is given in connection with his uncle, Robert (C, above); but more probably the Robert Bingham who died in Hopewell township, Washington county, Penn., June, 1804; m. Mary ――; had issue: 1. Hugh; 2. James; 3. Robert; 4. John; 5. Joseph; 6. Elizabeth; 7. Jane; 8. Mary; 9. Phebe.

IV. Hugh, d. in Hamiltonban township, May 11-15, 1793; had issue: 1. John-Armor, d. at Natchez, Miss., 1824; 2. Jean, d. at Freeport, Penn., 1857; m. her cousin, Hugh, son of Samuel (I. above); 3. Hugh, d. at New Wilmington, Lawrence county, Penn., 1865; m.

(1st) Oct. 13, 1807, Esther Bailey, daughter of Captain William and Mary Ann Duncan Bailey, of York, Penn.; m. (2d) Ellen Junkin Galloway; settled in Mercer, Penn., soon after 1800 (had issue by first wife: i. John-Armor, b. at Mercer, Penn., Jan. 21, 1815; settled in Ohio about 1841, and later, at Cadiz; served as a representative in Congress from 1854 to 1873, with the exception of one term; served as United States Minister to Japan from May, 1873, to 1885; d. at Cadiz, March 19, 1900; m. 1844, at Cadiz, his cousin, Amanda Bingham, daughter of Judge Thomas and Lucinda Stuart Bingham [had issue: Lucinda-Stuart, m. 1869, Rev. Samuel Robinson Frazier; Emma; Marie-Scott, m. at Tokio, Japan, 1876, James Robert Wasson]; ii. Marian; iii. William, a Baptist minister; iv. Martha, m. ―― Patterson, and settled at Pittsburgh; v. Hugh-Mason; had issue by second wife: vi. Thomas, settled in California; vii. Ellen-Mary. settled at Canton, Ohio). William Bailey, father of Esther Bailey Bingham, served, in 1775, as second lieutenant of the Independent Light Infantry Company of the first battalion of York county (Penn.) Militia, formed in Yorktown, December, 1775; the company was commanded in 1776 by William Bailey as captain, and was captured by the British at the fall of Fort Washington; settled in Yorktown after the Revolution; m. Mary Ann Duncan, probably daughter of ―― and Margaret Mason Duncan, the latter a native of Scotland, who d. Nov. 16, 1802, leaving funds with which to build the second United Presbyterian Church of Philadelphia; 4. Thomas, d. at Cadiz, April, 1853; m. Lucinda Stuart, d. at Cadiz, Nov. 6, 1844; daughter of James and Mary Ann McIlvaine (or McElwain) Stuart, of Newville, Cumberland county, Penn. (had issue: i. Martha-Armor, m. [1st] 1832, Henry Olmstead; m. [2d] Van Rensselaer Lee; settled at Cincinnati; ii. Lucinda, m. Joseph P. Wood; settled at Omaha, Neb.; iii. Mary-Jane, m. 1833, Josiah Scott; iv. Thomas-M., m. 1844, Rachel Sheets; v. John-Stuart, d. at Shippensburg, Penn., 1891; vi. Amanda, d. 1891; m. 1844, John Armor Bingham, her cousin, son of Hugh and Esther Bailey Bingham; vii. Emma-E., m. 1870, Judge John Stoneman Pearce, of Cadiz; viii. Isabella; ix. Belinda).

James Stuart (or Stewart), father of Lucinda Stuart Bingham, m. near Newville, Penn., Mary Ann McIlvaine (or McElwain); he was probably son of Alexander or Archibald Stewart, of Cumberland county; had issue: 1. Lucinda, m. Thomas Bingham, as above; 2. Mary, m. Samuel Patterson, of Newville, and settled at Cincinnati. V. Elizabeth. VI. Mary, m. ———— McKinley; had issue: 1. Mary; 2. John; 3. Hugh.

Thomas Bingham, a soldier of the Revolution, lived in Mercer county, Penn., as late as 1816; probably brother or son to Hugh, who d. 1777, although not mentioned in his will; but described in will of Thomas Armor, of Yorktown, who died 1785, as his " cousin," and brother to Robert.

Patrick Bingham, d. in Mount Joy township, Adams county, 1796, leaving a wife, Mary, and children: 1. Samuel; 2. Hugh; 3. Bryan; 4. Eleanor; 5. Agnes.

Agnes Bingham, d. in Manor of Maske, Adams county, Dec. 18, 1749, aged fourteen years.

Margaret Bingham is mentioned by her father, Alexander McVear, of Hamiltonban township, Adams county, in his will, dated April 13, 1799.

HUGH BIRNEY, a native of Ireland, son of John Birney, emigrated to America and settled in Chester county, Penn., in 1815; removed in 1819 to Green township, Harrison county, Ohio, where he d. September, 1862; m. 1800, ———— Brown, a native of Ireland; had issue: 1. William, settled in Rumley township; 2. Wesley; 3. Rebecca; 4. Martha, m. Samuel Hitchcock; settled in Indiana; 5. Jane, m. George Leese; settled in Coshocton, Ohio; 6. James, settled in Nebraska; 7. Elizabeth, m. Jacob Hitchcock; settled in Iowa; 8. Samuel, settled in Colorado; 9. Asbury, b. March 15, 1815; m. April 23, 1840, Ellen McCollough, b. May 29, 1821, daughter of Hugh and Isabella Cunningham McCollough, natives of Ireland, who settled in Jefferson county, Ohio, in 1810 (had issue: i. Isabella, d. May 22, 1863; ii. Oliver, settled in German township; iii. Almond, settled in Labette county, Kan.; iv. Hugh-W., b. March 17, 1849; m. (1st) June 15, 1883, Estella Montgomery, d. 1884; m. (2d) February 9, 1886, Hadassah Jack-

man, a native of Washington county, Penn., daughter of Andrew and Elizabeth Gaddis Jackman, natives of Ireland; v. Elizabeth, m. Joseph McCollough; settled in Archer township; vi. Rebecca-J., m. Henry K. Ford; settled in Salem township, Jefferson county).

ISRAEL BIRNEY, a native of German township, Harrison county, Ohio, removed to Nottingham township, where he d. May 11, 1862; m. in Franklin township, Martha Hedges, d. August 30, 1870, daughter of Samuel Hedges, of Cadiz township; had issue: 1. Samuel-H., b. October 28, 1838; m. March 3, 1863, Cynthia Johnson, daughter of Nathan Johnson, of Nottingham township; 2. Prudence, m. Slemmons Welsh; 3. William; 4. Elizabeth; 5. Israel.

JOHN BIRNEY, b. in Green township, Harrison county, Ohio; d. in Washington township, September 9, 1885; m. (1st) in Green township, Hannah McKee, d. 1872, daughter of Robert McKee; m. (2d) Sarah Eaton; had issue by first wife: 1. Rachel, m. Henry Pittis; 2. Nelson; 3. Robert-M.; 4. James-N., b. in Washington township, August 27, 1847; m. 1869, Anna R. McFadden, daughter of Robert McFadden, of Harrison county; 5. Rebecca-J., m. Matthew Simpson; 6. John-T.

ROBERT BIRNEY, b. in Ireland, about 1787; emigrated to America and about 1801 settled in Chester county, Penn.; removed with his family in 1807 to German township, Harrison county, Ohio, where he d. 1874; m. in Chester county, Penn., Margaret Northhammer, b. 1795, d. 1871; had issue: 1. Mary; 2. Zilla; 3. Wesley; 4. John; 5. Asbury; 6. Lot, settled in Washington county, Iowa; 7. Elizabeth, b. March 3, 1822; m. December 26, 1843, Robert W. Endsley, b. 1813, son of James and Elizabeth Walker Endsley; settled in Jewett, in Rumley township, Harrison county (had issue: i. Mary-M., m. William C. Adams; settled in Archer township; ii. Melissa; iii. Lucinda-J., m. Eli Caven; iv. Elizabeth-A., m. R. H. Freshwater, a minister, of Steubenville, Ohio; v. Rebecca-Frances, m. Charles A. Naylor, a minister); 8. Rebecca, settled in Washington county, Iowa; 9. J.-S., b. May 23, 1824; m. March 10, 1841, Susan Mummey, daughter of Charles and Rebecca Hedges Mummey, of Cadiz township (had issue: i. Margaret; ii. Mary, m. John B. Busby; iii. William-Asbury, settled in Cadiz; iv. Robert-M.; v. Charles-R., a minister, settled in New Philadelphia, Ohio; vi. Maria-B., m. Goliath Tedrow).

James Endsley, father of James Endsley, who married Elizabeth Birney, was a son of James Endsley, a native of Lancaster county, Penn., where he died; the son came with his widowed mother to Archer township before 1817, where he d. 1869; m. in Pennsylvania about 1815, Elizabeth Walker, d. 1865, a native of Columbiana county, Ohio; they were the parents of four children, three sons and one daughter, of whom: 1. Robert-W., b. 1813, m. Elizabeth Birney; 2. James, b. Sept. 7, 1817.

JANET BLAIR, see Family of Thomas Phillips.

JOHN BLAIR, a native of Ireland, emigrated to America, and d. about 1840, in Cadiz township, Harrison county, Ohio, where he had settled before 1804; had issue: I. John. II. Daniel. III. James. IV. Charity. V. William, b. March 14, 1804; d. January 29, 1867; m. Sarah Day, b. April 26, 1808; daughter of George and Margaret Moore Day, natives of eastern Pennsylvania, who were early settlers in Cadiz township; had issue: 1. George; 2. John-W., b. May 15, 1831, in Cadiz township; settled in Stock township; m. January 19, 1853, Melissa A. Carson, b. June 19, 1831, daughter of Elijah and Catherine Knight Carson; 3. Albert; 4. Mary.

JAMES BLACK, a native of Ireland, b. 1756; emigrated to America and first settled in Pennsylvania; removed to Green township, Harrison county, Ohio, about 1806, where he d. 1846; served in the Revolutionary War: m. about 1783, Jane Stewart, b. 1753; d. Aug. 22, 1835; had issue: 1. James, b. in Adams county, Penn., 1785; m. 1812, Isabella Hervey, b. 1785; d. Dec. 30, 1865; daughter of Margaret Hervey, an early settler in Harrison county, coming there after death of her husband (had issue: i. John-Hervey, b. in Green township, 1813; d. March 26, 1885; m. Feb. 22, 1838, Mary K. Work, daughter of Alexander Work, a resident of Green township; ii. James-S., b. June 20, 1816; iii. H.-Stewart, b. Nov. 22, 1819; d. Jan. 22, 1890; m. Oct. 31, 1843, Jane Thompson,

daughter of Samuel Thompson, of Green township; iv. Margaret-J., b. March 21, 1845; m. William Dunlap); 2. Mary; 3. Elizabeth; 4. Margaret; 5. Jane.

WILLIAM BOGGS, b. in the North of Ireland, 1716; removed to America about 1728, and afterward settled in Chester county, Penn., where he died; m. Jane Stein, a native of Ireland; had issue: James, b. July 21, 1735; John, b. February 19, 1737; Margaret, b. February 23, 1739; Robert, b. April 9, 1741; William, b. March 14, 1743; Jane, b. April 10, 1745; Elizabeth, b. July 31, 1747; Rebecca, b. January 31, 1749; Agnes, b. February 17, 1752; Mary, b. May 24, 1753; Joseph, b. October 1, 1754; Moses, b. May 6, 1757.

James Boggs (b.1735) settled in Newcastle county, Del.; served in the Revolutionary War; removed about 1790 to Washington county, Penn., settling near the present site of Cross Creek Village; m. (1st) in Newcastle county, Del., Hannah Rice; m. (2d) Sarah Brown; had issue by first wife: 1. William; 2. Rice; 3. Jane; had issue by second wife: 4. James, b. April 27, 1778; 5. Margaret; 6. Robert (twin brother to Margaret), b. November 17, 1779; 7. John, b. June 28, 1782; 8. Rebecca; 9. Mary (twin sister to Rebecca), b. February 15, 1784; 10. Sarah, b. April 21, 1786.

John Boggs (b. 1782), son of James, in 1839 removed from Washington county, Penn., to Harrison county, Ohio, where he d. December 21, 1848; m. September 17, 1812, Sarah Marshall, d. January 6, 1849; had issue: 1. Thomas-Marshall, b. June 26, 1813, in Washington county, Penn.; a Presbyterian minister; removed to Marietta, Lancaster county, Penn., thence to Mount Joy, in the same county, where he d. 1850; m. A. J. Cunningham, of Chester county, Penn.; d. January 6, 1849 (had issue: i. Elizabeth, m. Rev. Edgar, President of the Wilson College for women, in Chambersburg, Penn.; ii. John-C.; iii. William-M., settled in Chicago); 2. James-Brown, b. January 20, 1815; d. in infancy; 3. William, b. November 5, 1816; d. 1836; 4. John-M., b. October 20, 1818; a Presbyterian minister; served Paxtang and Derry congregations, near Harrisburg, Penn., thence removed to Millersburg, Ohio, and from there to Independence, Iowa, where he d. September 1, 1872; 5. Samuel-M., b. December 6, 1820, removed to Short Creek township, Harrison county, where he remained until 1884, when he settled in Athens; m. September 1, 1854, Margaret Parks; 6. Sarah-Ann, b. February 3, 1823; m. William H. Watson; settled in Belmont county (had issue: seven children); 7. Robert-W., b. August 1, 1825; removed to Short Creek township, where he remained until 1884, then settled in Athens; 8. James, b. July 23, 1828; d. February 13, 1840.

WILLIAM BOGGS, see Family of James Simeral.

SAMUEL BORLAND, a native of Ireland, emigrated to America and before 1785 settled near the present Manor Station, in Westmoreland county, Penn., where he m. Lydia Cary; both died in Pennsylvania; had issue:
I. Samuel, b. in Westmoreland county, 1785; d. 1862, in North township, Harrison county; m. (1st) Mary Little; m. (2d) Elizabeth Hevlin, daughter of Samuel and Elizabeth Hevlin; had issue, by first wife: 1. William, settled in Tuscarawas county, Ohio; 2. Washington, settled in Carroll county, Ohio; 3. Lydia, m. James Waddington, of Nebraska; had issue by second wife: 4. Mary, m. James Mackey; her family settled in Dennison, Ohio; 5. David, b. January 27, 1831, in North township; m. December 24, 1857, Ann Havnar, b. 1833; d. October 26, 1890; daughter of Dominick and Elizabeth Havnar, both of whom died in Monroe township.

JOHN BOYD, b. in Ireland; d. 1832; m. (2d) —— McMillan; emigrated to America about 1812 and settled in Freeport township, Harrison county, Ohio; had issue: 1. Samuel; 2. William, b. 1798; d. April 12, 1867; m. about 1864, Anne White, b. in Ireland, 1802; d. at Freeport, Jan. 7, 1879 (had issue: i. John, m. Sarah Fulton; ii. Hannah, m. William Williams; iii. George, b. 1827; m. Eliza Vail Markee, daughter of William and Hannah Norris Vail; iv. Sarah, d. young; v. Eliza, m. William Fulton; vi. Mary, m. James Fulton; vii. Margaret, m. —— Likes; viii. Belinda, m. James Carr; ix. William, m. Mary Phillips; x. Martha, m. R. Niblick; xi. Melancthon, d. young).

HENRY BOYLES, b. 1770; d. 1834; removed from New Jersey to Virginia, where he m. (1st) Rachel Barkhurst; m. (2d) in Chester county, Penn., Jane Filson, d. 1854; daughter of Robert Filson; removed to Bedford county, Penn., and thence, in 1821, to Steubenville, Ohio; had issue by first wife, three children; had issue by second wife: 4. John; 5. Samuel; 6. Elisha; 7. Margaret; 8. Henry, b. in Lancaster county, Penn., Jan. 5, 1814; d. July 8, 1892; removed to Harrison county, 1843; m. at Cadiz, Martha Grimes, b. May 12, 1826; d. April 4, 1874; daughter of William and Rebecca Grimes (who had settled in Harrison county about 1802), and both died at Cadiz, 1840; 8. Joseph-Filson, d. at Rockport, Ind., 1889.

GETTYS BRADEN, see Family of Jacob Stahl.

ROBERT BRADEN, of Irish descent, b. 1773, in Pennsylvania, of which State his paternal grandfather was a native, removed in 1800 to Short Creek township, Harrison county, Ohio, where he d. 1837; m. (1st) in Pennsylvania, —— Finney, daughter of James Finney, who settled in Short Creek township 1800; m. (2d) 1815, Catherine Hay, b. about 1775; d. 1845; had issue by first wife: 1. ——; 2. ——; had issue by second wife: 3. John, d. aged twenty-four years; 4. David-B., b. August 21, 1818, in Short Creek township; m. (1st) November 5, 1851, Susannah M. Groves, b. 1813; d. October 19, 1885, daughter of Francis and Jeanette Groves, of Cadiz township; m. (2d) in Canonsburg, Penn., September 2, 1886, Melissa Donnell, a native of that place; d. May 14, 1889; 4. Anna, m. Walker Patton; 5. Robert, settled in Washington, Iowa; 6. William, settled in Iowa; 7. Elizabeth, d. aged eight years; 8. Mary-Jane, m. Casper Devilbiss, and settled in Iowa.

JAMES BRADFORD, of Scottish descent, b. in Washington county, Penn., 1790, a son of James Bradford, a native of Lancaster county, Penn.; removed about 1800 to Cadiz. Harrison county, Ohio, where he d. 1830; m. Mary Morrison, who after her first husband's death returned to Washington county, Penn., where she m. (2d) David Watson, of Pennsylvania; she d. aged eighty-one years; daughter of James Morrison, of Washington county, Penn.; had issue (surname Bradford): 1.

James-M., b. February 28, 1821, in Cadiz; settled in Scio, about 1874; m. 1844, Julia Ann Lewis, of Jefferson county, Ohio, daughter of William and Mary Lewis (had issue: i. Ann-Eliza, m. (1st) Dr. Kennedy; m. (2d) Marian Coates; settled in Pratt county, Kan.); 2. David, settled in Washington county, Penn.; 3. Eliza, settled at Scio.

ABRAHAM BRANSON, a native of Virginia, of English descent, removed from near the vicinity of Winchester to central Ohio, about 1800; had issue: I. Reese, located in St. Clairsville, Belmont county, Ohio, where he died; had issue: 1. Abraham-Dow, b. June 13, 1806, in Belmont county, Ohio; located, 1831, at Kinsey's Mills, Belmont county, on the National Pike; settled near Georgetown, in Short Creek township, Harrison county, Ohio, about 1833, where he d. January 16, 1867; m. June 2, 1831, in Jefferson county, Ohio, Ann W. Wilson, b. 1806, near Mount Pleasant, Ohio; d. February 3, 1888, daughter of Jonathan and Hannah Wilson, pioneers of Jefferson county (had issue: i. Lindley-M., b. September 26, 1832, at Kinsey's Mills, Belmont county, Ohio; m. May 7, 1874, Anna M. Fox, daughter of Charles J. and Esther Cooper Fox, of Harrison county; ii. Elizabeth-S., m. Isaac Thomas; iii. Abraham-Wilson, b. December 9, 1846, in Short Creek township; m. May 25, 1875, Lucy Thomas, daughter of Isaac and Annie Ladd Thomas; iv. Rachel, settled in Iowa; v. William, settled in Kansas; vi. Jonathan, d. in infancy; vii. John-C., d. young); 2. William; 3. Maria; 4. Eliza.

Isaac Thomas, father of Annie L. Branson, was b. June 1, 1813; settled in Short Creek township; afterward removed to Mount Pleasant, Jefferson county, Ohio; m. January 1, 1834, Mary Ladd. b. near Richmond, Va., August 14, 1812; d. 1872; daughter of Robert and Mary Ladd.

ANTHONY BRICKER, of German ancestry, removed from Pennsylvania to Green township, Harrison county, about 1804, where he d. 1813; m. Margaret ———; had issue: 1. Henry; 2. George ———; 3. John, b. May 9, 1793; d. March, 1861; m. Anna Busby, b. 1812 (had issue: i. David; ii. John, m. ——— Holmes; iii. Elizabeth, m. Dr. William Beadle); 4. David; 5. Elizabeth, m.

(1st) ——— Hilbert; m. (2d) ——— Warfel.

JESSE BRINDLEY, a native of Germany, settled in Maryland about 1775, where he died; m. (1st) in Germany, ———; m. (2d) Julia Kent; had issue, among others: I. Benjamin, b. in Maryland; removed from Harford county, that State, to Archer township, Harrison county, Ohio, in 1825; afterward settled in Green township, where he died; m. in Maryland, Ellen Cooper, b. about 1759; d. 1824; had issue, ten children, of whom: 1. Priscilla, m. Caleb Low; settled in Steubenville, Ohio; 2. John, b. in Harford county, Md., March 16, 1806, came to Harrison county with his parents; settled in Cadiz, about 1873; m. 1830, Ann Brown, b. 1809; d. October 6, 1889; daughter of Hugh and Jane Brown, residents of Archer township (had issue: i. Hugh, settled in Kansas; ii. Benjamin; iii. Ellen, m. James Crawford; iv. Frank; v. Albert; vi. David; vii. Nathaniel; viii. Wesley; ix. Sarah, m. J. Rea Finney; x. John; xi. ———, d. in infancy; xii. ———, d. in infancy; xiii. Thomas, b. March 16, 1846; m. November 11, 1869, Hester A. Birney, daughter of Hamilton Birney, a resident of Archer township).

GEORGE BROKAW, of Huguenot descent, emigrated to America before 1775, with his brother, John, both of whom served in the Revolutionary War; located in Pennsylvania; removed about 1802 to Green township, Harrison county, Ohio, and afterwards settled in Athens township; m. about 1777 (?), Jane Custard (or Custer); had issue: 1. Abraham, b. April 8, 1778; 2. Benjamin, b. Sept. 28, 1779; 3. Sarah, b. Feb. 20, 1782; 4. George, b. March 27, 1784; 5. William, b. Feb. 10, 1786; 6. Judah, b. March 19, 1788; 7. Jane, b. July 15, 1790; 8. John, b. Sept. 23, 1793; settled in Athens township. where he d. March 25, 1876; m. July 10, 1823, Sarah Burwell, b. 1802; d. April 5, 1883, daughter of Job Burwell, a resident of Harrison county (had issue: i. Catherine, b. April 18, 1824; m. Benjamin Covert; ii. Jane, b. August 22, 1825; m. William Smith; iii. Mary, b. November 29, 1827; m. Isaac Fitch; iv. Margaret, b. November 19, 1829; m. William Price; v. Nancy, b. October 21, 1831; vi. George, b. December 5, 1833; settled in Iowa; vii. John-P., b. April 25, 1836; m. December 25, 1867, Mary E. McGrew, daughter of William McGrew, a resident of Green township; viii. Sarah, b. July 29, 1843; m. Wesley Van Horn; ix. Martha, b. September 1, 1845; m. Abraham Atzinger); 9. Mary, b. February 14, 1796; 10. Isaac, b. April 30, 1798; 11. Jacob, b. October 31, 1800; 12. Peter, b. December 25, 1802.

Some families of the name of Brocaw are found in the early records of Somerset county, N. J., and Adams county, Penn.

BASIL BROWN and THOMAS BROWN, two brothers, settled in Luzerne (then Springhill) township, Fayette county, Penn., about 1768. Thomas, b. about 1746, settled on the site of the present town of Brownsville about 1776, and began to lay out town-lots in 1785; he died in 1797, before March 27th, leaving issue: Ignatius, Thomas, Levi, Zachariah, Simeon, Elizabeth (m. ―― Cox), Eleanor, Ann, and Ruth; two of his daughters married William Crawford and ―― Ewing. Basil left issue: Thomas, m. (1st) Dorcas Goe, daughter of William Goe; m. (2d) Mrs. Philip Worley; Basil, d. unm.; Sarah, d. unm. Possibly descended from one of the above was Basil Brown, said to have been a native of England, who resided in Brownsville before 1800; had issue, among others: 1. Basil, b. at Brownsville, 1801; d. at Cambridge, Ohio, 1851, where he had settled in 1844; m. Nancy Johnson, b. 1809, d. 1888, a native of Pennsylvania (had issue, seven children, among whom: i. Turner, m. Mary E. Price; ii. Melford-J., b. in Brownsville, Jan. 16, 1832; removed to Ohio about 1850, and in 1853 settled at Cadiz; m. 1855, Martha Robinson, daughter of John Robinson, an early settler, who came from Pennsylvania).

JOHN BUCHANAN, a native of Londonderry, Ireland. settled in Carlisle, Penn., before 1776; served in the Revolutionary War, and after the close of that war located in Washington county, Penn.; m. ―― Ross; had issue: I. John. II. Jonathan. III. Mary. IV. Ross. V. Samuel, b. in Maryland, March 4, 1773; d. March 23. 1858; removed to the Connotton Valley, Harrison county, Ohio, before 1806; m. (1st)

in Washington county, Penn., 1799, Mary Neiper, a native of that county; d. July 15, 1818; m. (2d) Mrs. Mary Stanley Buchanan, b. 1778; d. January 21, 1838; of Mt. Pleasant, Ohio, widow of John Buchanan, who was a second cousin to Samuel Buchanan; had issue by first wife: 1. Jane; 2. Maria; 3. John, b. 1807; 4. Margaret; 5. Joseph, b. April 23, 1814; d. July 11, 1883; m. February 8, 1838, Elizabeth Hines, b. 1819; d. Jan. 5, 1883; daughter of Jacob and Susanna Brough Hines, of Archer township (had issue: i. Margaret, b. October 28, 1839; m. Johnson Montgomery; settled in Jefferson county, Ohio; ii. Susan, b. October 9, 1841; m. John Stringer; settled in Harrison county; iii. Samuel, b. October 25, 1843; d. September 5, 1863; iv. Mary, b. Dec. 19, 1845; m. William B. Anderson; v. John, b. March 11, 1848; settled in Pueblo, Colo.; vi. Thomas, b. November 8, 1850; a Presbyterian minister; settled at Ida Grove, Iowa; vii. Malinda, b. April 6, 1854; m. John Patterson; settled in Archer township; viii. James, b. October 5, 1856; d. December 11, 1857; ix. Albert, b. May 1, 1859; d. in infancy; x. Elizabeth, b. 1861; d. in infancy); 6. Nancy. VI. Thomas. VII. Joseph. VIII. George. IX. Margaret. X. Mary. XI. ――, m. ―― Harvey.

WILLIAM BUCHANAN, b. in Pennsylvania, 1790, of Scotch descent; served in the War of 1812; settled in Harrisville, Harrison county, Ohio, before 1853; m. in Ohio, Abigail Mercer, d. May 30, 1857, a descendant of Edward Mercer, of Anglo-Irish descent, who settled in America about 1720; had issue: 1. David; 2. Wilson; 3. William, b. May 1, 1853; settled in Hopedale, Harrison county; m. June 29, 1880, Virginia W. Maddox, a native of Short Creek township, daughter of Wilson and Mary Ladd Maddox.

Wilson Maddox, father of Virginia Maddox Buchanan, came to Harrison county in 1826, where he d. April 30, 1859; his wife d. January 17, 1875; came from Virginia and settled in Harrison county in 1833.

JOHN BUSBY, a native of Maryland; settled in Archer township, Harrison county, Ohio, in 1805; m. Agnes Wisner; had issue, fourteen children, among whom: 1. Abraham-H., b. in Archer township, Jan. 18, 1814; m. May 18,

1848, —— Marshall, daughter of James and Elizabeth Marshaii, natives of Pennsylvania, of Irish descent (had issue: i. John-B.; ii. Nancy-Jane, a. March 5, 1885; iii. Isaac-Jackson; iv. William-R.; v. James-W.; vi. Anna-Mary, m. Delmar Robinson); 2. Sarah, m. —— Healea; 3. Rachel, m. David Smith; 4. Belinda, m. 1819, Nathaniel Baker; 5. Elizabeth-Ann; 6. Eda, m. Zachariah Baker; 7. Mary-Ann, m. 1834, John McCombs; 8. Dorcas, m. 1833, Aaron Conaway; 9. Deborah, m. 1838, Albert Singhaus; 10. Jane, m. 1840, William Strawsbaugh.

JOHN CADY, a native of county Tyrone, Ireland (son of Joseph Cady, who settled in Reading, Penn., in 1783), settled in Washington county, Penn., and thence removed to Cadiz township, where he died, 1824; m. Margaret Parr; had issue, among others: 1. James, b. in Washington county, Penn., March 2, 1812; removed to Virginia in 1832, and thence to Flemingsburg, Ky., in 1838; returned to Cadiz, 1842, and settled at Cadiz Junction, 1856; m. October 2, 1834, Caroline T. Purdy, a native of New York City (had issue: i. Isabel; ii. William-H.; settled in Dennison, Ohio; iii. Dorcas-C., m. William H. Randall, of Southern California; iv. Adaline-E.; v. Caroline-T.; vi. Elizabeth-A.; vii. Ella, m. R. J. McCarty; viii. Lucinda-M., m. John S. McKay; settled in Memphis, Tenn.; ix. John-E., settled at Cadiz Junction; x. James-R.); 2. Mary, b. 1790; d. July 8, 1865; m. Hiram Conwell; 3. William, settled at Cadiz (had issue, among others: i. James; ii. Isabel, m. —— Lupton; iii. Ida).

JOHN CALDWELL, b. near Redstone Creek, Fayette county, Penn., 1781, of Scotch-Irish descent; in 1808 removed to Green township, Harrison county, Ohio, where he d. Dec. 10, 1859; m. (1st) in Pennsylvania, Elizabeth Birney; d. in Harrison county; m. (2d) Sarah Reed, b. 1791; d. Feb. 16, 1871; daughter of Robert Reed, a pioneer in Harrison county; had issue by first wife: 1. Robert-Reed, settled in Wood county, Ohio, where he died aged seventy-five years; had issue by second wife: 2. Samuel-Mitchell, settled in Clarke county, Ohio; 3. Elizabeth-Rea, m. James Davidson; 4. Ankrum; 5. William-H., b. Aug. 22, 1825; settled in Cadiz township; m. 1856, Mary-Ann

Cochran, daughter of Robert and Sarah Cochran, of Harrison county; 6. John, settled in Marshall, Kan.; 7. Isaac-Shannon; 8. Martha-McCrea, m. James English; 9. James, settled in Fort Wayne, Ind.; 10. David-Hilbert; 11. Albert-Hamilton. David and Albert Caldwell settled in Guernsey county, Ohio.

JOHN CAMPBELL, see Family of Samuel Patton.

JOHN CAMPBELL, a native of Scotland, had issue, among others:
I. John, probably b. in Pennsylvania; removed to Guernsey county, Ohio, before 1818, where he resided for four years; then settled in Green township, Harrison county, where he died; m. (1st) Margaret Fogle; d. 1844; m. (2d) —— ——, of Tuscarawas county; had issue by first wife: 1. George; 2. Nathaniel; 3. Andrew; 4. Elizabeth; 5. Margaret; 6. Abraham; 7. Frederick; 8. John, b. Feb. 26, 1822; m. Malinda Dennis, daughter of Jacob Dennis, a resident of Green township (had issue: i. William; ii. Rebecca, m. William Ford; iii. Jennie, m. James Rutledge; iv. Margaret, m. Merchant Ault; v. John; vi. Laura, m. William Abraham; vii. Edward; viii. Josiah-P.-Scott; ix. ——, d. in infancy; x. James; xi. Nellie); 9. Hester; 10. Robert; 11. Henry.

JOHN CAMPBELL, d. in Windsor township, York county, Penn., 1775 (before Sept. 18), leaving a wife, Anna, and children, William, John, James, Charles, and Ann; of these:
John Campbell, b. 1744; d. Aug. 13, 1807; served in the Revolutionary War (probably as a militia lieutenant); removed with his family to Washington county, about 1780, and settled in Cross Creek township, where he died; m. March 31, 1772, Mary Hammond, of York county, b. 1752-53; d. March 18, 1817; had issue:
I. Ann, b. March 27, 1773; probably d. young.
II. Griselda (" Gracie ") b. Feb. 19, 1775; m. Major Benjamin Bay, and removed to Belmont county, Ohio, about 1812.
III. John, b. Jan. 22, 1775; d. July 24, 1844; m. Elizabeth Lyle, and removed to Wheeling township, Belmont county, Ohio.
IV. William, b. Aug. 11, 1779; m.

Eleanor (?) Smith, and removed to Wheeling township, Belmont county, Ohio.

V. James, b. Dec. 29, 1781; d. July 17, 1842; m. Margaret Smith, b. Oct. 16, 1784; d. Oct. 8, 1878; removed to Wheeling township, Belmont county, Ohio, in 1803; served as a captain in the War of 1812; had issue, among others: 1. John, a physician, b. Nov. 21, 1804; d. Sept. 17, 1882; m. May 11, 1830, Jane Irwin, b. 1808; d. 1883 (had issue: i. Mary, b. Jan. 24, 1833; ii. Margaret-A., b. Feb. 17, 1836; iii. James-B., b. Nov. 14, 1839; iv. Rachel-J., b. April 14, 1842; v. Maria-L., b. March 29, 1848; vi. Martha-E., b. Jan. 18, 1852); 2. William-M., b. 1808; m. (1st) Mary Kerr, b. 1820; d. Dec. 13, 1874; m. (2d) Louisa Dixon, b. May 8, 1835; d. July 19, 1889.

VI. David, b. March 25, 1784; m. Ann Rea, daughter of William and Jane Mason Rea, of Lower Mount Bethel township, Northampton county, Penn. (the former b. Sept. 13, 1762; d. in Cross Creek township, Washington county, Penn., Sept. 28, 1835; son of the Revolutionary Col. Samuel [b. 1732; d. 1816] and Ann McCracken Rea).

VII. Charles, b. Oct. 31, 1786; d. June 4, 1832; m. Feb. 22, 1810, Esther Mason, of Cross Creek township; had issue: 1. Lucinda, b. 1811; 2. Mary, b. 1812; 3. Elizabeth, b. 1813; 4. John, b. 1815; 5. William-Mason, b. Nov. 10, 1816; m. (1st) 1842, Isabella Ramsey; m. (2d) 1856, Anna E. McIlvaine; 6. Louisa, b. 1818; 7. David, b. 1820; 8. Hannah, b. 1822; 9. Esther, b. 1824.

VIII. George-H., b. June 5, 1789; m. Elizabeth Rea, sister to Ann Rea; had issue: 1. Jane, m. John Wilson, of Noble county, Ohio; 2. John, m. Eliza Moore, of Hickory, Penn.; 3. Mary, m. John Graham, of Knox county, Ohio; 4. William, m. Elizabeth Nichols, of Greene county, Penn.; 5. Elizabeth, d. unm., aged fifty-eight; 6. Samuel-Scott, b. 1822; d. 1895; removed to Harrison county, Ohio; m. (1st) —— Wright; m. (2d) Ann E. Wallace, of Washington, Penn.; m. (3d) Mrs. Mary Law Long, of Harrison county; 7. George-W., b. 1826; d. 1885; 8. Esther-I., removed to Cadiz, Ohio (three other children died young).

IX. Mary, b. Feb. 4, 1792; m. William Fulton, of Mount Pleasant township, Washington county.

X. Elizabeth, b. Oct. 9, 1793; m. William Mason Rea, brother to Ann and Elizabeth Rea.

CHRISTIAN CANAGA (originally spelled Gnaegi), emigrated from Berne province, Switzerland, to America before the Revolution (1750-70), and afterwards settled in Somerset county, Penn., whence he removed to North township, Harrison county, Ohio, about 1807, where he died 1813; had issue, among others: 1. Jacob, b. Feb. 23, 1780; d. 1872; m. 1804, Susanna Livingstone, d. 1830, daughter of Christian and Anna Livingstone, of Somerset county; removed to North township, Harrison county, about 1806; had issue: 1. Anne-D., b. May 19, 1805; d. 1889; m. 1823, Rev. D. Strayer; 2. Catharina, b. May 23, 1807; m. Michael Firebaugh; 3. Levi, b. Aug. 29, 1809; 4. Joseph, b. Feb. 21, 1811; 5. Jacob, b. Jan. 15, 1813; d. 1857; m. Sarah Fisher; 6. Salome, b. Aug. 10, 1814; 7. Elias-Greene, b. April 23, 1816; d. Sept. 4, 1888; m. June 27, 1844, Jane McClintock, b. 1818; d. 1894; daughter of Thomas and Elizabeth McClintock, of Carrcll county (had issue: i. Silas-Wright, b. June 2, 1845; m. 1868, Elizabeth Wight, daughter of George Adam and Biddy Gordon Wight; ii. Orlando-Loomis, b. July 11, 1846; iii. Milton-Addison, b. 1848; d. young; iv. Alfred-Bruce, b. Nov. 2, 1850; v. Elizabeth-Ellen, b. June 21, 1852; vi. Melissa-Anna, b. Feb. 18, 1854; vii. Josephine, b. Dec. 14, 1855; viii. Emma-Jane, b. June 9, 1857; ix. Heber-Edson, b. Jan. 3, 1860; x. Thomas-McClintock, b. March 12, 1863; xi. Barton Livingston, b. Dec. 19, 1865; xii. Ira-Atilla, b. Jan. 31, 1867; xiii. b. Sept. 25, 1870); 8. Lydia, b. Aug. 1, 1819; m. Napoleon B. Fisher; 9. Manassas, b. May 17, 1821; 10. Susanna, b. June 5, 1823; 11. Mary, b. 1825; 12. John, b. Feb. 10, 1830.

ERASMUS CANNON, b. in Maryland, March 3, 1763; settled about 1815, in Athens township, Harrison county, Ohio, where he died; m. Mary Bowman, d. aged ninety years, a native of Maryland; had issue: I. Mary. II. Rachel. III. Maria. IV. Euphemia. V. Harriet. VI. Moses, b. in Maryland. Oct. 15, 1794; settled in Athens township, where he d. Aug. 26, 1851; m. October 15, 1819, Rachel Turner, d. December 11, 1864; daughter of Joshua and Priscilla

Turner, of Moorefield; had issue: 1. Sarah-Ann, m. Joseph Dickerson, and settled in New Athens; 2. William, settled in Cadiz; 3. James, b. March 31, 1824; m. Oct. 21, 1848, Mary Trimble (daughter of John Trimble, whose father was killed while serving in the Revolutionary War; his mother, Eliza McCall Trimble, settled in Belmont county, Ohio, in 1805); (had issue: i. Mary-E.; ii. Sarah-T.; iii. Rett-A.; iv. John-A.; v. Hayes, settled in Butte City, Mont.; vi. Jeanette; vii. A.-A.); 4. John; 5. Rachel-Jane; 6. Thomas; 7. Moses; 8. Allen; 9. Caroline, m. Basil Bowers; settled in New Martinsville, W. Va. VII. Ewell. VIII. John. IX. Erasmus. X. Thomas.

JOHN CARNAHAN, a native of the North of Ireland, d. at Cadiz, May 20, 1806, being the fourth person buried in the old graveyard at that place; had issue, among others: I. George. II. Samuel, b. 1764; d. Oct. 13, 1851; m. Sarah ———. III. Joseph, b. 1770; d. Feb. 21, 1852; m. ——— Slater; had issue: 1. Joseph; 2. Samuel; 3. James; 4. John, b. 1806; d. 1882; m. 1831, Martha Henderson, b. 1800; d. 1880, daughter of Alexander and Mary Bell Henderson (had issue: i. Mary-Belle, m. Lawson Scott; ii. Andrew-Henderson, m. 1860, Elizabeth Wood, daughter of Sylvanus and Amanda Tingley Wood; iii. Elizabeth, m. Dr. William T. Sharp; iv. Thomas-Lee, m. Sarah Emerson; v. Martha, m. George Black); 5. Margaret; 6. Sarah; 7. Isabel, d. May, 1816. IV. John. V. James.

JAMES CARRICK, a native of Adams county, Penn., of Scotch-Irish descent, removed to Harrison County, Ohio, about 1811, settling in Short Creek township, where he d. 1820; m. in Adams county, Penn., 1775; his wife d. 1833; had issue, among others: 1. David, b. April 1, 1782; d. Dec. 25, 1863; served in the War of 1812; m. Elizabeth ———, b. 1794; d. Nov. 15, 1873 (had issue, among others: i. Agnes-E., m. 1845, John Hanna Hammond); 2. John, d. 1854; 3. Laura, m. ——— Andrews; 4. Nancy, m. ——— Carr; 5. James-W., b. October 14, 1799; removed with his parents to Short Creek township, where he d. March 10, 1885; m. (1st) 1825, Martha Pennel, d. Jan. 7, 1833; m. (2d) 1834, Mrs. Sarah Campbell Boggs, a native of Belmont county, Ohio, d.

1870, daughter of William Campbell, an early pioneer of Belmont county (had issue by first wife, three children; had issue by second wife, eight children, of whom: i. Ezra-L., b. December 15, 1843; served in the Civil War; m. 1872, Martha Jamison, daughter of Andrew Jamison).

GEORGE CARROTHERS, b. in Ireland, 1784; emigrated to America and first located in Washington county, Penn., 1803; removed, about 1813, to Nottingham township, Harrison county, Ohio, and in 1836 to Moorefield township, where he d. December 4, 1863; m. (1st) in Pennsylvania about 1810, Jane Hall, b. in Ireland, February 2, 1791; d. February 2, 1828; m. (2d) 1828, Ann Hastings, a native of county Fermanagh, Ireland, b. May 1, 1798; d. January 14, 1886; had issue by first wife: 1. James; 2. John; 3. George; 4. William; 5. Margaret; had issue by second wife: 6. Sarah, m. James Wilson; 7. Beatty, b. March 14, 1832, in Nottingham township; settled in Moorefield township; m. (1st) Nov. 26, 1856, Martha J. McClintock; d. March 26, 1859; m. (2d) June 21, 1860, Elsie Johnson, b. July 10, 1839; 8. Eliza, m. Jackson Kennedy; 9. Mary; 10. Christopher; went to Japan as a missionary in 1869.

JOHN CARSON, a native of Maryland, b. 1780; d. May 13, 1858; settled in Nottingham township, Harrison county, Ohio, about 1800; m. Hannah Rogers, also a native of Maryland, b. 1777; d. Nov. 2, 1852; had issue, among others:

I. Franklin, b. July 8, 1808; d. June 16, 1874; m. (1st) Oct. 20, 1829, Sarah Hines; d. 1844; daughter of John and Rebecca Deacon Hines, who were among the early settlers in Harrison country, coming from Westmoreland county, Penn.; m. (2d) Nov. 25, 1852, Tabitha Hines, sister of his first wife; had issue by first wife: 1. Louisa-A., b. September 2, 1830; 2. John, b. November 2, 1831; settled in Lucas county, Iowa; 3. Hannah, b. December 6, 1833; 4. William-F., b. August 4, 1835; settled in Lucas county, Iowa; 5. Elijah-R., b. June 13, 1837; m. Drucilla P. Johnson, b. Sept. 13, 1840, daughter of Abiram and Lydia Turner Johnson, pioneers of Nottingham township; 6. Walter-B., b. August 20, 1838; 7. Rebecca, b. December 8, 1839; 8. Harvey-L., b. September

19, 1841; served in the Civil War and died in that service; 9. Isaac, b. February 15, 1844; settled in Lucas county, Iowa.

II. Elijah, b. 1810; d. November, 1887; m. 1832, Margaret Mahaffey, b. in Washington county, Penn., 1803; d. 1884; had issue, among others: 1. ——, m. Joseph G. Rogers; 2. Elmira-J., m. James M. Hines; 3. ——, m. Thomas Benton Huffman. III. William. IV. Walter. V. John.

JOHN CARSON, see also Family of Rudolph Hines.

WILLIAM CARSON, b. in Ireland, 1803; d. there, 1865; m. Jane Noble, b. 1792; d. 1812; had issue, among others: 1. William-N., b. 1822; d. 1899; m. in Ireland, 1845, Margaret Tiernan, b. 1821, d. 1885, daughter of Henry and Jane Abram Tiernan.

JOHN HENRY CARVER, b. in Germany; came to America as a drummer boy with a regiment of Hessian soldiers who served on the British side in the Revolutionary War; about 1779 m. Talitha Mitchell, d. March 14, 1845, a native of North Carolina; he settled in Mt. Pleasant, Jefferson county, Ohio, about 1798, removing thence to Flushing township, Belmont county, where he resided until 1812, and then located at Freeport, Harrison county, where he died March 15, 1841; had issue: I. John. II. Rebecca, m. —— Thompson. III. Henry. IV. Elizabeth, m. —— Carrington. V. Jane. VI. Ann, m. —— Bailey. VII. Abner, b. Jan. 23, 1805; d. May 13, 1884; m. (1st) 1829, Eliza Norris, d. July 23, 1855, daughter of Thomas Norris, of Freeport; m. (2d) Rachel Cullen, d. Aug. 14, 1882; had issue, among others: 1. Thomas-P., b. Sept. 19, 1843; served in the Civil War; m. November 15, 1868, Mary A. Johnson, daughter of William Johnson, of Smyrna. VIII. Mary, m. —— Cox, and settled in Iowa. IX. Elijah, b. July 17, 1810, in Belmont county; settled in Freeport; m. (1st) Nov. 26, 1835, Nancy Boals, d. Jan. 24, 1854; dau. of James Boals, of Freeport; m. (2d) April 25, 1871, Narcissa E. Bevan, daughter of Joseph Bevan; had issue by first wife: 1. Henry-B., b. October 17, 1836; d. June 25, 1890; settled in Washington township; m. (1st) April 8, 1858, Sarah Phillips; d. Aug. 20, 1876; daughter of John Phillips, of Washington town-

ship; m. (2d) March 20, 1878, Nancy E. McCullough, daughter of Jonathan McCullough, of Tippecanoe; 2. Mary-J., m. Thomas Sloan. Elijah Carver had. issue by second wife: 3. Anna; 4. Thaddeus.

JOHN CASSELL, a native of Germany, emigrated to America and settled in Frederick county, Maryland, where he married and died; had issue, among others: 1. Jacob, b. April 15, 1799; d. near Hopedale, 1881; m. in Maryland, 1821, and removed from Unionville, that State, to Green township, Harrison county, about 1835 (had issue: i. John-Wesley, m. 1893, Elizabeth Jones; ii. Chelnissa, d. 1888; m. —— Decker; iii. Mary, d. young).

PHILIP CECIL, born in Maryland, son of Kingsbury Cecil, also a native of Maryland, who afterward settled in Kentucky, where he died; the son removed to Harrison county, Ohio, before 1823, where he died in 1850; m. Mary Logan; d. 1845; daughter of John Logan; had issue: 1. Richard, b. in Harrison county, May 23, 1823; m. Feb. 25, 1847, Jane E. Bliss, daughter of Zadoc Bliss, of Franklin township (had issue: i. Sarah-Jane, b. April 16, 1848; m. A. Oliphant; ii. George, b. July 17, 1850; iii. Mary-K., b. May 19, 1853; iv. Emma-L., b. April 9, 1856; v. John-B., b. Dec. 11, 1858; vi. Jesse-F., b. March 21, 1861; vii. Clara, b. Sept. 10, 1863; viii. ——, d. in infancy; ix. Clarence-A., b. June 8, 1867; x. Merritt-R., b. March 31, 1870); 2. John, m. Dec. 10, 1846, Susanna Donahey; 3. William; 4. Kingsbury; 5. Margaret; 6. Jesse, m. 1838, Elizabeth Goddard; 7. Wesley.

Zadoc Bliss, father of Jane E. Cecil, was a native of Connecticut; b. Feb. 26, 1788; d. July 8, 1850; settled in Franklin township, about 1826, having removed thither from Columbiana county, Ohio; m. Keziah Hoskins, b. April 4, 1786; d. May 31, 1851; had issue: 1. Ralph; 2. Sarah-C.; 3. Mary; 4. Emily; 5. James; 6. George-W.; 7. Zebulon; 8. John; 9. Keziah; 10. Jane-E., m. Richard Cecil.

NATHAN CHANEY, d. 1837; a native of Maryland; removed from Virginia to Cadiz township, Harrison county, Ohio, about 1805; m. in Virginia, Sarah Mansfield; d. 1847; had issue, among others: I. Thomas, b. Oct. 28, 1803, in Vir-

2

ginia; d. July 1, 1890, in Archer township; served in the War of 1812; m. Sept. 25, 1836, Elizabeth Clark, had issue: 1. James; 2. John; 3. William; 4. Sarah; 5. Martha; 6. Samuel, b. Dec. 14, 1846; m. Aug. 5, 1875, Clarinda Edwards, daughter of John Edwards, of New Athens, Harrison county; 7. Mary-Ann; 8. Elizabeth-Ann; 9. Mary-Ellen; 10. Thomas-W.; 11. Hannah; 12. Nancy.

James Clark, father of Elizabeth Chaney, was a native of Fayette county, Penn., where he married Sarah Watson; served in the War of 1812; had issue: 1. Martha; 2. Elizabeth, m. Thomas Chaney; 3. Mary; 4. John; 5. William.

ROBERT CHRISTY, of Scottish descent, b. about 1732-35; emigrated to America and first settled in New York City; removed to Jefferson county, Ohio, before 1800, and later located in Archer township, Harrison county, Ohio, where he d. 1830; served in the Indian wars; m. Margaret Marshall, a resident of New York; had issue: 1. George, d. aged eighty-four years; served in the War of 1812; 2. William; 3. Robert, b. in Jefferson county, 1799; settled in Nottingham township, Harrison county, about 1832, where he d. Oct. 9, 1853; m. 1831, Jane M. McCleary, b. 1812, daughter of Andrew McCleary (d. in Jefferson county, 1812) and sister to James McCleary (b. 1809) (had issue: i. David, b. Nov. 12, 1832; settled in Stock township; m. April 7, 1864, Elizabeth Spiker, daughter of Christopher Spiker); ii. Elizabeth, m. John R. Hines; iii. Margaret; iv. James; v. Sarah-A., m. Meredith Barrett; vi. George; served in the Civil War; vii. Jane-Anne; viii. Mary, m. George Garver; ix. Lydia-C., m. Elias Hines; x. Joanna-Matilda, m. Pinckney Moore); 4. David; 5. John; 6. Sarah, d. aged eighty-three years; 7. Nancy, d. aged over eighty years; 8. Margaret.

JAMES CLARK, b. probably in Virginia; d. in Pennsylvania; m. Margaret Trimble; had issue: 1. James; 2. Matthew, b. 1800, in Virginia or Pennsylvania; d. in Cadiz township, 1852; m. in Washington county, Penn., Jane Barr, b. 1801; d. Oct. 5, 1865; daughter of John and Sarah Gailey Barr, of Scotch-Irish descent (had issue: i. John-Barr, b. Oct. 9, 1827; d. Jan. 13, 1872; a United Presbyterian minister; served as colonel of the 193d Pennsylvania Volunteer Infantry in the Civil War; m. (1st) Lydia Collins; m. (2d) Frances Florence; ii. Eleanor-Margaret, m. John C. Jamison, of Cadiz, Ohio); 3. Samuel, m. Jane Hawthorne; 5. John; 6. Thomas, m. Ellen Barr; 7. Sarah, m. James Hunter; 8. Elizabeth, m. James Carnahan; 9. Rebecca, d. young; 10. Anne, d. young.

JOSHUA CLARK, a native of Fayette county, Penn., of the family of Walter Clark; removed, in 1804, to Belmont county, Ohio, and in 1808 to Short Creek township, Harrison county, thence to Freeport, in the year 1839, where he d. Jan. 17, 1868; m. in Pennsylvania, Susannah Flaugh, of English descent; d. July 6, 1853; had issue: 1. Elizabeth; 2. John; 3. Abisha, settled in Maynard, Ohio; 4. Mary; 5. James; 6. Hannah; 7. Margaret, m. Augustus Harris; 8. Susan, m. James Reeves, and settled in Washington township; 9. Joshua, b. April 9, 1823; settled in Freeport; m. Feb. 28, 1862, Sarah Covington; d. July 5, 1887; daughter of Elijah Covington.

ROGER CLARK, b. 1726, in Ireland; d. 1765; settled in Cumberland county, Penn.; m. (1st) in Pennsylvania, ―― Agnew; m. (2d) ――; had issue by first wife: Elizabeth, James, Nancy, and Jane; had issue by second wife: Joseph and John.

James Clark, the second child by the first wife, was b. 1751, in Cumberland county, Penn., removed to Westmoreland county, Penn., 1776; settled in Jefferson county, Ohio, in 1810, where he died, in 1833; served in the Indian and Revolutionary Wars; m. 1775, Jane Jack, a native of Cumberland county, b. 1753; had issue:

I. John. II. Joseph, b. in Westmoreland county, Penn., Feb. 12, 1778; removed to Jefferson (now Harrison) county, Ohio, in 1808, and settled in Green township, where he d. Oct. 3, 1861; m. March 4, 1811, Rachel Johnson; b. Dec. 31, 1793; d. Sept. 3, 1854; had issue: 1. James, b. 1812; d. 1847; removed to New Philadelphia; 2. Mary, b. Aug. 22, 1813; 3. Johnson, b. Aug. 31, 1814; settled in Cadiz; 4. Ingram, b. Sept. 21, 1816; d. Feb. 18, 1876; served in the Ohio Legislature, 1866-68; m. Feb. 16, 1842, Sarah Moore, daughter of William Moore, a resident of Green township (had issue: i. Rachel, b. Nov. 10, 1842; d. April 22, 1865; ii. Alfred-W., b. Aug. 27, 1845; settled in Nebraska; iii. John, b. April, 1849; d. April 12, 1871; iv. Joseph-A., b. Nov. 16, 1852; settled in Nebraska; v. Clara-J., b. Feb. 27, 1855; d. April 22, 1880; m. Lee Johnson; vi. Charles-G., b. July 10, 1860; settled in Nebraska; vii. Ella-B., b. December 5, 1862; m. George Mills); 5. Jane, b. Sept. 26, 1818; m. David Moore (had issue: i. James-Clark, settled in Cadiz); 6. Rachel, b. March 4, 1824; 7. Ephraim, b. Feb. 19, 1826; d. at Cadiz, Oct. 10, 1885; served in the Ohio Legislature, 1855-57; m. Isabella Kennedy, daughter of Dr. Moses and Catherine Snyder Kennedy (had issue: i. Oliver, removed with his parents to Cadiz, in 1871; m. (1st) Sept. 13, 1871, Clara S. Cochran; d. Jan. 20, 1878; daughter of Samuel Cochran; m. (2d) March 20, 1879, Elizabeth Agnes Kerr, daughter of James Kerr, of Cadiz; ii. Frances, d. aged six years; iii. Ida, m. George D. McFadden, of Cadiz; iv. Cora-V., d. aged seven years); 8. Joseph, b. June 4, 1830; settled in Cadiz; 9. Oscar, b. March 10, 1833; m. Margaret Hamilton; settled in Walton, Kan.; 10. Albert, b. Jan. 16, 1836; m. Amanda Kerr, daughter of John C. Kerr, of Harrison county; settled in Nebraska. III. William. IV. Mary. V. James. VI. Andrew. VII. Thomas. VIII. Robert. IX. Francis.

Samuel Kerr, grandfather of Elizabeth Kerr Clark, was b. Oct. 25, 1792; d. in Short Creek township, Harrison county, where he was among the pioneers; served in the War of 1812; m. (1st) Sept. 28, 1815, Annie Smith; m. (2d) September 8, 1835, Agnes Hamilton; had issue by first wife: 1. Sarah-J., m. James McLaughlin; 2. James, b. April 19, 1818; d. in Cadiz, Jan. 21, 1886; m. Julia Ann Carrick (had issue: i. Samuel-Mason; ii. David-Ramsey, a minister; iii. Elizabeth-Agnes,m. Oliver Clark; iv. James-A.; v. Adda-Zilla, m. Charles G. Clark, and settled in Nebraska; vi. Mary-M.; vii. Julia-Ella, m. ―― Matson, and settled in Short Creek township); 3. Mary, m. William Campbell, of Belmont county, Ohio; 4. Joseph-S.; 5. Ellen, m. Stewart Carrick; 6. Robert, a Presbyterian minister; had issue by second wife: 7. Thomas-H.; 8. Samuel-C., a Presbyterian minister; 9. Margaret-Ann, m.

John Calderhead; 10. William-J.; 11. Effie-J.

JAMES CLEMENTS, a native of Maryland, settled in Cadiz township, Harrison county, Ohio, before 1819; later removing to Athens township, where he died; m. Plessey Merritt, a resident of Belmont county, Ohio; had issue: 1. Nancy; 2. Josiah; 3. Daniel, b. in Athens township, Dec. 24, 1819; d. Sept. 1, 1872; m. 1842, Elizabeth Dickerson; d. Jan. 22, 1888; daughter of Baruch Dickerson, a resident of Cadiz township (had issue: i. Thomas-W., b. June 14, 1846; m. June 19, 1883, Josephine Smith, a resident of Harrison county; ii. John-M., b. June 4, 1848; m. June 20, 1888, Mary Sloan, daughter of John Sloan, a resident of Moorefield township; iii. Samuel; iv. Jane-Elizabeth, m. Robert Bartow; v. Josiah; vi. Louisa; vii. Clara-P., m. ―― Dunlap; settled in Belmont .county, Ohio); 4. John; 5. Esther; 6. Eliza; 7. Mary; 8. Merritt; 9. James.

JOHN CLEMENS, a native of county Tyrone, Ireland, died aged one hundred years, his wife also having attained the same age when she died; first settled in Eastern Pennsylvania; removed from Raccoon Creek, Washington county, Penn., to Harrison county, Ohio, about 1837, and later to Tuscarawas county, where he died; m. in Ireland, Frances Scott, a sister of Alexander Scott, later of Scott's Mills, Tuscarawas county, Ohio; had issue: 1. David; 2. John; 3. Joseph; 4. William; 5. James, d. aged seventy-two; first located in Washington county, Pennsylvania; removed to Harrison county, Ohio, in 1836, and subsequently settled in Athens township; m. in Pennsylvania, Mary Campbell, a native of that State, d. aged seventy years, daughter of James Campbell and wife, of Scotch descent, who died in Pennsylvania (had issue: i. John, m. Elizabeth Moore; ii. Eliza-Jane; iii. Frances, m. Simpson Bethel; iv. Samuel-C., b. June 28, 1833, in Washington county, Penn.; removed to Athens township, Harrison county, Ohio, and later to Cadiz township; m. May 12, 1864, Sarah J. Dunlap, daughter of Hugh B. Dunlap, of Athens township; v. Mary-J., m. Thomas Furbay, of New Athens, Ohio; vi. Alexander-S., settled in Newport, Tuscarawas county; vii. Rebecca; viii. Gillespie); 6. Samuel, d. 1887, in Iowa; 7. Elizabeth; 8. Mary; 9. Frances; 10. Rebecca.

SAMUEL COCHRAN, of Scotch-Irish descent, b. in Lancaster (now Dauphin) county, Penn., 1738; d. 1818; served in the Revolutionary War; located on the Monongahela River, ten miles above Pittsburgh, before 1800; m. 1770, Mary Shearer, b. 1754; d. 1805; had issue, among others:
1. Robert, b. in Lancaster (now Dauphin) county, Penn., Sept. 15, 1771; d. Feb. 1, 1861; settled near Cadiz, Ohio, about 1801; m. (1st) 1800, in Pennsylvania, Dorcas Neal, d. 1801; m. (2d) 1807, in Allegheny county, Penn., Sarah Calhoun; b. Jan. 8, 1787; d. April 4, 1867; daughter of David and Eleanor King Calhoun; had issue by first wife: 1. Dorcas, b. 1801; d. 1853; m. Isaac Whittaker; had issue by second wife: 2. Eleanor, b. Feb. 11, 1808; d. Sept. 17, 1867; 3. Samuel, b. March 30, 1811; d. September, 1899; m. (1st) 1839, Sarah J. Hedges, d. 1841; m. (2d) 1849, Margaret Thompson, b. July 11, 1820, daughter of Samuel Thompson, of Green township (had issue by first wife: i. an infant, d. 1841; had issue by second wife: ii. Clara-S., d. 1878; m. Oliver Clark, of Cadiz; iii. Robert-Byron, m. 1886, Flora Morgan, daughter of M. Morgan, of Short Creek township; iv. Belle, m. William Morgan, of Cadiz township; v. Martha); 4. David, a United Presbyterian minister; b. Aug. 1, 1814; d. Oct. 30, 1883, in Leavenworth, Kan.; m. Martha Shearer (had issue, three sons and six daughters, of whom: i. William; ii. Martha—both removed from Leavenworth with their mother to San Jose, Cal., after 1883; iii. James, settled in Oregon; iv. ——, m. —— Shearer, and settled in Kansas City, Mo.; v. ——, m. —— Bissett and settled in Leavenworth, Kan.; vi. George; settled in Kansas City, Mo.; vii. ——, m. —— Pierson, and settled in Tonganoxie, Kan.; viii. ——, m. —— Monks, and settled in Chicago; ix. Elizabeth, settled in Lawrence, Kan.); 5. Mary, b. Dec. 11, 1817; d. July, 1899; m. W. Harvey Caldwell, and settled near Cadiz; 6. Robert-Reed, b. Sept. 14, 1822; m. Oct. 10, 1867, Rachel Hedges, daughter of William and Mary Jane McClellan Hedges, of Cadiz township (had issue: i. John-William; ii. Robert-

Emmett; iii. Mary-Eleanor; iv. Frank McClellan; v. Rees-Burchfield); 7. Sarah-Jane, b. Oct. 9, 1825.

DAVID COLLINS, m. Mrs. Ann Workman Glasgow; had issue: 1. John, m. Ellen Patterson (had issue: i. Patterson; ii. David; iii. Jane; iv. Elizabeth; v. Ellen); 2. Martha, d. 1847; m. (1st) James Bowland; m. (2d) 1822, John Maholm (had issue, by first husband, surname Bowland: i. Robert, b. 1798; d. 1880; ii. Anna, b. April 18, 1810; d. May 16, 1844; m. Robert Lyons; had issue by second husband, surname Maholm; iii. Eliza-Jane, m. 1848, Joseph Sharon; iv. Martha-Matilda, m. 1845, Rezin J. Bennett; v. James-B.); 3. Elizabeth, m. Robert Gilmore (had issue: i. Ephraim, m. Julianna Dennison; ii. John; iii. Arabella, m. Theodore Jennings; iv. Joseph, m. Letitia A. Brady; v. Ann-W., b. April 16, 1817; d. Oct. 30, 1880; m. John M. Richey; b. Nov. 2, 1803; d. Jan. 30, 1897); 4. Ruth, m. George McFadden.

GEORGE COLLINS, b. in Maryland, about 1796; d. in Moorefield township, Harrison county, Jan. 1, 1870, where he had settled in 1832; m. in Frederick county, Maryland, Eliza Johnson, b. 1803; d. 1890, daughter of Joseph and —— Bain Johnson; had issue: 1. Elizabeth; 2. Israel; 3. William; 4. Amanda; 5. Mary; 6. Zachariah, b. in Maryland, 1828; d. 1884; m. Rachel Willoughby (daughter of Henry Willoughby), b. in Knox county, Ohio, 1831 (had issue: i. George-H., m. Elizabeth A. Hilbert; ii. William; iii. Nicholas-B.; iv. Elizabeth, d. young; v. Ann-Eliza, m. David N. Reynolds; vi. Parley-A., m. Frank J. Mead); 7. Catharine; 8. George-P.; 9. Nicholas; 10. Battelle; 11. John-W.; 12 Cyrena; 13. Eliza; 14. Thomas-L.

DAVID COMLY, b. in Washington county, Penn., Aug. 8, 1798; removed in 1814 to what is now Carroll county, Ohio; settled near Mount Pleasant, Jefferson county, about 1817, where he d. 1886; m. 1821, Sarah Whinnery, a native of Pennsylvania; had issue, among others: 1. John-W., a physician; b. June 24, 1823; settled in Harrisville, Harrison county, m. 1849, Mary C. Armstrong, a native of Ohio, of Scotch-Irish descent; d. 1863; daughter of Charles and Sarah Armstrong (had issue: i. Sarah-J., m. Dr. N. R. Coleman, and settled in Columbus; ii. Marietta; iii. William-J., d. in infancy).

CHARLES CONAWAY, see also Family of William Johnson.

MICHAEL CONAWAY (brother to Charles [1751-1837] and Samuel Conaway) b. 1737, near Baltimore, Md., of Scotch-Irish descent; m. 1779, Elizabeth Davis, a native of Scotland; had issue: I. Michael-C., b. near Baltimore, Md., 1780; removed about 1800 to Pennsylvania; in 1805 settled with his parents in what is now Stock township, Harrison county, Ohio; m. in Pennsylvania, 1805, Martha Hoagland, daughter of James and Mary Hooey Hoagland; had issue: 1. Eli, b. 1806; d. 1832; 2. Aaron, b. Oct. 13, 1807; settled in Archer township; m. March 28, 1833, Dorcas Busby, daughter of John Busby, of Archer township (had issue, fourteen children, of whom: i. Michael; ii. ———; killed in the Civil War; iii. ———; iv. John-B., settled in York, Neb.; v. Henry-O., settled in Omaha, Neb.; vi. Alpheus-B., settled in New Sharon, Iowa; vii. ———, m. R. M. Welch; viii. ———, m. C. B. Burrier); 3. Elizabeth, m. 1828, George McKinny (had issue, five children); 4. Henry, m. Rosanna Mosholder (had issue, three children); 5. Susanna, m. Joel Smith (had issue, three children); 6. Rachel, m. Alexander Picken (had issue, seven children); 7. Enoch, d. 1861, in West Virginia; m. (1st) Amanda Granfel; m. (2d) Charlotte Loman (had issue by both wives); 8. Mary, d. 1855; 9. Moses-H., b. Aug. 6, 1817; d. Oct. 3, 1890; m. (1st) July 15, 1856, Mary J. Crozier, b. Feb. 15, 1829; d. Nov. 19, 1862; m. (2d) Sept. 13, 1883, Kate Gallaher, b. Sept. 28, 1843. II. John, b. 1790, in Kent county, Md.; came with his parents to Stock township, Harrison county, where he d. 1861; served in the War of 1812; m. Elizabeth Hoagland, b. 1797, in Pennsylvania; d. 1886, in Stock township; had issue, nine children, of whom: 1. Charles, b. Sept. 12, 1819; m. April 1, 1847, Mary Given, b. Sept. 1822, daughter of Robert and Rebecca Evans Given, pioneers of Harrison county (had issue: i. Rebecca-J., d. aged fourteen years; ii. Robert, settled in Conneaut, Ohio; iii. John-W.; iv. Ella-E., m. Samuel Milliken, and settled in Tuscarawas county, Ohio; v. Mary-Martha); 2. Elizabeth; 3. Jemima; 4. Susanna; 5. Rachel; 6. Cynthia, m.

——— Layport; 7. Hannah, m. ——— Whitaker; 8. Martha, m. ——— Patterson. III. Charles, m. Frances Arnold; had issue, nine children. IV. Catharine, m. Henry Barnes. V. Susan, m. Gabriel Holland (see Holland Family). VI. Elizabeth, m. Archibald Virtue.

James Hoagland, father of Martha Conaway, was of Dutch descent; settled in Harrison county; his wife, Mary Hooey, was of Irish descent; had issue, among others: 1. Martha, m. Michael Conaway (b. 1780); 2. Mary, m. Harvey Tumbleson; 3. Jane, settled in the South; 4. Ann, m. Piatt Martin. James Hoagland's brother, Aaron Hoagland, settled in Ashland county, Ohio; another brother, Moses, settled in Holmes county, Ohio.

PATRICK CONNOR, b. in Ireland, 1807; d. in Pennsylvania, 1890; m. Margaret Gallagher, b. 1813; d. 1889; had issue: 1. Bryan, b. 1835; settled at Salineville, Ohio, 1871; m. in England, Mary Morris, daughter of James Morris (had issue: i. James-V.); 2. Mary, m. ——— Cordy; 3. Margaret, m. ——— Whalen; 4. John, m. Mary McCann.

HIRAM CONWELL, a native of Virginia, of Scotch descent; settled in Harrison county before 1816; about 1830 he went to New Orleans, and never returned, having died, it is thought, of cholera, which was epidemic at that time; in Ohio he had married Mary Cady (b. 1790; d. July 8, 1865), a daughter of John and Margaret Parr (1761-1864) Cady; had issue, among others: 1. John, b. 1827, in Cadiz; served as an officer in both the Mexican and Civil Wars; he was one of a party that went to the gold fields of California in 1849, returning to Cadiz in 1851; m. (1st) October, 1848, Mary J. Gordon, a native of Ireland (had issue: i. Jesse-L.; ii. Frances-May; iii. William-Henry, who died in infancy; iv. Charles-Emmett; v. Minnesota, m. Wesley Holmes, of Harrison county; vi. Caroline, m. John F. Kennedy; vii. Ella, m. (1st) Charles B. Pearce; m. (2d) Dr. Campbell); John Conwell m. (2d) Elizabeth McConnell, of Cadiz. Mrs. Mary Cady Conwell married (2d) Joseph Forker, by whom she had issue, surnamed Forker: 1. Isabella-Belinda, m. John Shauff; 2. Henry-G., settled in Cadiz; 3. Mary-Jane, m. Dr. C. Thomas; settled in Des Moines, Iowa.

JAMES COOKE, a native of Ireland (son of Robert Cooke, a native of Scotland, who removed to Ireland), emigrated to America and, about 1788, settled in Washington county, Penn., thence removed to Athens township, Harrison county, Ohio, about 1805; d. 1815; m. in Ireland, Nancy Moore, d. 1829; had issue: I. Mary, m. John Love. II. Elizabeth, m. John Henderson. III. Robert. IV. William. V. James. VI. John. VII. Thomas. VIII. George, b. in Washington county, Penn., May 5, 1804; settled in Athens township; m. July 10, 1824, Nancy Anderson, daughter of Col. William Anderson, an early settler in Cadiz township; had issue: 1. Nancy, m. William Gillespie, and settled in Guernsey county; 2. Melila, m. James Crossan; 3. Ruth-E., m. David McConaughey; 4. Mary; 5. Jane, m. Thomas Morrow; 6. James, b. Dec. 28, 1835; m. March 4, 1858, Jane McCracken, daughter of William McCracken, of Belmont county; 7. William; 8. George; 9. John, settled in Bridgeport, Ohio; 10. Thomas, twin brother to John; 11. Mary-N., m. John H. Rourk; .12. Matilda, m. William Walker.

JOSEPH COOK, b. in Pennsylvania; settled in Freeport township about 1820; had issue: 1. Jesse, b. 1810; d. 1898; m. 1825, at Westchester, Ohio, Susanna Wilson, b. 1814; d. 1896; daughter of James Wilson (had issue: i. William, b. 1837; removed to B'oomington, Ill.; m. Temperance Persgoy; ii. T.-H.; settled in Scio); 2. Joseph, b. 1812; 3. David, b. 1815; 4. Jane.

WILLIAM C. COOPER, a native of England, emigrated to America and first settled in Pennsylvania; later removed to near Deesville, Harrison county, Ohio, where he died; his widow d. in Cadiz township; had issue: 1. Sarah, m. ——— Lafferty, and settled in Cadiz township; 2. William, settled in Carrollton, Ohio; 3. Benjamin; 4. Stephen, settled in Oregon; 5. John, settled in Rising Sun, Ohio; 6. Thomas, d. in the army; 7. Michael, removed to Indiana; 8. Louisa. m. John S. Clevender, and settled in Dakota; 9. Mary.

JOHN COPE, a native of Virginia (great grandson of Oliver Cope, who emigrated from Wiltshire, England, to Pennsylvania. 1687. and d. 1701), removed from Virginia to Belmont county, Ohio, in 1812; located in Short Creek

township, Harrison county, in 1813, where he died; m. in Virginia, Grace Steer, b. 1763; d. March 30, 1885; had issue:
I. William, b. Aug. 1, 1796; d. in Iowa, Sept. 27, 1869. II. Joseph, b. in Virginia, Jan. 9, 1799; d. April 22, 1885; m. in Fayette county, Penn., 1825, Ruth Griffith, of Welsh descent, b. in Westmoreland county, Penn., Jan. 1, 1801; daughter of William and Sarah Cooke Griffith; had issue: 1. Amos-A., settled in Poweshiek county, Iowa; 2. Benjamin-T., b. May 15, 1828; m. 1855, Rachel Lukens, b. 1834, in Guernsey county, Ohio, daughter of Moses and Elizabeth Barber Lukens; 3. Israel, d. in infancy; 4. Oliver-G., b. Aug. 11, 1830; served in the Ohio Legislature, 1880-1881; m. March 6, 1856, Sarah Williams, d. May 19, 1859, daughter of Nathan and Sarah Williams, of Harrison county; 5.———, d. in infancy. III. Isaac, b. Feb. 1, 1801; d. Dec. 19, 1883. IV. John, b. in Virginia, April 25, 1803; m. 1832, Mary Lukens, b. in Pennsylvania, Nov. 4, 1804; d. July 19, 1876; daughter of Moses and Sarah Lukens; had issue: 1. Sarah-T., b. June 2, 1833; 2. Lemuel, d. young; 3. Hiram, b. Dec. 16, 1843; m. 1872, Martha Thomas, daughter of Isaac and Anna Thomas, early settlers in Harrison county. V. James, b. Nov. 9, 1806; d. in Hopedale, Jan. 17, 1868.
Moses and Elizabeth Lukens, parents of Rachel Cope, removed to Harrison county from Guernsey county, in 1838. The father of Elizabeth Lukens was Samuel Barber, b. 1777; d. in Harrison county, in January, 1851; m. Ann Schooley, b. 1766; d. Oct. 1, 1863.

SAMUEL COPE, b. in Frederick county, Va., 1762; d. November, 1854; settled in Green township, 1823; m. in Frederick county. Va., 1797, Sarah Steer, b. Feb. 27, 1778; d. 1828; daughter of James and Abigal Steer; had issue: 1. John, b. 1799; 2. Elizabeth, b. 1801; 3. Susannah, b. 1803; m. 1830, Lloyd Case of Pennsylvania (had issue: i. James; ii. William; iii. Thomas; iv. Sarah-Elizabeth; v. Rhoda-Jane); 4. Abigail, b. 1805; 5. Joshua, b. 1808; 6. Jane, b. 1811; 7. Sarah, b. 1814: 8. Anna, b. 1816; 9. Mary, b. 1819; 10. Rachel, b. 1823.

JAMES COPELAND, a native of Ireland, emigrated to Pennsylvania and settled in Westmoreland county, thence

removing to Wayne township, Jefferson county, Ohio, in 1800; had issue:
I. Thomas, b. in Westmoreland county, Penn., 1795; settled in Green township, Harrison county, Ohio, in 1814, where he d. 1879; m. Nancy Shepler; had issue: 1. Christina; 2. Mary; 3. Jacob; 4. Lucinda; 5. James, b. Sept. 4, 1823; settled in German township; m. 1846, Margaret Gutshall, daughter of Daniel and Mary Hospelhorn Gutshall, who settled in Harrison county, in 1800—the father served in the War of 1812—(had issue: i. Mary-M.; ii. Thomas-D.; iii. Nancy-J.; iv. Elizabeth-A.; v. Christina-L.; vi. Rebecca-S.; vii. Sarah-S.; viii. James-A.; ix. Emma-A.; x. Adaline; xi. Evaline, twin sister to Adaline last named; xii. Laura-B.; xiii. Samantha-M.); 6. Samuel; 7. Peter; 8. Joseph-L.; 9. John-M.; 10. Henry; 11. Thomas-F.; 12. George. II. James. III. Susan. IV. Samuel. V. Mary. VI. Jennie. VII. Joseph. VIII. Nancy. IX. John. X. Iba.

JOHN COPELAND, a native of Ireland, emigrated to America and settled in Maryland or Pennsylvania, whence, in 1805, he removed to Jefferson county, Ohio; d. 1840; m. Isabelle Leach, a native of Pennsylvania; had issue: 1. Samuel; 2. Thomas, b. in Jefferson county, Ohio; removed to Franklin township, Harrison county, Ohio, before 1837, where he d. July 4, 1877; m. in Harrison county, Nancy A. Dick; d. April 1, 1880, daughter of William Dick, a resident of Harrison county (had issue: i. Jane, m. John Hilton; ii. Isabelle, m. Nathaniel Lukens; iii. John; iv. Mary; v. William, b. Sept. 4, 1837; m. 1863, Mary Cruin, daughter of George Cruin, of Franklin township); 3. Joseph; 4. James, b. in Maryland, Aug. 7, 1801; settled in Washington township, where he d. April 30, 1859; m. 1837, Mary A. Walters, daughter of Leonard and Rachel Ruby Walters, of Jefferson county (had issue: i. Thomas-W., b. in Franklin township, Aug. 25, 1838; settled in Washington township; served in the Civil War; was a prisoner at Andersonville; m. Aug. 29, 1869, Mary E. Ramsey, of Washington township; ii. Matilda; iii. Rachel; iv. Amanda; v. Isabelle: vi. Leonard: vii. S.-S.; viii. Nannie-E.; ix. John, served in the Civil War; d. about 1865); 5. David; 6. William, settled in Franklin township,

where he d. 1870; m. 1833, in Harrison county, Mary Dempster, daughter of Robert and Elizabeth Hunter Dempster, of Jefferson county (the former a native of Pensylvania; the latter a daughter of John Hunter, who settled in Jefferson county in 1820); (had issue: i. John-W.; ii. William-D., b. Jan. 8, 1836; m. March 10, 1867, Lucy Burns, daughter cf John M. and Elizabeth Hilbert Burns; iii. Joseph; iv. Albert; v. Elizabeth; vi. Isabelle; vii. Mary-M.; viii. Margaret-J.); 7. Archibald.

John M. Burns, father of Lucy Burns Copeland, was a native of Westmoreland county, Penn.; removed to Smithfield, Jefferson county, Ohio; afterward settled in German township, Harrison county; m. Elizabeth Hilbert, daughter of John Hilbert; had issue: 1. Frances-Samantha, m. Alexander Henderson; 2. Letitia, m. Joseph Courtright; 3. Lomida, m. Henry Taylor; 4. Lucy, m. William D. Copeland.

Leonard Walters, father of Mary Walters Copeland, was an early settler in Jefferson county; m. Rachel Ruby; had issue: 1. Thomas; 2. Joseph; 3. Mary-A., m. James Copeland; 4. Catharine; 5. Martha; 6. Maria.

ROBERT COULTER, a native of county Antrim, Ireland; emigrated to America and settled with three brothers in Chester county, Penn., 1780-1790; thence removed to Lancaster county, Penn.; m. Isabella Mayes, a native of the North of Ireland, daughter of Joseph Mayes, who after the death of her first husband, m. Robert McCoy; removed in 1816 to Jefferson county, Ohio; thence in 1828 to Perry township, Tuscarawas county, Ohio, where she d. June, 1849; had issue: 1. Andrew, b. June 14, 1796, in Lancaster county, Penn.; d. Sept. 30, 1872, at Smithfield, Ohio; removed in 1816 to Jefferson county, Ohio; m. (1st) Jane Reed. a native of Jefferson county; m. (2d) June 9, 1844, Nancy Mayes, b. Sept. 15, 1815; d. June 17, 1859; had issue. among others: 1. Robert-McCoy, b. March 19, 1849, near Bethel, Ohio; a Presbyterian minister; m. Sept. 27, 1881, Janet E. McCoy, daughter of Matthew McCoy, of Archer township, Harrison county.

Joseph Mayes, father of Nancy Mayes Coulter, was b. June 6, 1785. in Washington county, Penn., of Scotch-Irish descent; settled near Folks' Station,

Green township, Harrison county, where he d. Dec. 29, 1845; m. Sarah Miller, daughter of John Miller, of Beech Spring, Ohio.

WILLIAM COULTRAP, a native of Virginia, of Scottish descent, settled in Stock township, Harrison county, Ohio, in 1816, where he d. 1823; m. in Virginia, Mary Woods; d. 1842; had issue: 1. William, b. in Virginia, 1800; d. 1845; m. in Jefferson county, Sarah Moore; b. 1796; d. Sept. 8, 1889 (had issue: i. Nathaniel; ii. Nancy; iii. Mary; iv. Richard-M., b. 1840; m. Mary E. Moore; v. David; vi. Ruth; vii. Oliver; viii. Nathan; ix. William; x. Susannah; xi. Margaret; xii. Charles); 2. Henry; 3. David; 4. Matthew; 5. Elizabeth, m. —— Hall; 6. Sarah, m. —— McGeel; 7. Margaret, m. —— Hall.

JOHN COURTRIGHT, b. in New Jersey, Sept. 7, 1774; removed to Washington county, Penn., and thence to near the present site of Salineville, Columbiana county, Ohio, before 1809; had issue:
I. Jacob-V. II. James. III. Samuel, b. April 30, 1809; removed in 1829 to Carrollton, Ohio, later to Short Creek township, Harrison county, and in 1856 to Smithfield, Jefferson county; m. (1st) 1829, Frances Zollars; d. 1862; daughter of Frederick Zollars, of Harrison county; m. (2d) 1867, Mary E. Stonebraker; had issue by first wife: 1. James; 2. Franklin; 3. Z.-Z., b. July 12, 1832; settled in Freeport in 1875; m. 1858, Mary A. Crew; 4. Vail, settled in Illinois; 5. Mary-Jane, m. George D. Walcott; 6. Charles; 7. Ann-Rebecca, m. Thomas Penny; 8. John; 9. Sarah, m. William Carrick; 10. William, settled in Franklin; 11. Joseph-W., b. Jan. 6, 1847, in Short Creek township; settled in Freeport township; served in the Civil War; m. (1st) Sept. 28, 1866, Letitia Burns; d. Aug. 17, 1875; daughter of John M. Burns; m. (2d) Oct. 15, 1881, Laura Steadman, of Freeport; 12. Melissa, m. Wilson Lugar. IV. Isaac. V. William. VI. Milo. VII. Judith. VIII. Rebecca.

GEORGE COX, see Family of David Smylie.

PETER CRABTREE, a native of England, emigrated to America and first settled in western Pennsylvania;

removed to Rush Creek, Jefferson county, Ohio, where he remained until about 1812, and then settled in Nottingham township, Harrison county, Ohio, where he d. 1829; had issue:
I. Rhoda. II. Sarah. III. Rachel. IV. Ann. V. Amy. VI. Cornelius. VII. Gabriel. VIII. William, b. in Pennsylvania, about 1795; m. Rachel Moore, b. about 1811; daughter of Loami Moore, who served in the Revolutionary War; had issue: 1. Sarah; 2. Keziah; 3. John-D., b. June 12, 1825; m. May 27, 1847, Elizabeth Moore, b. Feb. 6, 1829, in Moorefield township, Harrison county, daughter of David and Sarah Kidwell Moore (had issue: i. William; ii. Sarah; iii. Martha; iv. Gabriel; v. Mary; vi. Edmond; vii. Elmer); 4. Loami; 5. Gabriel; 6. Shepard; 7. James, served in the Civil War; 8. William, served in the Civil War; 9. Peter; 10. Mary-A.

WALTER CRAIG, a native of Ireland, of Scotch descent, settled at West Middletown, Washington county, Penn., about 1791; m. in Ireland, Jane McCleon; had issue:
I. David. II. Thomas. III. Ann, b. 1780; d. Aug. 30, 1847; m. John Jamison (see Jamison Family). IV. Rebecca. V. William. VI. John, b. in Ireland, Aug. 1, 1775; emigrated to America with his parents, and afterwards settled at Hardscrabble (now West Alexander), Penn., removed in 1803 to Green township, Harrison county, Ohio, where he d. Aug. 22, 1825; m. in Pennsylvania, Elizabeth Johnson, b. June 23, 1781; d. Feb. 28, 1864; had issue: 1. Jane, b. June 14, 1802; d. 1890; m. Joshua Hamilton; 2. Johnson, b. in Green township, Dec. 19, 1803; d. 1888; m. 1834, Martha Thompson, b. 1810; d. July 16, 1890; a daughter of Samuel Thompson of Green township (had issue: i. John, d. in infancy; ii. Thompson; settled in Nebraska; iii. Rachel-A., m. George W. Brown; settled in Nebraska; iv. Eliza-J., m. M. K. Turner, and settled in Nebraska; v. William-S.; settled in Nebraska: vi. John-A., b. May 6, 1852; m. Oct. 20, 1881, Elizabeth J. Mills, daughter of James and Nancy Davis Mills); 3. Rachel, b. Sept. 16, 1805; d. Aug. 22, 1825; 4. Mary, b. July 16, 1808; m. Nathaniel Gilmore; settled in Ford county. Ill.; 5. Ann. b. Feb. 22, 1811; d. Feb. 27, 1887; m. James Tag-

gart; 6. Rebecca, b. July 27, 1813; m. Andrew Patterson, of Pickaway county, Ohio; 7. William, b. March 15, 1816; d. Feb. 8, 1872, in Fulton county, Illinois; 8. Walter, b. July 4, 1819; m. (1st) 1844, Jane Moore, b. 1824; d. 1859; daughter of William and Sarah Moore, of Green township; m. (2d) 1860, Hannah Henderson, d. 1879; m. (3d) Florence Welch, daughter of William Welch (had issue by first wife: i. Sarah-Jane, d. aged thirteen years; ii. Amanda, m. Cassius M. Nichols; iii. John, settled in Nebraska; iv. Elizabeth, m. W. H. Oglevee, and settled in Illinois; had issue by second wife: v. William; vi. ——, d. in infancy); 9. John, b. July 31, 1822; d. Sept. 16, 1825. VII. Walter. VIII. Jane. IX. Susan.

EDWARD CRAWFORD, b. in Virginia, about 1760; d. in Archer township, Harrison county, 1831; removed there from Brooke county, West Virginia, in March, 1806; m. Mary Wiggins, b. 1770; d. 1864; daughter of Edward and Charity Wiggins, of Brooke county; had issue: 1. Ellen, m. James Hagerty; 2. Mary, m. James Harper; 3. Alexander, d. in Carroll county; 4. Thomas, b. Dec. 3, 1804, in Brooke county, Va.; removed with his parents to Archer township; m. (1st) 1829, Jane Kelly, daughter of Hugh and Mary Kelly, residents of Cadiz; m. (2d) March 5, 1839, Mrs. Eleanor Forbes, widow of Joseph Forbes, a former resident of Harrison county (had issue by first wife: i. Hugh; ii. Edward; iii. Isabella; iv. Thomas; had issue by second wife: v. John-A.; vi. Elizabeth; vii. Jane; viii. Robert; ix. James-F.; x. Jason); 5. Isabella, m. William Welch; 6. Charlotta; 7. Josiah; 8. Nancy, m. William Lewis; settled in Holmes county; 9. Margaret; 10. Elizabeth, m. Joseph McGonigal; 11. John, b. in Archer township, Nov. 29, 1816; m. in 1849, Elizabeth Hedges, b. 1827; d. 1877; daughter of Samuel and Prudy Hedges (had issue: i. Mary, m. Hamilton Lisle, of Archer township; ii. Samuel-E., in Archer township, 1853; settled in Cadiz township; m. 1874, Emma E. Barrett. a native of Nottingham township, daughter of William H. Barrett; iii. Alexander; settled in Archer township: iv. Harriet, d. 1878: v. Martha, m. John Holland, of Cadiz; vi. Margaret); 12. Harriet, m. Matthew McCoy, of Archer township. Alexander Wiggins, the father of Edward Wiggins, was of Scotch descent, having come to America from the North of Ireland a short time before Edward was born. Edward Wiggins died in Virginia.

ROBERT CREE, a native of Pennsylvania, m. Elizabeth Villars, b. in Pennsylvania, Oct. 12, 1763; daughter of John and Mary Villars; had issue:
I. Ann, b. Nov. 13, 1788.
II. Mary, b. Dec. 17, 1789.
III. Janet, b. Feb. 5, 1790.
IV. Robert, b. April 12, 1791.
V. George, b. Dec. 28, 1793.
VI. Eleanor, b. April 20, 1795.
VII. John, b. Sept. 18, 1796.
VIII. James, b. in Pennsylvania, May 12, 1798; d. May 16, 1859; removed to Freeport township, Harrison county, Ohio, about 1817; m. Dec. 27, 1817, Sarah Woods, b. March 10, 1803; d. Sept. 23, 1860; had issue: 1. William-A., b. Dec. 31, 1818; d. Oct. 17, 1881; 2. Elijah-V., b. April 22, 1826; d. Oct. 17, 1843; 3. James-H., b. Aug. 29, 1829; d. Dec. 6, 1855; 4. John-W., b. Jan. 30, 1832; 5. ——, b. April 24, 1833; d. in infancy; 6. Thomas-M., b. April 24, 1835; m. March 6, 1859, Caroline A. Grant, b. Nov. 20, 1839; daughter of Mead and Elizabeth Grant, of Carroll county, Ohio; the former d. June 7, 1883; the latter d. Feb. 8, 1886; 7. Sarah-J., b. May 20, 1837; 8. George-W., b. April 4, 1839; 9. Robert-B., b. Nov. 5, 1841; served in the Civil War; d. May 10, 1863, in the army; 10. Mary-M., b. Sept. 7, 1844; 11. Elizabeth-V., b. June 16, 1847.

ROBERT CROSKEY, a native of Ireland, emigrated to America and later, in 1802, removed to Green township, Harrison county, Ohio; had issue:
I. William. II. John, b. in New Jersey, Oct. 7, 1775; d. March 16, 1862; m. in Pennsylvania, Feb. 9, 1801, Catherine Fry, b. June 25, 1781; d. in Iowa, Jan. 22, 1863; daughter of Samuel Fry, a resident of Pennsylvania; had issue: 1. John, b. April 19, 1802; d. Oct. 20, 1867; m. Esther ——; 2. Christina, b. Feb. 13, 1804; 3. Rachel, b. Feb. 22, 1806; 4. Samuel-F., b. Dec. 11, 1808; 5. Sarah, b. Jan. 12, 1811; 6. Jackson, b. Feb. 6, 1815; d. Feb. 7, 1890; 7. William, b. Oct. 11, 1817; m. Jan. 16, 1840, Susan Baxter, b. May 11, 1822, daughter of Samuel P. Baxter, a pioneer of Green township

(had issue: i. Nancy-Jane, b. June 25, 1841; m. Edward Hall; ii. Clarinda, b. Oct. 9, 1846; m. Rezin B. Mansfield; iii. Louisa-Caroline, b. Sept. 9, 1848; d. June 28, 1869; iv. Susan-Amanda, b. Feb. 7, 1856; m. William F. Houser); 8. Abraham, b. Jan. 24, 1820; settled in Chicago; m. Mary Phillips, daughter of Thomas and Elizabeth William Phillips (had issue: i. Thomas, m. Martha Osburn).

WILLIAM CROSKEY, b. in Ireland, 1795; d. 1873; son of Robert Croskey, who emigrated to Maryland, in 1775; removed to Washington county, Penn., and thence, in 1812, to Green township, Harrison county, Ohio; m. 1848, Margaret Crabb, of Jefferson county, Ohio; had issue: 1. Robert; 2. Margaret, m. James Thompson; 3. Henry, settled in McLean county, Ill.; 4. Anna, m. John Clifford, and settled in Green township; 5. Mary, m. George McFadden; 6. Sarah, m. Thomas Groves, of Jefferson county; 7. John, died in infancy; 8. ———; 9. ———.

THOMAS CRUMLEY, a native of Virginia, b. Dec. 31, 1776; d. July 3, 1861; settled near what is now the village of Harrisville, Harrison county, Ohio, in 1802, coming into Ohio with the Dickersons and Dunlaps; m. in West Virginia, Elizabeth Gardner, of English descent; d. 1856; had issue: 1. Samuel; 2. Sarah; 3. Mary, m. Joshua Dickerson; 4. William; 5. Thomas; 6. Ira, b. Oct. 7, 1809; settled near Freeport, in Washington township; m. Jan. 31, 1840, Jane Dickerson (had issue: i. Mary-E., m. David McFadden, and settled in Iowa; ii. Sarah, m. William Wilson, and settled in Freeport, Harrison county; iii. Hiram; iv. Clara; v. Thomas, m. Oct. 9. 1888, Abbie Kirkpatrick, daughter of G. W. Kirkpatrick, of Moorefield township, Harrison county); 7. Elizabeth; 8. John; 9. Hannah, m. ——— Glazener; 10. James; 11. Aaron-W.; 12. Emily, m. ——— Barkhurst; 13. Joseph; 14. David.

ROBERT CULBERTSON, b. in Ireland, 1743; emigrated to Ohio in 1811, and settled one mile northeast of New Athens, in what is now Harrison county, Ohio, where he died Dec. 23-24, 1840; m. (1st) in Ireland, ———; m. (2d) in Ireland, ———; d. aged sixty-seven; had issue by first wife:
I. James. II. John. III. Samuel.

IV. Ezekiel; had issue by second wife: V. Thomas. VI. Robert. VII. Benjamin. VIII. William. IX. Hugh. X. Joseph. XI. George, settled in Muskingum county, Ohio. XII. Annie, m. Thomas Pollock, and settled in Guernsey county, Ohio. XIII. Mary, d. aged eight. XIV. Gillespie, b. in Athens township, October, 1816; m. (1st) Dec. 17, 1840, Dorcas Holt, of Guernsey county, b. 1818; d. Aug. 15, 1865; m. (2d) Nov. 8, 1866, Eliza J. Duncan, a native of Guernsey county, daughter of James Duncan (d. 1835), and Elizabeth McKinney Duncan (d. 1861); had issue by first wife: 1. John, b. Sept. 20, 1841, in Athens township; m. Nov. 8, 1866, Sarah Jane McDowell, b. 1845; d. 1890; daughter of William and Hannah Watters McDowell, early settlers in Athens township; 2. Mary, m. Jeremiah Brown, of Monroe township; 3. Sarah-Ann, m. F. M. Cooper, and settled in New Athens; 4. Robert, d. aged seventeen; had issue by second wife: 5. Dorcas-Eliza, m. Samuel A. Kirkland.

JOHN CUNNINGHAM, a native of Ireland, of Scottish descent, emigrated to America, and first settled at Baltimore; thence removed to Fayette and Westmoreland counties, Penn.; d. in Westmoreland county, April 19, 1797; m. Elizabeth ———, d. in Westmoreland county, March 2, 1816; had issue: I. James, b. 1780; d. at Mansfield, Ohio, 1870; served as a captain in the War of 1812. II. Ezekiel, m. Feb. 25, 1813, Mary Dregoo; settled near Chillicothe, Ross county, Ohio. III. David, b. May 6, 1783; d. May 27, 1849; m. (1st) Dec. 23, 1806, in Fayette county. Penn., Mary McLaughlin, b. Sept. 28, 1782; d. April 6, 1829; daughter of John and Elizabeth McLaughlin; m. (2d) Ann Barricklow, b. May 8, 1808; d. Aug. 13, 1887; had issue by first wife: 1. John, b. Oct. 29, 1808; d. Aug. 18, 1870; m. Feb. 3, 1829, Nancy Sharp, b. 1810; d. Oct. 10, 1875; daughter of William (d. 1835) and Mary McFadden Sharp, who removed from Hopewell township (?), Washington county, Penn., to Harrison county (had issue: i. Mary, m. 1850, Eldred Glencairn Holliday, son of Robert and Eliza White Holliday; ii. David, b. March 1, 1837; m. 1859, Laura Phillips, daughter of Thomas and Elizabeth Williams Phillips, natives of Chester county, Penn., who settled at Cadiz about 1820-25. IV. Joseph, d. May 18, 1807. V. Robert, d. in West Virginia.

EMANUEL CUSTER, d. at Jessups, Maryland, of which State he was a native, aged over one hundred years; removed to Harrison county, Ohio, early in the century, afterwards returning to Maryland; had issue:
I. John, a native of Frederick county, Md., d. at Cresaptown, Allegany county, that State, 1830; had issue, among others: 1. Emanuel-H., b. at Cresaptown, Dec. 10, 1806; removed to Rumley, Harrison county, Ohio, about 1824, and later, to Monroe, Mich.; m. (1st) Aug. 7, 1828, Matilda Viers, d. July 18, 1834; m. (2d) Feb. 23, 1836, Mrs. Mary Ward Kirkpatrick, b. near Burgettstown, Washington county, Penn., May 31, 1807; daughter of Thomas and Sarah Ward, of Cross Creek township (she m. 1st, Israel R. Kirkpatrick, and by him had issue: i. David; settled in Wood county, Ohio; ii. Lydia-A., m. David Reed, and settled at Monroe, Mich.) (had issue by first wife, three children, of whom: i. Brice-V., settled at Columbus, Ohio; had issue by second wife: iv. George-Armstrong, b. Dec. 5, 1839; served as general in the Civil War, and afterwards killed by the Indians at the battle of the Little Big Horn, June 25, 1876; m. Feb. 9, 1864, Elizabeth Bacon, daughter of Judge Daniel S. Bacon, of Monroe, Mich.; v. Nevin, b. July 29, 1842; settled near Monroe, Mich.; vi. Thomas-Ward, b. March 15, 1845; lieutenant U. S. A.; killed at battle of the Little Big Horn, June 25, 1876; vii. Boston, b. Oct. 31, 1848; killed at the battle of the Little Big Horn, June 25, 1876; viii. Margaret-Emma, b. June 5, 1852; m. Lieut. —— Calhoun, killed at the battle of the Little Big Horn, June 25, 1876).
II. Jacob, b. 1790, at Jessups, Md.: d. 1862, in Rumley township, Harrison county, where he had settled before 1816; m. Sarah Webster, b. 1798; d. 1835; daughter of William Webster, a pioneer of Ohio; had issue: 1. William-Webster, b. in New Rumley, July 1, 1816; settled at Scio, about 1850; m. in New Hagerstown, Frances Amelia Phelps, b. in Massachusetts, daughter of Eben and Mary Kibbee Phelps, who settled in Franklin (now Kent), Portage county, Ohio, when Frances was five years old; (had issue: i. Mary-E., m. Dr. D. J. Snyder; ii. Caroline-A., m. W. N. McCormick; settled in Florida; iii. James-A., served in Civil War; killed at Mount Sterling, Ky.; iv. Albert-O., b. 1850; d. April 1, 1870, in Steubenville, Ohio; v. Clarence-P.); 2. Alexander, d. aged four years; 3. Stewart-F., settled in Connotton, Harrison county; 4. John; 5. Henry-L., settled in New Philadelphia; 6. Robert, settled in Scio; 7. Isaac, settled in Westerville, Ohio; 8. Vincent, d. in infancy.
III. Emanuel, d. in Maryland.
IV. Charlotte, b. 1796; d. 1854; m. Robert Cummings, b. 1789; d. 1823.
V. Susan, m. John Hendricks.
VI. Mary, m. Joseph Cummings.

ROBERT DAVIDSON, a native of Pennsylvania, removed to Green township, Harrison county, in 1802; m. about 1804, —— Croskey, sister of John Croskey, with whom he came to Ohio; had issue: 1. Margaret; 2. Elizabeth; 3. Robert; 4. James; 5. Rachel; 6. William, b. 1822; removed to Iowa in 1877; m. Oct. 10, 1849, Christian Shepler, daughter of Samuel Shepler, of Green township (had issue: i. Samuel-F., b. March 19, 1850; m. Nov. 18, 1869, Caroline M. Bell, daughter of Francis Bell, a resident of Wayne township, Jefferson county, Ohio; ii. James-H.); 7. Mary.

SAMUEL DAVIDSON, b. in Allegany county, Md., 1771; was one of a family of thirteen children; his father was a native of Ireland, who emigrated to Maryland; settled in Washington township, Harrison county, Ohio, in 1812, where a cousin had preceded him; m. Mary Drake, a native of Pennsylvania; had issue:
I. Lewis. II. Jesse. III. Jonah, b. in Allegany county, Md., July 4, 1804; d. June 16, 1889; m. 1829, Sarah Joice, d. 1859; had issue: 1. Eliza, b. in Washington township, Oct. 26, 1832; m. Aug. 4, 1864, James Wilson; d. 1873; son of James and Sarah Brock Wilson, natives of Virginia, who were among the early settlers of Moorefield township. IV. Mary. V. Hannah. VI. Nancy.

WILLIAM DAVIDSON, b. Nov. 20, 1747, son of William Davidson, a native of Ireland, who settled in Pennsylvania before the Revolutionary War; m. (1st) Rosanna Hutchinson, a native of

Wales; m. (2d) Barbara McDale (by whom he had issue, five sons and three daughters); had issue by first wife, three sons and two daughters, of whom:
I. Lewis, b. March 23, 1773, in Fayette county, Penn.; removed in 1801 to the present site of Catlettsburg, Kentucky; a year later located on the French grant, in Scio county, Ohio, where he remained until 1809, and thence removed to Freeport, Harrison county, Ohio; served in the War of 1812; m. his cousin, Mary Davidson, b. in Allegany county, Md., Sept. 23, 1778, daughter of Lewis and Nancy Todd Davidson; the former was a brother of William Davidson, Jr.; the latter a native of England. Lewis and Mary Davidson were m. in Fayette county, Penn., in July, 1798; had issue: 1. William; 2. Nancy, d. in Scioto county, Ohio; 3. Rosanna, d. in Scioto county; 4. John-S.; 5. Mordecai-W.; 6. Lewis-H., b. 1809, in Scioto county; removed with his parents to Harrison county; settled in Freeport township, Harrison county; was licensed to preach Feb. 8, 1845; m. Jan. 7, 1830, near Moorefield, Harrison county, Lucinda Latham, b. Sept. 18, 1810, in Fauquier county, Va. (had issue: i. Isaiah, d. in infancy; ii. Lucy, d. in infancy; iii. Sarah, d. in infancy; iv. James-M., killed Sept. 20, 1863, in the battle of Chickamauga; v. Mary, m. ―――― McPeck, and settled near Jewett, Harrison county; vi. Latham-A., settled in West Milford, Harrison county, W. Va.; vii. Alexander-J., settled in Tucson. Ariz.); 7. Susanna; 8. Mary; 9. Jesse; 10. Thomas-L.; 11. Joseph-C.; 12. Jonathan-S.

JESSE DE LONG (son of Solomon De Long), of French descent, b. about 1776, on Short Creek, Jefferson county, Ohio, where his parents came from Pennsylvania; d. near Dennison, Ohio, May 8, 1882; his family served in the Revolutionary War and the War of 1812; removed to Tuscarawas county, Ohio, where he m. Nancy Wagner; afterward settled near Dennison; had issue, among others: 1. Espy, b. May 11, 1832; removed to Monroe township, Harrison county, Ohio, 1872; served in the Civil War; m. March 6, 1864, Sarah A. Carmack, b. May 1, 1847, in Canal Dover, Ohio, daughter of Jacob and Clarissa Carmack, natives of Maryland.

DANIEL DEWEY, b. in Lebanon, Conn., June 19, 1731; d. March 9, 1816; served as ensign, lieutenant, and captain in Company 4, Twelfth Connecticut Militia, 1767 to 1772; a personal friend of "Brother Jonathan" Trumbull (Governor of Connecticut); m. Feb. 22, 1753, Temperance Bailey, b. Feb. 2, 1731; d. March 31, 1795; daughter of Isaac and Abigail Hunt Bailey; had issue, nine children (Temperance, Esther, Daniel, Eliphalet, Philena, Ebenezer, Joshua, Experience, and Anna), of whom:
I. Eliphalet, b. at Lebanon, Conn., Dec. 13, 1762; d. at Cadiz, 1838; removed to Hartwick, Conn, 1798, where he was instrumental in building Hartwick Seminary; emigrated to Ohio in 1835, where he joined his son, Chauncey, who had preceded him; m. at Lebanon, Conn., Aug. 25, 1793, Rachel Ann Hyde, b. Dec. 3, 1761, at Norwich West Farms, Conn.; d. at Cadiz, 1847; daughter of Silas and Martha Waterman Hyde; had issue, nine children (Eliphalet, Susan, Lucy-Williams, Martha, Chauncey, Josiah, Henry, Harriet and Silas), of whom: 1. Chauncey, b. March 27, 1796, at Norwich West Farms, d. Feb. 15, 1880; removed to Cadiz, September, 1821; m. Feb. 11, 1823, Nancy Pritchard, b. Oct. 27, 1804, at Uniontown, Pa.; d. Sept. 6, 1897; daughter of John and Sarah Bromfield Pritchard (the former a native of Wales, b. 1775; d. 1844; the latter b. 1782); (had issue: i. Eliphalet-C., b. Dec. 16, 1823; d. 1886; m. 1845, Virginia Affleck); ii. Harriet-Eliza, b. 1825; d. 1831; iii. Henry, b. 1828; d. 1830; iv. John-Henry, b. 1830; d. 1848; v. Orville-C., b. Nov. 12, 1833; m. 1868, Elizabeth Good Tingle; vi. Mary-Pritchard, b. March 6, 1836; d. 1869; m. 1857, Edward Fulton Moffett; vii. Martha. b. 1839; d. 1840; viii. Charles-Paulson, b. Oct. 24, 1843; m. (1st) Emma Scott; m. (2d) Mrs. Gertrude Osborne Jewett: ix. Albert-B., b. 1846; m. 1880, Louise Shufeldt, of Chatham, N. Y.; x. Clara-Hyde, m. Charles Mather Hogg. Daniel Dewey (1731-1816) was the son of John (b. 1700; d. at Lebanon. Conn., 1774) and Experience Woodward Dewey (m. 1726); grandson of Josiah (b. 1666 at Northampton, Mass.) and Mehitable Miller Dewey (m. 1691); and great-grandson of Josiah (b. at Windsor, Conn., 1641, where he was a fellow-townsman of President Grant's

immigrant ancestor, Matthew Grant) and Hepzibah Lyman (daughter of Richard and Hepzibah Ford Lyman) Dewey. Josiah Dewey, last named, was the son of Thomas Dewey (b. about 1597, at Sandwich, Kent county, England) who immigrated to Dorchester (now South Boston), Mass., in 1630, on the vessel, " Mary and John," with Matthew Grant and others, whence he removed to Connecticut, in 1635, and helped to found the town of Windsor.

ASA DICKERSON, b. 1814; d. 1864; a native of Washington county, Penn., probably of the immediate family of John or Henry Dickerson; removed to Harrison county, Ohio, where he m. Jane Dunlap, b. in Harrison county, 1814; d. 1873; had issue: 1. Samuel-D.; settled at Peabody, Kan.; 2. William-H.; 3. Sarah-J., m. Adam Dunlap; 4. Lydia-E., m. J. E. Carnahan, and settled in Pawnee county, Neb.; 5. Dunlap, d. in the army during the Civil War; 6. Granville, settled at Maryville, Mo.; 7. Rebecca-Caroline, m. Joseph McFadden Hamilton; 8. Adam-J., settled in Lyons, Kan.

JOHN DICKERSON and HENRY DICKERSON settled in Amwell (now Franklin) township, Washington county, before 1780, John apparently having come from Dunbar (now Tyrone) township, Fayette county, where his name appears on the tax-list in 1772, and where Joshua Dickerson (1740-1827) had settled about 1770; Joshua and John were doubtless brothers, and Henry may have been a third brother, although more probably the son of John.

John Dickerson d. in Washington county in 1785 (before March), leaving a widow, Ruth (d. before December, 1807), and children, of whom the following were mentioned in his will, written more than seven years before his death: 1. Susannah; 2. Henry (may have been the Henry mentioned below); 3. Gideon, d. unm. September-November, 1789; 4. Baruch; 5. Asa, d. January, 1794; m. Lydia —— (had issue: i. John; ii. William, d. 1860; m. (1st) Sarah Jolly; m. (2d) Martha Clark); 6. Drusilla.

Henry Dickerson, of Morris township, d. before Aug. 13, 1825; m. Ann ——; had issue: 1. Joshua, b. in Washington county, May 3, 1781; d. April 30, 1853;

m. (1st) Margaret McPherson; m. (2d) Cornelia Craig (had issue: i. Joshua-D.; ii. Nancy; iii. Alexander; iv. John, b. April 13, 1810; d. April 10, 1865; m. [1st] Mary Adams, daughter of Robert; m. [2d] Mary Johnson; v. Jane, m. Samuel Walters; vi. Ruth, m. Lewis Barker; vii. Henry; viii. Lydia, m. Howard Trusell; ix. Margaret, m. William Hazlett; x. Matilda); 2. George; 3. Gideon, m. Eliza Gunn, and removed to Ohio; 4. Henry, m. Catharine Beck, and removed to Illinois; 5. Leonard, m. Susan Wolf, and removed to Ohio; 6. Asa; 7. Margaret, m. —— McLaughlin; 8. Ruth, m. —— Reynolds.

JOSHUA DICKERSON, b. 1740; d. in Fayette county, Penn., Oct. 10, 1827; came from New Jersey; settled on what is now called Dickerson's Run, in Dunbar township, near East Liberty, Fayette county, Penn., about 1770; here, in 1780, he built a grist-mill on the site of the mill now owned by the Oglevee brothers; from this settlement and its vicinity emigrated to Harrison county the families of Dunlap, Oglevee, Barricklow, Rankin, and others; Joshua Dickerson had six sons, Thomas, William, John, Joshua, Levi, and Eli, all of whom removed to Ohio near the beginning of the present century. Joshua Dickerson also had, among other daughters, one, Sarah, who m. Samuel Dunlap; of the sons:

Eli, b. 1768; d. in Harrison county, Nov. 24, 1834; m. Mary ——, b. 1776; d. April 28, 1831.

Thomas, b. May 19, 1764; d. Dec. 24, 1852; m. in Fayette county, Mary Curry, b. Jan. 16, 1766; d. March 30, 1853; emigrated to Harrison county about 1802, and settled at the present site of Dickerson's church; had issue:

I. Baruch, b. May 21, 1786; d. Oct. 2, 1824; m. in Harrison county, Elizabeth Holmes, b. near Wellsburg, W. Va., daughter of William Holmes and sister of Joseph Holmes; served as a captain in the War of 1812; had issue: 1. Joshua, b. Nov. 9, 1808; m. (1st) 1834, Elizabeth Crumley (d. 1839), whose parents removed from Western Virginia to Harrison county early in the century; m. (2d) Mary Elliott, b. Dec. 10, 1820, daughter of Samuel (d. 1828) and Nancy Grimes (d. 1830) Elliott, of Belmont county (had issue by second wife: i. Aaron-M., b. 1845; d. 1875; ii.

Baruch, b. 1846; d. 1864; iii. Thomas; settled near Flushing, Ohio; iv. Sarah; v. Elizabeth; vi. Theodore; vii. Samuel, d. in infancy; viii. Hiram, settled near New Athens; ix. Charles, settled in Colorado); 2. Susanna, m. Edward Lafferty; 3. Mary, d. in infancy; 4. Thomas; 5. Mary, m. Arrison Shotwell, and settled at Glenville, Ohio; 6. Jane, m. Ira Crumley, and settled in Washington township; 7. William-Wilson, b. April 12, 1818; settled in Athens township; m. Oct. 17, 1839, Susan McCoy, daughter of Thomas McCoy, of Athens township (had issue: i. Baruch, d. in infancy; ii. Thomas, d. in infancy; iii. Hannah; iv. Granville; v. Winfield; vi. William; vii. Elizabeth; viii. Clara; ix. Alvin); 8. Elizabeth, m. Daniel Clemens; 9. Baruch, d. in infancy.

II. Joshua, b. in Fayette county, Penn.; d. April 12, 1850; m. Sarah Dunlap, b. 1779; d. Feb. 25, 1871; had issue: 1. Rebecca, m. Samuel Porter; 2. Joshua; 3. Adam; 4. John, b. Aug. 10, 1810; d. Feb. 20, 1878; m. Elizabeth McFadden, d. March 21, 1887, daughter of Samuel McFadden of Cadiz township (had issue: i. Joshua; b. Dec. 15, 1832; ii. Elizabeth, b. March 2, 1834; m. Thompson McFadden; iii. Sarah, b. Sept. 24, 1836; m. Jacob Webb; iv. Jane, b. April 24, 1838; m. Hiram Lafferty; v. Samuel-C., b. May 19, 1840; vi. John-J., b. April 29, 1842; vii. Rebecca, b. Nov. 16, 1843; m. Joshua Dickerson; viii. Margaret, b. March 20, 1845; m. Samuel B. Porter; ix. William-N., b. Dec. 3, 1846; settled near New Athens; m. Oct. 14, 1880, Mary B. McFadden, b. July 19, 1857, daughter of Robert and Rebecca Dunlap McFadden; x. James-M., b. Dec. 2, 1848; xi. Susan-C., b. Dec. 26, 1851; m. Gilmer Richey; xii. Mary-A., b. May 2, 1853; m. Watson Dunlap); 5. Susan; 6. Sarah; 7. William, b. Oct. 7, 1815; m. (1st) 1838. Jane Lafferty, b. 1817; d. Sept. 11, 1864; daughter of Samuel Lafferty, of Moorefield township; m. (2d) Mary McMillan; m. (3d) 1881, Margaret Bartow (had issue by first wife: i. Samuel; ii. Joshua, b. Sept. 2, 1842; m. 1864, Rebecca Dickerson, daughter of John and Elizabeth McFadden Dickerson; iii. William, settled in Moorefield township; iv. John, settled in Illinois; v. Joseph-B., b. Oct. 30, 1848; m. 1874. Mary Barrett, daughter of Erasmus Barrett, of Cadiz township; vi. Margaret, m. John Dickerson.

and settled in Kansas; vii. Sarah, m. ------ Scott; viii. Mary, m. John Lafferty; ix. Edward); 8. Mary, m. William Knee; 9. Jane, twin sister to Mary.

III. Thomas, settled in Harrison county.

IV. John.

V. Joseph, b. 1796; d. in New Athens, 1877; m. (2d) Mrs. Sarah Ann Cannon Mills, b. July 27, 1820.

VI. Eli.

VII. Levi.

VIII. Hiram.

IX. Jane.

X. Susan.

JOHN DOWNS, a native of Ireland; settled in Pennsylvania before 1800; removed to Carroll county, Ohio, where he died; had issue, among others: 1. Richard, b. in Pennsylvania, 1800; d. 1860, in Stock township, Harrison county, where he came from Carroll county, before 1832; m. in Stock township, Elizabeth McKinney, b. in Ireland; d. Jan. 19, 1886; daughter of George McKinney (had issue: i. Mary-J., m. Percival Adams; ii. George-M.; iii. John; iv. James; v. John-F., b. March 2, 1832; m. Nov. 9, 1860, Sarah West; d. May 18, 1879; daughter of Amos West; vi. Richard; vii. Margaret).

George McKinney, father of Elizabeth McKinney Downs, was a native of Ireland; settled in Stock township, Harrison county, before 1832, where he d. 1845; his wife d. 1841; had issue: Elizabeth, John, Nancy, Jane, George, Fryer, James.

ADAM DUNLAP, b. 1752; d. Jan. 10, 1830; removed from Dunbar township, Fayette county, Penn., to Athens township, Harrison county, before 1809; m. Rebecca Work, b. Dec., 1745; d. March 9, 1846; had issue:

I. Samuel, b. Sept. 11, 1772; d. Oct. 2, 1839; settled in Athens township, Harrison county, Ohio, before 1805; m. about 1800, Sarah Dickerson, a native of Fayette county, Pa.; d. Nov. 11, 1858; daughter of Joshua Dickerson; had issue. among others: 1. ------, m. Nelson Pearce, and settled in Cadiz township; 2. Adam, b. April 8, 1805; d. Feb. 20, 1883; m. (1st) Margaret Thompson; b. 1824; d. 1863; daughter of David Thompson; m. (2d) Elizabeth J. Sprott, b. 1829; d. 1871 (had issue by first wife: i. Sarah, m. John Porter; ii. Martha. m. Samuel Porter; iii. Mary,

m. J. D. Barricklow; had issue by second wife: iv. Nancy, m. A. Farrell, and removed to West Virginia; v. Samuel, d. Jan. 4, 1859; vi. Elizabeth-J., m. Robert Holliday, and settled in Moorefield township; vii. Amanda-Adaline, m. Henry Barto; viii. John-A., b. Dec. 11, 1859; m. Mary H. Chaney, daughter of James and Margaret Chaney; ix. William-S.; x. Clara-B., d. young).

II. William, b. 1780; d. Feb. 24, 1865; settled on the Brushy Fork of Stillwater Creek about 1812-13, later returning to Fayette county, Penn., and thence removing to Belmont county, Ohio; m. Margaret Rankin, b. in Fayette county, Penn., 1787; d. May 19, 1838; had issue: 1. Adam, settled in Missouri; 2. James; 3. William, settled in Missouri; 4. Samuel, b. June 25, 1825; removed to Belmont county, Ohio; m. (1st) 1844, Elizabeth Jane Bethel, b. 1827; d. 1858; daughter of James and Mary Brock Bethel; m. (2d) 1859, Mary E. Bethel; d. 1872; daughter of John and Elizabeth Oglevee Bethel (had issue by first wife: i. William-J.; ii. Margaret, m. A. Dunlap; iii. Lycurgus-M.; iv. Thomas-A.; v. Joseph-C.; had issue by second wife: vi. O.-E.; vii. Eliza-J., m. ——— Compher; viii. Isaac-E.; ix. Samuel-A.; x. Cora-B.); 4 Margaret; 5. Rebecca.

III. John, b. Jan. 28, 1787; d. Feb. 24. 1874; m. Nancy Dickerson, a native of Fayette county, Penn.; had issue: 1. Adam; 2. Susan; 3. Mary; 4. Rebecca; 5. Joshua, b. 1822; d. Sept. 4. 1879; m. 1847, Nancy G. Watson; d. 1884; daughter of Robert S. Watson (had issue: i. Watson, b. Oct. 13, 1849; m. Sept. 4, 1874, Mary A. Dickerson; ii. Adam-C.; iii. Rachel-A., m. J. L. Scott, and removed to Missouri; iv. Mary-J., m. Winfield Scott, and removed to Missouri; v. Louisa-B., m. John Webb; vi. Susan, m. John P. Dunlap): 6. John.

IV. Adam, b. Sept. 15. 1790; d. Sept. 20, 1863; m. 1817, Jane Patterson: had issue: 1. Joseph, b. June 29, 1818; m. February, 1846, Julia Ann Hayes, d. Sept. 3, 1878; daughter of John and Hannah Hayes, natives of Pennsylvania (had issue: i. Adam-B.; settled in Freeport township: ii. John-A.; iii. Harriet-J., m. Israel Howells; iv. Patterson; v. William-H.; vi. Harriet-F., m. Israel Shepard; vii. Mary, m. John Stephenson; viii. A.-M., b. 1860; m.

Laura J. Moore, daughter of R. L. and Sophia Moore; ix. James-V.; x. Cora-B.; xi. Robert-S.; xii. LeGrand-E.); 2. Hugh-B., b. Feb. 15, 1820; m. Feb. 15, 1844, Elizabeth Dunlap, daughter of Joseph and Sarah Gilmore Dunlap (had issue: i. Sarah-J., m. Samuel Clemens; ii. Joseph-G.; iii. Mary-E.; iv. William-A.; v. John-P.); 3. Rebecca, d. in infancy; 4. Nancy; 5. Mary-J.; 6. Sarah-A., b. 1828; 7. Adam, b. 1834; 8. Patterson; 9. Samuel; 10. John; 11. Robert; 12. William.

V. Joseph, b. in Fayette county, Penn., Oct. 12, 1792; d. March 23, 1878; m. (1st) 1819, Sarah Gilmore, b. Jan. 14, 1800; d. May 18, 1837; daughter of Samuel and Elizabeth Buchanan Gilmore; m. (2d) Mary Anne Roberts, d. 1856; m. (3d) 1859, Susan Webb; had issue by first wife: 1. Samuel, b. May 20, 1820; d. Oct. 19, 1889; m. Oct. 22, 1844, Mary Rea, b. Dec. 14, 1821, daughter of Joseph and Jane McConnell Rea, of Green township (had issue: i. Martha, m. J. McKibben; ii. Sarah, m. ——— Dickerson; iii. Mary, m. H. Dunlap, of Athens township; iv. Clara-B.); 2. Joseph, b. May 30, 1834; m. 1855, Elizabeth Dickerson, daughter of Adam Dickerson (had issue: i. Sarah, b. 1856; ii. Jane, b. 1858; iii. Lee-D., b. 1861; iv. Crittenden, b. 1862).

VI. Robert, b. May 11, 1794; d. March 2. 1860; m. 1819, Mary Patterson, d. Sept. 29. 1852; daughter of Hugh and Nancy Patterson, natives of Ireland, who emigrated to Pennsylvania, where the father died; had issue: 1. Adam, b. Oct. 2, 1820; d. 1895; m. (1st) 1845, Margaret McFadden, d. 1863. daughter of Samuel McFadden; m. (2d) 1874, Sarah Jane Dickerson, d. 1875 (had issue by first wife: i. Robert, b. Nov. 14, 1845; m. April 20, 1871, Margaret McFadden. daughter of John J. McFadden. of Athens township; ii. Samuel, b. Nov. 13, 1847: m. March 16, 1876, Annie R. McFadden. daughter of John J. McFadden; iii. Mary: iv. Elizabeth; v. A.-J.. b. June 14, 1859; m. June 9, 1887, Annie McAdam): 2. Hugh-Patterson. b. Oct 17, 1822: d. March 29. 1894; m. 1856, Sarah Jane Kennedy. b. 1832; daughter of Napoleon B. and Mary Gilmore Kennedy (had issue: i. Robert-Kennedy; ii. Mary. m. William B. Scott, and removed to Missouri: iii. John-A.. d. young; iv. Joseph-B : v. Amanda-B.; vi. Samuel-P.; vii. Albert-C.); 3. Sam-

uel, b. Dec. 24, 1825; d. June 29, 1882;
m. 1857, Mary J. Dunlap; d. 1900;
daughter of Adam Dunlap (had issue:
i. William-F., b. Aug. 2, 1858; m. Oct.
29, 1885, Mary H. Dunlap, daughter of
Samuel Dunlap, of Nottingham township; ii. Emily-J.; iii. James-P.); 4.
Nancy; 5. Rebecca; 6. Mary; 7. Robert.
    VII. Mary, b. 1788; d. March 22, 1858;
m. John McFadden, son of John and
Margaret Sharp McFadden (see McFadden Family).
    VIII. Sarah, b. Dec. 31, 1779; d. Feb.
25, 1871; m. Joshua Dickerson (see
Family of Joshua Dickerson).
    IX. Esther, m. ——— Rankin.
    X. Rebecca, b. March 31, 1786; d.
March 24, 1864; m. (1st) ——— Rankin;
m. (2d) Alexander (?) Hamilton.
    XI. Rachel, m. Baruch Oglevee.

JAMES EDGAR, of Scotch-Irish
descent; removed from Washington
county, Penn., to Wellsburg, Va., and
thence to Nottingham township, Harrison county, Ohio, where he died in
1845; had issue:
    I. James, b. in Washington county,
Penn., Feb. 22, 1794; d. March 16, 1882;
m. Charity Bartow, b. in Washington
county, N. Y., July 24, 1798; d. March
16, 1882; daughter of Zenas and Elizabeth Carpenter Bartow (the former
born about 1750, was an officer in the
Revolutionary War, and settled about
1809 at Connotton, Harrison county,
Ohio); had issue: 1. ———, d. in infancy; 2. Elizabeth; 3. Adam; 4. Cyrus,
settled in Monroe county; 5. Margaret;
6. James, killed in the Civil War; 7.
Phœbe, m. ——— Petty; 8. Francis; 9.
Matilda, m. ——— Kidwell; 10. Elijah-
G.; 11. Charity, m. ——— Hanlon; 12.
Samuel-D., b. Aug. 30, 1842, in Monroe
county, Ohio; settled in Nottingham
township, Harrison county; served in
the Civil War; m. Jan. 14, 1869, Susan
Poulson, b. March 14, 1852, in Nottingham township, daughter of John and
Rachel Rogers Poulson.
    II. Jane. III. William. IV. Adam.
V. Elizabeth. VI. Nancy.

ANDREW EKEY, see Family of
Obediah Holmes.

JOHN ELDER, see Family of William Scott.

SAMUEL ELLIOTT, a native of Ireland, emigrated to America, and, about
1800, settled in Belmont county, Ohio;

m. (1st) Mary Grimes; m. (2d) ———;
had issue by first wife: 1. Joseph, settled in New Athens, Harrison county;
2. Samuel, b. in Belmont county, about
1817; settled in Short Creek township,
Harrison county, in 1847, where he died
Jan. 15, 1884; m. 1845, Sarah Thomas,
b. Oct. 28, 1828 (had issue: i. Mary-
Elizabeth, settled in Guernsey county,
Ohio; ii. Hameline, settled near Cadiz,
Ohio; iii. Martha-J., m. ——— Thomas,
and settled near Mount Pleasant, Jefferson county; iv. Susann-A., m. ———
Anderson, and settled in Short Creek
township; v. Reason-Wilson, settled
near Harrisville, Ohio; vi. Malinda, m.
Samuel Brokaw, and settled in Belmont
county; vii. Aaron, settled in Short
Creek township; viii. Harvey, b. 1864;
d. 1883; ix. Taylor); 3. James; 4. Mary,
m. Joshua Dickerson; 5. Nancy, m.
Joshua B. Dickerson, and settled in
Short Creek township.
    Isaac Thomas, a native of Virginia,
father of Sarah Thomas Elliott, was
one of the first settlers of Short Creek
township, Harrison county, Ohio, locating there in the early part of the
century; had issue: 1. Peter; 2. Isaac,
b. 1785; d. 1867, in Washington county,
Iowa, where he had settled in 1843; m.
Elizabeth Holmes, b. 1800; d. 1852 (had
issue: i. Aaron; ii. Asa; iii. Abram, a
Methodist Episcopal minister; iv. John,
settled in Iowa; v. Taylor; vi. William,
settled in Colorado; vii. Sarah, b. Oct.
28, 1828; m. Samuel Elliott; viii. Susan,
m. David Twinand); 3. Susan; 4. Ruth;
5. Anna; 6. Sarah; 7. Aaron.

JOHN ENDSLEY, see Family of
George McPeck.

PATRICK ENGLISH, a native of
Great Britain, served in the Revolutionary War, and afterwards settled at
Redstone, Fayette county, Penn.;
thence removed to Cadiz, Harrison
county, Ohio; from there he went to
Coshocton county, where he died; had
issue, among others:
    I. James, b. Oct. 17, 1791, either in
Virginia, or Baltimore county, Md.;
d. in North township, Harrison county,
Ohio, June 6, 1869; m. (1st) Jane Pickens, d. 1842; m. (2d) Ann McCarroll, b.
Jan. 25, 1809; d. Oct. 17, 1884 (daughter
of John McCarroll, a native of Scotland,
who died in Harrison county); had issue by first wife: 1. Talitha; 2. John,
settled in Tuscarawas county, Ohio; 3.

James, d. aged seventeen; 4. Matthew, settled in New Philadelphia, Ohio; 5. Thomas, served in the Civil War; d. at Nashville, Tenn; 6. Susannah; 7. Alpha, settled in Iowa; 8. Nelson, d. in Iowa; 9. Nancy, m. William Donaldson. and settled in North township; 10. William, settled in Kansas; 11. Jane, m. Samuel McLean, and settled in Iowa; 12. Alexander, settled in Harrison county; 13. James (second), settled in Brilliant, Ohio; 14. Mary-E., m. John Morgan, and settled in Iowa; had issue by second wife; 15. Martha, b. July 2, 1845; m. James Price; settled in Leesville, Carroll county, Ohio; 16. George, b. Feb. 11, 1847, settled near Scio; m. Sept. 4, 1877, Julia A. Lewis, daughter of Griffin Lewis, of Jefferson county, Ohio; 17. Isaiah, b. Dec. 5, 1848; settled in North township; 18. Malida, b. Aug. 17, 1850; m. T. W. Smith, and settled in North township; 19. Scott, b. Aug. 13, 1852, in North township, where he settled; m. Oct. 29, 1879, Ida Masters, daughter of Isaac and Ann Overholtz Masters.

JAMES ERVIN, a native of Maryland, settled in Short Creek township, Harrison county, Ohio, about 1812; afterward removing to Franklin township, Harrison county, where he d. 1850; m. in Maryland, Elizabeth Bann, d. 1870; had issue: 1. William; 2. James; 3. John; 4. Henry, b. April 6, 1815; settled in Washington township; m. 1840, Elizabeth Watts, of Harrison county (had issue: i. James; ii. John; iii. Mahala; iv. Ann; v. Margaret-H.; vi. Sarah-J.; vii. Isabelle; viii. Thomas; ix. Actia-A.); 5. Phœbe; 6. Isaac; 7. Nancy.

JOHN ESTEP, d. aged about eighty-four years; removed from Pennsylvania to Short Creek township, Harrison county, Ohio, before 1826; m. in Pennsylvania, Sarah Smith; d. aged about eighty-four years; daughter of Edward Smith; had issue: 1. Harrison, settled at Lloydsville, Ohio; 2. William, a physician, settled in Lloydsville; 3. Robert; 4. Harriet, m. Taylor Lynn; 5. Andrew, b. 1826; settled in Kansas City, Mo., where he d. 1884; m. 1850, Sarah Henderson, daughter of Andrew and Martha Nichol Henderson. The Nichol family was of Scotch origin; during the religious persecution in Scotland they passed from

Scotland to county Derry, Ireland, thence emigrated and settled in Cumberland county, Penn., 1789; afterward located in Westmoreland county, Penn.; and about 1800 removed to Colerain township, Belmont county, Ohio; the parents of Martha Nichol Henderson were Andrew (1798-1861) and Jeanette (b. 1801) Nichol. Andrew and Martha Nichol Henderson had issue: 1. Martha; 2. John-N.; 3. Anna; 4. Agnes, m. Thomas Love, and settled at Aledo, Ill.; 5. Margaret, m. Robert C. McConnell, and settled at Brady, Ohio; 6. Mary-J., m. John Mintier, and settled at Shepherdstown, Ohio; 7. Andrew-Jackson; 8. Sàrah, m. Andrew Estep; 9. Isabelle, m. John Anderson, and settled in Iowa; 10. Andrew, settled at Hardy, Neb.; 11. Elizabeth, m. R. W. Castle, and settled in Iowa; 12. Harriet, m. John Sweeney, and settled in Iowa; 13. William-T.; 14. Thomas-Jefferson; 15. M.-N.

ROBERT ESTEP, a native of New Jersey, settled in Peters (now Union) township, Washington county, Penn., before 1784; had issue, thirteen children, among whom: 1. Nathan, died without issue; 2. William (had issue, among others: i. Joseph); 3. Ephraim (had issue: i. Elmira); 4. James-S., a Baptist minister; m. Sarah Gaston (see Gaston Family), b. about 1808; d. 1875; daughter of Samuel and Margaret Penny Gaston, of Peters township (Samuel, b. 1772; d. 1853; son of John and Charity Cheeseman Gaston, who removed to Washington county from Upper Freehold township, Monmouth county, N. J., before 1783) (had issue, at least six children, of whom: i. Josiah-Morgan, b. Feb. 19, 1826; d. May 5, 1888; settled in Cadiz, Ohio, about 1853; m. 1857, Amanda J. Crabb, b. September, 1837; d. March 23, 1898; daughter of Jacob and Jane D. Crabb; ii. Harrison, removed to Marion, Ind.; iii. James, removed to Marion, Ind.).

ISAAC FINICAL, a native of Pennsylvania, of German descent, b. 1779; removed from Washington county and settled in Cadiz township, Harrison county, Ohio, in 1831; afterwards removed to Short Creek township, where he d. 1854; m. in Pennsylvania, Margaret Anderson, b. 1797; d. 1885; daughter of Robert Anderson, of Washington

3

county, who served in the Revolutionary War; had issue: 1. Eliza-May, m.
William Spiker; 2. Margaret, m. Alexander Henderson; 3. Jane, m. William
Miller; 4. Frances-C., m. David Stewart; 5. Mary-E., m. Calvin Rodgers; 6.
Rachel-A., d. in infancy; 7. Robert; 8.
John, b. in Washington county, Penn.,
April 4, 1829; m. April, 1856, Martha
Irwin, daughter of William Irwin, who
afterwards removed to Iowa (her
mother was a native of Ireland, her
family having settled in Harrison
county when she was six years of age);
9. Thomas.

MICHAEL FINLEY, b. in Scotland
or Ireland about 1680-90; emigrated
from county Armagh, Ireland, to
America, landing at Philadelphia Sept.
28, 1734, with his wife and seven or
eight sons; first settled on Neshaminy
Creek in Bucks county, Penn., afterwards in New Jersey, and later in
Sadsbury township, Chester county,
Penn., where he lived from 1737 to 1747
or later; had issue, among others:
1. John, b. in county Armagh, Ireland,
killed by Indians about 1757-59, in Lurgan township, Cumberland county,
Penn., where he had settled near Middle
Spring Church before 1744; m. Martha
Berkley; had issue: 1. James, settled in
upper South Carolina; 2. Mary, m. (1st)
John Thompson; m. (2d) James Leonard, d. in South Huntingdon township,
Westmoreland county, Penn.,1791; (had
issue by first husband: i. Martha, d.
unm., aged twenty-eight years; ii.
Anthony, m. Rachel Henley, d. in Davis
county, Ky., aged seventy-five years;
iii. Jane, m. Charles Foster, and both d.
1796 in Cincinnati; iv. Mary, d. 1806; m.
Adam Carnahan; had issue by second
husband; v. Catharine, m. —— Wil-
liams; vi. Elizabeth, b. March 4, 1772;
d. June 25, 1863; m. (1st) March 3, 1796,
Capt. Alexander Buchanan, b. 1760; d.
May 8, 1810; m. (2d) Nov. 19, 1811,
David Compton, of Meadville, Penn.,
had issue by first husband: Robert;
James; Mary; Thomas; Alexander;
Sarah; John; and by second husband:
Rebecca and Nancy-Hanna; vii. Ann,
or Nancy, b. June 7, 1775; d. at Cadiz,
Ohio, March 23, 1818; m. Dec. 6, 1796,
John Hanna, of Greensburgh, Penn.,
son of John Hanna, and had issue:
James-Leonard, 1797-1820; Catharine,
1799-1801; Mary Leonard, 1800-1820;

John-Evans, 1805-1894; Jane-Finley,
1811-1833; Andrew-Finley, 1813-1847,
and David-Wilson, 1843; viii. John-
Berkley (or Barclay), b. 1777; m. ——
Austin, and removed South; ix. James-
Finley, m. Sarah Barber, and settled at
Bath, Summit county, Ohio); 3. Michael,
b. about 1747; d. near Chillicothe, Ohio;
4. Ann, m. Thomas Johnston, who lived
in Westmoreland county, Penn., in
1775; 5. Elizabeth, b. about 1748; m.
(1st) John Prebles (or Peebles), m. (2d)
William McCracken; m. (3) Capt. Wil-
liam Rippey, of Shippensburg, Penn.;
6. Andrew, b. 1750; d. July 5, 1829, in
South Huntingdon township, West-
moreland county, Penn.; served as first
lieutenant in the Revolution (8th
Pennsylvania, 1777); m. Jane Jack,
daughter of John and Eleanor Jack, of
Westmoreland county (had issue: i.
John, m. Mary Stokeley, daughter of
Nehemiah Stokely, of Westmoreland
county, and had issue: Nehemiah and
Stokeley; ii. Andrew, removed to
Indiana; iii. Mary, m. —— Bell; iv.
Nancy, m. —— Bell; v. Jane); 7.
Samuel, b. April 15, 1752; d. April 2,
1829; served as major of a Virginia
Cavalry regiment during the Revolu-
tion, and as a brigadier-general in the
War of 1812; m. May 5, 1789, at Newville, Cumberland county, Penn., Mary
Brown, daughter of James Brown (had
issue: i. Martha, b. March 16, 1792; m.
Rev. W. L. McCalla, of Philadelphia;
ii. James-Brown, b. June 7, 1794; d. May
14, 1851; m. (1st) Mary Theresa Brown;
m. (2d) Mary E. Moore; lived in Chillicothe, Ohio, until 1829, and at South
Bend, Ind., in 1836; iii. Clement-Alex-
ander, b. May 11, 1797, at Newville,
Penn.; d. Sept. 8, 1879, at Philadelphia;
surgeon-general U. S. A., 1861, and brigadier-general, 1876; m. (1st) Elizabeth
Moore, daughter of Samuel Moore, of
Philadelphia; iv. Samuel-Berkley, b.
Feb. 10, 1800; d. about 1877; thrice
married; v. John-Knox, b. Jan. 13,
1806; d. about 1885; m. Margaret
Nevin); 8. John, b. 1754; d. 1837 or 1838,
in Fleming county, Ky.; served as lieutenant and captain in the Revolution
(Pennsylvania Line, 2d, 5th, and 8th
regiments, and as major in Wayne's
army, 1793); settled at Upper Blue
Lick, Ky., before 1800; m. Hannah
Duncan, daughter of David Duncan, of
Ft. Pitt (had issue: i. David-Duncan,
lived in Nicholas county, Ky., as late

as 1871); 9. Clements; settled in South Carolina (?). (See Clements, VI.)

II. Samuel; a minister; b. in county Armagh, Ireland, 1715; d. in Philadelphia, July 17, 1766; m. (1st), Sept. 26, 1744, Sarah Hall, b. 1728; d. July 30, 1760; m. (2d), Ann Clarkson, daughter of Matthew Clarkson, of Philadelphia; President of Princeton College, 1761 to 1766; had issue: 1. Rebecca, b. about 1743; m. about 1760, Samuel Breese of New Jersey (had issue, among others: Elizabeth-Ann., b. Sept. 29, 1766; m. May 14, 1789, Rev. Jedediah Morse, of Connecticut, and among their children was Samuel Finley Breese Morse, of Connecticut, the inventor of the telegraph); 2. Joseph, b. about 1745; d. unm.; 3. Sarah, b. about 1747; m. Isaac Snowden, of Philadelphia; 4. Samuel, b. about 1748; d. unm.; served as surgeon in the Revolution (Massachusetts Line); 5. John-Hall, b. about 1750; served as first lieutenant in the Revolution (Fifth Pennsylvania Battalion, 1776); 6. Ebenezer, b. about 1754; served as captain in the Revolution (on staff of General Smallwood, Maryland Line, 1777); 7. James-Edwards-Burr, b. May 15, 1758; d. June 3, 1819; served as surgeon in the Revolution (Massachusetts Line, 4th, 5th, and 15th regiments), m. Jan. 2, 1798, Mary Peronneau, daughter of Arthur Peronneau, of Charleston, S. C. (had issue: i. Samuel-Benjamin-Rush, a physician; b. Dec. 13, 1801; d. without issue, 1833; m. Mary Ancrum; ii. William-Peronneau, b. Jan. 3, 1803; d. April 9, 1876; m. (1st) Nov. 14, 1833, Clelia Peronneau; m. (2d) Anna M. Harris Gibson; iii. Mary-Hutson, d. young; iv. Sarah-Anna, d. young; v. James-Edwards-Burr, a physician; b. June 28, 1808; d. May 11, 1844; m. Feb. 14, 1832, Maria Ancrum); 8. ———, d. in infancy.

III. William, d. 1800; lived in Sadsbury township, Chester county, 1737 to 1747, in West Caln township, 1750 to 1764, or later; removed from Chester to York (now Adams) county, Penn., after 1764, and thence to Augusta county, Va.; m. (1st) ———; m. (2d) Catharine Culbertson (mother of William and Michael Finley), daughter of Samuel Culbertson, of Londongrove township, Chester county; m. (3d) Ann Cowan, daughter of David Cowan, of Lancaster county; m. (4th) Eleanor ———; had issue by first three wives: 1. William,

lived in York county (now Adams county) in 1771; 2. Michael, b. 1744; d. Aug. 13, 1821; m. Nov. 29, 1772, Mary Waugh, daughter of William and Mary Waugh, and removed to Rockbridge county, Va. (had issue: i. William, b. Oct. 4, 1773; m. (1st) June 28, 1796, Margaret Horner; m. (2d) Elizabeth Christian, and had issue: David-Horner; John-Horner; Matilda, m. Rev. James Paine; Drusilla, m. John S. Leech; Elizabeth, m. James Johnston, and Margaret, m. Joseph Bell; ii. Samuel, b. June 9, 1775; m. Sept. 22, 1796, Mary Tate, daughter of John Tate, of Virginia, and had issue: Maria-Waugh, 1779-1849, m. Rev. Isaac Jones; John-T., 1801-1848; Jane-Tate, 1803-1854, m. John B. Christian; George-W., 1806-1834; Nancy McClung, b. 1807; William, 1812-1871; Lavinia, 1812-18; Caroline-Ellen, m. James Harper; Samuel-B., 1818-1874; and Mary McClung, d. 1829; iii. John, b. Sept. 2, 1778; m. April 21, 1807, Ellen Tate, and had issue: Clarinda-J.; Eliza, d. 1856; m. Dr. Thomas S. Bouchelle; Augustus-Washington, 1813-1889; William-Waugh, 1815-1874, and John Tate, b. 1817; iv. Mary, b. Sept. 2, 1778; d. Dec. 29, 1804; m. Aug. 22, 1797, Samuel Patterson, of Rockbridge county, Va.; v. Elizabeth, m. Jesse Scott, and removed to Indiana; vi. Esther, b. Sept. 30, 1780; d. unm., July 26, 1804; vii. Catharine, b. Sept. 30, 1780; d. in infancy; viii. Michael, b. March, 1783; d. June 6, 1823; m. April 26, 1808, Ruth Irvine, and had issue: Augustus-C., 1809-1858; Maria-Waugh, 1812-1891; m. Jonathan Brooks; Caroline-E., 1812-1832, m. Samuel Patterson; and Harriet-Newell, 1822-1842, m. David C. Gilkeson); 3. Aaron, d. before 1794; m. Margaret Withrow; 4. Andrew, b. Feb., 1764; d. May 8, 1844; m. (1st) Ann McClain, of Pennsylvania; m. (2d) Jane Lyle, of Virginia; 5. James, d. young; 6. Samuel, d. young; 7. ——— (a daughter), m. ——— Morrow (?); 8. Margaret, m. 1770, D. C. Humphreys, and settled in Augusta county, Va.; 9. Elizabeth, m. David Blythe, of York county, Penn.; 10. Anna, d. before 1794; m. Robert Campbell, of Berkeley county, West Va.; 11. Susan, m. Robert Rowan, and removed to Ohio; 12. Mary, living in 1794; m. John Martin.

IV. Michael, of Chester county, lived in Sadsbury and West Caln townships about 1737-1758, and in Londonderry township, 1764; m. Ann Lewis, of Chester county; had issue: 1. Joseph-Lewis, b. 1760 (?); d. May 23, 1839; served as lieutenant, captain, and major in the Revolution (Miles' Rine Battalion, and 13th, 8th, and 2d regiments, Pennsylvania Line); lived in Adams county, Ohio, in 1833 (had issue: i. John-Blair, lived in Lewis county, Ky., in 1841); 2. Ebenezer; a merchant of Baltimore; m. (1st) Jane, daughter of Rev. John McKnight, of Franklin county; m. (2d) Mrs. Catharine (Allen) Marshall, of Kentucky.

V. James, a minister; b. in county Armagh, Ireland, February, 1725; d. in Rostraver township, Westmoreland county, Penn., Jan. 6, 1795; minister of Rock or East Nottingham Church, Cecil county, Md., 1752 to 1783; and of Rehoboth and Roundhill churches, Westmoreland county, Penn., 1783 to 1795; m. 1752, Hannah Evans, b. 1715; d. April 1, 1795; daughter of Robert Evans; had issue: 1. John-Evans, a minister; b. July 6, 1753; d. in Ohio after 1813; pastor of Fagg's Manor church, 1781 to 1793, when he removed to Bracken, Mason county, Ky., and thence to Red Oak, Ohio; m. —— Ruston, daughter of Job Ruston, of Londonderry township, Chester county, Penn.; 2. Samuel-Robert, b. Dec. 19, 1758; d. Oct. 25, 1839; 3. Margaret, b. Sept. 5, 1756; d. May 10, 1836; m. Col. John Power, of Westmoreland county, Penn., b. 1757; d. July 29, 1805; 4. Ebenezer, b. Dec. 30, 1758; d. Jan. 18, 1849; settled on Dunlap's Creek, Fayette county, Penn., in 1772; m. (1st) Jane Kinkaid, b. 1762-4; d. June 5, 1793; m. (2d) Violet Lowrey, d. Nov. 11, 1804; m. (3d) Margery Cunningham, b. 1770; d. Jan. 27, 1822; m. (4th) Mrs. Sarah Jones, b. Sept. 14, 1769; d. Jan. 24, 1848 (had issue: i. John-Evans, b. November, 1783; d. March, 1793; ii. James, b. November, 1784; d. 1861; iii. Elizabeth, b. December, 1786; d. July, 1860; iv. Joseph, b. March, 1788; d. December, 1848; v. Hannah, b. October, 1791; d. March, 1793; vi. Rebecca, b. October, 1795; vii. Hannah, 2d, b. Oct. 10, 1796; viii. William, b. August, 1798; d. January, 1865; m. Rhoda Harris; ix. Samuel, b. July, 1800; d. in Ohio; x. Jane, b. 1802; d. August, 1890; m. —— Hibbs; xi. Ebenezer, b. Oct. 24, 1804; d. Dec. 28, 1891; m. Feb. 9, 1826, Phœbe Woodward; xii. Eli-H., b. April 6, 1807; d.

Jan. 7, 1892; xiii. Robert, b. April, 1809; d. October, 1874; m. Ann ——; xiv. Margaret, b. Nov. 29, 1810); 5. Hannah, b. June 20, 1764; d. before 1820; m. John Robinson; 6. Joseph, b. Dec. 13, 1766; d. June 3, 1860; m. (1st) —— Veech; m. (2d) Frances Moore; 7. James, b. Jan. 14, 1769; d. Nov. 17, 1772; 8. William, b. June 10, 1772; d. Aug. 20, 1857; m. (1st) Sarah Patterson; m. (2d) Margaret Wilson; 9. Michael, b. March 24, 1774; d. July 29, 1850; m. (1st) Eleanor Elliott, daughter of William Elliott; m. (2d) Mrs. Mary Plumer Smith.

VI. Clements, b. March, 1735; d. Aug. 11, 1775, in South Huntingdon township, Westmoreland county, Penn.; m. Jan. 12, 1761, Elizabeth Carnahan (sister of John Carnahan); had issue: 1. Elizabeth, b. April 9, 176—; 2. John, b. May 18, 1766 (had issue: i. James-Power, b. Aug. 6, 1792; ii. Jane, b. July 16, 1794; iii. Clements, b. Nov. 17, 1796; iv. Mary, b. Jan. 28, 1799); 3. Martha, b. June 12, 1775; d. May 27, 1847; m. 1793, Reynolds Ross, of Westmoreland county; b. in Ireland, April 2, 1755; d. Feb. 11, 1847 (had issue: i. Clements, b. June 6, 1795; ii. John, b. Aug. 31, 1797; iii. Elizabeth, b. Feb. 21, 1800; m. —— Boyd; iv. William, b. Aug. 15, 1803; v. Samuel, b. Sept. 11, 1805; vi. Mary, b. Nov. 29, 1807; m. —— McCurdy; vii. Jane, b. April 5, 1809; viii. Martha, b. March 12, 1811; m. —— Wallace; ix. Andrew-Finley, b. June 4, 1813; d.——; x. James, b. Jan. 27, 1816). It is possible that this Clements Finley was a son and not a brother of John Finley (I.), who married Martha Berkley. John's son removed to South Carolina, but there are many circumstances leading to the conclusion that he may afterwards have settled in Westmoreland county, Penn., and died there in 1775.

HENRY FERGUSON, of Scotch-Irish descent, settled in Indiana county, Penn., about 1778; removed in 1802 to Green township, one mile west from Hopedale, in Harrison county, Ohio; had issue: I. Samuel. II. John. III. Joseph. IV. Thomas. V. Henry, b. in Indiana county, Penn., 1788; d. in Green township, 1863; served in the War of 1812; m. 1810, Elizabeth Johnson; d. 1856; had issue: 1. Vincent, b. July 12, 1812; d. May 20, 1876; removed to Germano, Harrison county, in 1835; m.

March 19, 1835, Mary Amspoker, b. Dec. 21, 1816; daughter of Samuel and Mary Norris Amspoker (had issue: i. Amelia; ii. John-H., b. Jan. 20, 1838, in Germano; served in the Civil War; m. Oct. 6, 1881, Addie Plummer, b. July 18, 1849, in Washington county, Ohio; daughter of Robert L. and Charlotte Faires Plummer; iii. Elizabeth, m. Martin Overholt; settled in Custer county, Neb.; iv. Samuel-J.; v. Mary-Jane; vi. Rebecca-A.; vii. Susan-P., m. Henry Redman; settled in Iowa; viii. Mary-I.; ix. Margaret-A., settled in Iowa; x. Henry-W., settled in Colorado; xi. Sarah-C.; xii. Etta-R.); 2. Samuel; 3. John, settled in Kansas; 4. Isabelle; 5. Mary; 6. Eliza-A., m. —— Ferguson, and settled in Archer township.

Samuel Amspoker, father of Mary Amspoker Ferguson, settled in Harrison county, Ohio in 1803, locating five miles north from Cadiz; had issue: 1. John; 2. Alexander; 3. Samuel; 4. Elizabeth; 5. Susan; 6. Mary, m. Vincent Ferguson; 7. Sarah; 8. Charles-N.; 9. James.

DANIEL FIERBAUGH, a native of Germany, settled in Pennsylvania about 1779; removed to what is now North township, Harrison county, Ohio, but afterward returned to Pennsylvania, where he died, his widow settling in Ohio after his death; had issue, among others:

I. David, b. either in Pennsylvania or Maryland, 1787; settled in North township, where he d. June 14, 1864; m. in Harrison county, Magdalena Gundy, b. 1797; d. 1878; daughter of Rev. Joseph and Fannie Coffman Gundy (the former a Mennonite minister, who settled in Harrison county, in 1804); had issue: 1. Frances, m. John Weimer, and settled in Austin, Neb.; 2. Daniel, b. April 27, 1817; d. Oct. 14, 1885; m. 1841, Elizabeth Boor, daughter of Michael and Caroline L. Barence Boor (the former came to Harrison county with his parents in 1838; d. in Defiance, Ohio) (had issue: i. Caroline-L., d. Jan. 26, 1866; m. Rev. B. F. Rinehart; ii. Mary-M.. m. Ebenezer W. Laughridge; iii. Michael-B., b. Aug. 7, 1845; served in the Civil War: m. Nov. 18, 1869. Sarah E. Smith, b. 1852; d. Feb. 10. 1890; daughter of Thomas and Mary Smith; the former b. 1809; d. February, 1881; the latter b. 1813; d.

1882; iv. David-G., d. April 13, 1870; v. Clara-E., d. Oct. 27, 1879).

JOHN FIREBAUGH, a native of Pennsylvania, of German descent, b. 1786; d. April 8, 1872, in North township, Harrison county, Ohio, where he had settled before 1825; served in the War of 1812; m. Elizabeth Friend, b. 1793; d. Feb. 19, 1872; daughter of Jacob and —— Bowers Friend; had issue: 1. Mary, m. John Shiltz; 2. Jacob, m. Catherine McCarroll, and settled on the Kanawha River, Virginia; 3. John, m. (1st) Nancy Capper, a native of Ohio; m. (2d) Amanda Rippeth, also of Ohio; 4. Elizabeth; 5. Catherine, m. (1st) Joseph Heaston; m. (2d) J. Overholtz; 6. Margaret, m. Isaac Heaston; 7. David, b. March 11, 1825; served in the Civil War; m. 1854, Christina Heaston, b. in Monroe township, daughter of John and Christina Heaston, pioneers of Harrison county, both having died in Monroe township (the former a native of Maryland; the latter born in what is now a part of Philadelphia); 8. Samuel, settled in Southern Kansas; m. (1st) Julia True, of Ohio; m. (2d) Jemima Schooly, of Iowa; m. (3d) Emily Tucker, of Kansas; 9. Susan, m. David Addleman; 10. Frances, m. John Heaston; 11. Elias, settled in Nebraska; m. Mary Boor, of Ohio; 12. Sarah, m. Andrew Hale, of Carroll county, Ohio; 13. Joseph, b. 1838; d. Jan. 26, 1879, in Uhrichsville, Tuscarawas county, Ohio.

JOHN FORD, removed from Redstone, Fayette county, Penn., and settled in Nottingham township, Harrison county, Ohio, before 1827; had issue, among others: 1. Lewis, b. in Washington or Fayette county. Penn., 1794; d. in Nottingham township about 1846; m. Rebecca Dodd, b. about 1795 (had issue: i. Slemmons; ii. William; iii. Lewis; iv. Emily; v. Piety-A.; vi. Ruth; vii. John-E.. b. in April, about 1832; m. Dec. 2, 1870, Viney R. Hudson, b. in Indiana, June 3, 1843.

ADAM FORKER, b. in Scotland, 1793; d. in Mercer, Penn., 1837; m. Jane Green. d. 1836; had issue: 1. Jacob, b. 1786; d. July 19, 1842; 2. George, b. 1788; 3. Hannah. b. Oct. 21. 1791; 4. Joseph, b. Dec. 30. 1799; d. at Cadiz, 1841: m. Mrs. Mary Cady Conwell, b. in Reading, Penn.. 1792; d. 1865: daughter of John and Margaret Parr Cady (had issue: i.

Belinda, m. John Shauf; ii. Mary-Jane, m. Dr. Chalkley Thomas, and settled in Des Moines, Iowa; iii. Henry-G., b. Nov. 19, 1838; d. Jan. 25, 1896); 5. Samuel, b. 1805; d. Sept. 5, 1866; 6. James, d. July 18, 1852; 7. John, d. Jan. 17, 1865; 8. Mary, d. June 14, 1856; m. —— Harris; 9. Israel, d. April 28, 1866; 10. William, d. April 6, 1871.

ABRAHAM FORNEY, b. 1740; d. Aug. 27, 1824; a native of Germany; m. Susanna ——, b. 1752; d. May 28, 1842; emigrated to America about 1798, and in 1801 settled in Cadiz township, Harrison county, Ohio; had issue: 1. John. II. Abraham. III. Catharine. IV. Mary, b. 1775; d. Aug. 5, 1850; m. about 1793, probably near Martinsburg, West Va., Charles Timmons, b. 1751; d. 1820 (see Timmons Family). V. Susanna, m. —— Rabe. VI. Frederick, b. Aug. 28, 1787, in Germany; removed to Nottingham township, 1827, where he d. 1854; served in the War of 1812; m. Oct. 29, 1812, Deborah Harris, d. June 21, 1873, whose parents were pioneers. in Harrison county; had issue: 1. Sophia, b. Sept. 6, 1813; 2. Susanna, b. Nov. 3, 1814; 3. Mary-Ann, b. Aug. 6, 1817; 4. John, b. Nov. 29, 1820; settled at Deersville; m. Nancy Johnson, daughter of Ephraim Johnson, of Moorefield; 5. Eliza-M., b. July 6, 1825; 6. Catherine, b. July 8, 1827; 7. Alice, b. July 4, 1829. VII. Sophia.

JOHN FORSYTHE, a native of Ireland, of Scotch descent, emigrated with his wife and settled in Fayette county, Penn., before 1800; had issue: I. John. II. Robert. III. Jesse, b. in Fayette county, Penn.; d. in Washington township, Harrison county, Ohio, Nov. 5, 1857; m. (1st) Mahala Patterson, in Pennsylvania, where all his children but the youngest one, were born; m. (2d) 1811, Sarah Colvin, d. June 24, 1854; had issue by first wife: 1. William, b. March 10, 1800; 2. Maria, b. Sept. 25, 1801; 3. Elizabeth, b. Sept. 21, 1803; 4. Matilda, b. Sept. 21, 1805; had issue by second wife: 5. Samuel, b. Jan. 19, 1812; 6. Harrison, b. Jan. 15, 1813; 7. Joseph, b. Dec. 22, 1814; 8. Nancy, b. Nov. 19, 1816; 9. John, b. June 15, 1818; 10. Benjamin-F., b. March 15, 1820; 11. Levi-C., b. Aug. 2, 1822; 12. Rebecca, b. Dec. 1, 1824; d. Aug. 19, 1872; m. Judge Amon Lemmon; 13. Jesse, b. Nov. 6, 1826, in Washington township, Harrison county, Ohio; served in the Civil War; served as a member of the Ohio Legislature, 1877; m. Oct. 26, 1854, Eliza Dean, b. 1829; d. Jan. 17, 1890; daughter of Samuel and Mary Dean, of Cross Creek township, Jefferson county, Ohio. IV. Eli. V. Nancy. VI. Elizabeth.

GEORGE FOSTER, a native of England, b. Sept. 24, 1794; settled near Scio, Harrison county, Ohio, 1816, where he d. June 8, 1849; m. (1st) Jerusha Wortman; m. (2d) 1837, Jane Shouse, a native of Pennsylvania, of German descent, b. 1810; d. June 16, 1889; had issue by first wife: 1. George; 2. Jane, m. Joseph Cummings; 3. Jerusha, m. —— Custer; 4. Sarah, m. —— Reed; 5. Elizabeth, m. —— Kent; 6. Lavina; had issue by second wife: 7. Joseph-B., d. Aug. 18, 1889; 8. William, settled in Superior, Neb.; 9. Madison-J., b. June 22, 1842; settled in North township; m. July 9, 1863, Margaret J. Somerville, daughter of Christopher and Jane L. Somerville; 10. John, d. in infancy; 11. David-C., settled at Uhrichsville, Ohio.

JOHN FOWLER, a native of Maryland, whose father was killed in the Revolutionary War, removed to West Virginia in 1800, settling opposite Steubenville, Ohio; afterward located near Hopedale, Harrison county, Ohio, and, before 1819, settled near Hanover, where he died about 1840; m. in Maryland, Mary Huff; had issue, among others:
I. Garrett, b. in Maryland, Feb. 28, 1799; settled in Monroe township, Harrison county, Feb. 15, 1828, where he d. March 21, 1867; m. April 23, 1819, Hannah H. Eagleson, b. near Waterford, Erie county, Penn., March 21, 1805; daughter of John and Mary Simpson Eagleson (the former a native of Maryland; served in the War of 1812, settling near Cadiz, in Harrison county, in 1813; the latter a native of Ireland, her parents having settled in Allegheny City, Penn., where she was married); Garrett and Hannah Fowler had issue: 1. Mary-Ann, m. Joel Cramblet, and settled in Franklin township, Harrison county; 2. John-E., settled in Columbus, Ohio; 3. Asenath-T.; 4. Thomas-E., b. Dec. 6, 1820; served in the Civil War; m. Nov. 27, 1856, Maria McBeth, a native of Harrison county,

daughter of John and Mary McBeth
(had issue, seven children); 5. Richard-
P., settled in California; 6. Isaiah, settled in Brown county, Neb.; 7. Jeremiah, b. July 10, 1837; m. 1859, Catherine Auld, of Franklin township,
daughter of Stewart (b. in Pennsylvania, 1792; d. September, 1883) and
Sarah McConnell (d. 1844) Auld; settled in Scio; 8. Joseph-C., b. Aug. 30,
1841; served as an officer in the Civil
War; m. Oct. 14, 1869, Maria C. Simmons, daughter of George and Sophia
Simmons (had issue, nine children);
9. Malachi, d. in infancy; 10. Joel-C.,
d. aged four years; 11. Garrett-H., settled in Dennison, Ohio; 12. Clarissa, m.
John Spray, and settled in Franklin
township.

II. John, d. April, 1847; m. Elizabeth
———; had issue: 1. Andrew; 2. James;
3. John; 4. Mary, m. ——— Cells; 5.
Sarah, m. ——— Leaters; 6. Nancy; 7.
Hannah.

III. Benjamin, b. in Pennsylvania,
Oct. 31, 1802; d. May 15, 1891; settled
in Monroe township; m. Jane Whittaker; b. 1793; d. April 20, 1880; had
issue: 1. Mary; 2. Jane; 3. John; 4.
James-W., b. Oct. 12, 1829; settled in
Stock township; m. June 7, 1852, Elizabeth Crawford, daughter of Andrew
Crawford, of North township (had issue, nine children); 5. Rebecca; 6.
Francis; 7. Benjamin-B.; 8. William;
9. Arabella.

IV. Francis, d. 1838; m. 1830, Mary
Giles; had issue: 1. Francis.

V. Joel, m. 1836, Esther Fisher.

VI. Jeremiah.

VII. Cena.

JOSIAH FOX, b. at Falmouth, England, 1763, son of John and Rebecca
Steevens Fox; d. in Colerain township,
Belmont county, Ohio, 1847, where he
had settled in 1814; m. at Philadelphia,
1794, Anna Miller, b. 1768; d. 1841; of
German descent; daughter of Peter
Miller; had issue: 1. Charles-James, b.
in Washington, D. C., 1805; d. 1895;
settled in Short Creek township, Harrison county, Ohio, about 1839; m. Feb.
7, 1837, at Flushing, Ohio, Esther
Cooper, b. near Baltimore, April 10,
1810; d. 1896; daughter of Nicholas and
Sarah Balderson Cooper (had issue: i.
Anna-Miller, m. Lindley M. Branson;
ii. William-Spicer, b. 1839; m. 1876,
Esther J. Moore, daughter of Jeremiah

and Sarah Moore; iii. Sarah-C.; iv.
Francis-C.); 2. John, d. young; 3.
Elizabeth-Miller, m. Moses Chapline;
4. Anna-Applebee, m. Robert I. Curtis;
5. Rebecca-Steevens, m. Elijah Picker-
ing; 6. John-Charles, d. young; 7.
Sarah-Scantlebury, m. B. E. Dungan; 8.
Francis-Drake.

JOHN FULTON, b. Aug. 26, 1777, near
Havre de Grace, Maryland, of which
place his parents were residents, removed in 1816 to Green township, Harrison county, where he d. Oct. 2, 1856;
m. Dec. 12, 1799, Lydia Mitchell, b. Aug.
26, 1777; d. July 18, 1844; daughter of
Samuel Mitchell, a resident of Maryland; had issue: 1. Mary, b. Sept. 13,
1800; 2. Margaret, b. Feb. 21, 1802; 3.
William, b. July 29, 1803; d. July 30,
1884; 4. John, b. Nov. 26, 1805; 5. Elizabeth, b. Dec. 2, 1808; 6. Susannah, b.
Jan. 1, 1811; 7. Miriam-Jane, b. Jan.
29, 1813; d. April 13, 1886; 8. Sophia, b.
March 6, 1816; d. July 27, 1889; 9.
Phœbe, b. July 13, 1819; 10. James, b.
Jan. 25, 1825; m. (1st) April 4, 1855,
Maria Louisa Simpson Gibson; d. Sept.
20, 1875; daughter of William Gibson, a
resident of Holmes county, Ohio; m.
(2d) Oct. 12, 1889, Charlotte Branson
Pittis, daughter of George Pittis, of
Scio (had issue by first wife, eight
children).

PHILIP FULTON, b. in Cecil county,
Md., June 24, 1777; d. Sept. 14, 1841 (his
father, of Scottish descent, had settled
in Maryland before the Revolution);
about 1805 he removed to Washington
county, Penn., thence to Steubenville,
Ohio, in 1810, and in 1814 settled in the
southeastern part of Nottingham township, Harrison county; served in the
War of 1812; m. in Maryland, April 2,
1801, Sarah Hanna, b. in Harford county, Md., May 8, 1782; d. Sept. 3, 1845;
had issue: 1. Jane-S., b. Dec. 15, 1801;
2. Alexander, b. in Maryland, Sept. 12,
1803; d. March 15, 1881; m. Nov. 2,
1826, Sarah Ramsay, b. in Maryland,
Feb. 12, 1804, only child of Samuel and
Elizabeth Cochrane Ramsey (had issue: i. Samuel, b. Aug. 17, 1827; m.
March 13, 1860, Caroline Watson, b. Oct.
11, 1838, in Marion county, Ohio, daughter of William and Sarah Kennedy
Watson [the former born in Ireland,
1798; d. in Illinois, 1870]; ii. Elizabeth,
m. ——— Yarnall, and settled in Moore-

field township; iii. Alexander; iv. Albert; v. Philip, settled in Nottingham township; vi. Mary-J.; vii. Sarah-A.); 3. William, b. April 28, 1806; 4. Philip-S., b. July 10, 1808; 5. Hannah, b. Feb. 4, 1811; m. —— Kirkpatrick; 6. Harrison, b. May 11, 1813; 7. Elizabeth, b. Feb. 9, 1815; m. —— Lantz; 8. Sarah-Anne, b. July 20, 1818; m. —— Davison, and settled in Freeport township; 9. Mary-Ann, b. April 14, 1821; m. —— Moore, and settled in Moorefield township; 10. Julianna, b. May 3, 1823; m. —— Pickering, and settled in Moorefield township; 11. John, b. March 2, 1827; settled in Nottingham township; 12. Calvin, b. Aug. 19, 1833.

Samuel Ramsey, father of Sarah Ramsey Fulton, was a son of Charles Ramsey; b. in Chester county, Penn., May 23, 1780; d. in Harrison county, Ohio, March 14, 1858; m. 1802, Elizabeth Cochrane, b. in Chester county, Penn., Oct. 28, 1768; d. Nov. 18, 1857; in 1804 the Ramsey family removed to Allegheny county, Penn., remaining there until 1814, when they settled in Harrison county, Ohio.

JOHN GASTON, b. about 1600, in Scotland (or France), of Huguenot descent; m. in Scotland, and had, among others, three sons: John, William, and Alexander, who emigrated to county Antrim, Ireland, about 1660-1668; of these, probably John (whose name appears on hearth-money rate list for Ireland in 1669, is of Magheragall, county Antrim) had issue, among others, several sons, some of whom remained in Ireland, and some emigrated to America, as did also the sons of other brothers; of the emigrants of that generation the names of eight are known (and the children of William, son of John last named), viz., Hugh of New Jersey, Joseph of New Jersey, Joseph of Pennsylvania (probably a son of Hugh), William of Pennsylvania (probably a son of Hugh), John of New Jersey (probably a son of Hugh), James of New Jersey (probably a son of Hugh), John of Connecticut, Alexander of Massachusetts. Of these, the last two were brothers, and are said by Marshall Gaston's account to have first landed in New Jersey, with one or more other brothers, who remained there; it is probable that they may have been brothers of Hugh and

Joseph of New Jersey; they have also been identified in part as brothers of the William who remained at home, his residence being Caranleagh (Carnlough?), Cloughwater, county Antrim (near Ballymena), Ireland. In the account given below, these nine progenitors of the Gaston family in America will be designated as follows:

William Gaston of Antrim (whose children emigrated to South Carolina).
Hugh Gaston (1st).
William Gaston (1st).
Joseph Gaston of Pennsylvania (1st).
John Gaston of New Jersey (1st).
James Gaston (1st).
Joseph Gaston of New Jersey (1st).
John Gaston of Connecticut (1st).
Alexander Gaston (1st).

Another of the Gastons who remained in Ireland (living at Gastontown, Killycowan, county Antrim), had a daughter, who m. Gavin MacArthur; their son, William, b. 1796, emigrated to America after 1818, settling in Vermont; m. Malvina Stone (had issue, among others: i. Chester Alan Arthur, twenty-first President of the United States).

First will be given the family of William Gaston of Antrim, who remained in Ireland, but whose children all emigrated to America and eventually settled in South Carolina.

William Gaston of Antrim, b. at Caranleagh, Cloughwater, county Antrim, Ireland, about 1680-90; d. about 1770; m. —— Lemon; had issue: I. John, d. 1782; m. Esther Waugh, d. 1789; emigrated to Pennsylvania, and thence removed about 1751-52 to Chester District, South Carolina, settling on Fishing Creek; served as King's Justice before 1776; and as leader of the patriots of his vicinity during the British incursion, 1780-81; had issue: 1. Margaret, b. Aug. 29, 1739; m. James McCreary (had issue: i. John, served in the Revolutionary War, and as a member of Congress; ii. Samuel; served in the Revolutionary War; became a Baptist minister); 2. Martha, b. June 11, 1741; m. her kinsman, Joseph Gaston, great-grandson of the first Irish William (had issue, among others: i. Alexander, m. Mary Blair); 3. William, b. June 5, 1743; served as a captain in the Revolutionary War (had issue: i. William; ii. James); 4. John, b. June 24, 1745; d. about 1806, leaving descendants, who emigrated to Illinois (had issue, among others: i. William); 5. James, b. April 15, 1747 (had issue: i. Stephen; and several daughters, who removed to Ohio about 1801-02); 6. Robert, b. March 11, 1749; served in the Revolutionary War; killed at the battle of Hanging Rock (S. C.), Aug. 6, 1780; 7. Hugh, b. March 12, 1751; m. his cousin, Martha McLure; removed to Wilcox county, Ala., 1826, and thence to Mississippi (had issue: i. John; ii. Ebenezer; iii. James; iv. William; v. Hugh; vi. Mary; vii. Martha; viii. Esther; ix. Margaret); 8. Alexander, b. Aug. 24, 1753; killed at the battle of Hanging Rock; 9. David, b. July 7, 1755; killed at the battle of Hanging Rock; 10. Ebenezer, b. Sept. 15, 1757; killed at the battle of Hanging Rock; 11. Esther, b. Oct. 18, 1760; m. her kinsman, Alexander Walker, son of —— and Jane Gaston Walker (the latter a great-granddaughter of the first Irish William); (had issue: i. John-Gaston); 12. Joseph, b. Feb. 22, 1763; d. Oct. 10, 1836; m. 1790, Jane Brown, b. 1768; d. 1858; served in the Revolutionary War, and wounded at the battle of Hanging Rock (had issue: i. John-Brown, b. Jan. 23, 1791; m. Mary Beaufort McFadden; ii. Narcissa, b. Nov. 17, 1792; m. —— Lewis; iii. Eliza, b. Sept. 20, 1794; m. —— Neely; iv. Esther, b. Dec. 4, 1796; m. D. G. Stinson; v. Margaret, b. April 29, 1798; vi. Jane, b. Aug. 17, 1800; m. —— Crawford; vii. James-A.-H., b. Oct. 17, 1801; viii. Robert, b. Jan. 1, 1808).

II. Elizabeth, m. John Knox; settled in South Carolina; had issue: 1. William, a minister in 1768; 2. James, a physician (had issue, among others: i. Jane, possibly the same who m. Samuel Polk, of Mecklenburg county, N. C.); 3. John; 4. Hugh; 5. Sarah, m. John Johnston.

III. Hugh, d. Oct. 20, 1766, a minister; emigrated to America about 1766, and died at the house of his brother, John, shortly after landing; had issue: 1. William; a physician; b. Feb. 6, 1749; 2. Alecia, b. Feb. 16, 1750; d. 1825; m. —— Nelson; 3. Martha, b. June 11, 1752; m. James Ross (had issue: i. James, emigrated to America, but returned to Ireland, and settled at Londonderry; ii. —— (a daughter), m. and had issue, who settled at Balti-

more; iii. Hugh-Gaston, emigrated to America, and served in the War of 1812; iv. Rebecca, m. —— Latimer, of New Jersey); 4. James, b. Oct. 6, 1754 (had issue, eight children); 5. Mary, b. Dec. 7, 1756; d. young; 6. Elizabeth, b. June 16, 1759; m. —— Rogan, a physician, of the North of Ireland; 7. Thomas, emigrated to America, and settled in New York (had issue, two daughters, of whom: i. ——, m. —— Lindsay, and settled at Orange, N. J.); 8. Mary, b. April 4, 1763; d. unm.; 9. Hugh, b. April 27, 1765.

IV. Mary, m. James McLure; emigrated to America, and settled in South Carolina; had issue: 1. John; served as a captain in the Revolutionary War; killed at the battle of Hanging Rock (S. C.), Aug. 6, 1780; 2. William; a physician (had issue: i. Hannah, d. 1813; m. 1805, Judge William Gaston, son of Dr. Alexander Gaston); 6. Mary, m. Samuel Lowry; 7. ——, m. Edward Martin.

V. Robert, emigrated to America, and settled on Lynch's Creek, Lancaster county, S. C.; had issue: 1. William, b. July 23, 1755; d. 1838; served in the Revolutionary War; removed to Kentucky, and thence to Walnut Hill, Marion county, Ill. (had issue, four sons and five daughters, of whom: i. Samuel, d. 1826; settled in Marion county, Ill., 1819; ii. William; served in the War of 1812; iii. John, settled in Bond county, Ill.; iv. Robert, settled in Bond county, Ill., 1822; v. Margaret, m. Thomas Kell, and removed to Marion county, Ill., 1822); 2. James; 3. John; 4. Hugh; 5. Joseph; 6. Margaret, d. 1816; m. her second cousin, John McCreary.

VI. Janet, m. Charles Strong; emigrated to America, and settled in South Carolina; had issue: 1. William; served in the Revolutionary War, and killed in that service; 2. Christopher; 3. Letitia, m. her cousin, James Strong; 4. Margaret, m. John Simonton (had issue: i. Charles-H.); 5. Janet, m. —— Gladney.

VII. William, drowned at Kell's Ford, Chester county, S. C.; m. after his fortieth year, —— Harbison, sister of James Harbison; had issue: 1. Hugh (had issue: i. William); 2. William, m. —— Beaufort; removed to Corinth, Miss., and thence to Memphis, Tenn.

(had issue: i. Leroy, a Presbyterian minister).

VIII. Martha, m. Alexander Rosbrough; emigrated to America, and settled in South Carolina; had issue: 1. William-Gaston, a minister; d. unm.; 2. Joseph, removed to Indiana about 1800; 3. Alexander, a physician, m. (1st) Mary Hemphill; m. (2d) Janet Porter (had issue by first wife: i. Mary-Martha; ii. William-Andrew; had issue by second wife, six sons and two daughters, of whom: iii. Alexander-M., removed to California in 1848, and became a judge at Eureka, that State; iv. Joseph-Brown, removed to California in 1848, and thence to Salt Lake City; v. David, settled in Texas; vi. John, settled in Tennessee; vii. Maclin, settled in Tennessee); 4. John, b. 1776; d. 1854; m. Eleanor Key (had issue, four sons and six daughters, of whom: i. John, killed in the Civil War; ii. William; settled at Sardis, Miss.); 5. ————, m. Rev. J. Bowman, and settled in Tennessee.

IX. Alexander, a physician, emigrated to America, and settled at Newberne, N. C., where he was killed by the British and Tories, Aug. 20, 1781; had issue: 1. Jane, m. Chief Justice John L. Taylor, of North Carolina (had issue: i. ————, m. David E. Sumner, of Gates county, Tenn.); 2. William, b. Sept. 19, 1778; d. Jan. 23, 1844; served in Congress, 1813-15; and as chief justice of North Carolina, 1834-44; m. (1st) 1803, Susan Hay, daughter of John Hay; m. (2d) 1805, Hannah McLure; m. (3d) 1816, Eliza Ann Worthington, daughter of Dr. Charles Worthington, of Georgetown, D. C. (had issue by first wife: i. Alexander; ii. Susan, m. Robert Donaldson, of New York; had issue by second wife: iii. Hannah, m. Judge Mathias E. Manley, of North Carolina; had issue by third wife: iv. Eliza. m. ———— Graham, of Maryland; v. Catherine, d. unm.).

Three brothers, Joseph, Robert, and Matthew Gaston, said to be great-grandsons of the first Irish William, emigrated to South Carolina, with their sister, Jane Gaston Walker, leaving a fourth brother, Alexander, in Ireland, b. about 1750; d. about 1840; of these Joseph Gaston m. Martha Gaston, daughter of Justice John (above).

The name of John Gaston appears on the tax-list of Lurgan township, Cumberland (now Franklin) county, Penn., in 1751, and the name of Robert Gaston on the tax-list of Sadsbury township, Lancaster county, 1754 to 1759. These may have been two of the brothers (sons of William of Antrim) recorded above.

————

Hugh Gaston (1st), b. in county Antrim, Ireland, 1687; d. in Bedminster township, Somerset county, N. J. (buried in Lamington graveyard), Dec. 23, 1772; m. Jennet ————, b. 1698; d. Aug. 1, 1777 (buried at Lamington); took up land in Mount Bethel township, Bucks (now Northampton) county, Penn., Feb. 10, 1746, and June 20, 1751; had probably a sister, Mary, m. to James Cauldwell (who emigrated to New Jersey from the North of Ireland about 1732, and settled on Long Hill addition to Elizabethtown; Hugh Gaston was probably the brother of Joseph Gaston, of New Jersey (1st), and the father of William and Joseph of Pennsylvania, of James and John of New Jersey, and of Margaret, who m. Nov. 8, 1750, Thomas Moffat (d. 1770), of Middlesex county, or one or more of them; also, either the father or grandfather of Hugh Gaston, Jr. (below), and of his sisters, Elizabeth Kirkpatrick and Mrs. William Logan; of these:

William Gaston (1st), took up land in (Upper) Mount Bethel township, Bucks (now Northampton) county, Penn., Feb. 20, 1751, on the same date as an entry made by Hugh (1st) above, of whom he was probably the son or possibly a brother; b. probably 1715-20; killed by the Indians in December, 1755, leaving a widow, who d. before September, 1762, and five children, as follows:

I. John, b. May, 1740; d. Sept. 10, 1823; m. in Monmouth county, N. J., Feb. 4, 1760, Charity Cheeseman, b. March 13, 1734; d. Feb. 15, 1821 (both buried at Mingo graveyard, Union township, Washington county, Penn.; Charity Gaston being the daughter of Joseph Cheeseman of Upper Freehold (now Millstone) township, Monmouth county, N. J., who d. 1783; and probably a descendant of the William Cheeseman who settled at Middletown, Monmouth county, 1667); removed from Monmouth county, N. J., after 1767, to Mount Bethel township, Northampton county, Penn., where he took up 275

acres of land in February, 1772; served
as a major in the Revolutionary War;
removed, about 1780-82, to Rostraver
township, Westmoreland county, Penn.,
and thence, about 1790, to Peters (now
Union) township, Washington county,
his wife's sister, Elizabeth Cheeseman,
accompanying them; had issue: 1. William, b. July 15, 1761; removed to Ohio;
2. Joseph, b. April 25, 1763; d. Nov.
21, 1821; removed to Abbeville District,
South Carolina; served as captain and
major of the Savannah regiment in the
Revolutionary War, 1782; m. Martha
Hutton, and thence, about 1807, removed to Butler county, Ohio (had issue: i. Rebecca, b. Feb. 20, 1784; m.
John Kerr; ii. Ann, b. Dec. 16, 1785; iii.
Margaret, b. March 17, 1788; m. Ezekiel
McConnell; iv. John, b. June 17, 1790;
v. Mary, b. Sept. 23, 1792; vi. William,
b. April 20, 1795; vii. Joseph, b. Oct. 9,
1796; viii. Matta-Ann, b. Feb. 6, 1799;
m. William Hayden; ix. Lydia, b. July
22, 1801; m. Ebenezer Wilson; x. Lucinda, b. May 9, 1804; m. Daniel
Symmes; xi. Eliza, b. Feb. 16, 1807;
m. Benjamin R. Symmes); 3. John, b.
Jan. 7, 1765; 4. Samuel, b. Feb. 18, 1767;
d. in infancy; 5. James, b. Feb. 18, 1767;
d. April 13, 1813; m. Mary Estep, b. Oct.
10, 1773, daughter of Robert and Dorcas
Estep; removed to Hamilton county,
Ohio (had issue: i. Nancy, b. March 25,
1794; m. ——— Spencer; ii. Dorcas, b.
Aug. 19, 1796; m. David Figley, and settled in Scott county, Iowa; iii. Charity,
b. Dec. 1, 1798; m. Enoch King, and
settled in Clark county, Ohio; iv.
Joseph; a minister; b. March 25, 1801;
d. Dec. 6, 1834; settled in Carroll county, Ohio; v. Maria, b. April 6, 1803; d.
Oct. 20, 1803; vi. Martha, b. Jan. 20,
1805; m. Enoch King (his second wife),
and settled in Clark county, Ohio; vii.
Rachel, b. March 18, 1807; d. Oct. 7,
1862; m. William S. Manfull. and settled at Steubenville, Ohio; viii. James-
Estep; a minister; b. April 14, 1809; d.
at Des Moines, Iowa, 1888-89; removed
from Warren, Trumbull county, Ohio,
about 1850. to Monmouth, Ill., and
thence to Davenport, Iowa, later settling at Des Moines [had issue:
Thomas-Kirk; William-Henry; Mary;
Joseph-James; John; Sarah-Kirk]; ix.
Robert, b. July 25, 1811); 6. Samuel. b.
Oct. 10, 1772; d. Feb. 21, 1853; m. Margaret Penny, of Allegheny county, b.
1776; d. Aug. 14, 1841 (had issue: i.

John, b. 1800; m. Patience Morrison; ii.
Charity, b. 1802; m. Robert Donaldson;
iii. Margaret, b. 1803; m. Thomas
Perry; removed to near Burlington,
Iowa, 1844; iv. Nancy, b. 1805; m. William Peppard, and removed to Ohio
about 1837; v. William, b. 1807; d. 1880;
m. Eliza Morrison; vi. Sarah, b. 1808;
d. 1875; m. Dr. James Estep—afterwards a Baptist minister—d. Feb. 26,
1861; son of Robert and Dorcas Estep,
who came from New Jersey [had issue,
six children, among whom: Harrison,
settled at Marion, Ind.; James, settled
at Marion, Ind.; Josiah-Morgan, b. Feb.
19, 1829; d. at Cadiz, May 5, 1888; m.
1857, Amanda J. Crabb]; vii. Eliza, b.
1810; m. Samuel Morgan; viii. Joseph-
Smith, b. 1811; d. 1870; m. Jane Hind-
man; d. 1879 [had issue, among others:
Samuel, b. 1831; m. 1st, Martha A. Mc-
Clure; m. 2d, Amanda M. Way]; ix.
Samuel, b. 1814; d. un-m., 1839); 7.
Elizabeth, b. May 8, 1778; d. Feb. 28,
1858; 8. Margaret, m. Samuel McClain,
a native of New Jersey; settled in Nottingham township, Washington county,
Penn., where they d. without issue.

II. William, b. 1742-48; d. in Upper
Mount Bethel township. Northampton
county, Penn., April-May, 1801; m.
Elizabeth ———; had issue: 1. Alex-
ander, m. Huldah ———: resided at
Richmond, Lower Mount Bethel town-
ship, until after 1811; 2. William; 3.
Charles; 4. Margaret, m. before 1806,
Elisha Everitt; 5. Elizabeth, m. 1806-97,
Simeon Hart.

III. Hugh, b. 1743-48; served in the
Revolutionary War from Mount Bethel
township; resided in Allegheny county,
Penn., in 1795.

IV. Jennet, b. 1744-48; m. Moses
Phenix.

V. James, b. 1748-55; lived in Mount
Bethel township in 1773.

———

Joseph Gaston of Pennsylvania (1st),
probably a brother of William Gaston
(1st) and perhaps a son of Hugh Gaston (1st), d. in Mount Bethel township,
Northampton county, Penn., October,
1775, where he had taken up land in
January, 1765; served as a King's Justice from 1766 to 1775; m. Isabel ———,
d. after 1775; had issue, five children.
Hugh, James, Elizabeth, John, and
Alexander, who were probably those
given below, although it is possible
these are not the same (it is possible (Joseph Gas-

ton's will names his "trusty friends, Hugh Gaston of East Jersey, Samuel Rea, and Major John Gaston of Mount Bethel township" [designated Major John Gaston in executors' deed made in 1779] as his executors, and makes provision for giving his five children an education):

I. Hugh, b. Jan. 18, 1764; d. in Columbiana county, Ohio, June 24, 1839; lived in Bedminster township, Somerset county, N. J., 1787; removed to Washington county, Lycoming county, about 1795-99, and thence to western Pennsylvania and Ohio; m. March 14, 1789, Grace Gaston, his cousin, b. Nov. 25, 1764; d. March 14, 1838; daughter of Robert (II. below) and Rosanna Cooper Gaston (had issue: i. Joseph, b. Dec. 24, 1789; m. Elizabeth Conkle [had issue: Samuel, Hamilton, Martin, Watson, Hugh, Jacob, Elizabeth]; ii. James, b. Jan. 20, 1793; d. March 13, 1872; m. Elizabeth Kilgore, sister to Daniel Kilgore, of Cadiz [had issue: William-Kilgore, m. (1st) Martha Graham; m. (2d) Andora Waage; Hugh-F., m. Elizabeth Stokes; Nancy, m. Stuart B. Shotwell, of Cadiz; Mary, m. her father's cousin, James W. Gaston, son of James Gaston, brother to Hugh (3d); Elizabeth, m. Joseph Lyons; Philander, m. (1st) Lucinda Conkle; m. (2d) Charity Moore; Narcissa, m. Albert Brockway; Daniel-O., d. unm.; Eleanor-Jane, m. John Geeting; John, d. unm.]; iii. Robert, b. Feb. 23, 1794; d. June 4, 1801; iv. Elizabeth, b. Sept. 7, 1797; d. Jan. 14, 1816; v. Hugh, b. April 9, 1804; d. March 27, 1854 [had issue: Hamilton, Martha, Elizabeth, Mary].

II. James, d. in Smith township, Washington county, Penn., May-June, 1813, where he had settled about 1788, having removed from Lower Mount Bethel township, Northampton county, m. Jane —— (she m. 2d —— Stewart) (had issue: i. William, d. unm., in Brooke county, West Va., 1830; ii. Mary, m. —— Anderson; iii. Jane, m. —— Gordon; iv. Eleanor, m. —— Moore; v. James-W., m. his cousin, Mary Gaston, daughter of Hugh (3d) above; vi. John; vii. —— m. Mr. Moore [had issue. William]).The name of the mother of Hugh and James Gaston last given was Simanton (probably a sister of the Robert Simanton, who settled in Bedminster township, Somerset county, N. J., before 1754; whose

land at that date adjoined the land of Hugh Gaston; and who removed to Pennsylvania and d. in Mount Bethel township, Northampton county, 1786, leaving children: James, Ephraim, Robert, Peter, Benjamin, Margaret Nelson, Jean Britton, and Esther Ross, of whom James and Peter settled in Washington county, Penn. The Simantons were closely connected with the family of Ephraim McDowell, who d. in Bedminster township, 1763, leaving, among other children, five sons, John, Matthew, Ephraim, Peter, and Benjamin).

III. Elizabeth.

IV. John, probably settled in Indiana.

V. Alexander, a physician, b. July 22, 1769; d. July 9, 1825; possibly the Alexander whose name appears in connection with that of John Gaston (son of William, 1st) as a taxpayer in Rostraver township, Westmoreland county, Penn. (that part now contained in Washington township, Fayette county), in 1783, when his household contained five persons; settled with his mother in Canton township, Washington county, about 1792; m. Rachel Perry, b. Sept. 1, 1773; d. Sept. 14, 1833; daughter of John and Jane McMillan Perry, who removed from West Nottingham township, Chester county, Penn., to Washington county, about 1787-99, settling in Buffalo township in 1799, and removing thence to Belmont county, Ohio, about 1800 (John, b. 1752; d. 1825; served in the Revolutionary War; Jane, b. 1744; d. 1819); removed to Brooke county, West Va., thence, about 1800, to near St. Clairsville, Ohio; and from there to Morristown, Ohio, 1811 (had issue: i. John-Perry, b. April 24, 1793; ii. Jane, b. April 10, 1795; d. Nov. 4, 1796; iii. Robert, b. Jan. 17, 1797; d. Sept. 27, 1834; m. Martha McClure; iv. Ephraim; a physician; b. June 26, 1799; d. May 30, 1868; m. (1st) Mary Wilson; m. (2d) Agnes Vance; v. Mary, b. May 20, 1801; d. Dec. 20, 1846; m. —— Tracy, and settled at McConnellsville, Ohio; vi. Charity, b. at St. Clairsville, July 27, 1803; d. 1887; m. John Lippincott, of Morristown; vii. Joseph, b. May 14, 1805; d. July 9, 1833; m. Nancy Fowler; viii. Alexander, b. Aug. 4, 1807; ix. Matthew, b. July 9, 1809; d. March 17, 1878; m. Drusilla Bute; settled at Plattsmouth, Neb.; x. Isaac, b. Sept. 16, 1811; d. at Colonna, Iowa, April 30,

1881; xi. James, b. Nov. 1, 1813). One account of Alexander Gaston (b. 1769) states that he was the son of Ephraim Gaston, who was the son of Ebenezer Gaston, who emigrated from Ireland to America in company with his brother, Matthew (d. unm.); and that Alexander Gaston had a brother, Joseph, who settled in southern Indiana; and another brother who settled in West Virginia. This account probably assumes Joseph, son of John, who married in South Carolina and settled in Butler county, Ohio, to have been the brother of Alexander.

———

Hugh Gaston, Jr., probably a son (or grandson) of Hugh Gaston (1st), b. 1734; d. June 25, 1808; m. (1st) Mary Sloan, b. 1742; d. Aug. 14, 1766; daughter of William and Mary Sloan, of Bedminster (?) township; m. (2d) Mary Adams, b. 1741; d. Feb. 16, 1793; daughter of John and Agnes Adams; m. (3d) Mary Kirkpatrick, b. in Bedminster township, Nov. 23, 1761; d. July 1, 1842; daughter of David and Mary McEowen Kirkpatrick (the former b. at Wattiesneach, Dumfriesshire, Scotland, Feb. 17, 1724; son of Alexander and Elizabeth Kirkpatrick, who emigrated to America with his family in 1736, and m. March 31, 1748, Mary McEowen); Hugh Gaston had issue by first wife: 1. William, b. April 12, 1763; d. Dec. 15, 1763; 2. Joseph, b. Dec. 18, 1765; d. Aug. 14, 1777; had issue by third wife: 3. Samuel Kirkpatrick, a physician; m. Nancy T. Cooper, daughter of Henry Cooper, of Chester, Morris county (had issue: i. Henrietta); 4. John, b. 1796; d. Feb. 17, 1800. Hugh Gaston, Jr., of Bedminster, had sisters: Elizabeth, b. 1737; m. Thomas Kirkpatrick; and ———, m. Captain William Logan, of Peapack; had issue, among others: 1. John.

Elizabeth Gaston, b. 1737, sister to Hugh Gaston, Jr., and probably daughter of Hugh Gaston (1st), m. Thomas Kirkpatrick, who settled near Liberty Corners, Bernard township, Somerset county, N. J.; had issue: 1. John, m. Anne Coriell, daughter of Elias Coriell (had issue: i. Sarah, m. John Layton, and settled at Plainfield; ii. Elizabeth, m. John King, son of John King, of Liberty Corners; iii. Thomas, m. Maria Hurd; iv. Elias, m. Jane Squier, daughter of Ludlow Squier, and settled at Plainfield; v. James, m. (1st) Aletta Van Arsdale, daughter of Philip Van Arsdale; m. (2d) Mary Stout; vi. Lydia, m. Stephen Woodard, son of Samuel Woodard, and removed to Chicago; vii. Jane, m. David Kline; viii. Mary, m. Tunis Van Nest; ix. John, d. at Newark, unm., aged thirty; x. Ann, m. Philip Van Arsdale, son of Peter Van Arsdale; xi. Hugh, m. Elizabeth King, cf Belleville); 2. Jane, d. unm., aged about sixty.

———

——— Gaston, sister to Hugh Gaston, Jr., and probably daughter to Hugh Gaston (1st), m. Captain William Logan, of Somerset county, N. J.

———

Margaret Gaston, probably daughter of Hugh Gaston (1st), m. 1750, Thomas Moffat, who d. 1770, Hugh Gaston serving as administrator of his estate.

———

John Gaston of New Jersey (1st), settled in Upper Freehold (now Millstone) township, Monmouth county, N. J., about 1741, where, in 1758, he was owner of a grist and fulling mill; a member of Dr. William Tennent's Freehold Presbyterian congregation; subscriber in 1758 to the fund for a parsonage for Allentown Church; deeded a tract of land to his son, Hugh Gaston, in 1793; probably the son of Hugh Gaston (1st) and brother of William (1st) who was killed by the Indians (as John Gaston, Jr., the son of the latter, made his home in Upper Freehold township from before 1760 until after 1767, marrying there); had issue, as shown by the records of Tennent Church, Freehold: I. Mary, baptized Dec. 9, 1739. II. James, baptized March 28, 1742; probably the same who m. April 20, 1773, Lydia Tapscott; and who contributed to fund for repair of Cranbury Church in 1785; had issue, probably, among others: 1. William, served in the Revolutionary War; m. Catharine English, daughter of Dr. James English, of New Brunswick (had issue, as shown by baptismal records of Cranbury Church: i. Lydia-Tapscott, b. Dec. 4, 1804; m. Aaron Allen; ii. John-Baird, b. May 25, 1806; iii. Mary-Ann, b. March 20, 1810; m., probably, John Perrine, Jr., also, iv. Letitia; v. Hannah). III. Hugh, bap. July 15, 1744; lived in Millstone township, Monmouth county, N. J., until after 1801. IV. Mary (2d), bap. March 8, 1747. V. Elizabeth, twin sister to Mary, bap. March 8, 1747. VI. Daniel, bap. April 3, 1749; served in the Revolutionary War; lived in Millstone township, Monmouth county, during the Revolution; had issue, among others: 1. John, bap. April 14, 1776. VII. Catharine, bap. June 2, 1751. VIII. John, bap. Jan. 20, 1754. IX. William, bap. July 18, 1756. X. Jane, bap. March 25, 1759.

James Gaston (1st), probably a brother to John Gaston of New Jersey (1st), his name appears as a subscriber to the fund for building Allentown Church parsonage, 1758, in connection with that of John Gaston of Upper Freehold (1st, above); possibly, he may have been the son of that John—whose oldest son, James, was baptized at Tennent Church, March 28, 1742. The name of James Gaston also appears as a member of the congregation of Lamington Church, in Bedminster township, Somerset county, N. J., during the pastorate of Rev. James McCrea, which terminated in 1766. A James Gaston also took up land in Mount Bethel township, Northampton county, Penn., in 1773 (probably son of William, 1st), and the name of James Gaston appears on tax-list of Cecil township, Washington county, Penn., 1787 and 1788; and on that of Rostraver township, Westmoreland county, Penn., 1789.

Joseph Gaston of New Jersey (1st), d. in Bernard township, Somerset county, N. J., shortly after March 31, 1777; member of Baskingridge Presbyterian congregation; m. Margaret ———, who survived him (probably his second wife, as a Joseph Gaston and Margaret Lines were married in Somerset county, about Nov. 2, 1772); emigrated from Ireland to New Jersey about 1720; probably a brother to Hugh Gaston (1st); had issue:

I. Margaret, m. Andrew Kirkpatrick, of Bernard township, Somerset county, N. J., son of Alexander and Elizabeth Kirkpatrick (the former of whom d. at Mine Brook, N. J., June 3, 1758); removed to Redstone, Fayette county, Penn.; had issue: 1. Alexander; 2. Jennet, m. Abner Johnson; 3. Elizabeth, m. Hugh Barclay (or Bartley); 4. Mar-

garet, m. Joseph McMartin; 5. Mary; 6. Sarah; 7. Anne; 8. Hannah.
II. John, b. Nov. 10, 1730; d. Oct. 3, 1776; m. (1st) June 27, 1758, Elizabeth Ker, b. March 19, 1738; d. May 6, 1765; daughter of William and Catherine Ker, natives of Scotland (the former b. 1700; d. July 4, 1777; buried at Lamington graveyard, Somerset county, N. J., son of Walter [1656-1748] and Margaret [1661-1734] Ker, who were exiled from Scotland about 1685, and settled at Freehold, N. J.); m. (2d) Sarah Ogden; had issue by first wife: 1. Catherine, b. May 12, 1759; d. April 14, 1762; 2. William, b. Jan. 13, 1761; d. Feb. 13, 1809; m. Dec. 10, 1782, Naomi Teeple, daughter of John and Margaret Teeple (had issue: i. John-W., b. Sept. 26, 1783; d. June 19, 1859; m. 1805, Sarah Castner; ii. Walter, d. in infancy; iii. William, b. Sept. 26, 1787; d. in New York City, Sept. 12, 1837; resided in Savannah, Georgia; iv. Margaret, b. Oct. 30, 1789; d. Nov. 3, 1827; m. 1819, John McCowen; v. Joseph, b. Feb. 13, 1792; d. April 5, 1814; vi. James, b. Jan. 8, 1795; d. March, 1820; vii. Oliver, b. Jan. 8, 1795; d. Jan. 21, 1823; viii. Abraham, b. April 25, 1797; d. Jan. 21, 1823; ix. Hugh, b. Aug. 27, 1800; d. March 30, 1821); 3. Joseph, b. May 2, 1763; d. Oct. 16, 1796; m. March 1, 1781, Ida Van Arsdale, b. April 28, 1762; daughter of Philip and Margaret Stryker Van Arsdale (the former b. 1734; d. 1776; the latter b. 1741; d. 1819) (had issue: i. Elizabeth, b. Nov. 17, 1782; d. Nov. 11, 1857; ii. Isaac-V., b. Sept. 9, 1784; d. February, 1811; iii. John-I., b. Feb. 14, 1787; d. March 23, 1846; iv. Margaret-B., b. Feb. 21, 1789; d. July 9, 1804; v. William-B., b. Aug. 9, 1791; vi. Sarah-E., b. Dec. 9, 1793; d. 1885; vii. Lydia, b. 1795; d. 1800); ———Lansing, and settled at Lansingburgh, N. Y.; 5. Stephen, settled in New York State; 6. Elizabeth, m. Elias Hodges, and settled at Colerain, Hamilton county, Ohio; 7. Isaac. b. March 25, 1773; m. March 17, 1803, Anna Hedges; settled near Morristown, N. J. (had issue, among others: i. Augustus-L., b. May 15, 1806; d. 1841; settled at Reily, Butler county, Ohio, in 1828; ii. E.-H., settled at Reily, Butler county, Ohio); 8. Margaret. m. Smith Scudder, of Elizabethtown, N. J. (had issue, two sons, of whom: i. Mansfield).

III. Robert, b. Jan. 23, 1732; d. in Turbut (now Delaware) township, Northumberland county, Penn. (buried in Warrior's Run graveyard), Sept. 2, 1793; m. May 15, 1762, in Bedminster township, Somerset county, N. J., Rosanna Cooper, b. March 23, 1742; d. Jan. 14, 1817; daughter of Daniel Cooper (b. at sea during the emigration of his parents from Holland to New York, May 1, 1695; d. May 2, 1795; m. six times, 1st, April 17, 1726, to Grace Runyon, b. January, 1706; d. November, 1755; lived at Piscataway; settled in Morris county, N. J., about 1732; had issue, ten children). Robert' and Rosanna Cooper Gaston resided in Bernard township, Somerset county, until about 1770; then in Pequannock township, Morris county, from before 1771 to 1777, returning thence to Bedminster township, Somerset county, and removing to Northumberland county about May, 1792; served in the Revolution as captain and lieutenant-colonel of New Jersey militia, and as captain in the Continental Line; had issue: 1. Joseph, b. Nov. 19, 1766; d. April 18, 1831; m. 1789, Margaret Melick, b. Dec. 22, 1767; d. Feb. 5, 1838; daughter of Aaron and Catherine Miller Moelich (had issue: i. Robert, b. March 30, 1790; d. Sept. 22, 1854; m. April 8, 1824, Eleanor Shannon, b. 1795; d. Oct. 12, 1867 [had issue: Martha-J.; Margaret-M.; Solomon-P.; Mary-E.; Charlotte-A.; Sarah-Ann; Sarah]; ii. Charlotte, b. Sept. 22, 1792; d. Aug. 13, 1824; m. James Durham; iii. Rosanna, b. June 7, 1795; d. Nov. 19, 1845; iv. Aaron, b. April 25, 1799; d. Oct. 24, 1868; m. [1st] Sarah Ann Clarke; m. [2d] Rosanna Camp; v. Daniel; a Presbyterian minister; who settled in Philadelphia; b. July 26, 1801; d. April 28, 1860; m. 1839, Rosa Morris, b. 1803; d. 1873; vi. Mary, b. May 14, 1804; d. July 11, 1880; vii. Anne, b. Dec. 20, 1808; m. William Sample); 2. Margaret, b. Dec. 17, 1768; d. Sept. 10, 1807; m. 1785, Daniel Melick, son of Aaron and Catherine Miller Moelich, of Bedminster township (had issue: i. Aaron; ii. Elizabeth; iii. Charlotte; iv. Rosanna; v. John; vi. Mary; vii. David; viii. William; ix. Daniel; x. Catherine); 3. Mary, b. Feb. 12, 1770; 4. Daniel, b. April 5, 1773; 5. Anne, b. March 25, 1774; 6. George-W., b. April 2, 1777; 7. John, b. Feb. 8, 1780.

IV. Joseph, b. 1738-39; d. 1803-04; served as paymaster of New Jersey militia from Somerset and Sussex counties, in the Revolution; named as executor of his father's will (dated March 31, 1777); settled in Hardwick township, Sussex county, N. J., about 1783; m. —— Linn, daughter of Joseph and Martha Kirkpatrick Linn (who removed from Bernard township, Somerset county, to Hunterdon county, thence to Hardwick township, Sussex county, and later to Hardyston township, Sussex county; he b. 1725; d. 1800; she b. 1723; d. 1791); had issue: 1. —— m. Dr. Elijah Everitt, b. in Kingwood township, Hunterdon county, 1770-80; d. Jan. 11, 1850; settled in Sparta township, Sussex county; 2. —— m. Rev. John Boyd.

V. Martha, m. —— Patterson.

VI. Priscilla, m. about Sept. 24, 1771, David McCain.

VII. ——, m. David Chambers; had issue: 1. Joseph; 2. William; 3. John.

————

John Gaston, of Connecticut (1st), b. in county Antrim, Ireland, probably near Ballymena (or, possibly, Ballymoney), 1703-04; emigrated to America, 1720-26, with his brother Alexander and perhaps a third brother, who settled in New Jersey; settled at Voluntown, Conn., 1726-27, where he d. March 29, 1783; m. about 1735, Janet Thomson, b. in Scotland, 1711; d. at Killingly, Conn., Nov. 3, 1806; daughter of Rev. Alexander Thomson, a native of Scotland, who lived for a time at Andover, Mass., and afterwards at Stonington, Conn.; had issue:

I. Margaret, b. 1734; d. Feb. 5, 1811; m. James Dickson, b. 1728; d. 1815; had issue: 1. James; 2. John; 3. Alexander; 4. Joseph ; 5. Nancy, m. William Church; 6. Phebe, m. Uriah Church (had issue: i. Andrew, m. Ruth Hall [their daughter, Clara, m. 1831, Horace White, of Syracuse, N. Y., and was the mother of Andrew Dickson White, b. at Homer, N. Y., Nov. 7, 1832]; ii. Gaston; iii. John; iv. Vesta; v. Nelson; vi. Diodata).

II. Alexander, b. 1739; served in the French and Indian War, and died, 1760, of disease contracted in that service.

III. John, b. at Voluntown, 1750; d. there Oct. 26, 1805; served in the Connecticut Legislature; m. about 1770, Ruth Miller, b. at Plainfield, Conn.,

1750; d. at Killingly, May 10, 1825; daughter of Rev. Alexander and Esther Miller (the former a Presbyterian minister, who settled at Plainfield, called to the Separatist Church at Voluntown, 1751, and imprisoned in the Windham county jail for a long time for refusing to pay the Established [Congregational] Church rates); had issue: 1. Alexander, b. at Voluntown, Aug. 2, 1772; d. at Roxbury, Mass., Feb. 11, 1856; where he had settled 1838; served in the Connecticut Legislature; m. (1st) April 1, 1803, Olive Dunlap, b. at Plainfield, 1769; d. at Killingly, Sept. 7, 1814; daughter of Joshua Dunlap; m. (2d) April, 1816, Kezia Arnold, b. at Burrillville, R. I., November, 1779; d. at Roxbury, Mass., Jan. 30, 1856; daughter of Aaron and Rhoda Hunt Arnold (the former a descendant of Thomas Arnold, b. 1599) (had issue by first wife: i. Esther, b. 1804; d. 1860; ii. John, b. 1806; d. 1824; had issue by second wife: iii. William, b. at Killingly, Oct. 3, 1820; d. Jan. 19, 1894; served as member of the Massachusetts Legislature; as mayor of Boston; and as governor of Massachusetts; m. May 27, 1852, Louisa A. Beecher, b. at Boston, Dec. 27, 1830; daughter of Laban S. and Frances Lines Beecher, natives of New Haven—the former a descendant of John Beecher, who emigrated probably from Kent, England, and d. at New Haven, 1637-38 [had issue: Sarah Howard, b. April 23, 1853; William-Alexander, b. May 1, 1859; m. 1892, May D. Lockwood; and Theodore-Beecher, b. Feb. 8, 1861; d. July 16, 1869]; 2. Margaret, b. Dec. 13, 1781; d. young.

Alexander Gaston (1st), b. 1714; m. Mary Wilson, b. 1718; emigrated to America with his brother John about 1720-26; said to have had a third brother in New Jersey; settled at Richmond, Mass.; had issue: I. William, b. Aug. 9, 1744. II. John, b. March 3, 1746. III. Robert, b. Dec. 28, 1747. IV. Mary, b. Sept. 20, 1749. V. Janet, b. Dec. 27, 1750; m. Robert Kasson. VI. Margaret, b. Jan. 5, 1753. VII. Alexander, b. Oct. 28, 1754; had issue, among others: 1. John, b. 1746, d. at Stockbridge, Mass., Sept. 6, 1834 (had issue, among others: i. John, b. 1786; d. March, 1873). VIII. David, b. Jan. 13, 1757. IX. Thomas, b. March 16, 1759. X. Phebe, b. April 22, 1765; m. —— Bacon. (Mr. Marshall

Gaston, of Oberlin, Ohio, made, before 1892, a nearly complete record of the descendants of the children of Alexander Gaston (1st) down to his own generation.)

JOHN WALLACE GILLESPIE, a native of Ohio, b. 1819; d. 1885; m. (1st) Nov. 29, 1842, Cordelia Dallas, b. in Wheeling, West Virginia, 1827; d. May 7, 1877; m. (2d) 1879, Mrs. Jane Dallas, widow of Henry Dallas; had issue by first wife: 1. Albert; 2. James; 3. Nettie; 4. Elosia, m. William McFadden; 5. Laura, m. John C. Spencer, and settled in Chicago; 6. John-W., b. May 1, 1857; m. April 15, 1890, Agnes Sheriff, daughter of Adam N. and Mary Vickery Sheriff; 7. Wayne.

FRANCIS GILMORE, a native of Ireland, settled in Archer township, Harrison county, Ohio, before 1815; m. in Harrison county, Sarah McBride, a native of Ireland, b. about 1790; d. March 30, 1840; had issue: 1. William; 2. Margaret, b. in Archer township, Jan. —, 1816; m. in 1833 John Welsh, b. in Pennsylvania, Nov. 20, 1808; d. Nov. 10, 1881 (son of Samuel and Catherine Welsh, natives of Ireland, who settled in Archer township before 1814); removed to Cadiz in 1874, where he died (had issue: i. Samuel, settled in Missouri; ii. Jason, settled in Iowa; iii. Sarah-Jane, m. John Adams, and settled in Archer township; iv. Amanda, m. Samuel F. Ross, a Methodist Episcopal minister, and settled in New Philadelphia, Ohio); 3. John, settled in Oskaloosa, Iowa; 4. Thomas, settled in Iowa; 5. Samuel, settled in Iowa.

NATHANIEL GILMORE, of county Cavan, Ireland; d. about 1771; m. Sarah McFadden, b. about 1748, at Coote Hill, county Cavan, Ireland; d. Dec. 29, 1835, near West Middletown, Penn. (Sarah McFadden Gilmore m. [2d] John Jamison, and emigrated to America about 1780-83, first settling in Shearman's Valley, Cumberland [now Perry] county, (?) Penn., thence removing to Independence township, Washington county, Penn.); had issue: 1. Jane, b. 1768; m. John Parr; removed first to Jefferson county, Ohio, and later to Illinois (had issue: i. John, m. —— Wheeler; ii. Mary; iii. Elizabeth, m. John Leech); 2. Samuel, b. 1770; d. Sept. 8, 1814; served as ensign in the War of 1812 (Capt. Baruch Dickerson's company, 2d Ohio Militia); m. Elizabeth Buchanan, b. 1777; d. Sept. 16, 1829; daughter of William and Nancy ?) Buchanan, of Washington county, Penn.; removed to Cadiz township, Harrison county, Ohio, about 1800-1 (had issue: i. Sarah, b. Jan. 14, 1801; d. May 18, 1837; m. Joseph Dunlap; ii. Samuel; iii. Nathaniel, m. Mary Craig; iv. Cyrus, b. 1811; d. April 14, 1883; m. Hannah Moore; v. William; vi. Mary, m. Napoleon B. Kennedy; vii. Eliza, b. Feb. 2, 1807; d. Jan. 14, 1873; m. May 1, 1828, John Phillips, b. June, 1797; d. at Cadiz, Ohio, May 5, 1859; son of William and Rachel Hamilton Phillips, of West Nottingham township, Chester county, Penn.

JOSIAH GLOVER, b. in Baltimore, Md.; removed to Smithfield, Jefferson county, Ohio; had issue: I. Josiah, m. 1833, Mary Barkhurst, a native of Maryland, b. 1817-18; d. February, 1872; had issue: 1. Sarah, m. Augustus Carter, of Jefferson county; 2. Nancy; 3. Susan, m. William Comly; 4. George-W.; 5. Josephine, m. John C. Brown; 6. Jefferson-C., b. March 3, 1845; m. 1869, Caroline I. Snyder, daughter of Samuel Snyder; 7. Elizabeth, m. Milton Hall, of Jefferson county; 8. Esther; 9. Quincy; 10. Leonora, m. John C. Brown (his second wife); 11. William-L.

JONAS GOTSHALL, emigrated from Perry county, Penn., to Harrison county before 1823; m. Mary Laler; had issue: 1. Jeremiah, m. Mary Long; 2. John; 3. Anna, m. William Arbaugh; 4. Jacob; m. (1st) Eliza Long; m. (2d) Ruth Hendrix; 5. Daniel, b. in Rumley township, 1831; m. (1st) Amanda Wortman, b. 1835; d. 1869; daughter of John and Rebecca Wortman; m. (2d) Eliza Wood; 6. Samuel, m. (1st) Margaret Carr; m. (2d) Harriet McClain; 7. Matilda, m. Alpheus Lowmiller; 8. Elizabeth, m. John Wood; 9. Katharine, d. young.

ALEXANDER GREEN, a native of Ire'and, settled in Belmont county, Ohio, 1808; m. (1st) in Ireland, Eleanor Chambers; m. (2d) Mary Bell; had issue by first wife: 1. Thomas; 2. John; 3. Samuel, b. in Ireland, Dec. 5, 1799; came to Ohio with his parents; settled in Washington township, Harrison county about 1829, where he d. June 2, 1879; m. Oct. 29, 1829, Ann Thompson, b. in Jefferson county, June 13, 1808;

daughter of Aaron and Sarah Balderson Thompson (had issue: i. William, b. Oct. 29, 1830; ii. James, b. in Washington township, Sept. 16, 1833; m. March 20, 1881, Clara M. Pittis, daughter of George Pittis, of Harrison county; iii. Aaron, b. May 6, 1836; iv. Sarah, b. Oct. 31, 1838; d. Sept. 16, 1844; v. Samuel-H., b. Dec. 5, 1840; d. Feb. 2, 1869; vi. Ruth-T., b. June 18, 1843; vii. Israel-J., b. Nov. 11, 1845); 4. James; 5. Elizabeth; 6. Abbie; had issue by second wife: 7. Isaac; 8. Alexander; 9. Sampson; 10. William; 11. Sarah; 12. Ellen; 13. Mary-Ann; 14. Maria; 15. Ruth.

Aaron Thompson, father of Ann T. Green, was a native of Ireland, b. Jan. 26, 1775; d. June 22, 1838; first settled in Chester county, Penn., 1790; removed to Jefferson county, Ohio, in 1802; son of William Thompson and Esther Chalfant; the former b. in Ireland, March 26, 1747; d. in Chester county, Penn., July 7, 1806; Aaron Thompson, m. in Chester county, Penn., 1797, Sarah Balderson, b. March 5, 1778; d. Sept. 26, 1846; had issue: 1. Esther, b. Nov. 19, 1798; 2. William, b. Jan. 3, 1801; 3. John, b. June 28, 1803; 4. Aaron, b. Sept. 13, 1805; 5. Ann, b. June 13, 1808; m. Samuel Green; 6. Ruth, b. Oct. 4, 1810; 7. Lewis, b. Nov. 21, 1813; 8. Israel, b. Jan. 4, 1818.

JOSEPH GRIMES, see Family of William McCullough.

WILLIAM GRIMES, removed from Washington (?) county, Penn., to Harrison county, Ohio, before 1805; about 1810 settled at Cadiz, where he d. May-August, 1840; m. Rebecca ———, d. about 1840; had issue: 1. James, b. 1817; d. July 10, 1841; 2. William, b. 1822; d. April 30, 1850; 3. Thomas-D., m. 1835, Margaret Lafferty (?); 4. Martha, b. May 12, 1826; d. April 4, 1874; m. Henry Boyles; 5. Elizabeth, m. 1830, Matthew M. Sloan (had issue, among others: i. William-Grimes, settled at Omaha; ii. Rebecca, m. Asbury F. Johnson, son of Henry and Catherine Johnson, of Moorefield township; settled at Laramie, Wyoming; iii. Elizabeth-J., b. 1838; d. 1843); 6. Nancy; 7. Anderson.

EDWARD HALL, b. March 4, 1760; son of Joshua Hall, of Howard Hill, Baltimore, Md.; an English sea-captain who served on the American side in the Revolutionary War; removed to

4

Jefferson county, Ohio, about 1803, settling near Smithfield; had issue: 1. Richard; 2. Harry; 3. Christopher-S.; 4. Edward-Thomas, b. Dec. 25, 1795, in Hailsboro, Baltimore county, Md.; settled with his parents near Smithfield, Jefferson county, Ohio; afterwards located in Washington, Guernsey county, Ohio, where he d. March 9, 1891; m. at York Haven, Penn., Dec. 20, 1827, Henrietta Catherine Roberts, b. April 12, 1804, at Fells Point, Baltimore, Md., daughter of Francis Cateby Roberts, an English sea-captain, who was drowned 1803, and Elizabeth Snyder Karg, a native of Baltimore (Edward and Henrietta Roberts Hall had issue: i. Francis-Spry, b. Oct. 3, 1828; settled in Washington, Guernsey county, Ohio; ii. Charles-Grafton, b. July 24, 1830; d. in California, Dec. 8, 1859; iii. Wilson-Roberts, b. July 8, 1832; d. March 16, 1849; iv. Thomas-Henry, d. in infancy; v. Sarah-Virginia, b. Oct. 6, 1835; m. William L. Houser; vi. Eliza-Jane, b. Feb. 9, 1838; d. Jan. 12, 1865, in Harrisburg, Penn.; vii. Edward-Harrison, b. April 12, 1840; served in the Civil War; d. Sept. 26, 1878; viii. Richard-Montgomery, b. Jan. 27, 1842; settled in Washington, Guernsey county; ix. George-Alfred, b. Dec. 9, 1843; d. March 31, 1849; x. Henrietta-Frances, b. Oct. 28, 1852; m. Dr. H. H. Harrison; settled in Wheeling, W. Va.).

After the death of her first husband, Elizabeth Snyder Karg Roberts, mother of Henrietta Hall, m. 1803, Charles Merrill Poor, a native of Greenland, N. H., of Puritan ancestry, son of John Poor; had issue, among others: Sarah-Ann, b. 1814; d. 1892; m. Robert Jackson Fleming, of Harrisburg, Penn.; George-A., settled in Vallejo, Cal.; Frances-Isabella, m. Henry S. McFadden, of Cadiz.

JOSEPH HALL, settled in the western part of Jefferson county, Ohio, about 1802, having come from North Carolina; d. 1825, in Jefferson county; m. in North Carolina, 1773, Christiana Peel; d. 1803; had issue, ten children, among whom:

I. Jesse, d. in Jefferson county, 1806; his wife died the same year; had issue, among others: 1. William, b. in Jefferson county, 1804; d. Dec. 14, 1883; m. April, 1826, Hannah Wharton, b. in Bucks county, Penn., 1807, daughter of Ezra and Martha Terry Wharton (who settled in 1818 on the present site of Harrisville, Harrison county, Ohio, where they died; the former b. Aug. 26, 1773; d. May, 1847; the latter b. May 19, 1778; d. Dec. 19, 1866; they were m. April 19, 1797); (William and Hannah Hall had issue: i. Ezra, d. 1852 in Minnesota; ii. Nathan-L.; iii. Penina; iv. Parker, b. June 6, 1829; settled in Short Creek township, Harrison county, Ohio, in 1853; m. [1st] August, 1853, Rebecca Hobson, a native of Belmont county, Ohio; d. 1866; m. [2d] 1872, Mrs. Tabitha D. Bundy, a native of Belmont county; v. Tilman, settled in Mahoning county; vi. Linton, settled in Columbiana county; vii. Martha, m. Thomas Dewees; settled in Morgan county, Ohio).

SAMUEL W. HAMILL, b. in county Antrim, Ireland, about 1787; d. in Monroe township, Harrison county, Ohio, Sept. 20, 1870; emigrated to America about 1820, first settling in New York City, where he remained for seven years; in 1824 m. Eliza Graham, b. in New York City, 1803; d. 1876; daughter of George and Rebecca Graham (the former a native of New York, the latter a native of Ireland); removed to Leesville, Carroll county, Ohio, in 1827, and located in Monroe township, Harrison county, in the spring of the following year; had issue: 1. Rebecca-J., m. William B. Edwards, of Plymouth, Ill.; 2. Catherine-A., m. Edward Greenlus, of Tuscarawas county, Ohio; 3. Samuel-S., b. June 22, 1840; settled in Monroe township; served in the Civil War, and as sheriff of Harrison county; m. March 21, 1872, Mary E. Heller, a native of Monroe township, daughter of Henry B. and Mary-A. Heller, early settlers in Harrison county; 3. Lindley-M., settled in Monroe township; served as an officer in the Civil War; 4. Wallace-S., served in the Civil War, and died in service August, 1861; 5. Robert-Emmet, served in the Civil War; d. in Sibley, Kan., Nov. 9, 1884; 6. Benjamin-G., settled in Kentucky; served as an officer in the Civil War.

FRANCIS H. HAMILTON, b. in Ireland, 1766; d. 1844; emigrated to America and first settled in Noblestown, Penn., about 1800; removed to Canonsburg, and afterwards to Mercer, where he remained until 1820, and then settled in Cadiz, Ohio; served in the War of 1812; m. 1806, Ruth Williams, b. 1788; d. 1842; of Scotch descent; had issue: 1. John, d. in Pennsylvania; 2. James, d. in Illinois; 3. David; 4. Jane; 5. Francis, b. Dec. 13, 1815; d. Jan. 28, 1887; m. Matilda ——, b. 1813; d. 1888; 6. William, b. Sept. 29, 1818; d. Nov. 14, 1892; 7. Samuel, b. in Cadiz, April 19, 1821; m. (1st) Aug. 6, 1843, Margaret J. Miller, of German descent, b. Aug. 10, 1826; d. Feb. 7, 1857; daughter of Michael Miller, of Harrison county; m. (2d) Bridget Downey, b. in Ireland, 1839 (her parents came to Vermont about 1842; her father d. in Kansas City, Mo., 1889); (had issue by first wife: i. ——, d. in infancy; ii. Samuel-D., settled in Harrisville, Ohio; iii. Henry-C., b. Dec. 29, 1850; iv. Eloisa-B.; had issue by second wife: v. Emma-Frances, m. William C. Leslie); 8. Sarah; 9. Mary, m. Jacob H. Herdman, and settled in New Concord, Muskingum county, Ohio; 10. Thomas.

JOSHUA HAMILTON, a native of Pennsylvania, of Scotch-Irish descent; settled in Harrison county, Ohio, before 1825; d. in Springfield, Ohio, Dec. 17, 1870; m. in Harrison county, Jane Craig, d. Nov. 9, 1889; had issue, eleven children, among whom: 1. Craig, b. April 16, 1825; d. in Cadiz township, Oct. 5, 1880; m. (1st) Feb. 21, 1850, Margaret McFadden, b. 1825; d. 1853, in McLean county, Ill., daughter of Joseph McFadden, of Harrison county; m. (2d) Jan. 28, 1858, Elizabeth McFadden, b. Oct. 29, 1836, daughter of Samuel and Margaret Rankin McFadden, of Cadiz township (had issue by first wife: i. Joshua, d. in infancy; ii. Joseph-McFadden, b. March 8, 1851; m. Dec. 25, 1873, Rebecca Caroline Dickerson, daughter of Asa and Jane Dunlap Dickerson; had issue by second wife: iii. Margaret-Jane, b. March 5, 1859; m. Eugene Watson, and settled in Belmont county; iv. Samuel-Rankin, b. March 17, 1863; m. Sept. 1, 1886, Georgianna Dickerson, a native of Noble county, Ohio, daughter of John and Catherine Lowe Dickerson; v. William-Sherman, b. Sept. 1, 1865).

The father of Craig Hamilton's second wife, Samuel McFadden, was b. 1815; d. 1863; his father, Samuel Mc-

Fadden, was a native of Ireland, who settled in Harrison county, where he d. 1837; Margaret Rankin McFadden, the mother of Elizabeth McFadden Hamilton, b. 1813; d. July 5, 1890, was a daughter of Robert Rankin, a native of Pennsylvania; the children of Samuel and Margaret Rankin McFadden were: 1. Robert; 2. Rebecca-J., m. Henry Barricklow; 3. Elizabeth, m. Craig Hamilton; 4. Sarah, m. Albert Moore; 5. Margaret, m. Thomas Richey; 6. Samuel.

ROBERT HAMILTON, d. before 1790; m. in West Nottingham township, Chester county, Penn., before 1770, Martha McMillan, b. 1748-49; d. March 18, 1831; daughter of John and Rachel McMillan; his widow removed with her four children to Buffalo township, Washington county, Penn., about 1795-98, in company with her brother-in-law and sister (John and Jane McMillan Perry), and, about 1803, settled at St. Clairsville, removing thence to Morristown, both in Belmont county, Ohio, where she died; had issue: 1. Rachel, d. 182—; m. about 1787, William Phillips, d. July 18, 1854; son of Thomas and Jane Blair Phillips, of West Nottingham township (had issue: i. Robert; ii. Martha, m. James Ross; iii. Thomas; iv. Jane, m. Samuel Lee; v. John; vi. William; vii. Mary, m. Jacob Grist; viii. Margaret, m. John Johns; ix. Eliza, m. —— Keatley); 2. Margaret, b. Nov. 26, 1776; d. Oct. 14, 1839; m. Edward Van Horn, b. 1777; d. Aug. 19, 1855; settled at New Athens, Harrison county, Ohio (had issue: i. Anne, b. 1803; d. 1815; ii. Martha, b. 1805; d. 1869; iii. Jemima; iv. Robert, d. 1895; v. Jane, b. 1809; d. 1888); 3. Martha, m. Alexander Morrison, and settled at Morristown, Ohio (had issue, among others: i. Robert, b. 1802; d. July 9, 1895); 4. John-Blair, d. about 1806; m. Mary Perry, b. ——; d. ——; daughter of John and Jane McMillan Perry (had issue, among others: i. Robert; a physician: b. Nov. 14, 1803; m. 1836, Margaret Wilson); 5. Jane, d. 1798; m. —— McClure (had issue, among others: i. Martha, b. Dec. 23, 1795; d. April 15, 1870; m. June 6, 1819, Robert Gaston, b. Jan. 10, 1797; d. Sept. 23, 1834; removed to Morgan county, Ohio, 1828, and thence to Knox county in 1831.

ROBERT HAMMOND, b. in county Tyrone, Ireland, 1765; d. in Belmont county, Ohio, 1845; m. Jane Cassell, b. in county Down, Ireland, 1764; d. 1852; emigrated to America and first settled in Pennsylvania, removing to Belmont county before 1809; both were members of the Seceder Church; had issue:

I. Mary, b. July 30, 1788.
II. Alexander, b. May 16, 1790; d. in Harrison county, 1874, where he had settled in 1809; in 1812 he located in Short Creek township, subsequently removing to Harrisville; was a member of the Seceder Church, and his house was a station on the "underground railroad," many slaves having been given shelter in his home before being taken to Canada; m. in 1812, Elizabeth Hanna, b. 1793; d. 1886; daughter of Samuel (b. in Cumberland county, Penn. 1763) and Elizabeth Duncan (b. in Scotland, 1766) Hanna, of Short Creek township; had issue, among others: 1. Esther, m. Robert Porter Hanna; 2. Margaret, m. S. J. Hawthorne, of Harrisville; 3. John-Hanna, b. in Harrison county, Ohio; settled in Cadiz in 1872; served as an officer in the Civil War; m. 1845, Agnes E. Carrick, daughter of David and Elizabeth Carrick, early settlers of Harrison county, the former having served in the War of 1812 (had issue: i. Alexander-James, b. Aug. 14, 1846; served in the Civil War; settled in Cadiz in 1878; m. in Cadiz, 1870, Charlotte Hunter, daughter of Joseph and Letitia McFadden Hunter; ii. Anderson-N., b. in Short Creek township, Harrison county, Ohio, 1848; settled in Cadiz, 1866; m. in Cadiz, 1870, Nancy Jane Moore, daughter of John Moore, removed to Chicago).

III. David, b. June 26, 1792.
IV. William, b. Aug. 2, 1794.
V. Margaret, b. July 8, 1795.
VI. Elizabeth, b. Oct. 24, 1797.
VII. Esther, b. Feb. 1, 1801.
VIII. John, b. March 10, 1803.
IX. Robert, b. March 20, 1805.
X. James, b. May 13, 1808.

ALEXANDER HANNA, b. in Ireland, 1737; d. in Somerset county, Penn., 1809; his son, James, b. in Ireland, 1770; emigrated to America when young; d. in Somerset county, 1819; served in the Pennsylvania Legislature; m. Ann Leech; had issue: 1. John, served in the Pennsylvania Legislature; 2. Mary; 3. Thomas; 4. James; 5. Alexander, b. 1802; d. 1881; 6. William; 7. Philo; 8. Jane; 9. Martha; 10. Anna.

ANDREW HANNA, settled in Paxtang township, Lancaster (now Dauphin) county, Penn., before 1737; d. in Hanover township, 1766; had issue: 1. Samuel, b. in mid-ocean; probably settled in Hopewell township, Cumberland county, see Samuel Hanna below; 2. Andrew, settled in Hopewell township, Cumberland county, Penn., about 1766; removing thence, 1772-75, to Guilford county, N. C.; m. Mary ———; 3. Margaret; 4. Isaac, b. 1743; d. in Aron, Livingston county, N. Y., 1816; m. April 15, 1766, Martha Bell, b. August, 1746; d. 1811; sister of Thomas, Lucy, Anna, and Walter Bell; removed from Dry Valley, Union county, Penn., to Livingston county, N. Y., about 1810 (had issue: i. Andrew, b. 1769; d. at Aronsburg, Centre county, Penn., Jan 24, 1835; m. Margaret Cook, b. 1776; d. 1841; their son Andrew settled in Canal township, Venango county, Penn.; ii. Samuel, m. ——— McPherson; iii. Elizabeth, m. Levi Van Fossen; iv. Matthew, b. 1780; d. at Aron, N. Y., Nov. 12, 1813; m. July 23, 1807, Catharine Pearson, b. Feb. 19, 1791; d. Sept. 9, 1882; v. Thomas, settled in Chautauqua county, N. Y.; m. Nancy Pearson, sister of Catharine, b. Feb. 11, 1797; d. May 8, 1817; vi. John, removed to Livingston county, N. Y.; vii. Anna, m. Alexander (or James) Beatty; viii. Martha, m. (1st) ——— McPherson; m. (2d) ——— Briggs; removed to Livingston county, N. Y.; and from there to Hyattsville, Ohio; ix. Isaac, m. Sarah ———); 5. Mary, m. William Woods; 6. John, removed to South Carolina; 7. Elizabeth, m. Moses Carson; 8. Matthew, settled in Hopewell township, Cumberland county, before 1771, where he resided as late as 1781.

JAMES HANNA, settled in Little Britain township, Lancaster county, Penn., before 1738, where he was living after 1769; had issue, among others: 1. James.

JAMES HANNA and his wife, Martha, emigrated from the North of Ireland, and settled in Pennsylvania; removed thence to Berkeley county, West Va., and from there to Mercer county, Ky., where he d. about 1798; had issue, six sons and six daughters, four of whom were born in Ireland; among others were: 1. Stephen; 2. James; 3. Adam, removed to Shelby county, Ky.; 4. Hannah, m. John Myles; 5. Thomas, m. Margaret Smith; removed to Shelby county, Ky. (had issue, among others: i. John-Smith, b. in Mercer county, Ky., March 27, 1798; d. ———; m. Aug. 11, 1825, Jane A. King, b. Oct. 10, 1805, daughter of Thomas and Anna McAfee King).

JAMES HANNA, b. in Washington county, Penn., 1792; settled in German township, Harrison county, Ohio, 1816, where he d. Jan. 14, 1877; m. in Pennsylvania, 1816, Mary McCleary, b. 1793; d. Oct. 31, 1872; had issue: 1. Mary, m. Robert Herron, a minister, and settled in Scio; 2. Esther, m. Robert Smiley, and settled in Archer township, Harrison county; 3. Tabitha-Jane, m. James Lawthers, of Bowerstown, and settled in German township; 4. Jerusha-Elizabeth, m. Wesley Brindley, and settled in Green township; 5. Ann, b. Aug. 27, 1818; settled in Jewett, 1877; 6. Alexander; 7. William-J.; 8. Sarah; 9. Dorcas.

JAMES HANNA, of Washington county, Penn. (probably of Hopewell or Strabane township), b. 1749; d. near Canonsburg, April 6, 1813; m. Anne ———, b. 1760; d. in German township, Harrison county, April 27, 1833; had issue: I. Moses. II. Matthew. III. William, b. 1780; d. April 6, 1830; settled in Green township, Harrison county, Ohio, about 1805; m. Mary ———, b. 1782; d. Nov. 19, 1853; had issue: 1. Robert; 2. John; 3. Esther; 4. Anne; 5. James, settled in German township, where he remained until 1858, thence removed to Monroe county, Ind., where he d. Oct. 12, 1886; m. 1835, Cynthia Shannon, daughter of William Shannon, of Jefferson county, Ohio (had issue: i. William, served in the Civil War; ii. Isaac; iii. James, served in the Civil War; iv. Robert-Porter, served in the Civil War; d. 1863, near Atlanta; v. John-N., b. about 1845; resided in Indiana until 1875, and then returned to Hopedale, Harrison county, where he settled; served in the Civil War; m. Dec. 30, 1872, Nancy J. Copeland, daughter of Jacob Copeland, of Hopedale; vi. Samuel-T.; vii. Moses-

K.; viii. Delmar-H.; ix. James-S.; x. Mary; xi. Jennie); 6. Martha; 7. Margaret; 8. William, b. 1812; d. Jan. 8, 1839; 9. Sarah, b. 1822; d. Jan. 13, 1842; 10. Louisa, b. 1823; d. April 27, 1834; 11. Samuel, b. 1824; d. May 6, 1834; 12. Prudence; 13. Mary; 14. Jane. IV. Joseph. V. Robert. VI. Samuel. VII. Prudence. VIII. Jean. IX. Anne. X. Martha. XI. John. XII. James.

JOHN HANNA and WILLIAM HANNA, probably brothers, emigrated from the North of Ireland, about 1731, and settled in East Fallowfield township, Chester county, Penn., about 1733, John first having located on Neshaminy Creek, in Bucks county, and about 1739, removed from Fallowfield township to West Nantmeal (now Honeybrook) township; of these two:

John Hanna, b. about 1700; d. March 8-13, 1770; m. Jane Andre, d. December, 1774; had issue:

I. John, a physician and minister, b. in mid-ocean, 1731; d. Nov. 4, 1801; m. about 1760, Mary McCrea, daughter of Rev. James and Mary Graham McCrea; served as minister of the Presbyterian churches of Bethlehem, Kingwood, and Alexandria, N. J., 1761-1801; had issue, thirteen children, six of whom died in infancy: 1. James, settled at Newtown, Bucks county; removed to Frankfort, Ky., after 1793; m. Mary Harris, of Newtown, daughter of John and Hannah Stewart Harris (had issue: i. John-Harris; ii. Sophia; iii. Charles-Stewart; iv. A daughter; one of the daughters m. John J. Crittenden, of Kentucky): 2. John-Andre, b. 1761; d. at Harrisburg, Penn., July 23, 1805; m. Mary Read Harris, b. Oct. 1, 1770; d. Aug. 20, 1851; daughter of John Harris, the founder of Harrisburg (had issue: i. Mary-Read, b. April 30, 1788; d. March 14, 1826; m. April 29, 1817, John Tod, of Bedford; ii. Juliana-Catharine, b. Nov. 8, 1789; d. without issue, April, 1861; m. Jan. 14, 1812, John Fisher; iii. Frances, b. April 27, 1791; d. 1868; m. Oct. 27, 1812, John Carson McAllister; iv. Caroline-Elizabeth, b. Feb. 5, 1794; d. Jan. 29, 1872; m. Dec. 8, 1812, Joseph Briggs, of Silvers' Spring, Cumberland county; v. Henrietta, b. Aug. 23, 1796; d. unm., Nov. 18, 1840; vi. Sarah-Elder, b. June 20, 1798; d. April 2, 1829; m. April 18, 1820, Richard Templin; vii. Eleanor,

b. Feb. 22, 1800; d. 1802; viii. Esther, b. July, 1801; d. 1801); 3. Catharine, m. Dr. Samuel Tolbert, of New York (had issue: i. Catharine, m. ——— Brooks; ii. Jane, m. ——— Sanford); 4. Mary, m. Dr. ——— Holmes, of Mansfield, Sussex county, N. J.; 5. William-R.; 6. Sarah, m. ——— Payne, of Mansfield, N. J.; 7. Jane.

II. William, a minister, settled at Albany, N. Y., about 1765, where he served as the first pastor of the Presbyterian Church of that place; became an Episcopalian clergyman and settled in Culpeper county, Va., about 1774, from whence, on account of his Toryism, he was obliged to remove to Montreal, Canada, at the breaking out of the Revolutionary War.

III. James, b. 1722; d. Jan. 21, 1807; m. Elizabeth ———, b. 1740; d. Dec. 12, 1821; had issue: 1. John, m. probably, Jane Guthrie, daughter of Adam Guthrie; 2. William, resided in Huntingdon county, Penn., in 1805; 3. Mary, m. ——— Gault; 4. Jane, m. William Irwin; 5. James; 6. Agnes.

IV. Robert.

V. Agnes, m. ——— Culbertson.

VI. Elizabeth, m. ——— McCool.

VII. Margaret, d. November, 1802; m. James Galt, of Salisbury township, Lancaster county; d. June, 1773.

William Hanna, d. after Sept. 22, 1766; had issue:

I. John, d. March-April, 1784; m. Abigail Wilson, b. 1739; d. 1833; daughter of Thomas Wilson, of Newlin township; had issue: 1. Elizabeth; 2. Mary, b. after 1766; 3. John, b. after 1763; 4. Abigail, b. after 1766; 5. Margaret, b. after 1766; 6. Phœbe, b. after 1766; 7. Jacob, b. 1771; d. Aug. 13, 1839.

II. William, m. Esther Wilson, daughter of Thomas Wilson, of Newlin township; settled in Newlin township, about 1776.

JOHN HANNA, b. in county Derry, Ireland, 1752; d. in South Huntingdon township, Westmoreland county, Penn., June 9, 1832; m. 1789, Elizabeth Miller, b. 1762; d. Oct. 4, 1835; daughter of John and Elizabeth Lindsey Miller; had issue: 1. Thomas, b. March 6, 1790; d. Dec. 29, 1855; m. Feb. 29, 1816, Esther Trout, b. Nov. 13, 1796; d. Oct. 24, 1876; daughter of Henry and Catharine Bossart Trout; 2. Martha, b. 1791; d. Sept. 18, 1862; m. 1817, Henry Lake,

b. 1777; d. Jan. 10, 1839; 3. Alexander, b. Feb. 15, 1796; d. Jan. 4, 1883; m. May, 1824, Eliza Hamilton; 4. John; 5. Elizabeth, m. Peter Broadsword; 6. James, b. 1800; d. 1829; 7. Margaret, b. May, 1803; d. Feb. 7, 1866; m. Dec. 30, 1830, John Hanna (a cousin); 8. Robert, b. 1806; m. 1833, Priscilla Hamilton.

JOHN HANNA, of Hopewell township, Cumberland county, Penn., d. after probably 1809; had issue:

I. John, d. Oct. 10, 1792 (or 1802).

II. Samuel, b. Nov. 29, 1763; m. Elizabeth Duncan, b. July 27, 1766; removed to Canton township, Washington county, Penn., about 1785; thence to Warren county, Ohio, about 1799-1800, and from there to Short Creek township, Harrison county, Ohio, 1801; had issue: 1. Jeanette, b. Feb. 22, 1786; d. young; 2. John, b. June 26, 1787; d. in Harrison county, Ohio, Aug. 12, 1849; m. 1826, Rachel Fulton; 3. Archibald, a minister; b. Feb. 12, 1790; d. in Wayne county, Ohio, June 9, 1875; m. April 4, 1816, Mary Ramage, daughter of William and Mary Ramage; 4. Elizabeth, b. Jan. 26, 1792; d. April 24, 1884; m. 1812, Alexander Hammond; 5. Samuel, b. Sept. 2, 1795; d. in Richland county, Ohio, June 2, 1862; 6. Isabella, b. June 25, 1797; d. 1846; m. Benjamin Ramsey; 7. Ezekiel, b. June 1, 1799; d. near Beech Spring, Harrison county, Ohio, May 10, 1861; m. Aug. 30, 1821, Elizabeth Anderson, b. Oct. 21, 1796; d. Jan. 24, 1845; 8. Robert, b. April 26, 1801; d. in Mansfield, Ohio, Dec. 2, 1886; 9. James, b. March 13, 1803; d. Harrison county, Ohio, Aug. 25, 1859; m. 1824, Margaret Fulton, b. in Fayette county, Penn., 1803; d. Aug. 10, 1859 (had issue, among others: i. John-Newton, settled in Short Cheek; m. [1st] 1861, Margaret A. Finley; d. March, 1871; daughter of Dr. Robert Finley, of Mount Pleasant, Ohio: m. [2d] 1878, Mahala Narragan, a native of Ohio); 10. William, b. Feb. 24, 1805; d. in Savannah, Ohio, Dec. 19, 1886; 11. Margaret, b. April 27, 1807; d. June 3, 1888; m. Levi Dickerson; settled near Malta, Ohio; 12. ———; 13.

III. Ann, m. Hugh Wylie.

IV. Esther, m. James Pitts.

V. Ezekiel, d. in Indiana county, Penn., 1817.

JOHN HANNA, removed from eastern Pennsylvania (probably from Cumberland county) and settled on Hendricks' Run, Fairfield township, Westmoreland county, before 1772; d. about September, 1788; had issue, among others: 1. John, b. in Fairfield township, Dec. 23, 1773; d. near Cadiz, Ohio, June 2, 1847; removed to Harrison county about 1814; m. (1st) Dec. 6, 1796, Ann (or Nancy) Leonard, b. June 7, 1775; d. March 23, 1818; daughter of James and Mary Finley Leonard (the last named a daughter of John and Martha Berkley Finley, of Lurgan township, Franklin county); m. (2d) Mrs. Margaret Wylie; had issue by first wife: 1. James-Leonard, b. Oct. 5, 1797; d. June 11, 1820; m. June, 1819, Mary Craig (had issue: i. Mary-Ann, m. 1839, Rev. Edward Small, of Mercer, Penn.); 2. Catharine, b. March 6, 1799; d. June 5, 1801; 3. Mary-Leonard. b. Feb. 5, 1800; d. unm. Sept. 11, 1820; 4. John-Evans, b. Dec. 19, 1805; d. Aug. 30, 1894; m. (1st) June 8, 1826, Susanna Robertson, b. March 9, 1804; d. April 15, 1865; daughter of Robert and Beulah Stanley Robertson, of Loudoun county, Virginia; m. (2d) Sarah E. Swayze, b. Sept. 4. 1819; daughter of Rev. William and Frances Peck Swayze (had issue: i. Neri-Augustus. b. April 3, 1827; m. June 7. 1849, Eliza Jane Phillips, b. Feb. 22, 1829; daughter of John and Eliza Gilmore Phillips; ii. James-Leonard, b. Aug. 25, 1829; m. Dec. 22. 1853, Harriet N. Wood; iii. Maria-Eliza, b. March 9, 1832; d. March 2. 1898; m. July 1. 1857, Sharon S. Heskett; iv. John-Edward, b. Aug. 12, 1834; d. Aug. 11. 1892; m. [1st] May 12. 1860. Harriet E. Perkins; m. [2d] Elizabeth ——; m. [3d] Alice Hill; v. Finley Robertson, b. Feb. 3, 1837; m. June 18. 1871. Ada M. Develing; m. [2d] Mrs. Mary Hyatt; vi. Mary-Ann. b. March 26. 1839; d. Aug. 26, 1840); 5. Eliza-Ann. b. Jan. 8, 1808; d. March 31, 1863; m. 183—. John Oglevee. b. in Cadiz township. Harrison county. Dec. 14. 1810; d. March 12. 1865; son of John and Agnes Oglevee, of Fayette county. Penn.. who emigrated to Harrison county. the father dying in 1815 (had issue: i. Mary-Ann. b. May 16, 1837; d. July 21. 1874; m. S. A. Osburn; ii. William-Hamilton. b. Sept. 10. 1838; m. June 20. 1867. Elizabeth A. Craig, daughter of Walter and Jane Moore Craig; iii. John-Finley. b. May 16. 1840; m. [1st] Jean Eagleson; m. [2d] Euphemia [Effie] Eagleson, sister of Jean; iv.

Baruch-Francis, b. June, 1842; d. June 12, 1844; v. James-Wilson, b. May 11, 1842; d. May 23, 1863; served in the Civil War, and died from disease contracted in that service; vi. George-Hopkins, b. February, 1847; d. April 12, 1857; vii. Nancy-Jane, b. February, 1849; d. June 25, 1865; viii. Susanna-Elizabeth, b. July 23, 1858; d. Feb. 10, 1880); 6. Jane-Finley, b. June 2, 1811; d. April 13, 1833; 7. Andrew-Finley, b. Feb. 21, 1813; d. April 12, 1847; m. Jan. 13, 1835, Susanna Craig (had issue: i. John-Rowland, b. Oct. 17, 1836; m. June 13, 1861, Ione Theresa Munger; ii. James-Wilson, b. April 13, 1843; m. May 30, 1867, Anna E. Carter; iii. William-Finley, b. March 23, 1846; d. Aug. 1, 1864; iv. Mary-Ann, d. in infancy; v. George-Edward, d. in infancy); 8. David-Wilson, b. Aug. 22, 1815; d. July 2, 1843).

PATRICK HANNA, of Hopewell township, Cumberland county, Penn., d. in Monaghan township, York county, about November, 1758; probably the same whose name occurs on tax-list of New Garden township, Chester county, Penn., 1739; had issue: 1. John (probably one of the two Johns last given above); 2. Joshua; 3. Samuel, d. in Hopewell township, about April, 1789: m. Mary Brady, daughter of Hugh and Hannah Brady: after his death, his widow removed, about 1790, with her family to Fairfield township, Westmoreland county, settling near her brother-in-law and sister, Archibald and Margaret Brady Hanna (had issue: i. Joseph; ii. Margaret; iii. Samuel; iv. Elizabeth; v. Mary; vi. Ebenezer. b. after 1770; vii. [a daughter], b. about May, 1785); 4. Archibald. d. in Fairfield township, Westmoreland county, June, 1794: m. Margaret Brady, daughter of Hugh and Hannah Brady (had issue: i. Hugh; ii. William; iii. Mary, m. Robert Williams; v. Martha; 6. Rosanna; 7. William; 8. ——. m. Moses Stuart. son of Andrew and Mary Stuart, of Hopewell township; removed to Peters township, Franklin county, before 1763.

ROBERT HANNA. died in Hempfield township. Westmoreland county, Penn.. about April-May. 1786; m. Elizabeth Kelly, daughter of John Kelly. of Donegal township. Lancaster county: settled in Hempfield township, about

1769-70, and founded Hannastown (which was attacked and burned by the Indians and British, July 13, 1782; when some of the inhabitants were killed and many carried to Canada as prisoners, among the latter being Elizabeth Hanna and her daughter, Jane, who were released at Montreal and returned home the following December; had issue: 1. Jane, b. May 13, 1764; d. June 11, 1816; m. Lieut. David Hammond, an officer in the Revolution; b. about 1749; d. April 27, 1801 (had issue: i. Elizabeth, b. June 21, 1786; d. May 5, 1822; m. John Watson, of Watsontown, Pa., b. Dec. 13, 1779; d. Jan. 13, 1856; ii. Mary, m. John Montgomery, and settled at Muncy, Penn.; iii. Grace, m. —— Montgomery, of Paradise, Penn.; d. without issue: iv. Robert-Hanna, b. 1791; d. 1848; major and paymaster, U. S. A., m. Elizabeth Clark Gloninger; v. Jane); 2. Elizabeth, b. about 1773; m. about 1797, her cousin, James Kelly, b. 1776, son of Col. John and Sarah Polk Kelly, of Buffalo Valley, Union county, Pa. (had issue: i. Eliza, m. John Bates; removed to Perrysburg, Wood county, Ohio; ii. John-Robinson, d. young; iii. Robert-H., d. unm.; iv. James-Andrew, d. unm.; v. Susan-Robinson, d. without issue; vi. Jane, d. unm.; vii. Maria (or Margaret), m. —— Hutchison, and settled in Huntingdon county, near Altoona, Penn.); 3. Susanna, m. William Robinson; d. without issue; 4. Margaret, d. young.

ROBERT HANNA, of Westmoreland county, Penn. (probably of Fairfield township); had issue: 1. William, settled on Chartiers Creek, three miles north of Canonsburgh, Washington county, before 1800; removed to Ohio, 1802 (had issue, among others: i. John; ii. Thomas; iii. Isaac).

ROBERT HANNA, settled in Lower Smithfield township, Northampton (now Monroe) county, Penn., before 1748, where he d. June-July, 1777; m. Margaret ——; had issue, among others: 1. Benjamin. Robert Hanna mentions in his will grandchildren, Robert Hanna and John and Eleanor Sealy.

ROBERT HANNA, b. about 1754; settled in what is now Greene county, Penn., before 1780, with his brother, Benjamin; had issue, among others: 1. Joseph, b. about 1786; m. Elizabeth

Hammer; removed about 1818-19, to Greene county, Ohio; and in 1820 to Jackson county, Indiana; 2. John; 3. Samuel; 4. Robert.

SAMUEL HANNA, probably son of Andrew Hanna, of Paxtang (above), d. in Hopewell township, August-September, 1808; m. Agnes ——; had issue: 1. Samuel; 2. Jean, m. —— White; 3. Martha, m. James Sharp; 4. Mary, m. James Sterret, son of James Sterret, of Donegal township, Lancaster county (had issue: i. James; ii. Samuel); 5. Elizabeth, m. —— Sterrett; 6. Rachel, m. —— Trimble; 7. Nancy, m. —— Williamson; 8. Sarah, m. —— White.

THOMAS HANNA, of county Monaghan, Ireland (probably from Ballybay), m. Elizabeth Henderson, and emigrated to America about 1763, supposed to have settled in Pennsylvania; d. about 1764-5; had issue:

I. John, d. about 1763; when the family reached Newcastle, Del.

II. James (twin), b. March 7, 1753; d. Oct. 31, 1827; m. (1st) in Maysville, Ky., Hannah Bayless, b. Aug. 13, 1761; d. Aug. 14, 1804; m. (2d) in Dayton, Ohio, Elizabeth ——; removed from Pennsylvania to Georgetown, Scott county, Ky., and about 1803 settled near Dayton, Ohio; had issue by first wife: 1. Thomas, d. in Massachusetts, without issue; m. three times; 2. James; a minister; settled in Crawfordsville, Ind. (had issue, among others: i. Bayless-W., U. S. Minister to Argentina, 1884-88); 3. Samuel. b. in Scott county, Ky., Oct. 18, 1797; d. at Ft. Wayne, Ind., June 11, 1866; m. Eliza Taylor, b. Feb. 2. 1803; d. Jan. 12, 1888; in 1819, settled at Ft. Wayne, Ind.; 4. Hugh, b. July 24, 1799; settled in Ft. Wayne, 1824, and, in 1835, laid off the town of Wabash, Ind.; 5. Elizabeth, m. (1st) John Johnson; m. (2d) —— McCorkle; settled at Thorntown, Ind.; 6. Martha, m. Andrew Telford (or Tilford), and settled in Troy, Ohio; 7. Sarah, m. Harvey Ward, and settled in Lafayette, Ind.; 8. Nancy-W., m. James Barnett, and settled in Ft. Wayne, Ind.; 9. Joseph-S., b. in Dayton, Ohio, Dec. 7, 1803; d. Aug. 4, 1864; m. (1st) ——; m. (2d) Hester Ann Sumwalt. James Hanna had issue by second wife: 10. Amos; 11. Harriet, m. —— McClure; 12. Benjamin; 13. Deborah.

OHIO VALLEY GENEALOGIES 57

III. Robert (twin), b. March 7, 1753;
d. at New Lisbon, Ohio, July 17, 1837;
m. Jan. 31, 1776, Catherine Jones, b.
Aug. 27, 1754; d. Sept. 28, 1835; dau.
of Benjamin Jones (b. in the Great
Valley, Chester county, Pa., d. 1754)
and his wife Esther Evans Jones, b.
in Chester county about 1734; d. about
1816 (m. 2d, John Jones). Robert
Hanna and his wife became Quakers
about 1780; removed from Pennsylvania to Lynchburg, Va., and about
1802-10 to Columbiana county, Ohio;
had issue: 1. Thomas, b. May 2, 1777;
d. Sept. 17, 1828; m. Anna ———; 2.
Benjamin, b. June 14, 1779; d. July
16, 1853; m. (1st) Dec. 15, 1803, Rachel
Dixon, b. July 19, 1785; d. Feb. 28,
1851; m. (2d) 1851-2. Hannah Kersey,
(had issue by first wife: i. Joshua, b.
Nov. 8, 1804; d. July 7, 1881; m. Feb.
3, 1830, Susan R. Lathrop, b. June 24,
1803; d. Dec. 17, 1875; ii. Leonard, b.
March 4, 1806; d. Dec. 15, 1862; m.
Sept. 10, 1835, Samantha M. Converse,
b. April 3, 1813 [and had issue, among
others: Marcus-A., b. July 11, 1838];
iii. Levi, b. Feb. 7, 1808; m. March 21,
1833, Nancy Watson, b. July 11, 1808;
d. April 1, 1879; settled at Greeley,
Col.; iv. Zalinda, b. Feb. 23, 1810; d.
Dec. 4, 1854; m. Feb. 28, 1828, Charles
D. Hostettor, b. April 29, 1802; d. Aug.
26, 1872; v. Robert, b. Aug. 15, 1812; d.
April 3, 1882; m. March 16, 1837, Harriet A. Brooks, b. March 8, 1815; d.
July 27, 1882; vi. Tryphena, b. June 12,
1814; d. Dec. 28, 1893; m. Sept. 4, 1833,
Samuel Nicols, b. Jan. 21, 1807; d. May
23 1873; vii. Rebecca, b. Sept. 21,
1816; d. Oct. 15, 1847; m. May 31, 1837,
Jesse Holmes; viii. Thomas-B., b. May
22, 1818; d. Nov. 9, 1885; m. March 2,
1843, Sophia T. Tabor, b. May 24, 1822;
d. Oct. 20, 1895; ix. Anna, b. March 3,
1821; d. Jan. 26, 1846; m. March 27,
1845, Hiram T. Cleaver; x. Benjamin,
b. March 14. 1823; d. April 3, 1881; m.
March 26, 1845, Catherine M. McCook,
b. Nov. 24, 1823; xi. Kersey, b. Oct. 6,
1824; m. March 15, 1849, Mary A. Mc-
Cook, b. Jan. 7, 1826; d. Feb. 7, 1891);
3. Esther, b. Aug. 6, 1781; d. Nov. 3,
1791; buried in South River graveyard,
Va.; 4. David, b. Jan. 9, 1784; d. Oct.
24, 1791; 5. Caleb, b. Sept. 4, 1786; d.
July 15, 1790; 6. Robert, a portrait
painter of Virginia; b. June 28,
1789; m. Roxanna ——— (had issue: i.
Raphael; ii. Fletcher); 7. Esther (2d),

b. April 10, 1792; d. Dec. 6. 1849;
m. Charles Hole, a Quaker minister;
(had issue, nine children); 8. Catherine,
b. Nov. 25, 1794; d. May 3, 1881; m.
John Hole (had issue, eight children);
9. Ann, b. July 30, 1797; d. 187—; m.
Benjamin Hambleton (had issue, living
in Iowa); 10. Joshua, b. Feb. 16, 1802;
d. Sept. 11, 1834.
  IV. Hugh, d. August, 1820; m. Rebecca
———, and settled on Ten Mile creek,
Morris township, Washington county,
Pa., about 1790; had issue: 1. John-
Vance, m. Lydia McCollum (had issue:
i. Thomas; ii. Matilda, m. John Braden,
and settled at Rankinville; iii. Margaret, m. Mathias Minton, and settled in
the village of Prosperity; iv. ———
v. ———; vi. ———); 2. James, m.
Phoebe, daughter of Benjamin Day;
removed to Carrollton, Ohio; 3. Elizabeth, m. Samuel Clutter; 4. Rebecca, d.
unm.; 5. Nancy, m. Jacob Hathaway;
6. Eleanor; 7. Martha, m. Dr. Spen-
cer Blachly, of Waynesburg, Pa.;
Hugh, settled at Connellsville, Fayette
county; 9. Thomas, d. young.
  V. Martha, b. Jan. 7, 1758; m. ———
Saunders, and settled on Ten Mile
Creek, Washington county, Pa.
  VI. Thomas, b. 1760; d. April 9,
1839; m. Jane Cowden, b. 1759; d. near
Cadiz, Ohio, April 4, 1839; settled in
Buffalo township, Washington county,
Pa., before 1793; removed to Harrison
county, Ohio, 1835; had issue: 1. John-
C., d. Sept. 13, 1865 (had issue: i.
James-Rankin; ii. Maria, m. W. G.
Maxwell and settled in Buffalo town-
ship; iii. Elizabeth-M., m. ——— Leiper,
and settled in Denver, Col.; iv.
Thomas, d. young; v. Thomas-H., a
minister; settled in Monmouth, Ill.;
vi. Margaret-M.; vii. Jane-C.; viii.
James-M.; ix. Hugh-Allison; x. ———,
died in infancy); 2. James, settled near
Cadiz, Ohio (had issue: i. Martha, m.
Rev. George C. Vincent); 3. Thomas, d.
young; 4. Thomas, a minister; d. Feb.
9, 1864; settled in Cadiz, Ohio, about
1821; removed to Washington, Pa.,
about 1848; m. (1st) Jemima Patterson,
b. Oct. 30, 1805; d. at Cadiz, July 14,
1847; m. (2d) Sept., 1848, Sarah R. Foster, of Washington, Pa., b. in Hebron,
Washington county, N. Y., Nov. 10,
1802 (had issue by first wife: i. Robert-
P.; m. Esther Hammond, and settled
at New Athens. Ohio; ii. Thomas-B.;
a minister; d. 1850-60; iii. Sarah-J., set-

tled at Salem, Washington county, N. Y.; iv. Mary, m. Dr. J. B. McMichael, of Monmouth, Ill.; v. Maria, m. Andrew J. Sweeney, of Wheeling, West Va.; vi. Martha, m. Dr. W. A. McKenzie; settled at Salem, N. Y.; vii. Joseph, d. young); 5. Elizabeth, m. —— McCune; 6. Mary, d. July 29, 1848; m. Rev. Joseph Scroggs, b. near Newville, Pa., March 1, 1793; d. in Fairfield township, Westmoreland county, Pa., April 21, 1873 (had issue, ten children, among whom: i. Joseph, a United Presbyterian minister, b. July 28, 1836).

WILLIAM HANNA, b. 1720; d. in Frankford township, Cumberland county, Penn., Oct. 3, 1807, where he had settled before 1764; had issue: I. John, d. June, 1824; had issue: 1. William; 2. John, d. October, 1839; m. Jane —— (had issue: i. William, d. August, 1861; ii. Eliza); 3. Mary, m. —— Mitchell; 4. Eliza. II. (possibly) Samuel.

WILLIAM HANNA, settled in Antrim township, Franklin county, Penn., before 1762, where he d. November, 1785; m. Elizabeth ——; had issue: 1. John; 2. ——, m. James Morrow; 3. ——, m. Henry Morrow; 4. ——, m. John Wherry; 5. ——, m. Samuel Adams.

HEZEKIAH HARRISON, of English descent, b. in Maryland, 1804; d. June 3, 1877; settled in Green township, Harrison county, Ohio, about 1820; m. 1829, Lydia Hilbert, b. 1813; d. May 28, 1869; daughter of David Hilbert; had issue: 1. David, settled in Marion county, Kan.; 2. Albert-J., d. May, 1889; served in the Civil War; m. Susanna Holmes, daughter of Asa and Mary McCoy Holmes; 3. Henry-H., m. (1st) ——; m. (2d) Henrietta F. Hall; settled in Wheeling, W. Va.; 4. William, b. in Short Creek township, Nov. 21, 1842; served in the Civil War; m. 1867. Sarah A. Hargrave, daughter of Joseph and Margaret Hargrave, of Harrison county; 5. Milton, d. in infancy; 6. Arabella.

JAMES HARRISON, b. in Ireland; m. Elizabeth Addy; d. 1872: had issue: 1. James; 2. Hugh; 3. Matilda, m. Seth Munn; 4. Sarah, m. Samuel Poulson; 5. Margaret, m. Richard Duncan; 6. Elizabeth, m. 1856, Patrick Lynch, b. in Ireland, 1833; d. 1887: settled in Cadiz, Ohio, 1856.

JOHN HARRISON, a native of England, b. 1758, emigrated to America and first settled in Pittsburg, Penn., about 1814; settled in North township, Harrison county, Ohio, about 1816; d. in England, 1833; his wife also d. in England; had issue: I. Joseph, b. near Otley, Yorkshire, England, 1800; came to Ohio with his parents in 1816, and settled in North township, where he died April 13, 1878; m. (1st) 1828, Ellen Hartley, a native of Carlton, England, b. 1806; d. 1853; daughter of Christopher and Mary Hartley, also natives of England (the former b. 1778; d. 1864; the latter b. 1789; d. 1867); m. (2d) 1857, Sarah Herron, b. 1813; d. 1890; had issue by first wife: 1. John, b. July 10, 1830; m. April 22, 1852, Euphemia Patterson, daughter of John and Isabella McMillan Patterson, early settlers of Carroll county, Ohio, who were m. 1824 (the former d. 1859; the latter, who was a daughter of Robenia McKelvey, and a granddaughter of Ann Shearer, a native of Scotland, d. 1846); (had issue, eight sons and four daughters); 2. William, b. Oct. 29, 1837: settled near Scio, m. 1860, Elizabeth Waddington, a native of Harrison county, daughter of William and Ann Wallace Waddington (had issue, ten children); 3. Joseph, b. 1840; d. 1847.

William Waddington, father of Elizabeth Harrison, was a native of Yorkshire, England, b. 1815; settled in Harrison county about 1835, where he m. 1839, Ann Wallace, a native of Pennsylvania who had settled in Harrison county; later they removed to Tuscarawas county, Ohio; had issue: 1. James; settled in Christian county. Ill.; 2. Elizabeth, m. William Harrison; 3. John; 4. William; 5. Henry; 6. Mary Jane; 7. Sarah; 8. Amos; 9. Isaac; 10. David.

JAMES HAVERFIELD, of Scotch-Irish descent, emigrated to America and settled in Huntingdon county. Penn.; located in what is now Harrison county after 1800; m. Nancy ——; had issue:

I. William, b. in Pennsylvania, 1774; d. in Harrison county, June 14, 1859; m. in Pennsylvania, Elizabeth Stitt, a native of that State; d. 1858; served in the War of 1812; had issue, ten children, among whom: 1. John, b. 1811; d. May 9, 1873; settled in Cadiz township; m. 1836, Nancy Richey, daughter of Thomas Richey, a native of Ireland, who had located in Harrison county (had issue: i. William-S., b. in Cadiz township, Oct. 2, 1838; served in the Civil War; m. 1865, Mary Haverfield, daughter of Alexander Haverfield, d. in Harrison county; ii. Eliza-Jane, m. R. A. McCormick, of Cadiz; iii. Alvin; iv. John; v. Mary; vi. Jessie, m. John S. Thompson; settled in Carroll county, Ohio).

II. John, b.1788; d. 1855; served in the War of 1812; m. Agnes Henderson, b. 1771; d. 1848; settled in Harrison county, Ohio; had issue: 1. Alexander, b. 1805; settled 1825, in Cadiz township, where he d. in January, 1875; m. Catherine Shimer, b. in Ohio, 1813; of Scotch descent; d. May, 1879 (had issue: i. Eliza, m. James M. McGaw; ii. James-H., killed at the battle of Snicker's Gap; iii. J. Calvin, b. March 12, 1842, in Cadiz township; served in the Civil War; m. 1870, Martha G. Thompson, daughter of R. G. and Jane Thompson, residents of Carroll county, Ohio; iv. Mary-H., m. W. S. Haverfield; v. Clarence-H.); 2. Jane, m. —— Clark; 3. Nancy; 4. James, b. 1814; d. April 2, 1880; m. Elizabeth Barr, b. 1829; d. Aug. 6, 1895; daughter of Hugh and Agnes Henderson Barr (had issue: i. Agnes, m. B. F. Oglevee; ii. Hugh; iii. Martha-Jane; iv. Caroline, m. C. O. Hines; v. Elizabeth-B., m. Henry S. Barricklow; vi. Ella; vii. John-Harvey; viii. Rheta-May; ix. Lulu-Irene).

III. Joseph, b. April 28, 1790; d. March 31, 1852; served in the War of 1812; had issue: 1. Gillespie, b. 1820; d. near Cadiz, March 17, 1882; m. May —, 1860, Sarah J. Hines, b. Oct. 29, 1830, daughter of William and Isabella Hitchcock Hines, of Cadiz township (had issue: i. William-H.. a minister, b. near Cadiz, March 14, 1861; ii. Mary-Belle, m. John Keesey; iii. Catherine-May, m. John Barger; iv. Gillespie-Sherman; v. Ida-Alice; vi. Melissa-Jennette; vii. Martha-Alberta); 2. George-L.; 3. Mary-Ann.

IV. James, served in the War of 1812.

V. Nathan, b. 1797; d. 1873. near Wheeling. W. Va.; came with his father to Harrison county, Ohio; m. in Pennsylvania, Harriett Barnett, d. 1877; had issue: 1. John-N., b. May 17, 1820, in Cadiz township; settled in Stock township, 1861; m. Oct. 27, 1842,

Emeline Laveley, b. April 30, 1822; daughter of John and Annie Gorsuch Laveley, natives of Maryland (had issue: i. Henry-L., b. July 29, 1843, in Cadiz township; served in the Civil War; m. April 17, 1866, Mary Elizabeth Barrett, a native of Harrison county, Ohio, daughter of William H. and Eliza Barrett; ii. Harriet-A., m. —— Birney; removed to Tuscarawas county; iii. William-Kinsey, b. Jan. 23, 1854; m. 1875, Anna Humphrey, daughter of William and Jane Law Humphrey; settled in Jewett; iv. Emmet-N., b. December, 1859; settled in Cadiz; m. 1875, Mary A. Finical, daughter of Robert Finical); 2. James-Nathan, b. Oct. 14, 1821, in Cadiz township; m. (1st) 1844, Martha Hitchcock, d. 1856; daughter of Samuel and Isabella Moore Hitchcock, of Harrison county; m. (2d) 1857, Eliza McDougall, born in Harrison county, daughter of Moses McDougall, who had married in Ireland before emigrating to Harrison county (had issue by first wife: i. Nathan; had issue by second wife: ii. Sarah-Alma, m. George F. Hanna; iii. Amanda, m. William H. Wiley; iv. Nancy-Estelle; v. James-Lloyd);3. William-B.;4. Thomas-H.; settled in Indiana; 5. Sarah-Jane; 6. Jemima-H., m. Jeremiah Weaver; settled in Franklin township. Harrison county; 7. Joseph, b. Nov. 15, 1832. in Cadiz township, m. March 15, 1855, Mary Jane Johnston, daughter of Samuel Johnston, of Harrison county (had issue: i. Harriet-Elizabeth, m. James A. Mitchell, of Cadiz township; ii. Kersey-Wood; iii. Bertha-Virginia); 8. Nathan-B., b. Jan. 29, 1835. in Cadiz township; served in the Civil War; m. Nov. 15, 1865, Mary A. Harper, daughter of Samuel and Cassandra Harper, who were among the early settlers of Harrison county; 9. Samuel-Patterson; 10. George-A., served in the Civil War; 11. Nancy-E., m. Neal McCaffrey; settled in Iowa.

JAMES HAWTHORNE, b. in Ireland, 1788; settled in Harrison county, Ohio, before 1819, where he d. 1844; two of his brothers settled in Jefferson county, Ohio; m. Rosanna Stewart, d. aged ninety-two years, daughter of Robert Stewart; had issue: 1. Hannah, m. —— McIlroy, and settled in Washington county. Iowa; 2. Margaret-Ann, m. John McNary, and settled near New

Athens, Harrison county; 3. Nancy-Jane; 4. Arabella, d. aged twelve years; 5. Robert-Creighton, b. Oct. 5, 1819; removed to Muskingum county, Ohio, in 1861, where he d. 1864; m. 1842, Margaret J. Grove, b. in York county, Penn., Aug. 26, 1817, daughter of Francis and Jeanette Grove (had issue: i. Arthur-Allison, b. Feb. 27, 1845; m. Jan. 3, 1878, Jane Eliza Maxwell, a native of Jefferson county, daughter of Samuel and Isabella McMillan Maxwell; ii. Francis-Grove, b. Jan. 25, 1847; iii. Emily-Arabella, b. Oct. 20, 1849; m. James Holmes; settled in Greene county, Ohio; iv. James-Stewart, b. Aug. 2, 1852; settled in Adena, Jefferson county); 6. Samuel-E.; 7. William; 8. Rosanna.

The parents of Margaret J. Hawthorne, Francis and Jeanette Grove, settled in Cadiz township, Harrison county, in 1833, where they resided until the time of their death; the former b. 1782; d. March, 1844; the latter b. 1789; d. 1873; had issue: 1. Emily; 2. Susan; 3. Maria; 4. Charlotta; 5. Margaret-Jane, m. Robert C. Hawthorne; 6. Eleanor-R., m. Oliver R. McNary, and settled in Leavenworth, Kan.; 7. Thomas-Cross, settled in Jefferson county, Ohio; 8. Sarah-Elizabeth, m. Samuel Kyle, and settled in Muskingum county, Ohio; 9. Francis-Pringle, settled in Cadiz township; 10. William-Scott, settled in Kansas.

LANCELOT HEARN, b. in Baltimore, Md., 1794, of Scotch-English descent; removed to eastern Ohio in 1815; settled in Cadiz, Harrison county, Ohio, about 1849; m. Barbara Sutherland Urquhart, daughter of Alexander and Francis Tucker Urquhart, who had settled near Cadiz in 1813 (the former was a native of Scotland, and served in the Revolutionary War; the latter, a native of West Virginia).; had issue: 1. Eliza, b. 1829; d. Feb. 25, 1879; m. Samuel Slemmons; 2. Wesley-Browning, b. in Jefferson county, Oct. 6, 1840; settled in Cadiz: served in the Ohio Legislature. 1890-92; m. 1868, Jane C. Beall. daughter of John and Agnes Vincent Beall. of Cadiz; 3. Albert, settled at Dodgeville, Wis.

JOHN HEASTAN. a native of Somerset county. Penn.; removed to Harrison county before 1827 and settled in Monroe township; m. 1833, Mary Hines, a

native of Westmoreland county, Penn., daughter of Christopher and Jane Jeffers Hines, who settled near Cadiz; had issue, among others: 1. John-Wesley, b. Jan. 8, 1840; m. 1863, Mary J. Bower, daughter of Jacob and Anne Bower.

JOHN HEBERLING, b. 1777; d. in Short Creek township, Harrison county, Ohio, 1864, where he had settled in 1823; served in the War of 1812; son of Andrew Heberling, a native of Germany, who settled in Virginia before 1784; m. in Virginia, Mary Crumley, b. 1780-83; d. 1864-67; had issue:
I. Henry, d. in Jefferson county, Ohio.
II. Eliza, m. James Ady, and settled in Muscatine county, Iowa. III. John, settled in Miles, Jackson county, Iowa.
IV. Hiram, settled in Osage county, Kan. V. William, settled in Greene county, Ill. VI. George-H., b. in Berkeley county, West Va., Feb. 6, 1814; settled in Short Creek township; m. 1835, Matilda Spurrier, a native of Maryland, d. Dec. 23, 1890; daughter of Ralph and Eleanor Cleary Spurrier; had issue: 1. Thomas; 2. William, served in the Civil War; killed at the battle of Perryville, Ky.; 3. Mary-Ellen, m. J. R. Watkins; 4. John; 5. Warner, m. Rosanna Hagan, d. 1881; 6. Andrew, settled in California; 7. Henry, m. Mary J. Stevens, of Short Creek township; 8. Hazlett; 9. Martha. VII. James, settled in Howard county, Mo. VIII. Andrew, settled in Iowa. IX. Rebecca, m. Thomas Lewis, and settled in Dubuque, Iowa. X. Mary, m. Joseph Holmes.
Ralph Spurrier, father of Matilda Heberling, was a native of Maryland, b. 1773; d. April 2, 1848, in Short Creek township, having settled there in 1801; m. March 3, 1801, Eleanor Cleary, b. Dec. 18, 1784; d. June 2, 1869; had issue: 1. John, b. April 3, 1802; 2. Samuel, b. Feb. 21, 1805; 3. Warner, b. Aug. 19, 1807; 4. Sarah, b. Nov. 10, 1809; 5. Richard, b. Sept. 5, 1812; 6. Ruth, b. March 24, 1815; 7. Matilda, b. Sept. 15, 1817; 8. Elizabeth, b. March 7, 1820; 9. Mary-Ann, b. Dec. 5, 1822; 10. Asenath, b. Sept. 20, 1824; 11. William, b. March 22, 1827.

SAMUEL HEDGES, b. in Virginia. Dec. 26, 1783; d. 1865; settled in Cadiz township about 1805; m. in Virginia. 1789, Prudence Dunlap, b. at West Liberty, (West) Virginia, Dec. 20, 1873; d.

Jan. 15, 1850; had issue: 1. Abraham, b. June 30, 1811; d. young; 2. William-Dunlap, b. 1812; d. June, 1867; m. Mary Jane McClelland, b. at Ballanahinch, Ireland, 1824; d. 1897; daughter of John and Jane Beatty McClelland (had issue: i. Rachel, b. 1844; m. Robert Reid Cochran; ii. Norwood, b. 1849; d. 1896; iii. Saran-Jane, b. 1851; m. Alexander Osburn; iv. Margaret-Anne, b. 1854; v. Samuel-Beatty, b. 1857; vi. Martha-Ellen, d. 1864; vii. Clara, d. 1864; viii. Cora, d. 1867; ix. Mary-Emma, m. Beatty Osburn; x. Infant; xi. William-Francis, b. 1867; d. 1870); 3. Sarah, b. Oct. 14, 1814; d. young; 4. Martha, b. April 27, 1816; d.1854; m.Israel Birney; 5. Rachel, b. Oct. 10, 1817; d. 1896; 6. Sarah, b. 1819; d. 1839; m. Samuel Cochran; 7. Margaret, b. January, 1820; d. young; 8. Prudence, b. Nov. 9, 1822; d. 1840; 9. Samuel, b. Jan. 20, 1825; d. 1886; m. 1851, Mrs. Sarah Rowley Welsh, b. in Carroll county, 1827; daughter of Luther Rowley (had issue: i. Martha, m. Samuel Richey; ii. Luther-R.; iii. William-P., b. 1858; m. 1879, Susan Ross, daughter of Aaron Ross; iv. Mary-E., m. William Boyles).

JOHN HENDERSON, a native of Ireland, d. February, 1862, in Rumley township, Harrison county, Ohio, where he had settled in 1817; after emigrating to America, first settled in Maryland, thence removed to Indiana county, Penn., and afterwards located in Harrison county; m. in Hagerstown, Md., —— Henderson, d. May 13, 1877; daughter of George Henderson; had issue, among others: 1. James, b. in Indiana county, Penn., Sept. 10, 1813; d. Nov. 1, 1889; m. October, 1838, Susanna McClintock, a native of Monroe township, daughter of Thomas and Elizabeth Fisher McClintock (had issue, among others: i. John-C., b. July 21, 1839; m. (1st) 1862, Hester Fisher, of North township, d. Jan. 4, 1865; m. (2d) April 2, 1866, Mahala P. Fisher, sister of his first wife, d. Oct. 8, 1877; m. (3d) March 27, 1879, Sarah McPeck, daughter of George McPeck, a resident of Archer township; ii. Thomas; iii. Alexander; iv. Elizabeth-Jane; v. George; vi. Lavina; vii. Barbara; viii. Henry; ix. Walter; x. William-Homer).

WILLIAM HENDERSON, a native of Pennsylvania, removed to Ohio, and, before 1813, settled in Cadiz township,

Harrison county, where he died; m. Nancy Wilkins, a resident of what is now Carroll county, Ohio; had issue, among others: 1. Sarah,m.—— Love; 2. Jane, m. —— Patterson; 3. Catherine, m. —— Trimbull; these three sisters settled near New Athens, Harrison county; 4. Alexander, b. Aug. 9, 1813; settled in Cadiz township; d. March 17, 1883; m. 1843, Margaret Finical, a native of Washington county, Penn., daughter of Isaac and Margaret Finical, who were early settlers in Harrison county (had issue: i. William, b. May 11, 1844; served in the Civil War; m. Dec. 7, 1871, Rachel H. Robison, daughter of James and Mary Barnes Robison, of Archer township, Harrison county; ii. Alvin, a physician, settled in New York; iii. James-O., b. Feb. 26, 1847; m. 1874, Belle Wells, daughter of Charles Wells, of Cadiz township).

JOHN HILBERT, emigrated from Adams county, Penn., to German township, Harrison county, Ohio, about 1833; had issue: 1. Peter; 2. John: 3. Daniel; 4. Henry, b. in Adams county, Penn., 1819; m. (1st) 1845, Anne Waddington; m. (2d) 1853, Margaret Finnicum, daughter of David and Elizabeth Lowmiller Finnicum; 5. Jacob, m. Mary Lowmiller; 6. Elizabeth, m. John Burns; 7. Mary, m. Frederick Trump; 8. Sarah, m. Jacob Bosley; 9. Lydia, m. Edwin Robinson; 10. Katharine, m. Jacob Unger; 11. Sophia, m. Edwin Robinson.

JOHN HINES, see Family of James Ramsey.

RUDOLPH HINES, b. in Germany; d. September-November, 1823, aged ninety; son of John Hines, who came to America before the Revolutionary War; removed to Steubenville, Ohio, in 1796, thence to Virginia in 1806; settled in Harrison county, Ohio, 1814; served in the Revolutionary War; m. Sarah Huff; had issue, twelve children, among whom:

I. William, b. in Allegany county, Md., March 19, 1800; d. September, 1887; m. Feb. 15, 1827, Isabella Hitchcock, b. Jan. 24, 1806; daughter of John and Jane McMahon Hitchcock (the former a native of Maryland, of Irish descent; the latter born in Ireland); had issue: 1. John-R., settled in Clark county, Iowa, 1879; m. 1853, Elizabeth Christy, d. at Murray, Iowa, 1880;

daughter of Robert and Jane Christy, natives of Harrison county; 2. Sarah-Jane, m. Gillespie Haverfield; 3. ———, d. in infancy; 4. Lemuel-Browning, settled in Redfield, Cal.; 5. William-Fletcher, b. February, 1839; served in the Civil War; m. Feb. 7, 1857, Christina Spiker, a native of Harrison county, daughter of Christopher and ªAra Carnes Spiker, early settlers in Harrison county (the former d. 1879; the latter 1870); 6. Mary-Ellen, m. Joseph Mc-Beth, and settled in Deersville; 7. Samuel-Montgomery, settled in Nottingham township; 8. James-McMahon, b. March 5, 1844; settled in Cadiz township; served in the Civil War; m. Nov. 3, 1868, Elmira J. Carson, a native of Harrison county, daughter of Elijah and Margaret Mahaffey Carson; 9. Thomas-Hogg, d. in infancy; 10. Ezra-Lawson, d. aged fourteen years.
II. Daniel. III. James. IV. John. V. Isaac. VI. Samuel. VII. Joseph. VIII. Mary. IX. Martha.

John Carson, d. in Nottingham township, was among the early settlers of Harrison county; Elijah, his son, father of Elmira Hines, was b. 1810; d. November, 1887; m. Margaret Mahaffey, b. in Washington county, Penn., 1808; d. 1884; her mother was a native of Maryland, of Welsh descent; had issue, seven children, of whom: 1. ———, m. Joseph G. Rogers; 2. Elmira-J., m. James M. Hines; 3. ———, m. T. B. Huffman.

THOMAS HITCHCOCK, a native of Maryland, removed to Jefferson county, Ohio, about 1792; settled in Archer township, Harrison county, after 1800; had issue, among others:
I. Samuel, b. in Maryland, 1787; removed to Cadiz township before 1812, where he d. Feb. 3, 1879; m. Isabella Moore; had issue: 1. Margaret; 2. Jane; 3. Isabella; 4. Harriet; 5. Maria; 6. Elizabeth; 7. Mary; 8. Martha; 9. John, b. March 12, 1812; settled in Franklin township, 1841; m. Jan. 8, 1835, Sarah Kelly, d. Sept. 10, 1889; daughter of Hugh and Mary Kelly, of Short Creek township (had issue: i. Isabella, m. Sept. 24, 1862, S. M. Birney; ii. John-A., settled in Cleveland, Ohio; iii. Mary-E., m. A. J. Lever, a minister; iv. Johnson, settled in Washington township; v. Mary; vi. Samuel, twin brother to Mary, m. 1875, Nancy Mc-

Gill, daughter of John McGill, of Franklin township); 10. Thomas.

JAMES HOAGLAND, see account of Michael Conaway.

GABRIEL HOLLAND, a native of Maryland, of English descent, settled in Archer township, Harrison county, Ohio, before 1814; m. in Maryland, Sarah Harriman; had issue, eight children, of whom:
1. Gabriel, b. in Maryland, 1789; d. in Archer township, 1871; m. Susannah Conaway; b. 1784; d. 1861; daughter of Michael and Elizabeth Conaway, of Archer township, pioneers of Harrison county; had issue: 1. John, b. September, 1814; he settled in Cadiz township; m. 1840, Esther West, of Cadiz township, b. 1820; d. April 13, 1889; daughter of Jonathan and Mary Comfort West (had issue: i. Sarah-Jane, m. J. Welling, and settled in Guernsey county, Ohio; ii. Samuel; iii. Elizabeth, m. D. B. Harrison, and settled in Iowa; iv. Martha; v. Susan, b. 1854; d. Feb. 22, 1889; m. C. McCune; vi. Gabriel, d. 1889; vii. Jonathan; viii. Amanda); 2. Sarah; 3. Elizabeth, m. A. Pickens, and settled in Iowa; 4. Mary-Jane; 5. Ellen; 6. Nancy, m. Martin Maholm, and settled in Archer township; 7. Harriet, m. ——— Lewis, and settled in Archer township; 8. Samuel, settled in Archer township.

ROBERT HOLLIDAY, son of Arthur Holliday, b. in the North of Ireland, 1758; d. at Martin's Ferry, Ohio, 1851; emigrated to America about 1793, first settling in the Cumberland Valley, and thence removing to Westmoreland county, Penn.; located in the western part of Harrison county, Ohio, about 1815; m. in Ireland, Rebecca Ramsey, d. 1826; had issue, nine children, of whom: 1. Nancy, m. ——— Cooper, and settled in Henry county, Indiana; 2. Robert, b. Aug. 1, 1792; d. July 5, 1885; served in the War of 1812; settled in Freeport about 1830; m. (1st) March 25, 1817, Frances Melton, b. Nov. 22. 1795; d. Dec. 22, 1818; m. (2d) March 29, 1821, Elizabeth White, b. Dec. 25, 1800; d. Aug. 16, 1872 (had issue by first wife: i. Frances-Melton, b. Nov. 28, 1818; had issue by second wife, thirteen children, of whom: ii. Theodore-Oscar, m. Susan Reaves; iii. Anne, m. 1846, David Winder; iv. Eldred-Glencairn, b. Jan. 19, 1822; m. Jan. 10, 1850, Mary Cun-

ningham, daughter of John and Nancy
Sharp Cunningham).

LEVI HOLLINGSWORTH, a Quaker,
great-great-grandson (through three
ancestors, each named Thomas Hollingsworth) of Valentine Hollingsworth, who emigrated from Belfast,
Ireland, to Pennsylvania, about 1683;
removed to Flushing township, Belmont county, in 1804; had issue: 1.
Elihu, b. in Belmont county, 1813; m.
1839, Lydia Ann Fisher, daughter of
Barrack Fisher, of Pughtown, Va. (had
issue: i. David, b. at Flushing, Ohio,
Nov. 21, 1844; m. April, 1875, Belinda
McBean, daughter of Dr. John Mc-
Bean).

REV. OBADIAH HOLMES, b. in
Manchester, England, about 1606; m.
1636; emigrated with his wife, Catharine, from Preston, Lancashire, and
settled at Salem, Mass., 21st of 11th
month, 1638; removed about 1643-44 to
Rehoboth, R. I., as he was a Baptist and
not allowed to live in the Puritan colony; publicly whipped by the Puritans
at Boston, in September, 1651, on account of his religious opinions, and "for
holding meetings on Lord's Day from
house to house;" served as minister of
the Baptist Church at Newport, R. I.,
from 1652 to 1682; d. Oct. 15, 1682; had
issue: 1. Jonathan, b. about 1637; 2.
John, b. about 1639; 3. Martha, b. 1640;
4. Samuel, b. 1642; 5. Obadiah, b. 1644;
6. Hope, m. —— Taylor; 7. Mary, m.
John Browne; 8. Lydia, m. Captain
John Browne. Of these, Jonathan, d.
1713; m. Sarah Borden; settled at Middletown, Monmouth county, N. J., 1667
(had issue: i. Obadiah; ii. Jonathan;
iii. Samuel; iv. Joseph; v. Sarah, m.
—— Oulde (?); vi. Mary, m. ——
Easton; vii. Catharine, m. —— Whit-
man; viii. Martha, m. —— Tilling-
hast). Obadiah m. —— Cole; settled
at Middletown, N. J., 1663 (had issue,
two sons and two daughters, of whom:
i. Samuel, d. young; ii. Jonathan, d.
Sept. 8, 1715). Rev. Obadiah Holmes,
the emigrant, had about 5,000 descendants living in America as early as
1790.

Descended from one of the above
was, Obadiah Holmes, b. at Trenton,
N. J., 1721; settled in the Virginia
Valley; living in Rockingham county,
Va., about 1768; in Jefferson county,
West Va., about 1771; in Bedford coun-

ty, Penn., about the time of the Revolution; in Strabane township, Washington county, Penn., 1784-85; and
later in Brooke county, West Va.,
where he d. about 1796; m. in New
Jersey, Mary Clum, d. in York township, Jefferson county, Ohio, 1812; had
issue:
I. John; served in the Revolutionary
War; was taken a prisoner and died
in service.
II. William.
III. Obadiah.
IV. Isaac, b. in New Jersey, April 29,
1764; removed with his parents to Virginia; served in the War of 1812; settled in what is now Carroll county,
Ohio, 1814, where he d. June 9, 1851; m.
in Virginia, 1794, Elizabeth McNabb, b.
July 24, 1772, in Shepherdstown, Va.;
daughter of George and Martha Mc-
Nabb and sister to Sarah McNabb; had
issue: 1. Martha, d. in Kenton, Ohio,
aged eighty-seven years; m. (1st) Joseph Wilson; m. (2d) William Leaper;
2. Clum, d. aged twenty-three years; 3.
Sarah, d. in Ottumwa, Iowa, aged
eighty-five years; m. Jacob Millisack;
4. Nancy, d. in infancy; 5. Mary, m.
James Price, and settled at Leesville,
Carroll county, Ohio; 6. Susannah, m.
Joseph Masters, and settled at Connotton, Harrison county; 7. George-Wash-
ington, b. Dec. 30, 1807; settled in
North township, 1843, where he d.
June 26, 1887; m. (1st) 1837, in North
township, Mary Cripliver; m. (2d)
Amanda Jenkins; m. (3d) Emily Stratton (had issue: i. Jacob-M.; ii. Isaac-
C., settled in Columbus, Ohio; iii.
Samuel-W., settled in Kansas; iv.
John-D.; v. Luther-L.; vi. Edward-S.;
vii. Martha-E.; viii. Phœbe-A.; ix.
Mary-Alice; x. Ora-A., m. J. M. Har-
rison, and settled in Washington State;
xi. Emma, m. Charles Crawford; settled
in New Philadelphia, Ohio); 8. Samuel,
settled in Leesville, Carroll county; 9.
Elizabeth, m. Sampson Jenkins, and
settled near Salem, Jefferson county,
Ohio; 10. John-McNabb, d. in Connotton, aged sixty-five years; m. Emily
——, who settled near Des Moines,
Iowa.
V. Jacob, b. in Rockingham county,
Virginia, Dec. 8, 1768; d. at Kenton,
Ohio, Oct. 14, 1841; m. on Buffalo Creek,
Brooke county, West Va., 1791, Elizabeth Huff, b. May 22, 1772; d. Jan. 27,
1857; shortly after his marriage he was

employed by the Government as an Indian scout, and in company with his brother-in-law, Kinsey Dickerson, and another man, was thus employed for three years, receiving for his services a section of land in Short Creek township, Jefferson county, near Mt. Pleasant; here he settled in 1796; had issue, among others: 1. (a daughter), m. —— Wilkin; 2. ——, m. Augustine Bickerstaff, of Steubenville, Ohio; 3. ——, m. Nathaniel Moore, of Little York, Jefferson county.

VI. Joseph, b. in Shepherdstown, Jefferson county, West Va., Jan. 27, 1771; removed to what is now Jefferson county, Ohio, before 1799; settled in Short Creek township, Harrison county, about 1800, where he d. April 20, 1868; served in the Indian Wars, and as an officer in the War of 1812; served in the Ohio Senate, 1832-34; m. in Jefferson county, Sarah McNabb, b. 1783; d. Feb. 10, 1862; sister to Elizabeth McNabb and daughter of George and Martha McNabb, of Scotch descent, early settlers near Mount Pleasant, Ohio; had issue: 1. George, b. 1799; d. 1886; m. (1st) Hannah Lynn; m. (2d) 1824, Tacy Thompson; m. (3d) 183—, Hannah Mansfield, daughter of Thomas and Mary Hill Mansfield (the former a native of England, b. 1757; d. 1844; the latter b. 1767; d. 1854) (had issue by first wife: i. Joseph, b. 1825; d. 1889; m. Mary McConnell; ii. Rezin, b. 1827; m. Emeline Mansfield; had issue by second wife: iii. Emma, m. 1864, Kersey Wood Kinsey); 2. Mary, m. John Glazner; 3. Elizabeth, m. (1st) William Dickerson; m. (2d) Isaac Thomas; 4. Cynthia, m. John Styres; 5. Asa, b. in Short Creek township, Dec. 4, 1806; d. Jan. 3, 1891; m. 1837, Mary McCoy, daughter of Thomas and Hannah McCoy, of Athens township, Harrison county (had issue: i. James-Taylor, served in the Civil War; settled in Columbus, Ohio; ii. Susanna, m. Albert Harrison, and settled in Cadiz; iii. Abram, served in the Civil War; settled in New Philadelphia; iv. Emeline; v. Sarah-Elizabeth, m. Henry Stringer, of Short Creek township; vi. Wilson; settled near Smithfield, Jefferson county; vii. Mary-Ellen, m. Samuel Dickerson, and settled in Athens township; viii. Henrietta, m. C. A. McCleary, and settled at Cadiz; ix. Oliver-Wendell, a Methodist Episcopal

minister, settled in Kent, Ohio; ix. Clifton-A.); 6. Abraham, b. in Short Creek township, Dec. 1, 1808; d. May 3, 1880; m. (1st) 1836, Rachel Mansneld, b. 1814; d. Feb. 12, 1854; daughter of Thomas Mansneld, of Jefferson county; m. (2d) 1856, Phœbe Ann Ekey, a native of Jefferson county, daughter of Andrew and Ann Howden Ekey (had issue by first wife: i. Joseph-M., b. 1847; d. 1871; m. 1870, Chloe A. McCleary, b. 1850, daughter of Ephraim and Mary A. Gillespie McCleary; ii. William; had issue by second wife: iii. ——, d. in infancy; iv. Wesley-A., b. in Short Creek township, Aug. 19, 1859; m. 1884, Minerva Conwell, daughter of John and Mary Conwell, of Cadiz); 7. Martha, m. John Webb, and settled at New Athens; 8. Joseph, m. Sarah Moore, and settled at Hopedale; 9. Sarah, m. James Haverfield; 10. Susan, m. (1st) Joseph Webb; m. (2d) Joseph Dunlap; 11. John, d. aged eight years.

VII. Samuel.

VIII. Elizabeth.

IX. Margaret.

Andrew Ekey, father of Phœbe Ekey Holmes, was b. in Pennsylvania, 1791; d. 1873; was of Irish descent; settled in Jefferson county, Ohio, 1801; m. Ann Howden, b. 1799; d. Feb. 5, 1890; had issue: 1. Andrew; 2. Margaret; 3. Mary-Ann, m. Benjamin Barkhurst, and settled in St. Clairsville, Ohio; 4. Phœbe-Ann, m. Abraham Holmes; 5. David; 6. Edward, settled in Jefferson county; 7. John-H.; 8. James, settled in Jefferson county; 9. Wesley.

WILLIAM HOLMES, b. 1782, son of William Francis Holmes, a native of Ireland, who settled in Pennsylvania, removed to Green township, Harrison county, Ohio, about 1802, where he d. Jan. 22, 1861; m. (1st) in Pennsylvania, Elizabeth Crouch, b. 1790; d. 1849; m. (2d) Matilda Thaker, d. in Mount Pleasant, Jefferson county; had issue by first wife: 1. Isaac, b. in Green township, where he d. Feb. 12, 1884; m. 1833, Jane Vincent; d. July 17, 1884; daughter of Dr. Thomas Vincent, of Green township (had issue: i. Sarah; ii. William-F., b. Dec. 25, 1836; m. (1st) Oct. 10, 1860, Amanda S. Baxter, b. April 25, 1836; d. Oct. 13, 1881; daughter of Samuel Baxter, of Green township; m. (2d) Dec. 24, 1884, Hannah J. Starr, daughter of William Starr, of Wayne township, Jefferson county, Ohio; iii. Thomas-V., b. March 14, 1840; m. Oct. 21, 1869, Melissa Jane Harrah, b. Feb. 13, 1847, daughter of John Harrah, of Jefferson county; iv. Eliza-Jane; v. Martha; vi. Matilda; vii. Mary; viii. Josephine; ix. Amanda; x. ———, d. in infancy; xi. ———, d. in infancy; xii. Winfield-S.); 2. Susan; 3. Sarah; 4. Elizabeth.

HARVEY HOST, a native of Germany, emigrated, before 1800, to Pennsylvania, where he died; m. Nancy Fulton (b. 1776; d. Jan. 11, 1845), who after the death of her husband, married (2d) John Moffat, and removed to Harrison county, Ohio; had issue by first husband (surname Host): 1. Harvey; 2. Samuel, b. in Pennsylvania, Dec. 20, 1801; settled in Green township, Harrison county, where he died Nov. 2, 1889; m. (1st) Aug. 27, 1825, Louisa Oxley; d. June 12, 1834; m. (2d) April 5, 1838, Jane Hines, a daughter of William Hines, of Harrison county (had issue by first wife: i. Henry; ii. James; iii. Mary-Ann; iv. John, b. in Jefferson county, Sept. 27, 1831; m. April 22, 1858, Ruth A. McMillan, b. Aug. 31, 1835; a daughter of John McMillan, of Carroll county, Ohio; v. Louisa; had issue by second wife; vi. William-H.; vii. Sarah; viii. David; ix. Amos; x. Eliza-Jane); 3. James; 4. John; 5. William; 6. Eliza.

HENRY HOUSER, b. in Kentucky, 1786; settled in Cadiz, Harrison county, Ohio, before 1825; d. Sept. 23, 1855; served in the War of 1812; m. at Bennett's Creek, Frederick county, Maryland, 1824, Susannah Ramsower, b. 1791; d. 1867; had issue: 1. William-Lambdin, b. June 17, 1825; m. Sept. 24, 1857, Sarah Virginia Hall, of Washington, Guernsey county, Ohio, daughter of Edward and Henrietta Catherine Roberts Hall (had issue: Francis-E., Mary-Virginia, Ellsworth-Wilson, William-Henry, Thomas-Edward, Isabel-McFadden, and Henrietta-Katharine); 2. Wilson- Lee, b. April 1, 1828; 3. Warnetta, m. William Stroud.

MICHAEL HUFF, of Brooke county, Va., m. Hannah Doddridge; had issue: 1. Joseph, an early Indian scout and fighter of Harrison county, d. in Short Creek township; 2. Michael, killed by the Indians on the Mississippi; 3. Elizabeth, b. May 22, 1772; d. at Kenton, Ohio, Jan. 27, 1857; m. 1791, Jacob Holmes, b. in Rockingham county, Va., Dec. 8, 1768; d. at Kenton, Ohio, Oct. 14, 1841; 4. William, an early Indian scout and fighter of Harrison county, d. in Short Creek township; 5. John, m. Sarah Johnson; d. at Columbia, near Cincinnati, Ohio, 1842; 6. Samuel, d. in Highland county, Ohio, about 1846; 7. Eleazer, d. in Highland county, Ohio, about 1833.

EDWARD HUGHES, of Scotch-Irish descent, settled before 1800 near Rising Sun, in Cecil county, Md., where he died; had issue: 1. Robert-M.; 2. Sarah, m. ——— Smith; 3. Rebecca, m. ——— Poole; 4. Edward, b. Oct. 30, 1814; removed about 1834 to Port Deposit, Md., thence to Philadelphia; located in Cadiz, Harrison county, Ohio, in 1839; afterwards settling in New Athens, where he d. April 5, 1889; m. in New Athens, Sarah Ann Brown, daughter of James and Jane Welch Brown (had issue: i. Hester-A.; ii. Eliza-Jane, m. Prof. Thomas M. Sewell, of New Athens; iii. Oliver-P.; iv. John-W., settled in Springfield, Ohio; v. George-W., settled in Hopkins, Mo.; vi. Mary-E., m. Rev. Oliver Holmes, and settled in Kent, Ohio; vii. James-C.; viii. Edgar; ix. Theodore, settled in Iowa; x. Vandorn; xi. and xii. Twins, d. in infancy.

James Brown, father of Sarah Ann Hughes, was b. in county Derry, Ireland, in 1785; settled near New Athens, Harrison county, about 1814; d. 1860; his wife was b. 1788; d. 1865; had issue: 1. George, settled in St. Clairsville, Ohio; 2. Joseph, settled near Flushing, Belmont county, Ohio; 3. Mary-Ann; 4. Jane; 5. Margaret, m. James Rankin, and settled in Missouri; 6. Sarah-Ann, m. Edward Hughes.

THOMAS HUNTER, d. in Newberry township, York county, Penn., before Nov. 19, 1777; m. Mary Canon; had issue, Nancy. James, Ephraim, Jane, Mary, of whom:

James, b. Dec. 6, 1738; d. Jan. 27, 1809; settled on Fourteen Mile Run, Unity township, Westmoreland county, Penn., about 1768-70; served in the Revolutionary War, and was one of the founders of Unity Presbyterian Church; m. Elizabeth McDonald; had issue: I. Ephraim. II. Joseph. III. Sarah. IV. William. V. Mary. VI. James, b. in

5

Westmoreland county, Penn., Feb. 4, 1777; d. in Wayne county, Ohio, Sept. 16, 1829; m. Agnes (Nancy) Sloan, b. March 28, 1777; d. Aug. 15, 1858; daughter of —— Sloan; had issue: 1. Elizabeth; 2. Samuel; 3. Joseph-R., b. in Westmoreland county, Penn., May 26, 1804; d. at Cadiz, April 4, 1886; m. March 16, 1835, Letitia McFadden, b. 1812; d. April 13, 1883; daughter of Samuel and Lydia Stafford McFadden, of Cadiz (had issue: i. Cyrus-James; a Presbyterian minister; settled in Uhrichsville, Ohio; ii. Samuel-McFadden; settled at Newark, Ohio, where he became a judge; iii. Mary, b. 1840; d. 1858; iv. Lydia, d. Feb. 28, 1886; m. William H. Arnold, of Cadiz; v. Charlotte, m. Alexander J. Hammond, of Cadiz; vi. William-Henry; settled at Chillicothe, Ohio; vii. George-Frederick; settled at Chillicothe, Ohio); 4. Isaac; 5. John-Sloan; 6. James; 7. Nancy-Sloan. VII. Thomas. VIII. Samuel. IX. Ralph.

JOHN HURFORD, b. in Culpepper county, Virginia, son of Samuel Hurford, whose father, John Hurford, was an English Quaker; m. in Virginia, Sarah Hayes, a native of that State; removed to Harrison county while it was still a part of Jefferson; had issue: 1. Evan, b. in Virginia; m. in Jefferson county, Sarah Hall, a native of North Carolina, who was a member of the Friends' Church; settled about five and one-half miles southeast of Cadiz, where they died, both in their ninety-first years (had issue: i. Aquila; ii. Joseph, b. in Cadiz township, 1809; m. Rebecca Ann Welsh, of Washington county, Penn.; d. in New Brighton, 1885; settled in Pittsburgh; had issue, one daughter and one son, both of whom died in infancy; iii. Mary-Ann; iv. Christian; v. Sarah; vi. John; vii. Hannah; viii. Rachel); 2. John; 3. Samuel; 4. Rachel; 5. Sarah; 6. Mary; 7. Ann.

SOLOMON INSLEY, b. in Maryland about 1770; d. in Guernsey county, Ohio; m. Britannia Dean, b. in Maryland; had issue:
I. Jemima.
II. Sarah.
III. Rebecca.
IV. Eunice.
V. Hudson.
VI. Micajah, b. in Maryland, 1791;

d. 1845, in Nottingham township, Harrison county, Ohio; came to Ohio with his parents; m. Clarissa Hawse, b. in Maryland, 1801; d. 1885; had issue: 1. Asbury; 2. Eunice; 3. Sarah, b. March 18, 1829; m. Jan. 1, 1857, James Barclay, b. in county Derry, Ireland, Sept. 23, 1823; d. April 21, 1885 (had issue: i. Joseph; ii. David, settled at Dennison, Ohio; iii. John; iv. Clara; v. William; vi. Benjamin, settled at Poughkeepsie, N. Y.; vii. James; viii. Annie); 4. Maria, m. —— Kennedy, of Tuscarawas county, Ohio; 5. Robert, settled in Kansas; 6. John, settled in Uhrichsville, Ohio; 7. Rachel, settled in Tuscarawas county; 8. Benjamin, served in the Civil War; killed at the battle of Petersburg, August, 1864.

JOHN JAMISON, b. in Ematris Parish, near Coote Hill, county Cavan, Ireland, 1743; d. near West Middletown, Washington county, Penn., Jan. 28, 1811; m. (1st) about 1765, ——; d. before 1772; m. (2d) about 1772, Sarah McFadden Gilmore, d. Dec. 29, 1835 (widow of Nathaniel Gilmore), of Coote Hill, county Cavan, Ireland; emigrated to America with his family and his wife's two children by her first marriage (see Family of Nathaniel Gilmore, p. 504) about 1773 (?), first locating in Shearman's Valley, near Newport, Perry county, Penn.; removed to Washington county and located in Chartiers Creek about 1782, afterwards settling near Buffalo Creek in Independence township, three miles southwest of West Middletown; with his second wife; buried in Mt. Hope graveyard, near West Middletown; had issue by first wife:
1. Andrew, b. 1766; d. at Cadiz, Ohio, March 30, 1859; m. about 1792, Nancy McKee, b. 1775; d. at Cadiz, Ohio, April 18, 1855; removed from Washington county, Penn., to Harrison county, Ohio, about 1830 (had issue: i. John, d. in Huron county, Ohio; m. Sarah Mulholm; ii. Barkley, b. 1795; d. Oct. 23, 1869; m. Margaret Patterson, d. 1875; iii. Elizabeth, d. about 1861; m. John Forbes and removed to Illinois; iv. Isabel, m. Levi Hamilton, b. 1805; d. April 6, 1881; v. Mary, d. about 1860; m. James Hutchison, and removed to Illinois; vi. Samuel, d. about 1825; vii. Isaac, b. 1808; d. Jan. 7, 1840; viii. Alexander, d. in Belmont county,

Ohio, March 18, 1856; m. Mary Mc-
Conahy).

2. Samuel, b. 1768; d. Nov. 4, 1855; m.
(1st) about 1797, Martha Barber, d.
about 1823; emigrated to America
about 1801; m. (2d) Mrs. Sarah Cope, d.
about 1850, all buried at West Middletown (had issue by first wife: i. John,
b. 1798; d. Feb. 14, 1875; m. [1st] about
1819, Mary Nealy, m. [2d] Ann Smith;
ii. Elizabeth, m. John Dinsmore, and
settled in Jefferson county, Ohio, near
Steubenville).

John Jamison had issue by second
wife:

3. Mary, b. 1773; d. 1850; m. about
1793, Robert Law, b. 1771; d. 1860; settled at New Lexington, Perry county,
Ohio, about 1835, where they are buried
(had issue: i. Thomas, b. 1794; d. 1878;
m. Mary Buchanan, and removed to
Iowa; ii. Sarah, b. 1795; m. about 1812,
Aaron Johnson; settled in Perry county, Ohio; iii. John, m. Mary Perry, settled in Perry county, Ohio; iv. Jane,
b. 1797; d. March 16, 1882; m. Robert
Welch, b. Feb. 26, 1787; d. Aug. 21,
1866; settled at Bloomfield, Muskingum
county, Ohio; v. Robert, d. about 1825;
vi. William, d. 1883; m. Sarah Dodan;
settled at Xenia, Ohio; vii. Mary, m.
about May, 1829, James McFadden, b.
1804; settled near Cadiz, Ohio; viii.
James, b. 1809; d. May, 1884; m. [1st]
Rebecca Patterson; m. [2d] ———
Skinner; settled at Monmouth, Ill.; ix.
Samuel, m. Hannah Brown; settled in
Iowa; x. Andrew, b. June 16, 1816; m.
[1st] ——— Hull; m. [2d] ——— Smith,
d. 1895; settled in Perry county, Ohio).

4. John, b. 1774; d. Oct. 16, 1848; settled near Cadiz. Ohio, about 1801; a
soldier of the War of 1812; m. about
1800, Ann Craig, b. 1780; d. Aug. 30,
1847, both buried at Cadiz (had issue:
i. Walter, b. Feb. 24, 1801; d. at Cadiz,
Ohio, 1883; m. [1st] 1828, Martha Beattie. daughter of James and Jane Reynolds Beattie. of Short Creek township,
b. 1807-8; d. Jan. 21, 1835; m. [2d] 1837,
Mary Snyder, daughter of Martin
Snyder).

5. Margaret. b. 1775; d. July 17, 1873;
m. about 1792, Thomas McKeaver, b.
1768; d. June 27, 1861; removed from
Washington county, Penn., to Perry
county, Ohio, 1834; both buried at
Iliff's M. E. Church, Perry county,
Ohio (had issue: i. Thomas, d. young;
ii. Sarah, b. 1798; m. about 1815, John

Dodds; iii. John, m. [1st] Elizabeth
Rogers; m. [2d] Emily Rogers, sister
of Elizabeth; settled near Morristown,
Belmont county, Ohio; iv. Ann, b. 1796;
m. Lewis Lunsford; settled near Wheeling, West Va.; v. Mary, m. George
Bushfield; settled in Illinois; vi. Margaret, d. 1873; m. Joseph Lane; vii.
Barbara, b. 1817; d. Dec. 13, 1876; m.
Jeremiah Driggs, b. 1804; d. May 25,
1867; both buried at Iliff's Church,
Perry county, Ohio; viii. Nancy, b.
1806; m. about 1831, Robert Scott; settled in Iowa; ix. Eliza, d. Nov. 5, 1885;
m. Ephraim Knoowy; settled in Perry
county, Ohio; x. Martha, m. ——— De-
Long; xi. Joseph, m. ——— Alexander;
settled at Olathe, Kan.; xii. Samuel,
m. ——— Wylie; settled in Perry county, Ohio; xiii. William, m. ——— Hol-
lenbach; xiv. Jane, m. John Yost).

6. Nancy, d. 1862; m. about 1798,
Robert McBroom, d. 1856; both buried
at Lower Buffalo, Brooke county, West
Va. (had issue: i. John, b. March, 1799;
d. Feb. 25, 1895; m. [1st] about 1827,
Elizabeth Griffa, d. Sept. 21, 1858; m.
[2d] 1860, Margaret Moore, b. 1808; d.
August, 1866; all three buried at Iliff's
Church, Perry county, Ohio; ii. Mary,
m. John Dickey; iii. William, d. in
Ohio; iv. Andrew, d. in Brooke county,
West Va., about 1850; v. Thomas, m.
[1st] Margaret Anderson; m. [2d]
——— Griffa; vi. Samuel, m. about 1834,
——— Henry; vii. Sarah, m. about 1835,
Christopher Hootman, d. in Brooke
county, West Va.; viii. Jane, d. about
1838; ix. Nancy, d. 1863; x. Robert, m.
about 1846, Rebecca Haggarty; xi.
David).

7. William, b. 1782; d. unm,. May 26,
1860; buried in Mt. Hope graveyard.

8. Elizabeth, b. 1785; d. Dec. 24, 1857;
m. 1803, Samuel McFadden, b. 1778; d.
July 2, 1837; settled near Cadiz, Ohio,
where both are buried (had issue: i.
James, b. 1804; d. June, 1874; m. May,
1829, Mary Law; ii. Sarah, b. 1807; d.
Oct. 14, 1841; m. Samuel Carnahan; iii.
Eliza, m. John Dickerson; iv. John, d.
July 4, 1881; m. about 1835, Margaret
McFadden; v. Samuel, d. March, 1863;
m. about 1834, Margaret Rankin; vi.
Jane, m. Adam Dickerson; vii. Alex-
ander, d. in California; m. about 1842,
Mary McFadden; viii. Margaret, m.
——— Dunlap).

9. Robert. b. 1788; d. Aug. 3, 1832; m.
(1st) 1812, Jane Hill, b. 1787; d. March

26, 1829; m. (2d) Dec. 3, 1830, Margaret Anderson, b. 1798; d. May 25, 1871; all buried at Mt. Hope graveyard, Washington county (had issue: i. John, b. April 8, 1813; d. Sept. 23, 1872; m. Feb. 8, 1840, Sarah Ralston; b. May 22, 1812; d. May 25, 1881; settled at Bloomfield, Muskingum county, Ohio; ii. Thomas, b. Aug. 31, 1815; m. April 18, 1848, Nancy Moore, b. Feb. 9, 1819; iii. Sarah, b. May 13, 1819; d. Sept. 15, 1893; iv. Samuel, b. Dec. 11, 1822; m. [1st] August, 1846, Susannah Herron, d. September, 1850; m. [2d] March 5, 1863, Mrs. Nancy [Lawrence] Patterson; v. William, b. Oct. 22, 1824; d. Jan. 26, 1893; m. [1st] Oct. 8, 1851, Mary Stewart; m. [2d] Margaret Anderson, b. 1798; d. 1871; settled at Keokuk, Iowa; vi. Robert, b. June 14, 1832; m. March, 1858, Elizabeth Hutchinson).

10. Sarah, b. 1789; d. June 25, 1880; m. 1813, Robert Graham, b. 1773; d. December, 1863; both buried in South Buffalo graveyard (had issue: i. John, b. May, 1814; ii. Robert, b. July, 1815; d. May 18, 1878; iii. Mary, d. November, 1887; m. about 1850, Robert Noble; iv. William, m. April, 1846, Susannah Jamison; settled at Indianola, Iowa; v. Sarah, m. —— Buchanan; settled near West Alexander, Penn.; vi. Margaret, m. about 1860, —— Chambers; vii. Jane, d. young; viii. Samuel, d. young).

PHILIP JARVIS, of German descent, b. in Baltimore county, Md., 1785; d. in Harrison county, Ohio, 1866; settled in Belmont county, Ohio, about 1811; m.in Baltimore county, Md., Mary Barnett, b. 1789; d. 1855; had issue: 1. Jacob, b. January, 1815; settled in Moorefield township, Harrison county, 1845; m. Oct. 6, 1842, Eliza M. O'Brien, b. 1814; daughter of Ezekiel O'Brien (had issue: i. Frank; ii. Mary, m. Samuel McConnell; iii. Jane, m. Albert Quigley; iv. Eliza-A., m. John Perry).

ALEXANDER JOHNSON, b. in county Tyrone, Ireland, 1772; emigrated to America and settled at Wilmington, Del., in 1783, thence removed to Butler county, Penn., and in 1814 settled near Jefferson, German township, Harrison county, where he d. 1869; m. in Pittsburg, Mrs. Eleanor Brown Work (widow of William Work), b. 1787, in Baltimore, Md.; d. 1862; had issue: 1. Andrew, d. in Sparta, Ill.; 2. John, b.

1814; d. 1875; 3. Nancy; 4. Alexander, b. Aug. 18, 1818; settled in Rumley township about 1883; m. Dec. 7, 1852, Margaret Galbraith, daughter of Samuel Galbraith, who with his wife, was a native of Ireland, and who removed from Pennsylvania to Harrison county (had issue: i. John; ii. Samuel; iii. Alexander, settled in Columbus, Ohio; iv. Ellen-Jane; v. Isabella-Ann, m. Michael Finical); 5. Mary, m. Joseph Hamilton.

HENRY JOHNSON, b. ——; d. 1850; removed from Allegheny county, Penn., to Harrison county, Ohio, before 1812, and settled in Moorefield township; m. Catherine ——, b. ——; d. ——; had issue: 1. Henry-M., m. 1824, Margaret Gibson (?); 2. William-C.; a physician; m. 1836, Jane McFadden, daughter of Samuel and Lydia Stafford McFadden; 3. Wesley; 4. Asbury-F., m. Rebecca Sloan, daughter of Matthew M. and Elizabeth Grimes Sloan; removed to Laramie, Wyoming; 5. Belinda, m. 1829, Dr. John McBean, of Cadiz, b. 1797; d. Jan. 7, 1875; 6. Julianna (?), m. James Tallman; 7. Harriet, m. 1836, George W.McPherson, b. 1811; d. Jan. 10, 1880; 8. Catherine, m. —— Price.

WILLIAM JOHNSON, b. in Pennsylvania, May 26, 1776; removed, 1804, to Short Creek township, Harrison county, Ohio, where he d. Jan. 7, 1855; m. Agnes Pickens, b. in Pennsylvania, May 15, 1781; d. Feb. 24, 1864; had issue: 1. Susanna, m. —— Fisher; 2. Mary-L.; 3. Margaret; 4. John; 5. Martha; 6. Josiah; 7. Basil; 8. Temperance, m. —— Neal; 9. William; 10. Elizabeth, m. —— Arnold; 11. Agnes, m. —— Wilson; 12. Rebecca; 13. Abram; 14. Albert, b. Nov. 30, 1823; d. Dec. 10, 1886; m. 1861, Rachel Conaway, daughter of Charles and Frances Arnold Conaway.

Charles Conaway, father of Rachel Conaway Johnson, removed from Maryland and located in Archer township, Harrison county, about 1805; removed with his wife to Richland county, Ohio, 1861, where he d. 1870; m. Dec. 17, 1819, Frances Arnold, d. 1872, daughter of Benjamin and Comfort Arnold, residents of Maryland; had issue: 1. Benjamin; 2. John; 3. Sophia; 4. Ann; 5. William; 6. Elizabeth; 7. Michael; 8. Mary; 9. Charles; 10.

Rachel, m. Albert Anderson; 11. Susannah; 12. Frances-Jane; 13. Enoch-W., served in the Civil War; killed August, 1862, in the battle of Perryville.

WILLIAM JOHNSON, a native of Ireland, d. June 4, 1829; removed from Washington county, Penn., to Short Creek township, Harrison county, Ohio, about 1814, where his son, John, had settled in 1802; m. in Westmoreland county, Penn., Elizabeth Laughlin, d. Jan. 10, 1816; had issue: I. John. settled in Harrison county, in 1802. II. William. III. Richard. IV. Alexander. V. Robert. VI. James, b. in Washington county, Penn., April 12, 1793; d. Nov. 9, 1863; m. March 19, 1818, Mary Simpson. b. May 28, 1794; d. Jan. 25, 1881; daughter of James Simpson; had issue: 1. Margaret, b. Oct. 6, 1819; m. Sept. 18. 1845, Samuel Muchmore, d. Aug. 21, 1889 (had issue: i. Albert, b. Nov. 6, 1847; d. Dec. 28, 1878; ii. Martha. b. July 29, 1850: m. Dec. 3, 1868, John Tallman; iii. William, b. June 29, 1853; m. March 11, 1886. Anna Tidball); 2. Elizabeth-J., b. Feb. 12. 1821; 3. Mary-Simpson, b. July 5, 1823; m. June 28. 1854, John Dickerson. d. April 12, 1865 (had issue: i. James-H., b. May 3, 1855; m. Oct. 1, 1879, Eva Parkinson; ii. Anna-M., b. Nov. 16, 1856; m. Feb. 1, 1882, William H. Hunter; iii. Ruth, b. Dec. 11. 1857; d. April 19, 1887; iv. Lewis, b. Jan. 16, 1859; d. Feb. 4, 1864; v. Flora-Bell, b. Oct. 15, 1865; m. Jan. 1, 1890, Isaac B. Scott); 4. Sarah, b. Dec. 30. 1825; d. April 8. 1887; m. Oct. 8, 1846, William Boals (had issue: i. James, b. April 24, 1848; m. Aug. 11. 1876. Mary Walker); 5. Catherine, b. Oct. 15, 1830; 6. William-H., b. May 4, 1833; m. Oct. 11, 1877, Mary Ann Parkinson. daughter of Thomas Parkinson, of Green township, Harrison county. VII. Samuel. VIII. Ann. IX. Catherine. X. Mary. XI. Elizabeth.

SAMUEL R. JOHNSTON, of Scotch-Irish descent, b. in Baltimore, Md., Dec. 3, 1798; removed with his mother to Charleston, S. C.. about 1800, where he remained until 1824, and then located in Monroe township, Harrison county, Ohio; d. Nov. 10, 1883; m. July 20, 1826, Rebecca Barnhill. b. 1807, in Harrison county; d. Aug. 23, 1873; daughter of William and Mary Barnhill, natives of Ireland, who settled in Harrison coun-

ty; had issue, eleven children, of whom: 1. William-B., settled at Connotton, Ohio; 2. Mary, m. Joseph McKelveen, and settled in Scio, Harrison county; 3. Joseph-E., b. Aug. 11, 1832; served in the Civil War; m. Jan. 26, 1865, Hannah S. Smith, b. near Laceysville, daughter of William P. and Margaret Smith, early settlers in Harrison county; 4. Margaret, m. Jacob Norrick; settled in Nodaway county, Mo.; 5. Rebecca, m. Simeon Smith, and settled at Tappan, Ohio; 6. Elizabeth, m. Daniel Smith, and settled at Laceysville; 7. Cecilia, m. Jonathan Manbeck, and settled at Des Moines, Iowa; 8. Samuel-R., served in the Civil War.

JOHN KAIL, b. in Pennsylvania about 1775, son of John Kail; d. March-May, 1821; settled in German township, Harrison county, Ohio, 1800; m. Catherine Rouch, b. in Pennsylvania about 1775-85; d. 1870; had issue: I. Henry. II. Frederick. III. John. IV. Mary. V. Margaret. VI. Nancy. VII. Anna. VIII. Elizabeth. IX. George. X. Jacob, b. in Pennsylvania, 1798; d. in German township, Harrison county, Ohio, 1874; served in the War of 1812; m. Mary Whitmore, b. 1798; d. 1852; had issue: 1. Elizabeth, m. Jacob Bosley; 2. George; 3. Lucinda, settled in the West; 4. Samuel; 5. John-R., b. Jan. 13, 1826; d. September, 1890; m. Nov. 1, 1853, Elizabeth Tedrow, of Rumley township, Harrison county, daughter of George and Elizabeth Hardsock Tedrow; 6. Lavina, settled in Kansas; 7. Hance-W., b. March 11, 1829; settled in Rumley township,1857; m. August. 1854, Elizabeth Bricker, b. May 2, 1838; d. Oct. 1, 1889. daughter of Henry and Mary Ann Smith Bricker; 8. Enoch,settled at Conrad Grove, Grundy county, Iowa.

JAMES KANE, b. in Ireland; d. in Zanesville, Ohio, about 1818; m. in Cadiz township, Anne Porter, whose parents were natives of Pennsylvania; had issue: 1. William, b. 1813; d. 1895; m. 1839, Mary Minerva Gray, b. 1823; d. 1882; daughter of Jeremiah and Margaretta Taylor Gray (the former from Long Island, the latter from Wales); (had issue: i. Rebecca, m. 1879. George Marple; ii. William-Henry-Harrison, m. Mary Kennedy; iii. James-Jeremiah, m. Ida McMillan; iv. Margaretta; v. Elizabeth-Phillips, m. 1888, Frederick

Carmen; vi. Mary-Maritia, m. William McGrew; vii. Jessie-Lee); 2. Hugh; 3. Margaret, m. Josiah Craig; 4. Martha-Anne, b. 1817; d. 1897.

MATTHEW KENNEDY, b. in Scotland, 1765-67; d. 1847; emigrated to America, and settled in Georgetown, D. C., before 1802, where he m. Christina Hines, d. 1836; removed to Harrison county about 1811; had issue: 1. William-C., m. Sarah Wyckoff; 2. Citizen-J., m. Maria Moore; 3. John-L., m. Matilda Ourant; 4. Mary-A., d. young; 5. Napoleon-Bonaparte, b. November, 1801; d. 1889; m. 1826, at Cadiz, Mary Gilmore, b. 1805; d. 1873; daughter of Samuel and Elizabeth Buchanan Gilmore (had issue: i. Samuel-Gilmore, b. 1827; m. Mary Ensley; ii. Elizabeth, b. 1829; d. 1851; m. Levi Morris; iii. Sarah-Jane, b. 1832; m. Hugh Patterson Dunlap; iv. Christina, b. 1834; d. 1883; m. Levi Morris (his second wife); v. Martha-A., b. 1836; m. John Heller; vi. Matthew-L., b. 1839; m. (1st) —— Haley; m. (2d) Mrs. —— Kramer; vii. Mary-F., b. 1844; d. 1863); 6. Return-Matthew, b. March 15, 1803; d. June 16, 1888; m. Feb. 19, 1824, Jane Moore, b. Sept. 20, 1792; d. Sept. 25, 1866; daughter of Robert and Margaret Armstrong Moore (had issue: i. Mary-A.; ii. Howard; iii. Robert; iv. Jackson, b. June 18, 1828; m. (1st) April 3, 1851, Eliza Carrothers, b. March 2, 1835; d. Sept. 4, 1876; daughter of George Carrothers; m. [2d] June 21, 1877, Mrs. Lucy Kennedy Heffling, widow of Walker Heffling, and daughter of Carroll and Mary Latham Kennedy; v. Maria; vi. Salathiel); 7. David-W., m. (1st) Buckington; m. (2d) —— Gibson; 8. Ahio-H., m. Elizabeth Harvey; 9. Thomas-J.; 10. Elizabeth, d. young; 11. Philip-H., m. Susan Jones; 12. Jacob-J., m. Matilda Smith; 13. Abraham-H.; 14. Christian-H., m. Matilda Todd; 15. Daniel, m. Mary Jane Johnson; 16 and 17. died in infancy.

ABSALOM KENT, b. in Virginia, 1777; son of Absalom Kent, a native of that State; removed to Stock township, Harrison county, Ohio, before 1810; d. in Illinois, 1875, where he had settled; had issue:

I. Absalom, b. in Stock township, 1810; d. 1876; m. (1st) Mary Walker, d. 1848; m. (2d) Sarah Traub; m. (3d) Margaret Worman; had issue by first wife: 1. Absalom, settled in Nottingham township; m. Jane A. Lee, b. July 17, 1837, daughter of Jesse and Harriet Mason Lee, natives of Virginia; 2. John-H.; 3. Joseph-W.; 4. Stewart; 5. William; 6. Tabitha; had issue by second wife: 7. Sarah-J., m. —— Toole; had issue by third wife: 8. Mary, m. —— Grimes, and settled in Cadiz. II. Abner. III. John. IV. Jacob. V. Jane. VI. Mary.

AARON KERR, see Family of William Scott.

JAMES KERR, see Family of Roger Clark.

JAMES KERR, b. 1751; d. June 2, 1825; emigrated from Adams and Westmoreland counties, Penn., settling in Short Creek township, Harrison county, Ohio, in 1805; m. Agnes (Nancy) ——, b. 1751; d. June 18, 1836; had issue, eight children, among whom:

I. James, b. 1787, in Adams county, Penn.; d. 1846, in Bellefontaine, Ohio; m. (1st) 1807, Catherine Duff; d. September 21, 1827; m. (2d) 1829, Martha Morrison, of Belmont county, Ohio; had issue by first wife: 1. John-C., b. April 15, 1811, in Short Creek township; settled in Belmont county; from whence he served as a member of the Legislature in 1846; m. (1st) March 23, 1836, Mary Henderson; d. 1847; m. (2d) Jan. 14, 1854, Sarah Newell; d. 1862; m. (3d) Nov. 3, 1863, Grizelle Taggart, daughter of Rev. William Taggart, of Cadiz, Harrison county (had issue by first wife: i. Martha-A.; ii. Amanda-K.; iii. James-H.-H.; had issue by second wife: iv. George; v. John; vi. Gilland; vii. Bentley; viii. Thomas-Corwin; ix. Vance-C.); 2. James; 3. William; 4. George; 5. Margaret-Ann; 6. Joseph; 7. Thomas-L.

II. Samuel, b. in York, now Adams county, Penn., Oct. 25, 1792; d. Feb. 27, 1882, in Short Creek township. where he had settled; served in the War of 1812; m. (1st) Sept. 8, 1815, Anne Smyth, d. 1833; m. (2d) September, 1835, Agnes Hamilton, a native of Ohio; d. March 28, 1885; had issue by first wife, seven children; had issue by second wife: 8. ——, d. in infancy; 9. ——, d. in infancy; 10. Thomas-H., b. Aug. 15, 1836, in Short Creek township. where he settled; m. Nov. 7, 1861, Letitia A. Calderhead, a native of Harrison county, daughter of William and Nancy McLaughlin Calderhead 11. Samuel-C., a Presbyterian minister, b. in Short Creek township, Sept. 9, 1838; settled in Franklin county, Kan., 1889; m. March 11, 1871, Elizabeth N. Rowley, daughter of Luther Rowley, of Bowerston, Harrison county; 12. Margaret-A., m. ―― Calderhead Hanna. III. John. IV. William. V. Mary. VI. Jane. VII. Elizabeth.

JOHN KERR, d. in Wigtonshire, Scotland, at the age of ninety-four; m. Grace McCracken, who d. aged ninety-six; had issue: 1. James, a Presbyterian minister, b. at Kirkcolm, Scotland, 1805; d. April 9, 1855; emigrated to America and first settled at Winchester, Virginia, removing to Cadiz, Ohio, in 1839; m. 1837, at Pittsburg, Margaret McWhirter, b. in Scotland, 1816; d. Nov. 1, 1890; daughter of David and Mary Fleming McWhirter, of Whithorn, Scotland (had issue: i. Mary; ii. Joseph; iii. David; iv. William; v. John, m. Ora Price; vi. James-W., b. 1850; m. 1881, Martha Lewis; vii. Eliza, m. Rev. Cyrus J. Hunter; viii. Agnes, m. J. W. Slemmons); 2. Grace; 3. Agnes; 4. Mary; 5. John; 6. Stair.

CONRAD KEESEY, b. in Pennsylvania, 1790; d. in Harrison county, Ohio, 1874, where he had settled 1816; m. (1st) in Pennsylvania, ―― Burkett; m. (2d) in White Cloud, Iowa, Ellen Brooks; had issue, among others: 1. ――, m. Erasmus Barrett, of Cadiz township; 2. James, b. 1821, in Harrison county; d. Jan. 6, 1884; settled about five miles northwest of Cadiz, Ohio; m. May 30, 1846, Margaret Layport, b. Dec. 22, 1826, daughter of John L. and Verlinda Harrison Layport (had issue: i. Jane-Ann; ii. Conrad, settled in Uhrichsville, Ohio; iii. Mary-Verlinda; iv. Amanda-V., m. (1st) A. Johnson; m. (2d) D. D. Bowman; v. John-L., b. Oct. 23, 1852; settled four and one-half miles from Cadiz; m. Nov. 24, 1881, Mary Belle Haverfield, daughter of Gillespie and Sarah J. Hines Haverfield; vi. Susan-H., m. James Milliken; settled in Cadiz; vii. Charles-W., settled in Peabody, Kan.; viii. Ella, m. Edward Trenner; settled in Arcola, Ill.; ix. Frankie, d. in infancy; x. Jessie-F., m. Elmer Bowers; settled in Arcola, Ill.; xi. Margaret-B.; xii. Bert-Q.).

DANIEL KILGORE, see Family of John Pritchard.

LEONARD KIMMEL, b. in Germany, 1741; d. in Rumley township, Harrison county, Ohio, 1825; emigrated to America, 1758, and later settled at The Glades, Somerset county, Penn., thence removed to the Cheat River, West Virginia about 1800, and settled in Rumley township a short time afterward; m. Susan Zimmerman, of The Glades, Penn., b. 1748; d. 1828; had issue:
I. John, emigrated from Somerset county, Penn., and settled in Rumley township, Harrison county, Ohio before 1814; m. Eve Turney, of Stone Creek, Penn.; had issue: 1. Susan, m. ―― Wallace; 2. Mary; 3. Sophia; 4. David, b. 1816; d. 1882; m. 1839, Eunice Belle Moore. b. March 17. 1818; d. Nov. 5, 1874; daughter of Thomas and ―― Bonnell Moore, of Pennsylvania (had issue: i. Maria, b. 1840; d. 1873; m. Frank Jamison; ii. John, b. 1842; d. 1863; iii. Daniel-Moore. b. 1843; d. 1865; iv. Royal. b. 1845; d. 1875; v. Thomas-Moore, b. 1848; m. 1872, Sarah Gotshall; vi. Steven, b. 1850; d. 1850; vii. Eunice-Mehitabel, b. 1851; d. 1852; viii. David-Patton, b. 1854; m. 1881, Sarah Schultz); 5. Adam; 6. Claytus; 7. Katharine.
II. Adam.
III. Henry, b. in Pennsylvania, 1789; settled in Rumley township; m. 1814, Christina Gidinger, b. at The Glades, Somerset county, Penn., 1794; daughter of Martin and Elizabeth B. Gidinger, natives of Germany. who settled in Harrison county, in 1808; had issue: 1. Susan; 2. Jonathan, b. July 15, 1815. in Rumley township; m. January, 1836. Mariah Catharine Nupp. daughter of John P. and Catharine Wolf Nupp. natives of Gettysburg, Adams county, Penn. (had issue: i. Sarah-Jane, m. Jacob Condo, of Germano, Ohio; ii. Elizabeth, m. Jacob Stall, and settled in Jewett, Ohio; iii. Nimrod. served in the Civil War; killed at the battle of Fisher's Hill; iv. Christina; v. Titus; vi. Simon-P.; vii. Jonathan; viii. George; ix. Isaac; x. Mary-Magdalena; xi. Martin).
IV. Leonard.
V. Frederick, b. in West Virginia. 1800; d. in Rumley township, March 24,

1885; m. 1826, Elizabeth Yingling; had issue: 1. Sarah, m. John Knoff, of North township; 2. Mary-Ann; 3. Rebecca; 4. Joseph, settled in North township; 5. Lydia-Ann, m. Jacob Binker, and settled in North township; 6. Henry; 7. William, b. Feb. 11, 1838; settled near Scio; m. Feb. 16, 1860, Louisa Sneary, b. May, 1844, daughter of Jacob and Mary Turney Sneary; 8. John; 9. Barbara; 10. Mahala; 11. Delila, m. Samuel Webb, and settled in Cleveland, Ohio; 12. Amos; 13. Joshua.
VI. Nancy, m. ―――― Harmon.
VII. Mary.
VIII. Susanna, m. 1819, Samuel Guthrey.

JOHN KINSEY, an English Quaker, native of London, emigrated to America, arriving at New Castle, Delaware, in the ship " Kent," June 16, 1677; one of the Commissioners for the settlement of New Jersey, under the purchase by Edward Byllinge; made selection and bargain with Peter Cock, the Swedish deputy, for purchase of 300 acres of land, situated above the mouth of the Schuylkill, near the place which afterwards became known as the site of Penn's Treaty and of the city of Philadelphia. John Kinsey, Jr., came to America in 1678, and settled on the tract of land purchased by his father, where he reared a family; his son John, was Chief Justice of Pennsylvania; Edmund Kinsey, another of his sons, removed in 1715 to Buckingham township, Bucks county, Penn., where he settled; was one of the founders of the Buckingham Monthly Meeting in 1720; m. Nov. 21, 1708, Sarah Osburn; his children were Samuel, David, Mary, Elizabeth, John, Joseph, Sarah, Benjamin, Jonathan. Of these, Benjamin, b. Oct. 22, 1727; m. (1st) 1749, Susanna Brown; m. (2d) 1776, Martha White; had issue, among others:
I. George, m. Dec. 22, 1773, Mary Gillingham; had issue: 1. Sarah; 2. Susanna; 3. Edmund; 4. James; 5. Aaron; 6. John; 7. George; 8. Charles. b. in Bucks county, Penn., May 19, 1786; removed with his parents to Mount Pleasant, Ohio. in 1798; located in the western part of Cadiz township, Harrison county, about 1815, thence, in 1832, removed to Moorefield; afterwards settling in Flushing. Belmont county, where he d. Feb. 11, 1884; m. (1st) in Philadelphia, June 1, 1815, Ann Wor-

rall, b. 1793; d. Oct. 26, 1832; m. (2d) in Moorfield, Talitha Gatchel; d. about 1838; m. (3d) 1842, Rhoda Boone, of Kentucky (had issue by first wife: i. Gillingham, d. aged twenty-two years; ii. Kersey-Wood, b. in Cadiz township, Nov. 2, 1823; settled at Cadiz, in 1847; m. (1st) May 6, 1847, Sarah Jane Haverfield; d. February, 1864; daughter of Nathan Haverfield; m. (2d) Nov. 9, 1864, Emma Holmes, b. Jan. 20, 1839, daughter of George and Hannah Mansfield Holmes; iii. Sarah-Jane, d. in infancy; had issue by second wife: iv. ――――, m. David Comly, and settled in Adena; v. ――――; vi. ――――; had issue by third wife: vii. Emily, m. Eli Davis, and settled in Pittsburg; viii. Charles-Wesley, m. Isabel McFadden, daughter of Henry S. and Isabel Poor McFadden; settled in Oakland, Cal.); 9. Ann.
George Holmes, father of Mrs. Emma Holmes Kinsey, was a son of Col. Joseph Holmes, a pioneer of Harrison county; m. (1st) Hannah Linn; m. (2d) Tacy Thompson; m. (3d) Jan. 7, 1834, Hannah Mansfield, daughter of Thomas Mansfield, of Jefferson county, Ohio; had issue by second wife: Joseph and Rezin, and two others; had issue by third wife: William, d. aged six years; Mary, d. aged three years; Emma, m. Kersey Wood Kinsey.

JAMES KIRKPATRICK, b. in Cecil county, Maryland, June 14, 1770; removed in 1801 to Washington county, Penn., where he remained until 1821, and then settled in Athens township, Harrison county, Ohio; settled, 1823, in Moorefield township, Harrison county, where he d. May 26, 1840; m. in Maryland, Mary Cochran, a native of Cecil county, b. Jan. 31. 1771; d. July 25, 1836; had issue: 1. Hugh, b. Sept. 21, 1795; 2. Robert, b. April 29, 1797; 3. Elizabeth, b. July 26, 1799; 4. William, b. in Cecil county, Dec. 11, 1801; d. in Moorefield township, May 1, 1888; m. Dec. 25, 1823, Sarah Guthrie; d. Jan. 14, 1885 (had issue: i. James, b. Nov. 21, 1824; m. (1st) Feb. 25. 1847, Ellen S. Wallace, b. June 17, 1827: d. Nov. 8, 1882; daughter of Rev. William and Mary McWilliams Wallace [natives of Pennsylvania, who settled in Ohio about 1817]; m. (2d) Oct. 12, 1886, Belle Guthrie, b. Dec. 10, 1835; daughter of Robert and Jane Cunningham Guthrie; ii. Robert-G.; iii. Joseph-C., b. Jan. 6,

1828; settled in Moorefield township; m. March 7, 1854, Margaret J. Wallace, b. Dec. 23, 1834, daughter of Rev. William and Mary McWilliams Wallace; iv. Hugh; settled in Iowa; v. Mary-J.; vi. Adeline, m. ——— Kirk, and settled at Flushing, Ohio; vii. Sarah, m. ——— Hays; viii. Elizabeth, m. W. E. Wallace; ix. John, b. 1839; d. 1845; x. Nancy; xi. Margaret, m. ——— Hays); 5. Mary, b. March 4, 1804 (had issue: i. Mary, m. ——— Douglas); 6. James. b. Jan. 10, 1807; 7. John, b. June 11, 1809.

WILLIAM KNOX, a Methodist minister, probably born in Ireland, 1767, of Scottish descent, settled in Maryland, about 1790; removed after 1800 to Harrison county, Ohio, where he d. June 16, 1851; m. Esther ———, b. 1785; d. March 2, 1863; had issue: 1. Jeremiah; 2. William; 3. David; 4. Sarah; 5. John, b. in Maryland; settled in Freeport; served in the War of 1812; d. May 16, 1863; m. about 1815, Mary Davis, a native of Ireland; d. April 12, 1887, daughter of Samuel Davis, who settled in Athens township (had issue: i. William; ii. Samuel; iii. Margaret; iv. Ann; v. Matthew-M.; vi. John-D.; vii. Sarah-J.; viii. James; ix. George-M.; x. E.-M., b. Aug. 16, 1840; settled in Freeport; m. (1st) Nov. 20, 1862, Abbie H. Bendore; d. April 25, 1884; daughter of John and Nancy Bendore, of Smyrna, Ohio; m. (2d) July 24, 1889, Mrs. Elizabeth Tipton Robinson; xi. Theodore); 6. James; 7. Arthur, d. Aug. 23, 1857 (had issue: i. William; ii. Clara); 8. Nancy.

WILLIAM LACEY, b. in Sussex county, Del., 1764; d. May 17, 1828; m. Elizabeth Stinson; removed to Ross county, Ohio, and thence to Harrison county; had issue: I. Robert, d. 1812; a soldier of the War of 1812. II. Anderson, removed West; had issue: 1. Joseph. III. John-Stinson, b. 1793; d. Jan. 16, 1873; m. Dec. 31, 1820, Anna Jeanette Hoyt, b. in New York City, July 21, 1802; d. Sept. 29, 1885; daughter of Jesse and Anna Hoyt; settled at Cadiz, Ohio, about 1816; had issue: 1. Elizabeth. b. Nov. 22, 1821; d. Feb. 16, 1823; 2. William-B., b. Dec. 11, 1820; d. Jan. 14, 1867; 3. Jesse-Hoyt, b. July 8, 1826; d. Sept. 29, 1899; 4. Henry-Brush, b. Nov. 11, 1828; m. (1st) Oct. 4, 1855, Frances Rebecca Stuart; m. (2d) Oct. 5, 1865, Mary Ann Beardsley; 5. John-S., b.

July, 1831; d. Dec. 22, 1832; 6. Robert-S., b. Sept. 22, 1833; 7. Anderson-Parker, b. Dec. 11, 1835; d. Jan. 21, 1895; 8. Lewis, b. Oct. 2, 1837; d. Jan. 22, 1843; 9. Anna-Jeanette, b. April 5, 1842; d. Jan. 4, 1866; m. Rev. W. B. Watkins.

EDWARD LAFFERTY (originally Lafetra), removed from Washington county, Penn. (probably Peters township), to Moorefield township, Harrison county, Ohio, some years before 1810, where he died; m. Elizabeth Ramage, b. 1733; d. 1844; had issue, among others:

I. Samuel, b. April 14, 1782; **d. Nov.** 29, 1857; m. Jan. 1, 1807, Margaret Figley, b. 1782; d. April 4, 1842; had issue: 1. Belijah, b. 1807; d. Aug. 11, 1887; m. 1830, Joshua Dickerson; 2. Jacob, b. Dec. 1. 1809; 3. Edward, b. March 14, 1812; 4. Elizabeth, b. Aug. 7, 1814: 5. Jane, b. Dec. 4, 1817; d. Sept. 11, 1864; m. 1839, William Dickerson; 6. Joseph, b. Oct. 26, 1819; 7. Margaret, b. March 15, 1822; d. May 22, 1847; m. Nicholas Familton.

II. Edward, b. in Pennsylvania, 1789; removed to Moorefield township with his parents, and afterward settled in Athens township. where he d. Nov. 8, 1836; m. Margaret McFadden, b. 1789; d. Sept. 14, 1864; sister of Joseph McFadden; had issue: 1. Samuel; 2. John; 3. Elizabeth, d. 1847; m. Thomas Grimes; 4. Margaret, m. Luke Vorhees, and settled at Loraine, Ohio; 5. George, d. 1860; 6. Joseph, settled in Belmont county; 7. Edward, b. Nov. 25, 1826; d. April 2, 1886; m. Sept. 7, 1865. Sarah A. Cooper, daughter of William C. Cooper; 8. Hiram, b. April 15. 1831; d. Aug. 31, 1875; m. 1857, Jane Dickerson, daughter of John Dickerson, of Athens township; 9. Finley, settled in Nebraska; 10. Mary-Jane.

The Laffertys may have removed to Washington county from Bedminster township, Somerset county, N. J., where a number of them lived during the Revolution. Edmund Lafetra, of Huguenot origin, settled in Monmouth county, N. J., in 1667; d. 1687; m. Frances ———; had issue: 1. Edmund; 2. Elizabeth, m. John West.

SYLVANUS LAMB, b. in Massachusetts, removed from Pittsburg, Penn., to Georgetown, Ohio, and thence in 1843 to Athens county, Ohio, where he

d. 1848; m. in Pittsburg, Isabella White, a native of that place, daughter of Samuel White, a native of Ireland, who afterward settled in Short Creek township; had issue, eight children, among whom: 1. Leonard, settled in Adalissa, Iowa; 2. Sylvanus, settled in Shickley, Neb.; 3. L———-B———, b. in Short Creek township, Jan. 27, 1833; removed to Athens county with his parents in 1843; subsequently returned to Short Creek township; served in the Civil War; m. 1854, Catherine Brooke. a native of Martin's Ferry; d. March 15, 1887; daughter of Benjamin and Martha Brooke, early settlers in Belmont county, where they came from Pennsylvania. (Benjamin B r o o k e served in the War of 1812.)

PETER LANTZ, a native of Pennsylvania, d. in Jefferson county, Ohio, 1821, where he had settled before 1809; m. Mary Patterson, a native of Pennsylvania, of Scotch-Irish descent; had issue: 1. Christopher-P.; 2. William; 3. John, b. May 24, 1809; d. Nov. 7, 1879; settled in Moorefield township, Harrison county, Ohio, about 1822; m. 1837, Eliza Fulton, b. Feb. 9, 1815; d. Feb. 8, 1887 (had issue: i. Dewey-S., settled in Belmont county, Ohio; ii. R.-W.; iii. Jasper-N., b. Jan. 22, 1843; served in the Ohio Legislature from 1883 to 1889; m. April 27, 1871, Sarah Sloan, b. April 20, 1848, daughter of John and Eliza Wherry Sloan; iv. A.-E., killed in the Civil War; v. Samuel-M., settled at Piedmont, Ohio; vi. Albert-C.); 4. Abraham; 5. Abigail; 6. Mary, m. ——— Beall, and settled at Coshocton county, Ohio; 7. Sarah, m. ——— Cramer, and settled in Medina county, Ohio.

EDWARD LAUGHRIDGE, a native of Ireland. emigrated to America and settled at Wilmington, Delaware, 1809; removed to Brooke county, Va., and thence to Jefferson county, Ohio; m. in Ireland. Margaret McConnell; had issue: 1. Robert; 2. Edward, b. in county Tyrone, Ireland, Sept. 10, 1803; d. in Green township, Harrison county. Ohio, June 16, 1889; m. (1st) Marjory McConnell, d. Aug. 26, 1868; m. (2d) Susannah Conaway of Stock township, daughter of John Conaway (had issue by first wife: i. Jane, b. Nov. 24, 1824; ii. Joseph, b. Sept. 20, 1826; iii. Margaret, b. Sept. 25, 1828; iv. Thomas, b. Feb. 2, 1831; v. Robert, b. Nov. 21, 1832; vi.

Edward, b. Aug. 16, 1834; vii. Elizabeth, b. May 2, 1836; viii. Nancy, b. April 21, 1838; ix. John, b. Sept. 27, 1840; x. William, b. Feb. 28, 1843; xi. Samuel, b. June 7, 1847; had issue by second wife: xii. James-H., b. Dec. 14, 1869; xiii. Susannah, b. Jan. 12, 1872); 3. James; 4. Matthew; 5. Joseph; 6. Jane; 7. Elizabeth; 8. Margaret.

JAMES LAUGHRIDGE, b. in Ireland, 1806, coming the same year with his parents to North township, Harrison county, Ohio, where he d. in 1866; m. Dec. 19, 1836, Anna Henderson, daughter of William and Sarah Henderson, of Harrison county (both of whom died in Tuscarawas county, Ohio, the former in 1852, the latter in 1850); had issue: 1. Sarah-Ann, m. Elias Stonebrook, and settled near Carrollton, Ohio; 2. E.-W., b. February 2, 1840; m. May 2, 1867, Mary M. Fierbaugh, daughter of Daniel and Elizabeth Fierbaugh, of North township; 3. Eliza-Jane, m. Henry Lutz. and settled near Carrollton; 4. James-Wesley, settled in Carroll county.

JOHN LAW, a native of Ireland, of Scotch descent, b. about 1765; d. about 1859; settled in Monroe township, Harrison county, Ohio, about 1826; m. in Ireland, Elizabeth Lynn, b. about 1781; d. about 1860; had issue. among others:

I. Matthew, b. in Ireland. 1806-8; d. in Monroe township, Sept. 9. 1878-79; m. March 31, 1836, Rebecca Birney, of Green township, b. 1816; d. September, 1864; had issue: 1. John, b. Aug. 26, 1837; m. Feb. 26, 1862. Sarah Jane Trimble, daughter of Robert and Sarah Evans Trimble; 2. William-B., b. Feb. 22, 1841; settled in North township; m. (1st) October, 1862, Rebecca J. Forbes; m. (2d) 1888. Florence Donaldson, daughter of William and Nancy English Donaldson; 3. Robert-B., settled in North township; 4. Jane, d. in infancy.

II. Jane, b. in Ireland. March 1. 1813; came to Harrison county with her parents; m. April 10, 1834, William Humphrey, b. in Ireland, June, 1812; settled with his mother and sister in Stock township, Harrison county, in 1832, where he d. 1884; had issue: 1. Elizabeth; 2. Thomas, d. March 31. 1886, in Saline county, Mo., where he had settled in 1865; 3. Margaret. m. Joseph Patterson, and settled in Missouri; 4. Mary-J., m. William Patterson, and settled in Greenwood county, Kan.; 5. Catherine, m. William Foster, a physician, and settled in Superior, Neb.; 6. John, settled in Labette, Kan.; 7. Ellen, m. Almond Birney, and settled in Labette, Kan.; 8. Martha, m. Marion Spiker, and settled at Cadiz; 9. Rebecca-Anne, m. W. K. Haverfield, and settled at Jewett. III. Henry. IV. Charlotte, m. William Beatty, and settled in Licking county, Ohio. V. Frances, m. John McMillan, and settled in Washington township. VI. Rebecca, m. Robert Irvine. VII. Margaret, m. John Simpson, and settled in Stock township. VIII. Mary, m. —— Simpson; d. in Illinois. IX. Elizabeth, m. Robert Birney.

Robert Trimble, father of Sarah Trimble Law, settled in Monroe township, about 1833; m. Aug. 7, 1825, Sarah Evans, of Jefferson county, Ohio; had issue: 1. Mary; 2. Ann; 3. Lucy; 4. John, settled in Union county, Ohio; 5. Martha; 6. George; 7. Rebecca, m. Frank Courtwright; settled in Franklin; 8. Sarah-Jane, m. John Law.

GEORGE LAYPORT (or Leporth, as originally spelled), of French Huguenot descent, emigrated from Maryland to the Beech Flats, near Steubenville, Ohio, before 1800; thence removed to Cadiz township, Harrison county, before 1806, settling on the farm now used as the county infirmary; his settlement at the first was on the frontier, and during the border wars with the Indians, his cabin was burned by them, and his son Thomas, aged eighteen, killed; after peace was declared, one of the Indians who had taken part in this attack, boasted of it in the presence of John Layport (Thomas's brother), during a general muster held in New Philadelphia. The brother attempted to kill the Indian on the spot, but was restrained. He afterwards followed him from New Philadelphia across Harrison county, to Salt Run in Jefferson county, and then despatched him while the Indian was stooping down to take a drink (from account of Rev. E. Layport; see also page 54, for a similar incident). George Leporth was one of the famous hunters of Harrison county in pioneer days, all kinds of wild game, turkeys, deer, wolves, and bears then being plentiful in his neighborhood.

He was also a skilled trapper; and set large steel traps for bear. "On one occasion," says Howe, in his "History of Ohio," "two of his sons, having trapped a wolf, skinned it alive, and then turned it loose," as an awful example to its fellows of what was in store for them in case they molested the settler's fold. George Leporth once set a trap for a bear, which was accustomed to follow a certain trail; and placed it by a log which the bear would have to step over, expecting it to step into the trap. But it happened that a Methodist missionary came along the trail that day on his way to a preaching station, near what is now Asbury chapel; and his horse stepped into the trap intended for the bear. Not being strong enough to release the trap by himself, the minister was obliged to wait until Leporth came along before he could proceed. George Leporth, or Layport, d. before Nov. 29, 1814, leaving a wife, Nancy, and children, John, Margaret Hevlin, Mary Hevlin, Dianna Spiker, Nancy Wilson, Isaac, and Susanna Babb; of these: 1. John, d. February-May, 1839; settled in Stock township (had issue: i. William, b. June 12, 1805; d. March 20, 1867; ii. Abraham, d. September-November, 1850; m. Sarah ——; iii. Isaac. b. Aug. 26, 1814; d. Aug. 3, 1882; m. Cynthia ——, b. 1815; d. May 2, 1895); 2. Isaac, d. August-October, 1825; m. Sarah —— (left issue).

JACOB LEMMON, a Methodist Episcopal minister, b. 1789; d. May 24, 1874; removed with his parents from Maryland, and settled in Freeport township, Harrison county, before 1821; m. Sarah Bosley; had issue: 1. Bosley; 2. Amon, m. 1852, Rebecca Forsythe, b. 1824; d. Aug. 19, 1872; daughter of Jesse and Sarah Colvin Forsythe, of Freeport township; 3. Moses. m. Mary Allen; 4. Sarah, m. —— Allen; 5. Rebecca; 6. Rachel; 7. Eliza.

ISAAC LEMASTERS, d. in Archer township, Harrison county, March, 1844; m. Jane ——; had issue: I. Nancy, m. 1815, John Rogers. II. Lydia, m. 1818, George Simonton. III. Jane, m. 1819, Samuel Pittinger. IV. Margaret. m. —— Ferrell. V. Susannah, m. 1829, John Robinson. VI. Elizabeth. VII. Abraham, m. 1824, Nancy Barnes. VIII. Isaac. IX. John, m. 1833, Mercy

Johnson. X. Ebenezer, m. 1840, Rebecca D. Nixon. XI. William, b. in Ohio, Dec. 20, 1816; removed from Short Creek to Archer township, Harrison county, where he d. March 8, 1877; m. 1839, Elizabeth Busby, daughter of Abraham Busby, of Archer township; had issue: 1. Abram-R., b. Sept. 7, 1840; d. Sept. 13, 1843; 2. Deborah-J., b. April 13, 1842; d. April 27, 1855; 3. Amanda-A., b. May 12, 1845; d. Oct. 11, 1854; 4. Isaac-K., b. Sept. 8, 1846; m. 1869, Elizabeth Devore, b. Aug. 9, 1850, daughter of Moses Devore, of Harrison county; 5. Melinda, b. Aug. 29, 1848; 6. ———, b. Feb. 12, 1850; 7. Mary, b. Aug. 23, 1853; d. Nov. 1, 1854; 8. John, b. May 1, 1855; 9. William-Jacob, b. Aug. 29, 1856; 10. Joshua-Ellsworth, b. Dec. 28, 1861; d. July 21, 1883.

ROBERT LISLE, b. 1774, a native of Pennsylvania, of Scotch-Irish descent, removed to Jefferson county, Ohio, before 1803, where he died, April 3, 1834; m. in Pennsylvania, Elizabeth ———, b. 1780; d. Sept. 12, 1852; had issue: 1. William; 2. Nancy; 3. Hannah; 4. Robert; 5. Jane; 6. Rachel; 7. Mary; 8. Eliza; 9. John, b. in Jefferson county, Ohio, Dec. 5, 1803; settled in Archer township, Harrison county, 1839, where he d. Oct. 30, 1890; m. in Jefferson county, 1829, Eliza A. Johnston, daughter of Robert Johnston (had issue: i. Johnston; ii. William, b. May 6, 1833; served in the Civil War; m. 1878, Rachel Beatty, daughter of Arthur Beatty, of Archer township; iii. Elizabeth; iv. Mary-Jane; v. John, b. Feb. 27, 1842; served in the Civil War; m. Nov. 6, 1873, Jennie Henderson, daughter of James Henderson, a resident of North township; vi. Hamilton, b. May 12, 1844; m. (1st) Nov. 11, 1869, Mary Crawford. d. March 29, 1875, daughter of John Crawford, a resident of Archer township; m. (2d) Oct. 2, 1882, Mrs. Elizabeth Haverfield, of Cadiz township; vii. Martha).

LISLE, see also Lyle.

SAMUEL LONG, of German descent, b. in Frederick county, Md., 1780; d. January, 1858; settled in Rumley township, Harrison county, about 1827; m. Anna Mary Myers, b. 1791; d. 1866; daughter of Jacob Myers; had issue: 1. Elizabeth, b. 1816; d. 1900; 2. Susanna, b. 1817; 3. Katharine, b. 1819; 4. Mary, b. 1820; d. 1892; m. (1st) ——— Got-shall; m. (2d) ——— Wood; 5. Jacob, b. 1822; d. 1899; 6. Rebecca, b. 1823; 7. Sarah, d. 1859; m. Joseph Graybill; 8. Eliza, b. 1829; d. 1876; m. Jacob Gotshall; 9. Joseph; a minister; b. 1832; m. Margaret Smith, daughter of Samuel and Margaret Axline Smith; 10. William, b. 1832; d. 1886; m. (1st) Sarah Nicholson; m. (2d) Celestia Redmond.

GEORGE LOVE, emigrated from county Tyrone, Ireland, to New York, 1791, and about 1792 settled in Washington county, Penn.; removed in 1800 to Wheeling township, Belmont county, Ohio, where he died; m. in Ireland, Isabella Smith; had issue: I. John, b. in county Tyrone, Ireland, about 1770, came with his parents to Belmont county; removed in 1808 to Athens township, Harrison county, Ohio, where he d. March, 1860; m. about 1807, Mary Cooke, d. Dec. 16, 1830, daughter of James Cooke; had issue: 1. George, b. March 29, 1810, in Athens township, where he d. Dec. 20, 1880; m. March 17, 1830, Jane McCracken, d. Feb. 21, 1879, daughter of Robert McCracken (had issue: i. Robert-M., b. Dec. 21, 1830, in Athens township; m. June 3, 1854, Sarah Henderson, daughter of William Henderson, of Cadiz township; ii. Mary, b. Sept. 20, 1832; m. David Lyle; settled in Uniontown, Belmont county; iii. John, b. Sept. 16, 1834; m. (1st) Eliza Tay'or, d. Jan. 28, 1869; m. (2d) Mary J. Mundell; iv. Martha, b. Dec. 24, 1836; v. James, b. Aug. 22, 1840; killed in the Civil War; d. Sept. 3, 1864, in Frederick City; vi. Nancy, b. Sept. 8, 1838; d. March 3, 1842; vii. George, b. Sept. 9, 1842; m. Dec. 6, 1865, Eleanor Haley, daughter of Samuel Haley, who removed from Belmont county to McLean county, Ill.; v'ii. Nancy-Jane, b. Sept. 13, 1844; d. March 19, 1849; ix. Margaret, b. Sept. 19, 1847; m. Dec. 15, 1870, Robert Henderson, b. Jan. 8, 1845; d. Feb. 14, 1887; son of William Henderson; x. Caroline-Jane, b. June 17, 1850; d. May 28, 1853); 2. James-C., b. Feb. 9, 1814 in Athens township, Harrison county, where he d. July 12, 1876; m. April 10, 1839, Jane McFadden, daughter of Samuel McFadden, a native of Ireland, who settled in Cadiz township (had issue: i. ———; served in the Civil War; d. in hospital in Fredericksburg, Va.; ii. John; iii. James; iv. Mary, m. ——— McCracken;

settled in Stearns county, Minn.; v. Elizabeth, m. —— McFadden; settled in Marion county, Kan.; vi. George, settled in Scio, Ohio; vii. Jennie; viii. Alexander, b. Nov. 21, 1846, in Archer township, where he settled; m. Nov. 16, 1876, Jennie L. Devore, a daughter of Andrew Devore, of Archer township); 3. Thomas, b. Jan. 31, 1820; settled in Aledo, Ill.; m. Agnes Henderson; 4. Mary, b. Feb. 15, 1825; d. Oct. 27, 1886; m. Joseph Wallace; 5. John, b. July 22, 1827; settled in Arkansas City, Kan.; m. Nancy Downing; 6. Nancy.

II. Thomas, engaged in river traffic on the Mississippi; place of death unknown.

III. George, b. about 1784, in county Tyrone, Ireland; came to Belmont county with his parents, where he d. Feb. 21, 1829; served as an officer in the War of 1812; m. Mary Moore, b. 1801, in county Tyrone, Ireland; daughter of John and Mary Smith Moore (she m. 2d, John A. Todd, of Nottingham township); had issue: 1. Thomas, settled in Madison county, Iowa; 2. John; 3. George, b. Aug. 14, 1827, in Belmont county; removed 1831, to Nottingham township, Harrison county; m. November 21, 1854, Barbara Barclay, daughter of David and Elizabeth Kissick Barclay, natives of Ireland.

IV. William.

V. Jane, m. Thomas Gillespie.

VI. Catherine, m. Joseph Haverfield.

VII. Mary, m. Jacob Morgan.

JACOB LUKENS, of Dutch descent, settled in York county, Penn., about 1780; later removed to near Havre de Grace, Maryland, where he died; had issue, among others: I. Eli, b. in York county, Penn., 1783; removed to Baltimore, Md., before 1804; afterward located in Bel Air, Harford county, Md.; in 1828, settled near Fairview, Guernsey county, Ohio, where he d. 1842; m. in Baltimore, 1804, Juliana Tollinger, of Dutch descent, b. 1765; d. in Franklin, Ohio, 1866; had issue: 1. Jacob, b. at Bel Air, Md., 1805; settled near Deersville, Ohio, where he d. May 27, 1884; m. 1830, Sarah C. Bliss, b. 1810; d. Feb. 21, 1886; daughter of Zadoc Bliss, of Hartford, Conn., who had settled in Ohio, in 1816 (had issue: i. Joseph-G., settled at Tippecanoe, Ohio; ii. Merriken-B., a physician, settled at Dalton, Ga.; iii.

Benjamin-F., a physician, settled at Philadelphia, Penn.; iv. William-H., b. Oct. 22, 1838; settled at Deersville; m. September, 1867, Rosa McKinney Clark, daughter of William and Louisa Clark; v. Charles-M., a physician, settled at Syracuse, N. Y.; vi. Thomas-J., b. May 1, 1843; served in the Civil War; m. Oct. 1, 1873, Jennie Thompson, daughter of James F. Thompson, of Montgomery county); 2. Naomi; 3. Elizabeth; 4. Eli; 5. George; 6. William; 7. Alexander; 8. Nathaniel.

MOSES LUKENS, see Family of John Cope.

ROBERT LYLE, b. 1698, a native of Ireland (son of John Lyle, who removed from Scotland to county Antrim, Ireland in 1681), in 1742, accompanied by his brother John, came to America; first settling in New York; John removed to New Jersey, near the present site of New Brunswick, where he died; Robert m. 1747, Mary Gilleland, thence removed to Northampton county, Penn., where he d. Dec. 9, 1765; had issue (all the sons but David serving in the Revolutionary War): I. John, d. April 17, 1826. II. Robert, b. 1753; d. Nov. 17, 1843. III. Moses. IV. Aaron, b. Nov. 17, 1759; d. in Washington county, Penn., Sept. 24, 1825, where he had settled in 1784; served in the Revolutionary War, in the Pennsylvania Legislature, 1797-1801, and in Congress, 1803 to 1816; m. 1782, Eleanor Moore, daughter of John Moore, of Northampton county Penn.; had issue: 1. Moses, b. 1783; d. 1840; m. Sarah Kerr; 2. James, b. 1785; d. 1860; m. Mary Campbell; 3. Mary, b. May 31, 1787; d. Sept. 25, 1853; m. John Campbell, of Washington county, Penn., b. 1775; d. July 24, 1844 (see Family of John Campbell); 4. Agnes, b. 1789; d. 1790; 5. Robert, b. 1791; d. 1820; 6. Jane, b. 1793; d. 1845; m. Samuel Ewing; 7. Margaret, b. 1798; d. 1883; m. William Patterson; 8. Aaron; 9. ——; 10. ——, b. 1805; d. 1807. V. David. VI. Jane. VII. Elizabeth. VIII. Rosannah. IX. Eleanor. X. Mary.

WILLIAM LYLE, of Scotch-Irish descent, m. Mary Maholm; had issue, among others: 1. William, b. Jan. 15, 1812; d. near Rumley, in Harrison county, 1861; m. July, 1836, Jane Lewis, b. near Manchester, England, March 1, 1817, daughter of George and Elizabeth

Powell Lewis (the former of whom emigrated to Harrison county in 1818); (had issue: i. Rosanna, m. George Schultz; ii. George, settled in Scio, Harrison county; iii. Elizabeth, m. Thomas McChannel; settled in Kearney, Neb.; iv. Mary, m. James McNab; settled in Jackson county, Wis.; v. Martha; vi. Sarah-E., m. Albert D. Finnicum; vii. Amanda, m. Edward L. Moore; settled in Cheyenne county, Neb.; viii. Emma-M., settled in Palestine, Texas).

Thomas and Elizabeth Smith Powell, parents of Elizabeth Powell Lewis, had issue: 1. James, b. March 17, 1785; 2. Jane, b. May 20, 1786; 3. Elizabeth; 4. Richard, b. Dec. 30, 1789.

LYLE, see also Lisle.

SAMUEL LYON, a native of Great Britain, emigrated to America about 1800, and first settled in Maryland; removed to Jefferson county, Ohio, about 1818, and afterward located in Harrison county; had issue, among others: 1. Samuel, b. in Jefferson county, 1818; d. in Washington township, Harrison county, Jan. 1, 1871; m. 1840, Catherine Hedges, b. 1811; d. Aug. 8, 1884 (had issue: i. Harriet, m. Leander Cramblett; ii. Aaron; iii. John-H.; iv. Elizabeth; v. Reuben-P., b. Nov. 8, 1847; m. Feb. 10, 1870, Eliza Jane Wiley, of Coshocton county, Ohio; vi. Jemima, m. David Meeks; vii. Robert-P.).

ROBERT LYONS, b. in Pennsylvania, Dec. 14, 1803; d. in Cadiz, Ohio, Aug. 17, 1887, where he had settled about 1818; m. (1st) 1832, Anne Bowland; b. April 10, 1810; d. May 16, 1844; m. (2d) Mrs. Anne Bowland Allison, of Washington county, Penn.; had issue by first wife: 1. James-Bowland, m. (1st) Sarah G .Thomas, b. April 4, 1838; d. April 21, 1871; 2. Nancy, b. 1835; d. 1837; 3. Richard, b. Aug. 21, 1840; d. Martha-Collins, m. 1857, David Barclay Welch, son of Rezin and Eliza Bayless Welch; 5. Ann-Eliza, b. 1843; d. 1844.

WILLIAM LYONS, a native of Ireland, emigrated to America before 1776; served in the Revolutionary War, receiving a wound which caused his death some years later in Morgan county, Ohio, whence he had removed from Harrison county; had issue: I. Thomas, b. in Pennsylvania; settled in Butler county, that State; removed to Ohio in 1820, first locating near the present site of Tippecanoe; later settled in Carroll county, where he died; m. Menie Lowrie, a native of Scotland, whose parents came to America when she was a child; sister of Walter Lowrie; had issue, ten children, among whom: 1. John-C., b. in Butler county, Penn.; settled in Bowerstown, Ohio; m. Susanna Forbes, d. Feb. 3, 1883 (had issue, four children, of whom: i. John-F., served in the Civil War and died at Resaca, Ga., 1865).

JAMES McAFEE, a native of Ireland, d. about 1795; emigrated to America, and about 1780 settled in Westmoreland (or Washington) county, Penn.; had issue: 1. Matthew; 2. James, b. in Washington county, Penn., 1785, where he m. Mary Wible, b. 1790; d. 1777; dau. of George and Mary Rummel Wible (natives of Germany, who removed from Pennsylvania to Ohio); settled in Rumley township, Harrison county, about 1823-28, where he d. 1876 (had issue, among others: i. Sarah; ii. Mary; iii. George, b. in Westmoreland county, Penn., Jan. 27, 1813; settled in Archer township, Harrison county; d. Nov. 20, 1889; m. June, 1835, Jane Hixon, daughter of Abner Hixon, a resident of Hanover; iv. James, b. in Washington county, Penn., 1817; settled in Rumley township; m. (1st) 1840, Letta Gordon; d. 1846, daughter of David and Elizabeth Archibald Gordon; m. (2d) 1849, Margaret Hendricks, b. Aug. 6, 1823; d. September, 1878, daughter of Peter and Catherine Webster Hendricks; m. (3d) 1880, Sarah Jane Gundy, daughter of William and Susanna Gatchell Gundy; v. John; vi. Matilda; vii. Hannah; viii. Rachel); 3 .John; 4. Mary; 5. Martha; 6. Jane; 7.——— (a daughter).

JOHN McBEAN, a physician, b. in Scotland, Oct. 22, 1797; d. at Cadiz, Jan. 7, 1875; m. March 18, 1829, Belinda Johnson, daughter of Henry and Catherine Johnson, of Moorefield township, both natives of Pennsylvania; had issue: 1. Jane, m. Armistead T. Ready, and settled at New Philadelphia; 2. William, b. 1833; d. 1884; 3. Catherine-L., m. Jesse H. McMath, and settled at Cleveland; 4. John-S.; a physician; b. 1840; m. (1st) 1876, Georgia Scott, b. 1849; d. 1883; daughter of George W. and Anna Scott, of Columbus; m. (2d) 1886, Alice Kennedy, daughter of Martin S. and Martha

McKee Kennedy; 5. Mary, m. Albert Lakin; 6. Harriet, m. Col. James M. Steele; 7. Julia, m. Dr. Milton Hoge, of Cambridge, Ohio; 8. Belinda, m. David A. Hollingsworth; 9. Laura, m. William S. Cessna; 10. Henry, b. 1848; d. Aug. 2, 1875.

JOSEPH McBETH, a native of Scotland, settled with his wife, Elizabeth, at Bolivar, Westmoreland county, Penn., before 1808, where he died; had issue, twelve children, among whom: 1. John, b. in Bolivar, Penn., Sept. 7, 1808; removed to Monroe township, Harrison county, Ohio, 1829, where he d. July 22, 1863; m. April 18, 1833, Mary Webster, b. in Harrison county, 1811; d. July 27, 1858; daughter of John and Katherine Webster, early settlers in Harrison county, where they came from Pennsylvania (had issue: i. Nancy, m. J. M. Ferrell, of Orrville, Ohio; ii. Mariah, m. Thomas E. Fowler; iii. Robert-C., settled in Clinton, Henry county, Mo.; iv. David-J., b. June 10, 1841; served in the Civil War; and a prisoner at Andersonville; m. June 22, 1871, Elmira Crim, a native of Franklin township, Harrison county, daughter of George and Catherine Crim, natives of West Virginia; v. William, d. in the Army Hospital, at Nashville, November, 1862; vi. Margaret-Ann, m. Garrett Fowler, and settled in Dennison, Ohio; vii. John; viii. Amanda, m. Thomas Bower, and settled in Bowerston, Ohio; ix. Mary, m. William J. Albaugh).

JOSEPH McCLAIN, removed from Westmoreland county, Penn., to North township, Harrison county, Ohio, in 1823; had issue: 1. James, b. 1801; d. 1851; m. Sarah Endsley, b. 1801; d. 1881; daughter of John Endsley, an early settler in Archer township (had issue: i. Jane; ii. Joseph, settled in Oregon; iii. John-E.; iv. Mary-Ann; v. Samuel, settled in Iowa; vi. James-Alexander, settled in Archer township; vii. Sarah, m. Edward Smith; viii. Harriet, m. Samuel Cutshall, and settled in Carroll county, Ohio; ix. Thomas-E., served in the Civil War and died in service, 1863; x. William; xi. Martha-Jane; xii. Nathan-S., b. 1848).

JOHN McCONNELL, of Scottish descent, emigrated from the North of Ireland, and probably before the Revolution settled in Pennsylvania; had issue:
I. James, settled in Athens township, Harrison county, Ohio; afterward removed to Louisville, Ky.
II. Elizabeth, settled in Athens township.
III. John, b. probably in the North of Ireland; came to Pennsylvania with his parents; probably settled in Washington county; removed to Athens township, 1801, where he was one of the first white settlers, and built one of the first horse-mills in that township; d. September-October, 1831; m. in Pennsylvania, Mary Morton, daughter of Edward Morton; had issue: 1. James; 2. William; 3. Margaret; 4. Elizabeth; 5. John, b. in Pennsylvania, May 5, 1796; settled in Athens township, where he d. Aug. 18, 1878; m. Oct. 20, 1823, Jane Robinson, d. April 10, 1887, daughter of Adam and Elizabeth Robinson, of Irish and German descent, who lived near Wilmington, Delaware (had issue: i. Robert, settled in Guernsey county, Ohio; ii. William; iii. James; iv. Margaret, m. William Howell; v. Mary, m. Joseph Holmes; vi. John; vii. Edward-S., b. April 3, 1836; m. Dec. 20, 1859, Cynthia Styers, daughter of John Styers, of Coshocton county, Ohio [a native of Pennsylvania, of German descent, whose parents were among the early settlers in Northwestern Pennsylvania]; viii. Elizabeth, m. John Cook, and settled at Bridgeport, Ohio; ix. Francis-M.; x. Adam, b. June 3, 1842; m. Oct. 3, 1865, Mary McFadden, daughter of John J. and Esther Clifford McFadden; xi. La Fayette; xii. Martha); 6. Jane.

ROBERT McCONNELL, a native of Pennsylvania, removed probably from Washington county, that State, to Belmont county, Ohio, 1807; and thence in 1814 to Washington township, Harrison county, Ohio, where he d. Aug. 22, 1850; served in the War of 1812; m. (1st) in Pennsylvania, Mary Caldwell; m. (2d) Prudence Coleman, d. 1867; had issue by first wife: 1. James, b. 1790; 2. Susan, b. 1793; m. ——— Lee; 3. David, b. 1795; 4. Alexander, b. 1796; 5. Martha, b. 1797; 6. Mary, b. 1800; m. ——— Vance; had issue by second wife: 7. Robert, b. Nov. 21, 1802; 8. Hannah, b. Sept. 20, 1804; m. ——— Coleman; 9. John-C., b. in Belmont county, Jan. 1, 1807; settled in Washington township with his parents; d. July 18, 1873; m. (1st) Jane Boles; d. May 29, 1841; daughter of James Boles; m. (2d) April 9, 1848, Rachel Browning, b. Jan. 25, 1825; daughter of Samuel Browning; 10. William, b. Jan. 6, 1809; 11. Wilson, b. April 13, 1811; 12. Prudence, b. March 22, 1813; 13. Margaret-Ann, b. Sept. 21, 1815; m. —— Farnsworth; 14. Sarah, b. Nov. 18, 1817; 15. Elizabeth, b. Nov. 6, 1819; m. —— Wilson; 16. Alexander-S., b. March 25, 1822; 17. David, b. Sept. 4, 1824.

Samuel Browning, father of Rachel McConnell, d. in Athens township, 1864; served in the War of 1812; m. Margaret Markee, whose parents were natives of England; had issue: 1. Julia-A.; 2. Elias; 3. Samuel; 4. Absalom; 5. Rachel; 6. Margaret; 7. Sarah; 8. Asbury-T.; 9. Susanna; 10. Wesley; 11. Zara; 12. Edward.

JOHN McCORMICK, b. in Pennsylvania, 1810; d. near Freeport, Ohio, Nov. 9, 1869; served as sheriff of Harrison county, 1846-48; m. Esther Allen, d. aged forty-seven; daughter of Reuben and Joanna McMillan Allen (both of Quaker origin, and both died in Washington township, aged respectively ninety-three and seventy-eight); had issue: 1. Reuben-Allen, b. in Washington township, June 19, 1839; served as an officer in the Civil War, as auditor of Harrison county, and as doorkeeper of the House of Representatives at Washington, D. C.; settled in Cadiz; m. 1863, Eliza Haverfield, a native of Cadiz township, daughter of John and Nancy Haverfield, of Cadiz township; 2. James-B., settled at Sidney, Neb.; 3. Henry-Clay, served in the Civil War, dying in the army; 4. John-T., settled at Columbus Junction, Iowa; 5. William-M., settled at Columbus Junction, Iowa.

JOHN and JOSEPH McCORMICK, brothers, emigrated from County Tyrone, Ireland, and probably first settled in Cumberland county, Penn.; removed about 1788, to North Huntingdon township, Westmoreland county; Joseph died unmarried, at the age of eighty-seven; John m. in Ireland, Sarah Sloan, sister to Dr. William Sloan; had issue, the first four of whom were born in Ireland: 1. William; 2. Andrew; 3. Jane, d. without issue; m. (1st) Robert Donaldson; m. (2d) ——

McDonald; m. (3d) Daniel Hellman; 4. Joseph; 5. John, b. Aug. 22, 1789; m. Esther Sowash, of Huguenot descent (had issue: i. William, d. in infancy; ii. Eli, b. May, 1820; iii. John-Calvin; iv. Sarah, d. young; v. George; vi. James-Irwin; a physician; vii. Silas; viii. Samuel; ix. Mary-Elizabeth, d. in infancy; x. Albert, d. young; xi. Rachel, m. John George; xii. Henry-H., speaker of the Pennsylvania House of Representatives in 1874; m. Martha Sharon, daughter of Joseph and Eliza Maholm Sharon; xiii. Horace-Greeley); 6. David; 7. Sarah, d. unm.; 8. Samuel, b. Feb. 8, 1793; d. Feb. 3, 1875; m. Margaret Kemerer; settled at Cadiz, Ohio (had issue: i. Albert-G.; ii. John, settled at Omaha; iii. Josiah-S.; iv. Finley; v. Hannah-J., m. Henry J. Dobbins; vi. Lucretia-S., m. James Barlow; vii. Mary-Belle, m. Benjamin Linton; viii. Adaline, m. George Elliott; ix. Sarah, m. Samuel Burns, and settled at Omaha; x. Clarissa); 9. Thomas; 10. Elizabeth, m. Samuel Osborne, and settled at Stewartsville (had issue, eight children).

JOHN McCOY, emigrated from Washington county, Penn., and settled in the northeastern corner of Athens township before 1806; d. 1820; m. Susanna ——; had issue: I. Joseph. II. John. III. Samuel. IV. Susanna, m. —— Robinson. V. Sidney, m. —— Counsel. VI. Thomas, m. Hannah Major; had issue: 1. John, b. Sept. 23, 1816; d. Dec. 3, 1890; m. about 1839, Eliza Walker, b. March 30, 1819; d. July 22, 1890 (had issue: i. Margaret-Jane, b. 1840; d. 1849; ii. Amanda, m. John Dickerson; iii. Thomas; iv. Mary, b. 1847; m. 1867, Davis Garvin; v. John; vi. Martin-J., b. Nov. 25, 1853; m. 1878, Isabella De Armond, daughter of David and Isabella De Armond; vii. Albert; viii. William, m. Alice McCoy; ix. Vincent-W., m. Ida Worstell, and settled in Morgan county, Ohio; x. Laura, m. John Anderson; xi. Olive, m. John McManus; xii. Isabel, m. Idelbert Burdette); 2. Thomas; 3. Ebenezer; 4. Susan, m. Wilson Dickerson; 5. Mary, m. Asa Holmes; 6. Lorilla, m. —— Dickerson; 7. Elizabeth, m. —— Anderson.

MATTHEW McCOY, b. Aug. 8, 1783; removed from Pennsylvania to Archer township, Harrison county, before 1820, where he d. Oct. 10, 1855; m. Jane ———, b. June, 1782; d. Sept. 18, 1855; had issue, among others: 1. Matthew, b. April 4, 1815; d. March 27, 1889; m. Harriet C. ———, b. May 28, 1820; d. Feb. 12, 1898 (had issue, among others: i. Edward-G., b. 1850; d. 1855; ii. Martha-J., b. 1851; d. 1851); 2. Thomas-M.; 3. James-S.; 4. William-M.

WILLIAM McCOY, removed from Washington county, Penn., to Carroll county, Ohio, about 1835; m. Jane ———; had issue: 1. William-H., b. in Canonsburg, Aug. 22, 1832; d. Sept. 19, 1884; settled in Cadiz, in 1857; served as an officer in the Civil War; m. March 24, 1857, Margaret A. Welling, b. in New Rumley, Harrison county, daughter of William and Margaret Welling.

JOHN McCULLOUGH, d. 1842, probably the son of William McCullough, who settled in Hopewell township, Washington county, Penn., before 1780; m. in Washington county, 1785, Esther Gamble, b. 1755; d. Aug. 8, 1841; removed to Wheeling township, Belmont county, Ohio, and, about 1813, settled near New Athens; had issue: 1. Esther; 2. William; 3. Alexander; 4. Margaret; 5. Joseph, b. Feb. 7, 1795; d. in Archer township, Harrison county, Jan. 31, 1870; m. (1st) 1817, Sarah Lyons, b. Sept. 27, 1797; d. March 24,1836; daughter of John and Elizabeth Beatty Lyons; m. (2d) Elizabeth ———, b. 1801; d. April 15, 1884 (had issue by first wife: i. Elizabeth. b. 1818; d. 1856; m. 1836, John Moore; ii. Esther, b. 1820; d. Sept. 24, 1892; m. 1841. Robert Anderson, b. near Claysville, Washington county. Penn., Oct. 11, 1815; d. April 25, 1891; son of Samuel and Catharine Forbes Anderson; iii. John, b. 1822; m. 1848, Jane Welch; iv. Mary, b. 1824; d. 1890; m. 1847. Martin Lee: v. Sarah-Jane, b. 1827; d. 1874; m. 1857, John Moore, husband of her deceased sister, Elizabeth; vi. Isabel, b. 1829; m. 1856, Daniel Mikesell; vii. James-Beatty; a physician; b. 1831; d. 1897; m. 1855, Martha Megaw; viii. Martha); 6. Samuel, twin brother to Joseph; 7. Martha; 8. James; 9. George; 10. Hannah; 11. John.

Three McCullough families seem to have settled in the vicinity of Crabapple Church near the beginning of the century, and the heads of the three families were either brothers, or very closely related. In addition to John McCullough, whose family is given above, Robert and William McCullough settled in Wheeling township, Belmont county, just south of New Athens, and were among the organizers of Crabapple Church, both appearing among the first bench of elders. They both also appear to have come from Hopewell township, Washington county, Penn., within the bounds of Upper Buffalo Presbyterian Church. In the call extended by the united congregations of Cross Creek and Upper Buffalo Churches to Rev. Joseph Smith, in 1779, are to be found the names of George, Robert, and William McCullough. William McCullough, of whom some account is given below, mentions in his will a brother, Peter.

ROBERT McCULLOUGH, b. 1756-57; d. June 17, 1823; removed from Hopewell township. Washington county, Penn., to Wheeling township, Belmont county, Ohio, before 1800; m. Jane ———, b. 1765; d. Oct. 15, 1835; had issue: 1. Margaret; 2. Mary; 3. Robert; 4. William; 5. Alexander; 6. James; 7. John; 8. Peter; 9. George; 10. Samuel.

WILLIAM McCULLOUGH, b. 1748; d. March 18, 1831; probably removed from York or Cumberland county to Hopewell township, Washington county. Penn., about 1779, where he (or possibly his father of the same name) appears as an elder of Upper Buffalo Presbyterian Church as late as 1793; served in the Revolutionary War; removed before 1800 to Wheeling township, Belmont county. Ohio, where, with Robert McCullough, he helped to organize Crabapple Church; m. Isabella ———, b. 1751; d. May 23, 1832; had issue, among others: 1. Mary, b. 1782; d. July 15, 1851; m. George Brokaw, b. March 27, 1784; d. Nov. 27, 1880; 2. Martha-E., b. Dec. 14, 1784; d. July 5. 1851; m. Nov. 2, 1820, Joseph Grimes (his second wife), b. November, 1782; d. Jan. 2, 1840 (had issue: i. George-D., b. April 13, 1808; d. Nov. 20, 1875; m. Jane ———-, b. March 27, 1812; d. Nov. 3, 1890; ii. Julia-Ann, b. 1809; d. March 16, 1884; m. William Campbell; iii. Joseph, a minister, removed to Independence, Kan.; iv. William-M., a minister; b. Sept. 23, 1821; d. Nov. 23, 1886; m. March 5, 1857,

6

Amanda S. Simeral; v. John; vi. Lucinda; vii. Isabella).

GEORGE McDIVITT, removed from Pennsylvania to North township, Harrison county, before 1817; d. 1837; m. Rachel ——— (possibly his second wife); had issue: 1. Charles, m. 1823, Frances Fisher; 2. George, b. 1797; d. February, 1869; m. (1st) 1817, Mary Johnston (?); m. (2d) Mrs. Susan Rutter Scott, of Leesville, Ohio (had issue by first wife, eight children; had issue by second wife: ix. Mary; x. Martha; xi. Eliza, m. Isaiah English; xii. Thursby, m. John Miner, of Pittsburg; xiii. John, settled in Stock township; xiv. Thomas-R., b. Dec. 8, 1837; served in the Civil War; m. 1865, Sarah Anderson, daughter of Robert and Hester Anderson; xv. Samuel; xvi. Lyle, b. October, 1846; m. 1869, Elizabeth Buxton, daughter of Haddon Buxton); 3. Lyle, d. March, 1838; m. Nancy ——— (had issue: i. William-E.; ii. Mary; iii. Jane); 4. John, m. 1827, Susanna Simpson (?); 5. Samuel; 6. Andrew, m. 1831, Jane Moody (?).

JAMES McDIVITT, removed from Westmoreland county, Penn., to North township, Harrison county, Ohio, about 1820; had issue, five sons, of whom the youngest: James, b. in Westmoreland county, Penn., Dec. 25, 1810; settled in North township, Harrison county, where he d. March 19, 1874; m. about 1830, Anna Birney, b. in Green township, 1808; d. Oct. 15, 1862; daughter of John Birney (had issue, ten children, of whom five died in infancy, of the others: i. Margaret, m. James Nixon; ii. Elizabeth, m. William Nixon, and settled in Stock township; iii. John, b. March 10, 1845; settled in Monroe township; m. June 24, 1875, Martha M. Easterday, a native of Harrison county, daughter of David and Mary Easterday; iv. Nancy, m. Thomas Cummings, and settled at Topeka, Kan.; v. ———).

SAMUEL McDOWELL, probably b. in Ireland, 1769; emigrated to America and settled in Washington county, Penn.; removed before 1808 to Athens township, Harrison county, Ohio, where he died; m. in Pennsylvania, Jane Moreland; had issue: 1. Nancy, m. James McAdams; 2. Samuel; 3. William, b. Nov. 6, 1808; d. May 21, 1869; m. Sept. 19, 1842, Hannah Watters,

daughter of John W. Watters, a resident of Delaware county, Ohio (had issue: i. Sarah-J., m. John Culbertson; ii. Mary-A., m. T. E. Johnson; iii. Samuel-Madison, b. March 6, 1851; iv. Emma, m. Dr. Thompson; v. Frances-A.; vi. Florence-A., twin sister to Frances); 4. James; 5. John; 6. Sarah, m. William Reed; 7. Susan-J., m. Smith Watson.

——— McFADDEN, of Coote Hill, county Cavan, Ireland, of Scottish descent; had issue:
I. John, b. about 1746; d. near Cadiz, Ohio, April 13, 1835; emigrated to America about 1774, and settled near West Middletown, Hopewell township, Washington county, Penn.; m. Margaret Sharp, b. 1751; d. April 26, 1826; daughter of John and Agnes Sharp, of Washington county, Penn. (or of George Sharp, who served from Washington county as a captain in the Revolution); removed to Cadiz township, Harrison county, Ohio, 1800; had issue: 1. Samuel-B., b. 1779; d. March 19, 1855; m. 1836, Sarah McFadden, daughter of Dr. Samuel and Nancy Logan McFadden; 2. George-S., b. 1784; d. Feb. 21, 1844; m. Ruth Collins, daughter of David and Ann Workman Collins; 3. John, b. 1789-90; d. Aug. 30, 1857; m. 1815, Mary Dunlap, b. in Maryland or in Fayette county, Penn., 1788-89; d. March 22, 1858; daughter of Adam and Rebecca Work Dunlap (had issue: i. Adam, b. 1815; d. July 17, 1873; ii. John-J., b. Oct. 21, 1820; settled in Athens township; m. Feb. 28, 1844, Esther Clifford, daughter of John Clifford, a native of Ireland [had issue: Mary, m. Adam McConnell; Margaret-Jane, b. July 12, 1846; m. Robert Dunlap; Rebecca-Ann, m. Samuel Dunlap; John-C.; George-D.; Edwin-Stanton; Sarah, m. Samuel McFadden; Adam; and Samuel-W.]; iii. Samuel-R., b. Oct. 10, 1825; m. May 7, 1851, Martha Robb, daughter of William and ——— Warnick Robb; iv. George; settled in Cadiz township; m. 1860, Mary Croskey, daughter of William and Mary Croskey, of Green township; v. Margaret, m. John McFadden, b. Oct. 10, 1810; d. in Cadiz, July 4, 1881; vi. Rebecca; vii. Mary, m. William Hamilton, and settled at Cadiz; viii. Sarah, m. John Porterfield, and settled at St. Clairsville; ix. Jane; x. Esther, m. ———

Phillips, and settled in Nebraska; xi. Rachel, m. William Hamilton, and settled in Belmont county; xii. Elizabeth, b. 1818; d. April 19, 1837); 4. Joseph, b. 1793; d. Feb. 26, 1859; m. (1st) 1826, Mary Thompson, d. March 2, 1844; daughter of David Thompson; m. (2d) Oct. 11, 1855, Catharine Henderson (had issue by first wife: i. Thompson, b. June 7, 1830; m. Nov. 23, 1854, Elizabeth Dickerson, daughter of John and Eliza McFadden Dickerson; ii. Joseph; settled in Cadiz township; iii. Mary, m. —— Fitch, and settled in California); 5. Mary, m. James Sharp, of Cadiz township (had issue: i. John, b. 1801; d. March 16, 1878); 6. Margaret, b. 1789; d. Nov. 29, 1857; m. 1813, Edward Lafferty, b. 1789; d. Nov. 8, 1836; son of Edward and Elizabeth Ramage Lafferty (had issue: i. Edward; ii. John; iii. Joseph; iv. George; v. Hiram; vi. Finley; vii. Elizabeth; viii. Margaret, m. 1835, Thomas D. Grimes; ix. Mary-Jane).

II. Sarah, b. 1748; d. near West Middletown, Pa., Dec. 29, 1835; m. (1st) Nathaniel Gilmore; d. in Ireland, about 1770-71; m. (2d) John Jamison, b. 1743; d. near West Middletown, Pa., Jan. 28, 1811; emigrated to America with her husband and children about 1773-83, and first settled near Newport, Perry county, Penn., afterwards removing to Independence township, Washington county; had issue by first husband: 1. Jane, b. 1768; m. John Parr; 2. Samuel, b. 1770; d. Sept. 8, 1814; a soldier of the War of 1812; removed to Harrison county, Ohio, about 1800-3; m. Elizabeth Buchanan (had issue: i. Sarah, m. Joseph Dunlap; ii. Samuel; iii. Nathaniel; iv. Cyrus; v. William; vi. Mary, m. Napoleon B. Kennedy; vii. Eliza, m. John Phillips); had issue by second husband: 3. John, m. Anne Craig, and settled in Harrison county, Ohio (had issue: i. Walter); 4. William; 5. Robert; 6. Margaret, m. —— McKeever; 7. Elizabeth, m. Samuel McFadden (had issue: i. John); 8. Nancy, m. —— McBroom; 9. Mary, m. —— Law; 10. Sarah, m. —— Graham.

III. Joseph, b. 1757; d. near Cadiz, Ohio, Nov. 17, 1835; settled near West Middletown, Penn., about 1774; and thence removed to Harrison county, 1800-03; m. Jane ——, b. 1760; d. May 5, 1827; had issue: 1. Samuel, b. in county Cavan, Ireland, 1785; d. near

Cassville, Nov. 12, 1869; m. (1st) Mary Milligan, b. 1775; d. 1842; a native of Adams county, Penn.; m. (2d) Jane ——, b. Jan. 3, 1799; d. Sept. 9, 1884 (had issue by first wife: i. Jane, m. James Love, and settled in Archer township; ii. Elizabeth, m. —— Mehollin; iii. Alexander, b. Sept. 19, 1818; settled at Cadiz; m. June 29, 1846, Elizabeth Barger, daughter of Valentine Barger [had issue: Joseph; Mary-Jane; Martha-A., m. J.-Law McFadden; and Elza]; iv. Mary; v. George; vi. Joseph); 2. Joseph; 3. George; 4. Margaret; 5. Jane.

IV. Samuel, a physician, b. 1757; d. April 26, 1834; m. Nancy Logan; emigrated to America before 1795, and first settled in Philadelphia; removing thence to West Middletown, Hopewell township, Washington county, Penn., and from there, soon after 1800, to Cadiz township, Harrison county, Ohio; had issue: 1. Sarah, d. at sea; 2. Margaret, m. —— Moore; 3. Mary, m. —— Wallace; 4. Thomas; 5. Benjamin, b. in 1795; d. Nov. 7, 1880; m. 1821, Mary Wilson, b. 1802; d. Sept. 9, 1882; 6. William; 7. Elizabeth, m. 1827, Robert McGonagle; 8. Sarah, m. 1836, Samuel B. McFadden; 9. Samuel; 10. Jane, m. —— Welling; 11. Nathaniel, b. October, 1811; m. 1833, Eliza Green; daughter of John and Mary Green, Pennsylvania Quakers (had issue: i. Samuel; ii. John; settled in Archer township; iii. William; settled in Kansas; iv. Hezekiah; v. George; settled in Archer township; vi. Mary, m. F. Crawford; vii. Henry; settled in Kansas; viii. Nancy-J.; ix. Elizabeth); 12. Nancy, m. —— Brothers; 13. Joseph; settled near Pittsburg.

V. ——, emigrated to America, and settled in Philadelphia, where he died, leaving among others, two sons, John and George, who both left issue.

VI. George, of Coote Hill, county Cavan, Ireland, m. Isabella McIntosh; d. in Cadiz; daughter of James McIntosh; had issue, among others: Samuel, b. 1782; d. 1861; m. Lydia Stafford, b. 1783; d. March 22, 1866; emigrated to America about 1820, and first settled at Philadelphia, removing thence to Cadiz, Ohio, 1831; had issue: 1. George, d. 1868; m. Charlotte Elliott; 2. Sarah, d. 1847; 3. Henry-Stafford, b. 1813; d. July 4, 1888; m. Dec. 6, 1842, Frances Isabella Poore, daughter of Charles M.

and Elizabeth Karg Poore (the latter a native of York county, Penn., whose parents had come from Brunswick, Germany; the former a descendant of John Poore, of Newburyport, who emigrated from England to Massachusetts, in 1635); (had issue: i. Charles-Poore, b. 1843; d. Oct. 7, 1866; ii. Henry-Hunter, m. [1st] Sarah Craig; m. [2d] Emma Beall; iii. Frances, m. John J. Hanna; iv. Isabelle, m. Charles W. Kinsey, and settled at Oakland, Cal.; v. Elizabeth-T.; vi. John-F., m. Laura Samson; settled at Columbus; vii. George-E., m. Iona Huffman; settled at Fresno, Cal.; viii. Samuel-Fleming); 3. Isabella, d. 1883; m. William L. Sharp, and settled at Steubenville; 4. Letitia, b. 1812; d. April 13, 1883; m. Joseph R. Hunter (see Hunter Family); 5. Jane, d. 1895; m. 1836, Dr. William C. Johnson, and settled at Marion. Ohio; 7. Margaret, d. 1895; m. 1838, Samuel Craig, and settled at Cambridge, Ohio; 8. Mary, d. 186—; m. Rev. Hugh Forsythe.

VII. ——, had issue, who came to America: 1. Alexander; 2. Samuel, b. 1778; d. July 2, 1837; m. near Middletown, Washington county, Penn., Elizabeth Jamison, b. 1785-86; d. Dec. 24, 1837; daughter of John and Sarah McFadden (II) Jamison; removed to Harrison county, Ohio, before 1815 (had issue: i. Alexander; settled in Kansas; ii. Elizabeth, m. John Dickerson, of Athens township; iii. Jane, m. Adam Dickerson, and settled in Athens township; iv. Margaret, m. Adam Dunlap, and settled in Athens township; v. Sarah, m. 1829, Samuel Carnahan, of Cadiz township; vi. James, b. Jan. 5, 1805; d. June 15, 1874; m. in Washington county, Penn., Mary Law, b. Nov. 19, 1808; daughter of Robert and Mary Jamison Law, the former a native of Scotland [had issue: Samuel, b. Oct. 12, 1830; m. (1st) 1854, Mary Richey, b. 1835; d. Feb. 24, 1872; daughter of John M. Richey; m. (2d) 1876, Eliza J. Richey, sister of Mary Richey: Mary; Robert; settled in Logan county, Ohio; William; James. b. Sept. 20, 1841; m. 1866, Arabella Richey, daughter of John M. and Ann Collins Richey; John, b. March 18, 1845; m. 1870. Margaret E. Morgan, daughter of Marshall and Ellen Morgan; Jamison-Law, b. July 16, 1851; d. Nov. 18, 1887; m. Aug. 26, 1874, Elizabeth Barger]; vii. John;

viii. Samuel); 3. Mary, m. Andrew Jamison.

John McFadden, probably a connection of the above family, m. Mary ——, and settled in Washington county, Penn.; their daughter, Mary, m. William Sharp; had issue: 1 ——, b. in Harrison county, 1807; d. at Millersburg, Holmes county, Ohio, 1893 (see William Sharp Family); 2. Nancy, b. 1810; d. Oct. 10, 1875; m. 1829, John Cunningham, son of David and Mary McLaughlin Cunningham.

SAMUEL McFADDEN, see also Family of Joshua Hamilton.

ROBERT McFARLAND, a native of Ireland, of Scottish descent, emigrated to America, and settled near Taylorstown, Washington county, Penn., in 1794, removing to Ohio some years later; m. Elizabeth Ferguson; had issue, among others: 1. William, b. 1795; d. 1878, near New Athens, Ohio, where he had located in 1824; served as a member of the Ohio Legislature; m. in Belmont county 1823, Elizabeth Henderson, b. 1800; d. 1867; daughter of Andrew and Martha Henderson, of Pennsylvania (had issue: i. Andrew; ii. Mary; iii. Martha; iv. Elizabeth, v. James; vi. William-Henderson, a United Presbyterian minister, b. June 14, 1832; settled at Cambridge, Ohio; m. —— Hanna; vii. Margaret, b. near New Athens; m. 1856, Rev. Jonathan Sharp McCready, b. near New Galilee, Beaver county, Penn., April 15, 1828; d. Sept. 7, 1864, from wounds received in the battle of the Wilderness, where he served as captain of Company H, 126th O. V. I.; son of Hugh McCready, of Pennsylvania; settled in Cadiz, Ohio, where he first served as minister in the Seceder (or Associate Presbyterian) Church, and later in the United Presbyterian Church; viii. Robert; ix. Nancy; x. Sarah); 2. Mary, died in Harrison county, in her eighty-seventh year; 3. —— (a daughter), d. in infancy.

JOHN McGAVRAN. a native of Ireland, b. 1737; d. 1770; emigrated to America and sett'ed in Maryland about 1755-60; m. Margaret Hill (m. 2d, —— O'Daniel), d. in Fayette county, Penn.; had issue:

I. Mary. II. Margaret. III. Mark. IV. William, b. 1767, in Harford county, Md.; d. 1853; removed to Springfield township, Jefferson county (now Lee township, Carroll county, Ohio) in 1818; m. March 17, 1791, Ann Thompson, b. in Harford county, Md., 1772; d. in Columbiana county, Ohio, 1863; daughter of Thomas Thompson; had issue: 1. Elizabeth, d. aged ninety-six; m. (1st) Thomas Magattogan; m. (2d) Benjamin Toland; 2. Mary, d. in Schuyler county, Ill., aged seventy-five; m. Charles Lucy; 3. Sarah, d. in Morgan county, Ohio; m. Samuel Hill; 4. John, d. in Columbiana county, Ohio; 5. Martha, d. in Illinois; m. John Mayes; 6. Margaret, d. in Kentucky; m. George Lucy, brother to Charles Lucy; 7. Thomas, d. in Colorado; m. Margaret Brown; 8. "Dillie"-Ann. d. aged twenty-two; 9. Mark, d. in Minneapolis, Minn., m. Louisa Daniels; 10. Stephen, d. in Harrison county, Ohio; 11. William-H., b. March 3, 1812, in Harford county, Md.; removed first to Jefferson county, and in 1843 to North township, Harrison county, Ohio; served as a member of the Ohio Legislature; m. in Stark county, Ohio. Elizabeth Brown, a native of Kentucky, of Scotch-Irish descent, daughter of James Brown (had issue: i. James-B.; ii. Henrietta, m. William H. H. Masters, of Scio; iii. George-W.; iv. Samuel-B., b. near Connotton, Harrison county. Nov. 25, 1847; settled in Cadiz; served in the Ohio Legislature; m. August. 1872, Jennie E. Johnson, of Carroll county; v. Elizabeth-Margaret, m. W. E. Clendenning, of Harrison county; vi. William-Thomas).

JAMES McGREW, a native of Western Virginia, settled in Jefferson county, Ohio, about 1832; m. April 26, 1824, Mary Pentecost, a native of West Virginia, d. in Harrison county, Ohio, 1840; had issue: 1. Alexander; 2. Murray; 3. William, b. in Hancock county, West Va., April 6, 1828; settled in Green township, Harrison county; m. (1st) Oct. 26, 1848, Cynthia Corbin. d. Jan. 26, 1885; m. (2d) March 31, 1887, Martha Kane, daughter of William Kane, of Cadiz; 4. James; 5. Joseph.

ROBERT McKEE, of Scotch-Irish descent, was a native of Redstone, Fayette county, Pennsylvania, where he m., 1806, Rachel Wills; was one of twelve children; settled in Archer townsh'p, Harrison county, Ohio, about 1807; had issue, among others: 1.

James, b. Feb. 11, 1811; settled in Green township, where he d. May 8, 1886; m. Nov. 24, 1834, Sarah Lewis, daughter of Joseph Lewis (had issue: i. Mary, b. Aug. 25, 1835; ii. Hannah, b. Nov. 20, 1836; d. Sept. 19, 1843; iii. Rachel, b. March 23, 1838; iv. Martha. b. Nov. 4, 1839; d. July 3, 1882; v. John. b. June 27, 1841; d. Sept. 11, 1864; vi. Henry, b. Feb. 16, 1843; vii. Joseph, b. July 17, 1845; viii. Amanda, b. Oct. 14, 1847; ix. Robert-M., b. March 17, 1849; d. June 24, 1857; x. Eliza, b. March 30, 1851; d. May 17, 1854; xi. Adeline, b. June 29, 1853; xii. Anna-Rebecca, b. Dec. 1, 1855).

Joseph Lewis, father of Sarah Lewis McKee, was born in New Jersey, Oct. 31, 1769; settled in Pennsylvania, where he died Sept. 4, 1853; was a Quaker, as was also his wife, Rachel Canby, b. in Pennsylvania; d. Sept. 1, 1852; removed from Chester county, Penn.. and first settled in Harrison county, Ohio, about 1829, but afterward returning to Pennsylvania; had issue: 1. Jesse, b. June 30, 1792; settled in Harrison county, 1817; 2. Jacob, b. Aug. 14, 1793; d. Feb. 5, 1883; removed to Harrison county with his brother Jesse; 3. Joseph. b. Jan. 5, 1795; d. March 1, 1882; settled in Harrison county in 1829; 4. Elizabeth. b. May 11, 1796; 5. David, b. Oct. 20, 1797; 6. Vernon, b. Oct. 23. 1798; d. April 5, 1882; 7. Lydia, b. March 10, 1800; 8. Rebecca, b. April 18, 1802; d. April 20, 1802; 9. Esther, b. April 21, 1804; 10 William, b. May 15, 1806; 11. Rachel. b. April 26, 1810; 12. Sarah, b. Nov. 24, 1812; m. James McKee; 13. Hannah, b. July 20, 1815.

RICHARD McKIBBEN, a native of Pennsylvania, of Irish descent; settled at Warrentown, Jefferson county, Ohio, about 1790: a short time afterward removed to Belmont county. Ohio; thence to Moorefield township, Harrison county. Ohio. and finally removed to Morgan county, Ohio. where he d. 1827; m. (1st) ——— Coulter; m. (2d) ——— Robison; m. (3d) Sarah Brokaw; had issue by third wife: 1. Richard: 2. Joseph; 3. Samuel; 4. Thomas: 5. William; 6. Rebecca; 7. Jane; 8. George, b. in Jefferson county, Ohio, Sept. 15, 1804; settled in Moorefield township, Harrison county; m. (1st) 1828, ——— Brashers; m. (2d) 1830, Martha Brokaw; m. (3d) Eleanor Morrison; m.

(4th) Jane Beall; d. 1887 (had issue by first wife: i. Jesse, settled in Illinois; had issue by second wife: ii. George, settled in Nottingham township, Harrison county; iii. John, b. Jan. 27, 1833; settled in Moorefield township; m. Jan. 3, 1856, Isabelle McMillan, b. Oct. 6, 1829; daughter of Charles and Rosanna Gilmore McMillan, natives of Ireland, who came to Harrison county from New York; had issue by third wife: iv. William; v. Eleanor; vi. Richard).

JOHN McLAUGHLIN, b. in Washington county, Penn., Nov. 4. 1774; d. at Adena, Jefferson county, Ohio, Nov. 10, 1860; settled in Ohio in 1801, removing to Adena the following year; served as a spy from Pittsburg to Wheeling, W. Va., during the Indian Wars; served in the Ohio Legislature for eight consecutive years, and in the State Senate the same length of time; m. about 1799, Anna Johnstone, d. June 6, 1849; had issue, thirteen children, among whom: 1. James, b. 1814; d. Aug. 25, 1865; m. Sarah J. Kerr, a native of Harrison county, daughter of Samuel and Annie Smith Kerr (had issue: i. William-B.; settled in Adena; ii. Ann-E., m. Lewis Bernhard, and settled in Harrison county; iii. Mary-E., m. William Courtright, and settled in Franklintown, Ohio; iv. Nancy-J., m. J. C. McNary, and settled in Unionport, Ohio; v. Samuel-K., b. in Adena, Sept. 12, 1846; m. May 22, 1872, Mary Belle Snider, a native of Green township, daughter of Samuel and Hannah Snider; settled in Harrison county, 1875; served in the Ohio Legislature, 1894-98); 7. Sarah-A., m. H. W. Parks, of Hopedale; 8. Joseph-S., settled in Jefferson county; 9. Mary-Emma, m. R. G. Dean, and settled in Omaha, Neb.

ROBERT McMILLAN, a native of Pennsylvania, removed to Jefferson county, Ohio, 1816, and in 1818 to Nottingham township, Harrison county, where he d. 1854; m. (1st) in Pennsylvania, Nancy Mitchell, d. 1840; m. (2d) Mary Boyd. d. 1844; m. (3d) Ellen Moore; had issue by first wife: 1. John, b. 1800; d. in Nottingham township, April 5, 1881; m. 1822, Elizabeth Peacock; d. Oct. 4. 1882; daughter of Eli Peacock (had issue: i. Robert-N.; ii. Thomas. b. June 9, 1826; settled at Deersville, in 1865; m. Dec. 23, 1852. Martha Ross, daughter of James and

Martha Phillips Ross; iii. Susan, d. Aug. 3, 1890; iv. Nancy, d. 1865; m. John Black); 2. Jane; 3. Nancy; 4. Margaret; 5. Mary; 6. Ann; 7. Robert; 8. Matthew.

ELIAS McNAMEE, of Scotch-Irish descent; emigrated from Pennsylvania, and settled in Freeport, Ohio; m. Mary Delaney, of French descent; had issue: 1. Amzi, b. Dec. 25, 1825; m. Mary Ellen Harvey, whose parents came from Maryland; b. 1823; d. 1886 (had issue: i. John; ii. Elias-B., m. Eva May Weeks).

ANDREW McNEELY (whose father emigrated from Ireland to America before the Revolution), b. in Berks county, Penn., 1772; d. in Cadiz township, Harrison county, Ohio, 1858, where he had settled in 1802; served as a member of the Ohio Legislature four years; m. in Philadelphia, 1800, Sarah Bettle, b. 1772; d. 1852, a native of that city; had issue, among others: 1. Cyrus, b. in Cadiz township, Harrison county, May 27, 1809; laid out the town of Hopedale, Harrison county, 1849, where he settled in that year; m. May 19, 1837, Jane Donaldson, b. 1807; d. 1887; a native of Cincinnati (had issue: i. Lorenzo; ii. Bryant; both died young).

JAMES McNUTT, d. in Green township, about May, 1822; m. Jane ———; had issue: 1. Benjamin; 2. James, d. 1855; m. Elizabeth Maholm, daughter of Samuel and Jane Maholm, of Cadiz (had issue: i. John; ii. Arthur-P., b. 1821; d. Dec. 15, 1895); 3. Joseph; 4. Sophia.

GEORGE McPECK, b. 1778; d. April 20, 1858; removed from Westmoreland county, Penn., to Harrison county, Ohio, in 1844; his wife b. 1785; d. April 27, 1869; they were m. Sept. 6, 1803; had issue, six sons and three daughters, of whom: I. William, settled in Union county, Ohio. II. George, b. in Westmoreland county, Penn., Oct. 24, 1808; came to Harrison county, Ohio, in November, 1829, and settled at Hanover, thence removed to Archer township, where he d. March 24, 1886; m. (1st) Oct. 6, 1831, Jane Endsley, d. Aug. 22. 1852. daughter of John and Jane Blaine Endsley; m. (2d) Oct. 6, 1853, Mrs. Barbara Endsley (widow of John Endsley). b. 1821; d. Nov. 1, 1854; m. (3d) Mrs. Catherine A. Lyons Caldwell, b. March 28, 1822; d. July 10, 1883; had issue, nine children, of whom: 1. John-Endsley, b. at Hanover, Aug. 1, 1832; settled in Archer township; served as an officer in the Civil War; m. Sept. 8, 1858, Mary Davidson, daughter of Rev. Lewis H. Davidson, of Washington township; 2. George-McKenney, b. 1836; d. Jan. 30, 1874; 3. David-Blair, b. 1845; d. in infancy; 4. William, b. 1859; d. July 24, 1875. John Endsley, father of Jane Endsley McPeck, was b. 1776; first settled in Cumberland county, Penn., where he m. Jane Blaine, b. in Ireland, 1773; d. Jan. 29, 1848; removed to Pittsburg, Penn., and thence, in 1808, to Archer township, Harrison county, Ohio, where he died April 29, 1835; had issue: 1. John, m. Barbara ———; 2. Jane, m. George McPeck; 3. Thomas; 4. James; 5. Mary, m. Nathan Shannon; 6. Sarah, m. Joseph McClain.

THOMAS MADDOX, b. in Virginia, 1778; son of Wilson Maddox, a native of Virginia; removed to Short Creek township, Harrison county, Ohio, about 1825, where he d. 1838; m. Jane Freeman, b. 1774; d. 1858; had issue: 1. Eliza, d. in Virginia, March 11, 1824; 2. Wilson, b. in Caroline county, Va., July 24, 1813; d. 1860; m. Nov. 30, 1836, Mary T. Ladd, b. in Virginia, 1818; d. 1874 (her parents were Robert and Mary T. Ladd, who came to Harrison county, about 1831, where they both died); (had issue: i. Eliza, m. G. B. Coutant; ii. Thomas, b. June 22. 1841; m. 1869, Henrietta T. Hague. d. Jan. 13, 1886; daughter of Henry and Sarah A. Thompson Woodward Hague, of Short Creek township: iii. Mary-Jane, m. Benjamin Chambers; iv. Virginia-W., m. William Buchanan. and settled at Hopedale, Harrison county).

SAMUEL MAHOLM, d. at Cadiz. November, 1838; m. Jane ———; had issue: 1. Jane, b. 1776; d. March 31, 1833; m. James Wilson. b. 1777; d. Dec. 6, 1839; 2. Nancy, b. 1779-80; d. Oct. 13, 1856; m. Walter B. Beebe, b. 1786; d. Jan. 24, 1836 (had issue: i. Walter-Butler, m. Maria B. Welch. b. 1822-23; d. Aug. 10, 1891; daughter of Rezin and Eliza Bayless Welch; ii. James): 3. Elizabeth. m. James McNutt, of Cadiz, d. May, 1855, son of James and Jane McNutt (had issue: i. John; ii. Arthur-P., b. 1821; d. Dec. 15, 1895); 4. Marga-

ret, b. 1790; d. 1858; 5. Hannah, m. ——— Phillips; 6. Mary, m. William Lyle; 7. Dorcas, m. John Bleaks; 8. Eleanor; 9. John, b. 1795; d. Sept. 9, 1854; m. April 4, 1822, Mrs. Martha Collins Bowland, daughter of David and Ann Workman Collins (had issue: i. Eliza-Jane, m. Joseph Sharon; ii. Martha-M., m. Rezin Bennett; iii. James-Bowland); 10. Sarah, b. 1803; d. 1848.

WILLIAM MALLERNEE, a native of Maryland, settled in Jefferson county, Ohio, 1809; m. Sarah ———; had issue:
I. Emanuel, b. in Maryland, Nov. 3, 1779; removed to Nottingham township, Harrison county, Ohio, about 1829, where he d. Feb. 23, 1839; m. (1st) Rachel Matthews, b. in Maryland, Nov. 3, 1788; d. June 24, 1828; daughter of Francis and Mary Karr Matthews, natives of Maryland who settled in Ohio in 1809; m. (2d) Hannah Eaton; had issue by first wife: 1. William, b. March 20, 1807; 2. Aquila. b. Jan. 6. 1809; 3. Mary-A., b. Aug. 17, 1811; 4. Matthew-F., b. Oct. 12, 1813; 5. Levi, b. Feb. 12, 1816; settled at Deersville, Harrison county, where he d. June 1, 1880; m. (1st) Dec. 6, 1838, Eleanor Johnson, b. Jan. 27, 1820; d. Dec. 23, 1863; daughter of Benjamin and Eleanor Johnson; m. (2d) Mrs. Jemima Garner Hines; m. (3d) June 1, 1879, Rachel Crabtree (had issue by first wife: i. David Turner, b. Nov. 18. 1839; ii. Emanuel, b. March 22, 1843; iii. Mary-A., b. March 25. 1846; m. J. H. Kent. and settled in Illinois; iv. Benjamin-J., b. Feb. 10, 1849; m. Jan. 17, 1872, Margaret Warman, b. in Illinois. March 15, 1850; daughter of William and Margaret Hoffman Warman; v. Lemuel, b. July 5, 1851: vi. Lydia-A., b. Aug. 3, 1854; vii. Caroline-L., b. Aug. 26, 1857; viii. Eleanor-J., b. July 18, 1860; m. L. D. Wells, and settled in Illinois; ix. Kinsey-C., b. Dec. 20, 1863: had issue by second wife: x. James-G., b. Oct. 10, 1866; xi. Levi-E., b. Oct. 20, 1868; xii. Ruth-J., b. Jan. 6, 1871); 6. Emanuel. b. Nov. 3, 1818; 7. Lewis, b. May 18. 1822; 8. Elizabeth. b. May 25, 1825; had issue by second wife: 9. Benjamin, b. Oct. 4, 1830; 10. Rachel, b. Aug. 13, 1832; 11. Jared, b. Sept. 10, 1834.
II. Mary.
III. Jared.

THOMAS MANSFIELD, a native of England, b. 1757; emigrated to America, and settled in Maryland before the Revolution; removed to Westmoreland county, Penn., and in 1797 settled on what was known as the Dorsey Flats, in Jefferson county. Ohio, where he d. June, 1844 (his two elder brothers served in the Revolutionary War; his brother Samuel served in the War of 1812); m. Mary Hill, b. 1767; d. 1854; had issue, among others: 1. William-L., b. in Jefferson county, November, 1810; settled in Green township. Harrison county, in 1866; m. 1840. Harriet Harrah, daughter of James G. Harrah (had issue: i. Margaret-J., m. A. Moore: ii. Thomas-B., served in the Civil War; settled in Iowa: iii. James-Harvey, d. 1876; iv. Mary-Ellis, m. Alonzo Hoobler; v. Nettie, m. John Mansfield. and settled in Steubenville; vi. Addie-R., m. William Hall).

ARTHUR MARTIN, b. in Ireland, 1771; emigrated to America and first settled in Lancaster county, Penn.; removed to Harrison county, Ohio, about 1817, locating in Cadiz township, where he d. 1826; m. in Lancaster county, Margaret Urey. a native of Pennsylvania, b. 1773; d. 1856; her grandfather, George Urey, served in the Revolutionary War; had issue: 1. Ann; 2. Mary, m. Washington Ourant, and settled in Cadiz township; 3. Edward; 4. John-H., b. in Pennsylvania; m. 1840, Harriet Hitchcock, b. in Harrison county, Nov. 6, 1819, daughter of Samuel and Isabella Moore Hitchcock (had issue: i. Albert, served in the Civil War; settled in Jay county, Md.; ii. Margaret; iii. Samuel; iv. Edward; v. John; vi. George; vii. Belle, m. John F. Mehollin; viii. Jane, m. John Jamison; ix. James, settled in Athens township; x. Mary, m. Joseph D. Clark; settled in Colorado); 5. George, b. in Harrison county, Ohio. March 1, 1817; m. Jan. 3. 1853, Rachel H. Kennedy, b. 1831, in Tuscarawas county, Ohio; d. 1881; a daughter of John and Matilda Kennedy.

Samuel Hitchcock, father of Harriet Martin, was b. 1788; d. Feb. 7, 1879, in Harrison county, where he had settled 1808; m. Isabella Moore, b. 1788; d. Feb. 2, 1851; they had twelve children, among whom were John and Harriet.

PETER MARTIN. a native of New Jersey, b. 1764; m. in Virginia, Eliza-

beth Heberling, a native of Maryland, b. 1770; removed to Short Creek township, Harrison county, Ohio, about 1822, where they died, the former in 1837, the latter in 1854; had issue: 1. Luther; 2. Nancy; 3. Sarah; 4. John, b. in Jefferson county, Va., Nov. 5, 1805; 5. Elizabeth; 6. Jacob; 7. Susan; 8. William; 9. George, settled near Zanesville; 10. Jesse, b. July 29, 1819; settled in Green township; m. Oct. 18, 1853, Elizabeth Scarborough, daughter of Thomas and Sarah Harris Scarborough, of Green township.

Thomas Scarborough, father of Elizabeth Martin, was b. in Pennsylvania, Feb. 1, 1796; d. in Green township, Harrison county, Sept. 4, 1867; m. Sarah Harris, d. July 6, 1855; had issue: 1. Charles, b. Oct. 5, 1824; 2. Mary-E., b. Feb. 5, 1828; 3. Elizabeth, b. Oct. 22, 1830, m. Jesse Martin; 4. Margaret, b. Nov. 21, 1832; 5. William, b. July 4, 1835; 6. Thomas, b. Dec. 12, 1839; 7. Asbury, b. Oct. 24, 1841.

JOHN MATTERN, removed from Westmoreland county, Penn., to Archer township, Harrison county, where he died June, 1861; m. Nancy ———; had issue: 1. Abraham, b. in Westmoreland county, Penn., Oct. 22, 1806; removed with his parents to Archer township, Harrison county, Ohio; located in Green township, April, 1837, where he d. Feb. 16, 1889; m. 1833, Mary Brown, b. April 14, 1808; d. Dec. 17, 1890; had issue: 1. Jane; 2. John; 3. Nancy-Ann; 4. Hugh-B.; 5. Wesley; 6. Alfred-S., b. Feb. 18, 1853; settled at Folks' Station, Green township; m. Sept. 14, 1881, Jennie R. Pry, daughter of Robert Pry, a resident of Pennsylvania, who afterward settled in Wellsburg, W. Va. II. John. III. Julia-Ann, m. ——— Smith. IV. Anna-Maria, m. ——— Hanna.

JAMES MAXWELL, a native of Ireland or Scotland, emigrated to America and settled near Baltimore, Md.; had issue: John, James, Hugh, George, Robert. Of these children, James Maxwell removed to Pennsylvania, where he was married; had issue:
I. John. II. Robert, b. July 30, 1769; settled near Bloomfield, Jefferson county, Ohio, 1798; m. in Pennsylvania. Deborah Wierman; had issue: 1. Robert, b. Jan. 20, 1794; d. Jan. 8, 1866; m. June 18, 1823; 2. Susannah, b. Aug. 5, 1795; d. Nov. 7, 1840; m. Oct. 13, 1813;

3. James, b. April 5, 1797; d. Jan. 13, 1860; m. June 27, 1822; 4. William, b. March 14, 1799; d. Oct. 5, 1884; m. Sept. 10, 1828; 5. John, b. Nov. 5, 1800; d. Oct. 3, 1821; 6. Mary, b. June 28, 1802; d. March 3, 1864; 7. Harmon, b. Feb. 1, 1804; m. May 23, 1833; 8. Thomas, b. May 20, 1805; m. Aug. 14, 1828; 9. Archibald, b. Dec. 2, 1806; d. Oct. 27, 1882; m. Feb. 7, 1832; 10. David, b. Nov. 19, 1808; d. Oct. 20, 1842; m. April 27, 1837; 11. Isabella, b. Sept. 15, 1810; d. June 21, 1872; m. July 10, 1835; 12. Matilda, b. June 15, 1812; d. July 5, 1813; 13. Hiram, b. Nov. 13, 1813; d. Aug. 8. 1852; m. Nov. 13, 1834; 14. Hezekiah, b. Aug. 21, 1815; d. Oct. 4, 1885; m. Oct. 5, 1843; 15. Allen, b. in Jefferson county, Ohio, May 7, 1817; settled in Harrison county, Ohio, 1856; m. 1843, Mary Ann Bell (had issue: i. Francis-B., b. April 25, 1845; d. June 26, 1845; ii. Martha-J., b. May 13, 1846; d. Dec. 21, 1870; m. Dec. 15, 1864, Henry Copeland; iii. Jackson-B., b. Sept. 4, 1849; m. Sept. 22, 1875, Esther Devore; iv. Elizabeth-D., b. July 13, 1852; d. Feb. 14, 1855; v. Nancy-A., b. July 10, 1855; m. Sept. 28, 1876, Emanuel Howard; vi. Mary-Belle, b. Dec. 2, 1857; d. Aug. 15, 1888; m. Sept. 23, 1887, J. F. Mattern; vii. Caroline-S., b. May 25, 1860; d. Jan. 21, 1863; viii. Vall-A., b. April 22, 1863; d. Nov. 27, 1886; ix. ———, b. and d. Dec. 11, 1865; x. Orpha, b. Jan. 22, 1873); 16. Margaret. b. July 5, 1819; d. June 28, 1841. III. Mary. IV. Margaret. V. Jane.

WILLIAM MAXWELL, a native of Ireland. as was also his wife, emigrated to America, and settled in Virginia before the Revolutionary War; had issue: 1. James, b. in Virginia; d. in Nottingham township, Harrison county, Ohio, 1868; settled in Jefferson county, before 1838, and thence removed to Harrison; m. in Virginia. Hannah Pollock, d. July 23, 1886 (had issue: i. David; ii. Mary-Jane; iii. Walker; iv. John; v. Elizabeth; vi. Margaret; vii. Henry; viii. James, b. in Nottingham township, April 26, 1828; m. (1st) Dec. 14, 1859, Elizabeth McCullough, of Nottingham township; m. (2d) Sarah Willison, of Washington township. Harrison county; ix. William; x. Rachel); 2. William; 3. Henry; 4. Alexander; 5. John; 6. Margaret; 7. Elizabeth.

JOSEPH MAYES, see Family of Robert Coulter.

SAMUEL MEARS, b. in Ireland, May 13, 1777, where he m. Leah Serges, b. May 8, 1786; emigrated to America and about 1790 settled at Baltimore, Md.; removed in 1818, to Perry township, Tuscarawas county, Ohio, where he died; had issue: 1. John, b. Nov. 2, 1805; 2. Alexander, b. Jan. 1, 1807; 3. William, b. April 1, 1809; d. Aug. 3, 1879; 4. Catherine, b. Nov. 23, 1810; 5. Jane, b. Oct. 2, 1811; d. March, 1879; 6. Robert, b. Oct. 26, 1813; settled at West Chester, Tuscarawas county, 1842, where he d. July 21, 1890; m. (1st) 1842, Anna Eliza Thompson, b. June 7, 1819; d. Sept. 28, 1861, daughter of Thomas and Mary Amelia Mitchell Thompson; m. (2d) Mary McCord (had issue by first wife: i. Elizabeth-Jane, b. July 29, 1843; d. Aug. 31, 1871; ii. Samuel-T., b. Oct. 1, 1845; settled in Freeport, Harrison county, 1882: m. Dec. 25, 1866, Sarah Arminda Stewart, of Freeport, daughter of Andrew and Mary A. Snider Stewart; iii. Robert-T., b. Nov. 24, 1848; iv. Mary-L., b. Oct. 20, 1851; d. July 17, 1873; v. Nathan-H., b. Oct. 19, 1856; vi. Harriet-A., b. Oct. 25, 1859); 7. Samuel, b. Sept. 28, 1815; 8. Rachel. b. Jan. 20, 1818; 9. Nathan, b. Sept. 27, 1820.

The parents of Ann Eliza Mears, Thomas and Mary Amelia Mitchell Thompson, were natives of county Down, Ireland, where they were m. 1816; emigrating to America and settling in New York the same year; removed to Harrison county, Ohio, 1820, locating three miles west of Freeport; the former was b. 1782; d. Sept. 12, 1828; the latter was b. Dec. 20, 1780; d. Aug. 17, 1865; had issue: 1. Ann-Eliza, b. June 7, 1819; d. Sept. 28, 1861; m. Robert Mears; 2. Robert, b. 1821; d. March 15, 1885; m. Louisa Carruthers; 3. James, b. 1823; m. Margaret Boles; 4. Harriet, b. 1825; m. Siles Stephens; 5. Julia, b. 1827; m. John R. Frazier.

JOHN MEGAW, a native of Ireland, emigrated to America about 1775; served in the Revolutionary War, entering the American army immediately after his arrival; removed from Westmoreland county, Penn., to North township, Harrison county, Ohio, about 1814; m. Jane Hamilton; had issue: I. John, b. in Pennsylvania, Feb. 18,

1784; came to Harrison county with his parents; settled in Archer township, 1822, where he d. March 9, 1865; m. in Westmoreland county, Penn., 1812, Catherine Best; b. in Pennsylvania, Jan. 31, 1789; d. Sept. 9, 1847; daughter of James Best; had issue: 1. Samuel, b. in Westmoreland county, Penn., Feb. 25, 1813; settled in Archer township; m. Nov. 13, 1834, Jane McCombs, d. July 2, 1885; daughter of James McCombs, a resident of Pennsylvania (had issue: i. Catherine-A., b. Oct. 9, 1835; ii. Margaret-M., b. Feb. 26, 1837; iii. John-C., b. May 20, 1838; d. May 30, 1864; iv. James-R., b. May 1, 1840; v. Samuel, b. Nov. 10, 1841; d. Sept. 30, 1845; vi. Mary-Jane, b. Aug. 19, 1843; vii. Eleanor, b. Dec. 24, 1845; viii. Sarah-E., b. Oct. 31, 1848); 2. Jane; 3. Sarah, b. in North township, Oct. 17, 1817; m. Dec. 31, 1843, William Maxwell, of North township; removed to Washington county, Iowa, in 1848 (had issue: i. Robert, d. near Hanover; ii. John; d. in Harrison county; iii. William-James; iv. Catherine-Jane; v. Nathaniel-McDowell; vi. ———, d. in infancy); 4. John; 5. James, b. in Archer township, Nov. 11, 1823; m. (1st) Oct. 5, 1851, Elizabeth Mitchell, d. April 7, 1880; daughter of John Mitchell, of Archer township; m. (2d) Oct. 30, 1884, Eliza Haverfield, daughter of Alexander Haverfield, of Cadiz township, Harrison county (had issue by first wife: i. J.-M., b. March 9, 1857); 6. John, b. in Archer township, Aug. 14, 1826; removed to Cadiz township, in 1856; m. 1852, Sarah Jane Christy, daughter of William Christy, who with his wife, was an early settler in Harrison county (had issue: i. John, d. 1866; ii. Martha-Ann, d. 1866; iii. Margaret-Jane, d. 1866; iv. Clara-Catherine; v. Everett-Grimes); 7. Jacob, b. Aug. 21, 1829; d. Feb. 15, 1888; m. June 22, 1867, Eleanor Robinson, d. May 21, 1882, daughter of James Robinson (had issue: i. James-R., b. May 4, 1865; ii. Minerva-R., b. Feb. 6, 1868; iii. John-B., b. May 17, 1871; iv. Catherine, b. Aug. 9, 1873; v. Lawson-E., b. Dec. 24, 1880).
II. Rebecca.
III. Jane.
IV. Samuel.
V. Sarah.
VI. James, b. Sept. 15, 1793; d. Oct. 24, 1851; had issue: 1. John; 2. James-G.; 3. George-T.; 4. Martha-Matilda; 5.

Eliza-Jane; 6. Eleanor; 7. Sarah-Ann, m. ——— Patterson.

JOSEPH MEHOLLIN, a native of Ireland, of Scottish descent; settled at Smithfield, Jefferson county, Ohio, before 1800, where he died; had issue: I. Joseph, d. aged sixty-five years; settled in Cadiz township; m. Margaret McFadden, b. 1789; d. 1877; had issue, among others: 1. John, b. in Cadiz township, 1818; d. 1900; m. Elizabeth McFadden (had issue: i. Samuel, b. Sept. 28, 1846; m. (1st) 1871, Mary Nash, b. 1853; d. 1879; daughter of Samuel Nash, of Cassville; m. (2d) Belle Smith, daughter of Archibald Smith, of Dickerson's Mills, Harrison county; ii. Joseph; iii. Mary-Margaret, m. Leonard Rowland, of Cadiz township; iv. John-Findley, b. in Cadiz township, March 17, 1856; m. 1878, Belle Martin, daughter of John and Harriet Martin, of Cadiz township); 2. Sarah, m. William Jamison, and settled in Cadiz township; 3. Margaret, m. George Tarbot, and settled near Moorefield.

MICAJAH MERRYMAN, of German descent, b. in Maryland, April 25, 1775; removed to Smithfield, Jefferson county, Ohio, about 1815; later settled in Archer township, Harrison county, and subsequently removed to Tuscarawas county, Ohio, where he d. 1847; served in the War of 1812; m. 1811, ——— Snyder, b. in Maryland, March, 1795, daughter of Martin and Mary Ann Snyder, natives of that State; had issue, among others: 1. John, b. in Cadiz township, July 26, 1823; settled in Archer township; m. Mary Shivers, b. in Nottingham township, Aug. 22, 1824, daughter of John and Elizabeth Shivers, pioneers of Harrison county, whence they came from Maryland (had issue: i. Martha, m. James B. Rogers, and settled at Cadiz; ii. Caroline; iii. Alexander; iv. Hannah, m. George English; v. Jackson; vi. Elizabeth, m. Lincoln Blair, and settled in Stock township; vii. Jeremiah-C., settled in Nottingham township; viii. Lafayette; ix. Sarah-M., m. James Love, and settled in Sauk Centre, Minn.; x. John).

JOHN PETER MIKESELL, a native of Frederick (now Carroll) county, Md.; d. in Rumley township, Harrison county, July 15, 1846, where he had settled in 1816; son of John Mikesell, a native of Germany; m. Mary Ann Long, b. in Maryland; had issue: 1. Joseph, b. March 25, 1811; settled at Jewett, Harrison county; m. Oct. 22, 1839, Magdaline Hoobler, b. Feb. 17, 1821; daughter of Adam and Elizabeth Lawyer Hoobler (had issue: i. Maria, b. May 6, 1843; m. James Aiken, of Jewett); 2. Andrew; 3. George; 4. Jesse, b. Dec. 11, 1819; d. Feb. 23, 1887; m. 1847, Mary E. Roby, daughter of John H. and Sophia Roby (both b. in Maryland, 1800); 5. Daniel; 6. Susanna; 7. Samuel.

JOHN MILLER, a native of Frederick county, Md.; removed to Rumley township, Harrison county, Ohio, about 1806, where he d. 1836; had issue:
I. Daniel, b. in Frederick county, Md., 1788; came with his parents to Harrison county; settled in German township, where he d. 1854; m. 1817, Susannah Lowmiller, b. in Dauphin county, Penn., 1796; daughter of John and Catherine Lowmiller, who settled in Harrison county before 1810; had issue: 1. Catherine; 2. Elizabeth; 3. Sarah; 4. John, b. Feb. 22, 1822; m. May 1, 1849, Susannah Mikesell, b. in Rumley township, Feb. 15, 1824, daughter of Peter and Mary A. Long Mikesell, who removed from Frederick county, Md., to Harrison county, before 1810 (had issue: i. O.-B.; settled at Germano, Harrison county; ii. Rebecca-Margaret; iii. H.-A., b. March 8, 1851; m. 1874, Sarah C. Wood, b. Sept. 22, 1852, daughter of Ellis and Elizabeth Shearer Wood, of Carroll county; iv. Andrew-B., settled in Rumley township; v. Daniel-D., a minister, settled at Parker's Landing, Penn.; vi. Samuel-H., settled in Greensville, Penn.; vii. John-O.; viii. Joseph-M., settled in Washington county, Penn.; ix. Clement-E.; x. Clayton-L.; xi. Jesse-L.); 5. Henry, b. Aug. 27, 1824; served in the Civil War; m. May 20, 1856, E. W. Gault, b. Feb. 28, 1831, daughter of John and Nancy McKinsey Gault, who settled in Harrison county, in 1839; 6. Susannah; 7. Rebecca; 8. Margaret; 9. Abigail; 10. Eliza-J. II. David. III. John, b. 1801; settled in Rumley township before 1828, where he d. 1836; m. Margaret Lowmiller, b. 1805; d. 1876; daughter of John and Susannah Ulerich Lowmiller; had issue: 1. Mary-Ann; 2. Susanna, b. in Rumley township, Oct. 11, 1828; m.

May, 1847, Thomas W. Ramsouer, b. in Rumley township, 1820; d. in Jewett, 1880; son of John and Catherine H. Ramsouer (had issue: i. Josiah-A.; ii. John-William; iii. Margaret-C.; iv. Sabella-J.; v. Harden-Miller, settled in Massillon, Ohio; vi. Daniel-D.; vii. Hester-A., m. Wm. Custer Edwards; settled in Dennison, Ohio; viii. Lauretta-F.; ix. Susan-Maria, m. Richey Osborn); 3. Isabella, m. William Manbeck; 4. Elizabeth, m. Isaac McCloud, and settled in Kansas; 5. Jacob; settled in Jefferson county, Ohio; 6. Daniel. IV. Jacob. V. Joseph. VI. Catherine. VII. Hannah. VIII. Mary. IX. Sarah.

WILLIAM MILLER, born in the North of Ireland; emigrated to America, and settled in Huntingdon county, Penn., about 1789; m. Rebecca Wylie; had issue: 1. James; 2. Samuel; 3. Joseph; 4. Benson; 5. Margaret; 6. Isabel; 7. Martha, d. 1873; m. John L. Martin, son of John and Elizabeth Livingston Martin, of Mifflin county, Penn. (had issue: i. Rebecca-Jane, m. 1861, Lyons F. Grider; ii. John, m. Jane Johnson; iii. Samuel; iv. William; v. Joseph); 8. Hester; 9. Rebecca.

ALEXANDER MILLS (whose father d. Feb. 10, 1776), was b. in county Down, Ireland, Dec. 11, 1738; d. Dec. 4, 1815; had issue:
I. John, b. in county Down, Ireland, Nov. 18, 1766; emigrated to America and before 1811 settled in Jefferson county, Ohio, removing thence to Carroll county, where he d. April 29, 1853; had issue, among others: 1. William, b. Sept. 1, 1811; removed to New Athens, where he d. 1864; m. 1844, Sarah Ann Cannon, b. July 27, 1820 (had issue: i. Rachel-Jane; ii. James-Allen; iii. Moses-Cannon; iv. John-Sullivan; v. Jesse-Lewis; settled in Kansas; vi. Mary-E., m. Dr. J. H. Irwin; settled in Oregon; vii. Nancy-Priscilla, m. Dr. James A. Calhoon, and settled at Pittsburg; viii. Robert-Emmett); 2. Alexander, settled in Carroll county (had issue, among others: i. Thomas; ii. Shane).

GEORGE MILLS, a native of Ireland or Scotland, emigrated to America and first settled in Pennsylvania. where he m. Elizabeth Caldwell, a native of Ireland; removed to Jefferson county, Ohio, before 1816; had issue: 1. George; 2. William; 3. John, b. Feb. 23, 1816; m.

March 21, 1850, Eliza J. Henderson, b. Aug. 28, 1827; daughter of John Henderson, of Jefferson county; 4. James; 5. Jane; 6. Nancy; 7. Eliza.

ROBERT MINTIER, b. in Pennsylvania, 1791, of Scotch-Irish descent; removed to Belmont county, Ohio, before 1819, where several of his children were born; located in Short Creek township, Harrison county, about 1831, where he d. 1870; m. in Belmont county, 1819, Elizabeth Hammond, b. 1798; d. 1863; daughter of Robert and Jane Hammond; had issue: 1. Alexander; 2. Joseph, b. in Jefferson county, Oct. 25, 1822; in 1854 located in Bureau county; settled in Short Creek township in 1862; m. (1st) 1846, Eleanor Campbell, d. 1853; daughter of William and Ellen Campbell, of Belmont county, Ohio (who had removed there from Washington county, Penn.); m. (2d) 1854, Eliza Jane Carrick, b. in Short Creek township; daughter of James (d. 1885) and Martha Pennell Carrick (the former having come to Ohio from Pennsylvania); (had issue by first wife: i. Elizabeth; ii. Martha, settled in Leavenworth, Kan.; iii. Robert; had issue by second wife: iv. Sarah-Belle; v. James-C., settled at Oberlin, Decatur county, Kan.; vi. Josephine, m. Alonzo Eli, and settled in Athens township; vii. Milton-S.; viii. Minerva-Jeanette; ix. Oscar-Glenn); 3. Thomas, settled in Muskingum county, Ohio; 4. William, d. in infancy; 5. John, settled in Belmont county; 6. James, b. March 9, 1829; served in the Civil War; settled in Short Creek township, Ohio; m. (1st) Oct. 26, 1854, Eliza Ann Kibble, d. 1855; m. (2d) Oct. 27, 1858. Mary Barnett, of Guernsey county, Ohio; d. 1865; m. (3d) Aug. 16, 1866, Elizabeth A. Davis, b. in Belmont county; daughter of John and Eleanor J. Israel Davis (the former d. in Jefferson county, in October, 1884; the latter also died in 1884; the maternal grandparents of Elizabeth Davis were Germans; her great-grandfather, Robert Israel, was an officer in the Revolutionary War); 7. Mary, m. John Hanna, of New Athens; 8. Martha, twin sister to Mary, d. young; 9. Eliza-Jane, m. James Henderson, and settled at Harrisville, Ohio; 10. Robert-Johnson, settled in Kansas; 11. Esther, m. Joseph Shepard, and settled in Iowa; 12. David, b. Feb. 3, 1841, settled in

Short Creek township; served in the Civil War; m. Sept. 26, 1867, Margaret Jane Richey, daughter of Alexander and Eliza Haneway (b. 1810; d. 1839) Richey (the former d. in Muskingum county, Ohio, March, 1867; the grandfather of Margaret Jane Richey, Andrew Richey, was one of the first settlers in Harrison county, and died there.

JOHN MITCHELL, b. 1774; a native of Ireland or Scotland; emigrated to America and first settled in Maryland; removed to Steubenville, Ohio, before 1816, and later located in Archer township, Harrison county, where he d. April 12, 1844; m. Mary Hines, b. 1782; d. 1850; daughter of Rudolph Hines, of Cadiz township, Harrison county; had issue, among others: 1. Robert, b. in Archer township, Jan. 5, 1816; m. Jan. 2, 1845, Eliza Jane Atkinson, b. June 16, 1823; daughter of James Atkinson, of Archer township (had issue: i. Jane, b. Oct. 31, 1845; d. June 30, 1871; m. Feb. 2, 1865, John Biggar; ii. John-R., b. March 11, 1847; iii. James-A., b. March 13, 1851; iv. William, b. Aug. 19, 1853; v. Mary-E., b. Sept. 2, 1855; m. (1st) Clarence Haverfield; m. (2d) Hamilton Lisle).

MATTHEW MITCHELL, b. in Ireland, where he m. Jennie McDill; emigrated to America, and, about 1785, settled in Washington county. Penn.; removed to Harrison county, Ohio, before 1806, subsequently returning to Pennsylvania, where both himself and wife died; had issue, among others:

I. John, b. April 6, 1787, in Washington county, Penn.; d. 1865, in Harrison county, where he had settled in 1816; m. Margaret McGee, b. about 1790; d. 1875; had issue: 1. Jane, m. Abraham Corban, and settled near Cassville; 2. Matthew, settled in Noble county, Ohio; 3. Nancy; 4. Rose-Ann, m. John Chamberlain, and settled in Poweshiek county, Iowa; 5. Morris, settled in Knox county, Illinois; 6. Elizabeth; 7. Margaret-Ann, m. John Nash; settled near Cassville, Ohio (had issue, six sons); 8. John-D., b. Nov. 22, 1825, near Cadiz; m. (1st) 1852, Rebecca Hammond, d. about 1865; m. (2d) Nov. 5, 1868, Elizabeth A. Kyle, daughter of Thomas and Jane McNary Kyle, of German township, Harrison county Ohio; 9. George; 10. Sarah, m. John

Houser, and settled in Mercer county, Ill., where she died, leaving six children; 11. Mary, m. Welling Calhoon, and settled in Crawfordsville, Ind.

AMMI MOORE, b. in New Jersey, 1767; removed to Greene county, Penn., about 1795, and in 1817 to Moorefield township, Harrison county, Ohio, where he d. 1823; m. Sarah Shepard, b. in Pennsylvania, 1777; d. 1841; daughter of William Shepard, a native of Pennsylvania, who had settled in the eastern part of Greene county; had issue: 1. Rebecca; 2. Mary; 3. Rachel; 4. Elizabeth; 5. Shepard; 6. John; 7. Uriah, b. in Greene county, Penn., March 4, 1814; m. Oct. 13, 1842, Mary Ann Fulton, b. April 14, 1821; daughter of Philip and Sarah Hanna Fulton, natives of Maryland, who settled in Harrison county, about 1819 (had issue: i. Sarah-A., m. ―――― Corbin; ii. John-F.; iii. William-A.; iv. Hannah-M., m. ―――― Dickerson; v. Albert-D., settled in Nottingham township; vi. Zephaniah; vii. Anderson-W.; viii. Vincent-C.; ix. Elliott-D.; x. Mary-E.).

ROBERT MOORE, b. in Ireland, 1771; emigrated to America and first settled in New York City, 1793, thence removed to eastern Pennsylvania, and in 1795, to Jefferson county, Ohio, locating ten miles west from Steubenville; about 1800 settled in Moorefield township, Harrison county, where he d. Feb. 1, 1835; m. Mary Armstrong, b. in Ireland, 1771; d. March 22, 1851; had issue: 1. Samuel; 2. Robert-A., b. in Jefferson county, about 1800; d. in Nottingham township, 1877; m. Elizabeth Peacock, d. 1864 (had issue: i. Mary-A., m. ―――― Adams, and settled in Freeport, Harrison county; ii. Susannah; iii. Eli-Peacock, settled in Freeport township; iv. William-C., b. April 20, 1836; settled in Moorefield township; m. March 21, 1861, Rebecca J. Adams, b. Jan. 21, 1842, daughter of Samuel and Elizabeth Johnson Adams; v. Eliza-J., m. ―――― Bartlett, and settled in Iowa; vi. Robert-B.; vii. Julia-A., m. ―――― Snyder; viii. Thomas-A.); 3. John, b. in Jefferson county, Aug. 4, 1809; d. May 14, 1874; settled in Moorefield township, Harrison county; m. Elsie Johnson, b. Oct. 6, 1811; daughter of William Johnson, an early settler of Moorefield township (had issue:

i. Mary, m. Jackson Rea, of Cadiz township; ii. Johnson, settled in Moorefield township; iii. Albert, b. July 7, 1841; m. June 13, 1867, Sarah McFadden, b. May 13, 1844, daughter of Samuel and Margaret Rankin McFadden); 4. William, b. Oct. 4, 1811; settled in Moorefield township; m. March 15, 1837, Lydia Delaney, b. June 7, 1820; daughter of John and Rachel Delaney, natives of Delaware, who had early settlers in Harrison county (had issue: i. Robert; ii. Sophia, m. Robert Moore; iii. Allen-D.; iv. Stewart; v. William, settled in Missouri; vi. Howard, settled in Cadiz; vii. Lucinda; viii. Lydia, m. Linard Fulton, settled in Missouri); 5. Jane; 6. Margaret; 7. Mary.

WILLIAM MOORE, b. 1779; d. at Cadiz, 1847; removed from Westmoreland county, Penn., to Harrison county, Ohio, about 1808; m. in Westmoreland county, 1802, Sarah Corey, b. in New Jersey, Jan. 12, 1783; d. at Cadiz, March 16, 1863; had issue: 1. Mary, b. 1803; d. 1882; m. William Fulton; 2. Rosanna, b. 1805; d. young; 3. Elizabeth, b. 1807; d. 1825; 4. Nancy, b. 1809; d. 1881; m. William Birney; 5. Samuel, b. 1811; d. 1880; m. Isabel Birney; 6. John, b. July 27, 1813; d. Feb. 2, 1883; m. (1st) 1836, Elizabeth McCullough, b. 1818; d. Sept. 9, 1858; daughter of Joseph and Elizabeth Lyons McCullough, of Archer township; m. (2d) Sarah J. McCullough, b. 1827; d. June 14, 1874; m. (3d) Phebe Gray (had issue by first wife: i. Sarah; ii. David-O., a physician, removed to Bloomington, Ill.; iii. William-A.; iv. Beatty; v. Mary, m. Thompson Craig; vi. Alice, m. Robert Watson Barricklow; vii. Nancy, m. Anderson N. Hammond, and removed to Chicago; viii. Joseph, a physician, removed to Omaha, Neb.; ix. Ingram-Craig); 7. Hannah, b. 1815; m. 1834, Cyrus Gilmore, son of Samuel and Elizabeth Buchanan Gilmore; 8. David, b. 1817; d. 1870; m. Jane Clark, b. 1818; d. June 23, 1879; 9. Rachel, b. 1819; d. 1845; m. Samuel Snyder; 10. Sarah, b. 1822; m. Ingram Clark (see Family of Roger Clark); 11. Alexander, b. 1824; d. 1885; m. Mrs. Susan Craig Hanna, widow of Andrew Finley Hanna, of Cadiz; 12. Jane, b. 1827; d. 1858; m. Walter Craig; 13. William, b. 1829; d. 1885; m. (1st) ―――― Saunders; m. (2d) ―――― Hurford; m. (3d) ―――― Purviance.

JAMES MORRIS, a native of Virginia or Maryland (whose grandparents are said to have come from England to Virginia before 1750), removed from Maryland to West Virginia with his family; had issue:

I. Daniel.
II. Thomas.
III. James.
IV. Zachariah.
V. John, b. in West Virginia, opposite the city of Marietta, Ohio, April 4, 1785; removed in 1813 to Cadiz, Ohio, and, in 1816, located at New Athens, where he d. April 4, 1865; m. in New Athens, Jan. 8, 1816, Charlotte Huff, daughter of Joseph and ———— Doddridge Huff (the former was a celebrated Indian scout and fighter during and after the Revolutionary War, and was also one of the first white settlers in Short Creek township, Harrison county; he was given a section of land in Athens township by the United States Government for services rendered in Indian wars; his wife was of the well-known Doddridge family, of Hopewell township, Washington county, Penn., where during Indian attacks she had molded bullets in the block-houses of the settlements); John and Charlotte Morris had issue: 1. ————, d. in infancy, Nov. 26, 1817; 2. Alexander, b. July 14, 1819; d. May 18, 1824; 3. Joseph, b. March 16, 1822; settled in German township; m. (1st) March 9, 1843, Mary Brock, d. Oct. 28, 1873, daughter of George S. Brock, of Belmont county; m. (2d) Feb. 17, 1875, Emma Moore, daughter of Cyrus Moore, of Jefferson county, Ohio (had issue by first wife: i. John-A., b. Jan. 11, 1844; ii. Mary-E.-C., b. June 27, 1847; iii. George-S., b. Oct. 31, 1850; iv. L.-V., b. June 12, 1854; d. Feb. 2, 1885); 4. Margaret, b. March 21, 1824; d. Sept. 25, 1846; 5. John, b. May 10, 1826; 6. Mary-Ann, b. May 26, 1828; 7. Prudence, b. July 23, 1830; d. March 2, 1838; 8. Philip-D., b. May 21, 1833; d. Oct. 28, 1835; 9. Charlotte, b. May 16, 1835; d. March 9, 1838; 10. Elizabeth, b. Jan. 12, 1840; d. Jan. 1, 1866.
VI. Elizabeth.
VII. Morgan, b. in Maryland; removed first to West Virginia, and thence to Jefferson county, Ohio, before 1812, where he d. June 4, 1864; served in the War of 1812; m. (1st) in West Virginia, Elizabeth Wood, d. 1837; daughter of Edward Wood, a pioneer; m. (2d) Ellen Smith, of Harrison county; had issue by first wife: 1. Nancy; 2. Mary; 3. Phœbe; 4. John, b. May 4, 1816; settled in Athens township, about 1850; m. (1st) March 20, 1846, Elizabeth Porter; d. July 11, 1852; daughter of James T. Porter; m. (2d) April 29, 1859, Elizabeth Maxwell, daughter of James Maxwell (had issue by first wife: i. James; ii. Elizabeth, m. Johnson Hughes; iii. Rebecca-Jane; iv. William; v. Margaret; had issue by second wife: vi. Alonzo, b. Jan. 12, 1860; m. June 13, 1881, Laura E. Dickerson, daughter of J. T. Dickerson, of New Athens; vii. John-O.; viii. Thomas-M., b. Feb. 1, 1862; settled in Belmont county; m. 1888, Mary E. Monahan; ix. Mary-Alice; x. Morgan; xi. Sarah-J.; xii. Charles); 5. Elizabeth; 6. Thomas; 7. Hannah; 8. William; 9. Morgan; 10. Eliza-Jane; had issue by second wife: 11. Rebecca-Ann; 12. James-S.
VIII. Phœbe.

MICHAEL MYERS, see Family of Ezra Wharton.

ANDREW NICHOL, see Family of John Estep.

JAMES OGLEVEE, emigrated from the North of Ireland and settled in East Nottingham township, Chester county, Penn. (now Cecil county, Md.) before 1722 (probably a son or brother of John Oglevee, who died in Cecil county, January, 1744, leaving a wife, Rachel, and children, James, Dorcas, and Jean); d. 1751-53; m. Sarah ————; d. May, 1753; had issue: John, Sarah, Jean, Margaret (m. ———— Boggs), and Violet (m. ———— Porter, and had two sons, James and John); his son, grandson, or nephew, John Oglevee, died in Cecil county, January, 1797, leaving children, John, Joseph, Mary, Sarah, Margaret, and Anne, of whom:

I. John, removed from Cecil county, Maryland, to Fayette county, Penn., and thence, soon after 1800, to Harrison county, Ohio, and settled on Boggs' Fork of Stillwater Creek, where he d. 1815; served in the War of 1812; m. Mrs. Agnes Passmore Patterson, b. 1771-72; d. Aug. 11, 1853 (she had issue by her first husband, ———— Patterson: 1. Jane, m. Adam Dunlap, and settled in Harrison county; 2. Mary, m. Robert Dunlap, and settled in Harrison county); John and Agnes Oglevee had issue: 1. Elizabeth, b. 1804; d. Dec. 5, 1881; m. 1827, John Bethel, son of Simpson and Nancy Holloway Bethel; 2. William, b. 1808; d. July 6, 1884; settled in Moorefield township; m. 1830, Susanna Price, b. near Stillwater, Belmont county, 1811; d. May 26, 1879; daughter of John Price, of English descent (a pioneer, who served in the War of 1812; his wife, of Scottish descent); (had issue: i. John; settled in Morgan county, Ohio; ii. George; iii. Agnes, m. Archibald Hammond, of New Athens; iv. David, b. May 10, 1837; settled at Cadiz, 1889; m. October, 1866, Jane Ramsey, daughter of William and Mary Ramsey [the former a son of John Ramsey, one of the early settlers of Harrison county; the latter, daughter of John Hines, also an early settler]; v. Hugh, b. in Moorefield township, Aug. 1, 1839; settled at New Athens; served in the Civil War; m. in Belmont county, Aug. 16, 1866, Mary Brock Morris, native of Harrison county; vi. Elizabeth-Ann, m. Dewey Lantz, and settled in Belmont county; vii. Jane; viii. James; ix. Baruch-Francis, b. March 3, 1848; settled in Cadiz township; m. 1885, Agnes Haverfield, daughter of James and Elizabeth Haverfield, of Cadiz township; x. Anna-E.; xi. Sarah-S., m. Oscar McFadden, and settled in Athens township); 3. Hugh; 4. John, b. Dec. 10, 1810; d. March 12, 1865; m. Eliza Ann Hanna, b. Jan. 8, 1808; d. March 31, 1863; daughter of John and Ann Leonard Hanna (who removed from Rostraver township, Westmoreland county, to Cadiz, in 1814); (had issue: i. Mary-Ann, b. May 17, 1837; d. July 21, 1874; m. Samuel A. Osburn; ii. William-Hamilton, b. Sept. 10, 1838; settled at Clinton, Ill.; m. 1867, Elizabeth A. Craig, daughter of Walter and Jane Moore Craig; iii. John-Finley, b. May 16, 1840; m. (1st) Jeanette Eagleson; m. (2d) Euphemia Eagleson; served as an officer in the Civil War, and as Auditor of the State of Ohio; settled in Chicago; iv. James Wilson, b. May 12, 1842; d. May 23, 1863; served in the Civil War, and died from disease contracted in that service; v. Baruch-Francis, b. May 20, 1844; d. June 12, 1845; vi. George-Hopkins, b. April 17, 1846; d. April 10, 1857; vii. Nancy-Jane, b. Feb. 8, 1849; d. June 25, 1866; viii. Susanna-Elizabeth, b. June 28,

1852; d. Feb. 10, 1880); 5. Nancy; 6. Baruch.

II. Joseph, b. in Cecil county, Md., 1765; d. in Franklin township, Fayette county, Penn., Sept. 14, 1835; m. Ann Barricklow, b. 1768; d. Oct. 16, 1845; daughter of Conrad and Sarah Farrington Barricklow (see Barricklow Family); had issue: 1. Jesse, b. 1804; d. Jan. 26, 1876; m. 1826, Elizabeth Galley, b. 1807; d. 1858; daughter of Philip Galley (had issue: i. Joseph, b. June 2, 1827; m. 1850, Rebecca Stoner; settled at East Liberty, Dunbar township, Fayette county; ii. John; iii. Philip); 2. John; 3. Farrington.

III. Margaret, b. 1776; d. May 25, 1851; m. James Porter, son of John Porter, of Pennsylvania; settled in Cadiz township, Harrison county; had issue: 1. Joseph; 2. Elizabeth; 3. John; 4. Ann; 5. James, b. Aug. 29, 1818; d. unm., Sept. 4, 1898; 6. Augustus, b. Feb. 18, 1822; d. unm., March 25, 1893.

ROBERT ORR, a native of county Tyrone, Ireland, b. 1769; d. Nov. 4, 1857; son cf Andrew Orr; emigrated to America, and in 1795 settled in Westmoreland county, Penn.; removed to Green township, Harrison county, Ohio, 1802; m. Ann Huston, a native of Ireland; had issue: 1. Martha, b. May 23, 1801; m. David Lindsay; 2. Esther, b. Aug. 15, 1802; m. Henry Maxwell; 3. Jean, b. April 1, 1804; m. John Maxwell; 4. Mary-Ann, b. Sept. 6, 1806; m. Matthew Hanna; 5. Miriam, b. Aug. 13, 1808; 6. Ziporah, b. March 13, 1809; m. 1837, Daniel Smith; 7. Bathsheba, b. April 2, 1810; 8. Dorcas, b. June 4, 1812; d. Oct. 8, 1866; m. 1846, John Reed (see Reed Family); 9. Elizabeth, b. July 7, 1814; m. Samuel Baker.

SAMUEL OSBURN, a native of county Derry, Ireland, of Scotch descent, emigrated to America, and settled in Westmoreland county, Penn.; served in the Indian wars; m. in Ireland, Susanna Garven; had issue, among others:

I. Alexander, b. May 14, 1785; removed to Athens township, Harrison county, Ohio, 1816; settled in Archer township, Harrison county, 1829, where he died Aug. 17, 1867; served in the War of 1812; m. (1st) in Pennsylvania, May 10, 1808, Mary Barnes, b. 1780; d. in Athens township, Jan. 5, 1824; daughter of James and Mary Barnes, natives of Ireland, who had settled in Pennsylvania; m. (2d) Martha Rankin, of Washington county, Penn., d. Dec. 25, 1848; had issue by first wife, among others: 1. Samuel, b. in Westmoreland county, Penn., April 4, 1813; settled in Archer township, Harrison county, Ohio; m. 1835, Elizabeth Welsh, daughter of John and Jane Welsh, of Scotch-Irish descent, who had removed from Lancaster county, Penn., to Archer township, in 1822 (had issue: i. Alexander, b. 1841; d. July 24, 1875; settled in Archer township; m. 1868, Sarah Hedges, daughter of William P. Hedges, of Cadiz township; ii. John-W., served in the Civil War; settled in Cadiz township; iii. Jane, m. Morrison Moorehead, and settled in Green township; iv. Martha, m. Granville Dickerson, and settled in Nodaway county, Mo.; v. Amanda, m. L. A. Welsh, and settled in Archer township; vi. Matthew-Beatty); 2. John; 3. Mary, m. William C. Mason; a Presbyterian minister; and settled in Illinois; had issue by second wife: 4. James-D., settled in Carroll county, Ohio; 5. Rebecca, m. —— Ramsey, of Scio, Ohio.

JOHN OURANT, settled in Columbiana county, Ohio, before 1808; m. Rachel Hewett; had issue: 1. Obadiah; 2. Matilda; 3. Harriet; 4. Washington, b. in Columbiana county, Sept. 15, 1808; removed to Moorefield, Harrison county, about 1822, and later settled in Nottingham township, where he d. Sept. 13, 1884; m. (1st) Jan. 22, 1830, Mary Martin, b. April 5, 1808; d. March 20, 1866; daughter of Arthur Martin; m. (2d) Ann Horn, b. March 21, 1813 (had issue by first wife: i. John-M., b. in Nottingham township, June 27, 1831; m. 1852, Harriet Kennedy, b. June 1, 1834, daughter of John L. and Matilda Ourant Kennedy; ii. James-K., b. Dec. 19, 1833; settled in Cadiz township; iii. Eliza-A., b. Feb. 20, 1836; iv. William-G., b. Oct. 11, 1839; settled in Cadiz township; v. George-W., b. June 10, 1842; vi. Enos-B., b. Sept. 5, 1844; settled at Omaha, Neb.; vii. Joseph-R.-T., b. Oct. 5, 1847; settled at Freeport; viii. Mary-M., b. Oct. 24, 1851; settled in Minnesota).

THOMAS PARKINSON, a native of Frederick, Md., b. 1762; removed to Green township, Harrison county, Ohio, where he d. 1838; served in the Revolu-

tionary War; m. in Maryland, Elizabeth Schleiff, b. 1758; d. 1847; had issue, four sons and three daughters, of whom:

I. John.

II. Jacob, b. in Maryland, 1787; removed, 1814, to Smithfield township, Jefferson county, Ohio; served in the War of 1812; m. in Maryland, 1810, Mary Kellar; d. 1876; had issue: 1. John; 2. Thomas, b. in Jefferson county, Feb. 19, 1818; removed to Green township, Harrison county, 1844; m. Oct. 1, 1844, Caroline C. Cuppy, daughter of Abraham Cuppy, a resident of Jefferson county (had issue: i. Mary-Ann, b. Aug. 6, 1845; m. William H. Johnson; ii. Susanna, b. Feb. 7, 1847; d. June 17, 1870; iii. Evaline-R., b. Aug. 25, 1853; m. James Dickerson); 3. Joseph; 4. William; 5. David; 6. Louisa; 7. Elizabeth; 8. Nancy; 9. Edward.

III. Edward.

IV. Margaret, m. —— Miller.

V. Elizabeth, m. 1818, Ephraim Smith.

VI. Mary, m. —— Michael.

JOSEPH PATTERSON, b. 1791; d. 1859; removed from Pennsylvania to Carroll county, Ohio, in 1825; m. (1st) at Harper's Mills, Pennsylvania, Isabella McMillan, b. in Scotland, 1809; d. Nov. 17, 1846; m. (2d) March 27, 1849, Catherine Adams, d. 1882; had issue by first wife: 1. James, settled in Linn county, Kansas; 2. Margaret, m. Matthew Nickle, of Beaver county, Penn. (had issue: i. William-P., settled at Scio); 3. Robenia, m. William Rutan, of Ashland county, Ohio; 4. Euphemia, m. John Harrison, of Harrison county, Ohio; 5. William, settled in Morgan county, Illinois; 6. Mary, b. in Carroll county; m. Aug. 25, 1853, Alexander M. Scott, b. 1826; d. Jan. 8, 1878; son of Benjamin and Susannah Scott, of Washington county, Penn., who came to Carroll county in 1851; his widow settled in Scio; 7. Isabella, m. William Hogue, and settled in Carroll county; 8. Adam, served in Civil War; killed in battle; 9. Thomas, d. in infancy; 10. Jane, d. in infancy; 11. Martha, m. Joseph Doty, of Richland county, Ohio; 12. John, d. in infancy; 13. Alexander; settled in Morgan county, Ill.; had issue by second wife: 14. Elizabeth, m. Dr. Cook, of Scio; 15. Jane, d. in infancy; 16. Samuel, settled in the West; 17. John, settled in Carroll county.

JOSEPH PATTERSON, of Scotch descent, b. in county Down, Ireland, April, 1799; emigrated with his parents to New York in 1811, thence removed to Pittsburg, Penn., and later to Harrison county, Ohio, settling in Cadiz township, 1852, where he d. 1879; m. Feb. 14, 1822, Jemima Hoagland, daughter of James Hoagland, of Stock township (had issue, eleven children, of whom: i. J.-C., b. Aug. 30, 1835; served as an officer in the Civil War; m. Sept. 7, 1865, Mary Ann Simpson, daughter of John and Margaret Simpson; ii. James-H., settled in Cadiz township).

JAMES H. PATTON, a native of Pennsylvania, b. 1785-6; d. Oct. 3, 1860; served in the War of 1812; settled in Short Creek township, Harrison county, Ohio, in 1816; m. Jane Walker, b. in Pennsylvania, Sept. 13, 1789; d. June 6, 1880; had issue, among others: 1. John-Walker, b. 1818; d. Sept. 7, 1890; m. Dec. 30, 1846, Anna Braden, b. near Cadiz, July 25, 1820; d. Feb. 10, 1883 (her parents were pioneers in Harrison county); (had issue: i. Robert-B., a United Presbyterian minister, settled in Columbus, Ohio; ii. Esther-M.); 2. Rachel-S., b. 1826; d. Nov. 20, 1845; 3. William, b. 1831; d. 1841.

JOSEPH PATTON, a native of Pennsylvania, removed to Rumley township, Harrison county, Ohio, 1816, where he d. 1851; m. in Fayette county, Penn., Sarah Burns, d. September, 1842, daughter of John Burns, a resident of Pennsylvania; had issue: 1. John; 2. Sarah; 3. Joseph; 4. Margaret (all born in Pennsylvania); 5. Matthew M., b. in Fayette county, Penn., Sept. 3, 1815; m. March 3, 1844, Sarah Jane McCullough, d. June 13, 1878, daughter of Samuel McCullough, of Carroll county, Ohio (had issue: i. Sarah-Margaret, b. Jan. 19, 1843; m. Adam Miller, and settled in German township; ii. James, b. Oct. 23, 1844; iii. John-H., b. Aug. 25, 1846; iv. Joseph, b. May 7, 1848; d. Aug. 22, 1851; v. Samuel-M., b. April 12, 1850; d. Aug. 31, 1857; vi. Addison, b. May 25, 1852; vii. William, b. Aug. 17, 1854; d. Feb. 27, 1858; viii. Fremont, b. Aug. 29, 1856; d. March 5, 1858; ix. ———, b. March 12, 1859; d. March 17, 1859; x. Ida, b. Feb. 9, 1860; xi. Fremont (2d), b. April 12, 1862; xii. Thomas-B., b.

Dec. 8, 1863; m. March 20, 1888, Harriet E. Finnicum, daughter of John Finnicum, of Rumley township); 6. James; 7. Mary; 8. Cynthia-J.; 9. David; 10. Ann.

SAMUEL PATTON, a native of county Down, Ireland, b. 1761; d. Oct. 15, 1828; emigrated to America, but returned to county Down in 1798, where he m. Jane Friar, of Scotch descent, b. 1756; d. April 23, 1841; settled at Wheeling, F. Va., in 1803, and the following spring settled in Belmont county, Ohio, near the junction of Wheeling and Crabapple Creeks; had issue: 1. James, d. in Ireland, in infancy; 2. William, b. in Ireland, 1799; d. May 2, 1873; m. Anna Clark, b. 1810; d. 1885; daughter of Alexander Clark, of Belmont county (had issue: i. Samuel, a Presbyterian minister; d. in Detroit, Mich.; ii. Margaret, m. Rev. J. P. Robb, and settled at Iberia, Morrow county, Ohio; iii. John, settled in Arkansas City, Kansas; iv. Ellen, m. Rev. Josiah Stephenson, and settled at Olathe, Kan.; v. Alexander-C., settled at Springfield, Ohio; vi. Caroline, m. Addison Lyle, and settled at Pittsburg, Penn.; vii. James-B., settled at Shepherdstown, Belmont county; viii. George-M., b. April 9, 1844; settled near New Athens; served in the Civil War; m. Jan. 1, 1868, M. Louise Campbell, daughter of Dr. John Campbell, of Uniontown, Ohio; ix. Calvin-W., settled at St. Clairsville; x. William-L., settled at Fairpoint, Belmont county; xi. Sylvanus; xii. Thomas-L., settled at Fairpoint); 3. John, d. in Cambridge, aged seventeen years.

Dr. John Campbell, father of Mrs. M. Louise Campbell Patton, was b. in Belmont county, Nov. 21, 1804 (his father, James Campbell, an officer of the War of 1812, came from Cross Creek township, Washington county, Penn., and settled at Uniontown, Belmont county); d. September, 1882; m. May 11, 1830, Jane Irwin, b. 1808; d. June, 1882; had issue: 1. Mary; 2. Margaret-A.; 3. James-B.; 4. Rachel-J.; 5. M.-Louise, m. George M. Patton; 6. Martha-E.

JOSEPH H. PENN, b. in England, April 25, 1813, son of Thomas and Hannah Penn, who emigrated to America and located at Cadiz, Harrison county, Ohio; settled in German township,

7

where he d. Sept. 21, 1881; m. Nov. 6, 1834, Jane Hamilton, b. June 28, 1813; d. Feb. 8, 1878; daughter of Francis and Ruth Hamilton; had issue: 1. Florella; 2. Thomas; 3. Francis-Hamilton; 4. Hannah-Mary; 5. Joseph-Rollins; 6. William-Boyce, b. April 9, 1849; settled at Bowerston; m. May 29, 1870, Martha Ann Weyandt, daughter of Abraham Weyandt; 7. Chastina-Ann.

HENRY PERRY, b. in the Wyoming Valley, Penn., about 1774; d. at New Athens, 1865; when about three years old, his parents were massacred by the Indians and himself carried off captive; afterwards liberated, and settled at Pittsburg; m. Sarah Franks, b. 1786; d. 1866, of Fayette county, Penn., of German descent; removed to Cadiz; had issue: 1. Martin, d. in Indiana; 2. Henry, d. young; 3. Adam, d. young; 4. Eliza, m. James Polen, and settled in Guernsey county; 5. John, d. young; 6. Thomas, d. young; 7. William-W., b. Dec. 18, 1823; d. Aug. 26, 1865; served in the Civil War, and died of disease contracted in that service; m. Dec. 18, 1845, Elizabeth Kelley, b. Oct. 14, 1816; daughter of James and Jane Kelley; settled in Short Creek township (had issue: i. John-H., b. Dec. 22, 1846; served in the Civil War; m. Sept. 9, 1871, Eliza Ann Jarvis, daughter of Jacob and Eliza O'Brien Jarvis; ii. James-A., b. May 3. 1849; m. 1881, Anna Norman, daughter of Daniel and Elizabeth Norman; iii. Albert-K., b. Nov. 14, 1852; m. Rebecca Riley, of Clermont county; iv. Samuel-L., b. 1855; d. 1858; v. William-T., b. Sept. 28, 1858; m. Sept. 5, 1878, Josephine M. Blackburn, daughter of John and Margaret Blackburn, of Franklin township; served as prosecuting attorney for Harrison county; vi. Joseph-D., b. Sept. 16, 1861; m. 1884, Lillian Walker); 8. James, removed to Illinois, where he d. 1882; 9. Mary, m. Joseph Howell, and settled at Hopedale; 10. Sarah-J., d. young; 11. Susan.

LEROY PETTY, of English descent; settled in Washington township, Harrison county, Ohio, before 1830, where he d. Aug. 31, 1882; m. (1st) Keziah Tipton; d. 1853; m. (2d) Hannah Hogue; had issue by first wife: 1. Henry, b. Nov. 11, 1835; d. Feb. 27, 1881; m. Nov. 23, 1858, Sarah J. Cree, daughter of

James Cree; 2. John; 3. Mary-Ann; 4. Elizabeth; 5. Martha; had issue by second wife: 6. Levi; 7. Harriet.

RICHARD PHILIPS, b. in Pennsylvania, 1772, where his parents had settled, having come from England before the Revolutionary War; removed to Jefferson county, Ohio, in 1803, where he remained until 1815, and then settled in Washington township, Harrison county, Ohio, where he d. December, 1856; m. Comfort Davidson, d. 1835; had issue: 1. Joseph, b. Jan. 14, 1803; d. April 19, 1886; m. May 9, 1833, Jemima Johnson, d. Sept. 3, 1888, daughter of Griffin Johnson (see below) (had issue: i. Comfort-Ann, b. Aug. 24, 1834; m. Warner Rogers; ii. Sophia, b. Sept. 10, 1836; iii. Amasa, b. Sept. 22, 1838; m. (1st) June 5, 1862, Elizabeth Hogue, d. May 30, 1880; m. (2d) Feb. 19, 1885, Mary Ellen Crouch; d. Aug. 30, 1885; m. (3d) May 26, 1886, Elizabeth Mears, daughter of William Mears; iv. Almeda, b. May 9, 1841; d. Sept. 9, 1844; v. John, b. June 14, 1843; vi. Elihu, b. Sept. 26, 1846; vii. Margaret, b. June 11, 1849; d. April 12, 1878; viii. Joseph, b. Aug. 19, 1851; d. Dec. 31, 1875; ix. Jemima, b. March 23, 1858); 2. John, b. near Smithfield, Jefferson county, Dec. 19, 1804, where he d. July 1, 1886; m. 1831, Eleanor Johnson, b. at Wheeling, West Virginia, Sept. 5, 1804, daughter of Griffin Johnson (had issue: i. Richard, b. Aug. 14, 1832; m. (1st) Oct. 1, 1862, Sarah Jane Jenkins, of West Chester, Tuscarawas county; d. June 16, 1878; m. (2d) Sept. 18, 1879, Nancy Carruthers, of Harrison county; d. April 10, 1888; ii. Mary, m. William Boyd; iii. Alfred, b. Dec. 26, 1835, in Washington township; removed, 1873, to Freeport township, Harrison county; m. Sept. 1, 1863, Rachel A. Mears, daughter of William Mears, of Tuscarawas county, Ohio; iv. Sarah, m. ——— Carver; v. Nancy); 3. Margaret; 4. Hannah; 5. Lewis; 6. Eleanor-Ann.

James Johnson, father of Griffin Johnson, and grandfather of Mrs. Jemima Johnson Phillips and Mrs. Eleanor Johnson Phillips, was a resident of Ohio (now Brooke) county, West Virginia, where some time between 1776 and 1790, he was captured by the Indians while in camp on McIntyre's Creek, in Jefferson county, in company with two neighbors, McIntyre and Layport, who were killed. James Johnson was carried to Sandusky as a prisoner, but afterwards released and returned home. Later he settled in Warren township, Jefferson county, Ohio, where, in October, 1788, his two sons, John, aged thirteen, and Henry, aged eleven, while searching in the forest for their cows, were captured by two Indians. When night came, the two boys arose, one of them secured possession of his captor's rifle, and the other, a tomahawk, with which they killed the two Indians while they slept. The two boys were afterwards donated a section of land by the Government for their bravery, it being located in Wells township, Jefferson county, the supposed scene of their adventure. James Johnson had several children, of whom: 1. John, b. 1775; 2. Henry, b. Jan. 4, 1777, settled in Monroe county, Ohio; 3. Griffin, removed from Wheeling to Washington township, about 1805 (had issue, twelve children, of whom: i. Eleanor, b. 1804; m. 1831, John Phillips; ii. Jemima, b. 1810; d. 1888; m. Joseph Phillips; iii. Nancy, m. Zera Davidson).

THOMAS PHILLIPS, d. October, 1790, in West Nottingham township, Chester county, Pa., where about 1763-5 he m. Jane Blair, dau. of —— and Janet Blair; served in the Revolution in Capt. Ephraim Blackburn's company of Col. Evan Evans's Battalion of Chester county militia; took up land in Nottingham township, Harrison county, Ohio, before 1809; had issue: William, John, Sarah, Mary, and Rachel, of whom:

William Phillips, b. about 1765-67; d. July 18, 1854; m. before 1787, Rachel Hamilton, d. 182—, daughter of Robert and Martha McMillan Hamilton (the latter born 1748; d. at Morristown, Belmont county, Ohio, March 18, 1831; daughter of John [d. 1778] and Rachel McMil'an, of West Nottingham township, Chester county, Penn.); had issue:

I. Robert, b. about 1787; d. April 20, 1850; m. 1814, Rosanna Mullen; had issue: 1. Rachel, b. Oct. 16, 1815; m. Morris Melrath (had issue: i. William-H., m. (1st) Thirza Chapman; m. (2d) Ella Oviatt; ii. Mary-E.; iii. Rosanna-J.; iv. Joseph-L., m. Emma Opdyke; v. Robert-A., m. Emma Reynolds; vi.

Sarah-M.; vii. Thomas-M., m. Ella Fitzgerald; viii. Martha-E.); 2. John-Arthur, b. Dec. 17, 1817; d. Oct. 22, 1819; 3. William, b. March 1, 1820; m. Martha Maria Lee, daughter of Samuel and Jane Phillips Lee (had issue: i. Samuel-Lee, m. Margaret Rissler; ii. Robert-Lee, m. Gertrude Rissler; iii. Oscar-Miles, m. Elizabeth Stacey; iv. William-Brummel, m. Luella Kelso; v. Edward-Wilson, m. Hannah Deal; vi. Charles-Hilbert; vii. Jane-Hamilton; viii. Thomas-Newton; ix. Emma-Bolton; x. Rosella); 4. Mary-Ann, b. Oct. 16, 1822; m. Josiah Brown (had issue: i. Sarah, m. Charles S. Jacobs); 5. Sarah, b. Nov. 19, 1825, m. Milton Brown (had issue: i. John-Milton, m. Rachel Ann Anderson; ii. Martha-Ann, m. Reed W. Anderson; iii. Henry-Clay, m. Sarah Martha Webb; iv. Thomas-Wood, m. Hannah Riley Jones); 6. Martha-J., b. Oct.17,1828; m. Montillion Brown (died without issue); 7. Rosanna-Rebecca, b. Oct. 17, 1831; m. William Phillips, grandson of John Phillips, Sr. (had issue: i. Joseph, m. Sarah Hilaman; ii. Mary, m. Harry Goodwin; iii. John).

II. Martha, b. 179—; d. December, 1836; m. James Ross, b. 1797; d. 1878; removed to Nottingham township, Harrison county, 1827; had issue: 1. Rachel, m. Immer Knight; 2. Deborah, m. William Poulson; 3. Jane, m. Isaac Drummond; 4. William-Phillips, d. young; 5. Mary-Eliza, d. young; 6. Thomas-Hamilton, m. Eliza Fulton; 7. Martha, m. Thomas McMillan, and settled at Deersville; 8. Barbara, m. Beall Pumphrey.

III. Thomas, b. 1792; d. Nov. 23, 1871; m. Elizabeth Williams, b. July 11, 1792; d. May 22, 1867; removed to Cadiz, Ohio, before 1820; had issue: 1. Adaline, m. William Welch, son of Daniel and Elizabeth Waits Welch, of Green township; removed to Mount Pleasant, Iowa, and thence, after the death of her husband, to Osceola, Neb. (had issue: i. William; ii. Thomas; iii. Daniel; iv. Ross, m. Anna Sherwood; also, four other children, who died in infancy); 2. Rachel, d. unm.; 3. Martha, d. in infancy; 4. Mary, m. Abraham Croskey, and settled at Chicago (had issue: i. Thomas, m. Martha Osburn); 5. Basil-Lee-Williams, b. Aug. 19, 1824; m. Feb. 25, 1846, Mary Pritchard, d. Nov. 27, 1896; daughter of John and Sarah

Bromfield Pritchard (had issue: i. Sarah; ii. Mary-Isabella, m. May 12, 1869, William Moseback, of Cnicago; iii. Ada-Welch, d. young; iv. Virginia-Anderson, d. young; v. Clara-Anderson, m. H. G. Cass); ö. William, m. (1st) Elizabeth Anderson; m. (2d) Sarah Lord, daughter of William Lord; m. (3d) Mrs. Lucretia Hilts (had issue, by second wife: i. Marcia); 7. Jonn, m. Sarah Hilligas (had issue: i. Mary, m. Henry Cruse, Jr.; ii. Jessica, d. young; iii. Thomas; iv. Elizabeth; v. Katharine; vi. George; vii. John); 8. Caroline; 9. Laura, m. David Cunningnam (had issue: i. Mary, m. John Maholm Sharon; ii. John, m. Mary Day Welch; iii. Ralph; iv. Elizabeth, d. young; v. Helen); 10. Caroline.

IV. John, d. young.

V. Jane, b. April 26, 1794; d. April 1, 1870; m. Samuel Lee; had issue: 1. Martha-Maria, m. William Phillips, son of Robert and Rosanna Mullen Pnillips, and settled at Charlestown, West Va.; 2. Esther-Ann, m. William Pennell (died without issue); 3. Josiah-Parker, m. Sarah-Wilson (had issue: i. Edwin-Kirk; ii. Addison, m. Ella McCann; iii. Rosella, m. James Kehoe; iv. Isaac, m. Sarah Kehoe); 4. Jane, m. Taylor Janney (died without issue); 5. Rachel-Hamilton, b. May 5, 1831; 6. Philena-Rebecca, m. Joseph Lincoln Stephens (had issue: i. Emma, m. Edward Haines; ii. Mary-Lincoln, m. Norville C. Brown; iii. Lydia-W., m. Elmer Vanneman; iv. Jane-Lee, m. Charles M. Riesler; v. Elizabeth-Rutledge; vi. John-Lincoln); 7. Samuel-Thomas, m. Anne Wilson (had issue: i. Leonard-W., m. Lydia Tollinger; ii. Frances, m. Francis Russell; iii. Charlotte, m. Joseph Brown; iv. Emma, m. William Steele; v. Rachel, m. Ellis Nelson; vi. Samuel; vii. William; vii. Minerva; ix. Anna); 8. Charlotte, m. Caleb Conner (had issue: i. Samuel-Lee, m. Emma Stoner; ii. Mary-Susan; iii. T.-Eugene).

VI. John (2d), b. June, 1797; d. May 5, 1859; m. May 6, 1828, Eliza Gilmore, b. Feb. 2, 1807; d. Jan. 14, 1873; daughter of Samuel and Elizabeth Buchanan Gilmore; had issue: 1. Eliza-Jane, b. Feb. 22, 1829; m. 1849, Neri A. Hanna, b. April 7, 1827, son of John-Evans and Susan Robertson Hanna, of McConnellsville, Ohio (had issue: i. Mary-Eliza; ii. William-Phil'ips; iii. George-Finley, m. Alma S. Haverfield; iv.

John; v. Charles-A.; vi. Harry-Gilmore, m. Alice Anderson; vii. Samuel-Edward, m. Katharine Jones); 2. William, d. young; 3. Martha, d. unm.; 4. Sarah, d. young; 5. Samuel, d. unm.; 6. Rachei-Anne, d. unm.; 7. William-Welch, m. Mary E. Craig, and settled at Lincoln, Neb. (had issue: i. William-Craig, m. Ada Guthridge; ii. John, d. unm.; iii. Lucy, died young; iv. Charles-Frederick, m. Miriam A. Parks; v. Francis); 8. Thomas, m. Frances Flagg, and settled at Chicago (had issue: i. William-Eugene; ii. Sarah).

VII. William, b. 1800; d. Dec. 11, 1884; m. Mary Eliza Smith; had issue: 1. George, m. Hannah Blake, and settled at Berryville, Va. (had issue: i. Nancy); 2. Robert, m. Susan McDonald; 3. William, m. Mary White, and settled at Wilmington, Del. (had issue: i. Ira-May, m. —— Applebee; ii. Willametta; iii. Roberta; iv. Elizabeth-Thomas); 4. Mary-Eliza, m. Samuel George, of Cadiz, Ohio, and removed to Des Moines, Iowa (had issue: i. Margaret; ii. William; iii. Eliza; iv. Laura; v. Beulah; vi. Murray).

VIII. Margaret, b. 1803; d. April 19, 1872; m. John Johns; had issue: 1. Rachel-Jane, m. Hiram McCrery (had issue: i. Jessie, m. Anna Ross; ii. Hiram-Jackson, m. Jane McVey); 2. Margaret, m. John Morris (had issue: i. John; ii. David; iii. Jane, m. ——Crompton; iv. Phineas; v. Sarah; vi. Walter-E.); 3. Mary, m. John F. Ferguson (had issue: i. Lydia; ii. Laura, m. Alfred Hannum; iii. James; iv. William; v. Emma; vi. Cleveland).

IX. Mary, b. 1800; d. April, 1878; m. Jacob Griest; died without issue.

X. Eliza, m. Thomas Keatley; had issue: 1. Thomas, m. Emma Magaw (had issue: i. Lydia, m. William Newlin); 2. William, m. Eliza Terry (had issue: i. Mary-Luella; ii. Monroe; iii. George-D.; iv. William-Thomas; v. Helen-Margaret; vi. Jane-C.; vii. Elizabeth-S.).

ABRAHAM PITTENGER, b. in New Jersey, about 1774; d. 1865; removed to Harrison county, Ohio, about 1812, and later settled in Cadiz township; son of Henry Pittenger, a native of New Jersey, of German descent; served in the War of 1812; m. Susanna Osborn, b. 1780; d. 1847; daughter of William Osborn, an early settler near Cadiz, who afterward removed to Richland county, Ohio; had issue: 1. Henry; 2. Samuel, b. 1798; d. Aug. 26, 1875; m. Jan. 10, 1820, Jane Lemasters; d. Feb. 14, 1874; daughter of Isaac Lemasters, of Archer township; had issue, among others: 1. Samuel, b. Aug. 15, 1830; d. Jan. 30, 1880; m. Oct. 11, 1849, Antoinette Thompson, daughter of Gabriel Thompson, of Carroll county, Ohio; 3. Peter; 4. Sarah; 5. Abraham; 6. Isaac-O.; 7. Mary; 8. Jacob, b. near Jewett, Aug. 19, 1812; m. April, 1842, Mary Ann Hendricks, d. 1884, daughter of Peter and Catharine Webster Hendricks, who were of Dutch descent and among the earliest settlers of Rumley township (had issue: i. Isabella, m. O. S. Dutton; ii. John-Wesley, d. 1882); 9. Phœbe, m. Robert Atkinson; 10. John; 11. Nathaniel, settled at Dennison, Ohio; 12. Nancy, m. James Foster, and settled in Jackson county, Ohio.

JAMES POULSON, a native of Maryland, b. about 1781; settled in Cadiz township, Harrison county, Ohio, before 1810; m. twice; had issue by first wife: 1. John, b. in Cadiz township, April 23, 1812; settled in Nottingham township, where he d. Feb. 19, 1863; m. Rachel Rogers, b. April 26, 1816, daughter of Samuel and Sarah Lewis Rogers (had issue: i. Samuel; ii. Elizabeth; iii. Sarah, m. ——— Russell, and settled in Belmont county, Ohio; iv. Thomas; settled in Nottingham township; v. Matilda; vi. Harriet, m. ——— Rogers, and settled in Nottingham township; vii. Susan, m. Samuel D. Edgar; viii. Salina-J.; ix. Evans); 2. James; settled in Jasper county, Iowa; 3. Jacob; 4. Elizabeth; 5. Jehu; settled in Jasper county, Iowa; 6. Wilson; 7. William; settled at Montpelier, Ind.; 8. Harriet; 9. Mary-Ann; had issue by second wife: 10. Samuel; 11. Robert; 12. Maria.

JOHN PORTER, a resident of Nottingham township, Chester county, or of Drumore township, Lancaster county, Penn., had issue, among others, three sons: Robert, Samuel, and James, of whom: Robert, settled in Washington county, and Samuel and James in Harrison county, Ohio. Of these sons:

Robert Porter, served in the Revolutionary War; settled near Canonsburg, Penn.; had issue, among others:

I. John, served in the War of 1812.
II. James-T., b. near Canonsburg,

Penn., 1786; d. in Cadiz township, Feb. 24, 1836; m. March 31, 1812, Elizabeth Porter, daughter of Samuel and Sarah Burns Porter; had issue: 1. Mary; 2. Sarah; 3. Elizabeth; 4. Samuel, d. young; 5. Samuel-T.; 6. Robert; 7. Elizabeth (2d); 8. Jane; 9. Rebecca; 10. Margaret.

Samuel Porter, a native of Pennsylvania, b. 1765, of Scotch-Irish descent; removed with his brother, James, to Cadiz township, Harrison county, Ohio, in 1802, where he d. Aug. 2, 1869; m. in Pennsylvania, Sarah Burns, b. Aug. 15, 1786; d. 1830; had issue:

I. John, d. 1831. II. James. III. Elizabeth, b. in Pennsylvania, April 1, 1794; d. in Cadiz township, May 4, 1863; m. 1812, James T. Porter, of Scotch-Irish descent, b. near Canonsburg, Washington county, Penn., 1786; d. in Cadiz township, Feb. 24, 1836, son of Robert Porter, who served in the Revolutionary War, and whose son, John, served in the War of 1812.

IV. David, b. in Washington county, Penn., Feb. 5, 1802; d. Dec. 22, 1885; m. Theresa Stone, b. in Belmont county; d. 1859; had issue: 1. Sarah; 2. John-D., b. Jan. 14, 1839; m. March 7, 1876, Mary Isabelle Porterfield, daughter of Alexander and Sarah Warnock Porterfield, of Belmont county; 3. Mary; 4. James, d. in infancy; 5. Samuel-B., b. in Athens township, Oct. 8, 1843; settled in Green township; m. 1864, Margaret Dickerson, daughter of John and Eliza McFadden Dickerson.

V. Samuel, d. Aug. 2, 1869. VI. Jane. VII. Mary. VIII. Smiley, b. 1807; d. in Morgan county, Ohio, 1865, where he had settled about 1853; m. Margaret Dugan, a native of Pennsylvania, b. 1808; d. 1875; had issue: 1. Caroline; 2. Margaret, d. in infancy; 3. Mary, twin sister to Margaret; settled in Noble county; 4. Catherine, m. Samuel Marquis, of Noble county; 5. Sarah-Jane, m. John Harper, of Morgan county; 6. Samuel, settled in Cadiz township; 7. John, settled in Belmont county; 8. Irwin, b. in Cadiz township, 1854; settled in Cadiz township; m. Dec. 25, 1888, Ida McFarland, a native of Harrison county. IX. Nancy, d. in infancy. X. Irwin, b. March 8, 1814; settled in Cadiz township. XI. Sarah.

James Porter, who came to Ohio with his brother, Samuel, in 1802, was born 1766; d. in Cadiz township, 1836; m.

1807, Margaret Oglevee, b. in Maryland, 1776; d. May 25, 1851; daughter of John Oglevee, of Scotch-Irish descent; had issue: 1. Joseph; 2. Elizabeth; 3. John; 4. Ann; 5. James, b. Aug. 29, 1818; d. unm.; 6. Augustus, b. Feb. 18, 1822, d. unm.

JOSIAH PRICE, a native of Wales, emigrated to America and settled in New Jersey before 1768; m. Mary Frazier; had issue: I. James. II. Benjamin, b. in New Jersey, Dec. 12. 1768; settled in Jefferson county, Ohio, before 1805; d. Sept. 18, 1853; m. Catherine Beebout, b. Sept. 5, 1766; had issue, among others: 1. Joel, b. in Jefferson county, Jan. 9, 1805; removed to Franklin township, Harrison county; m. in Jefferson county, May 24, 1836, Sophia Leas, a native of that county, daughter of Jacob and Elizabeth Zimmerman Leas, of German descent, who removed from Adams county, Penn. (had issue: i. Jacob-Leas, b. Sept. 13, 1837; ii. Catherine, b. Sept. 30, 1839; iii. William-H.-H., b. Oct. 14, 1841; iv. Elizabeth, b. Nov. 4, 1843; v. Sarah-J., b. Oct. 29, 1845; vi. Benjamin-F., b. Oct. 20, 1847; m. 1877, Mary Barkley, daughter of Andrew and Rebecca Welch Barkley; vii. George-W., b. Dec. 3, 1849; d. Oct. 28, 1864; viii. Leonard, b. Aug. 23, 1852; ix. John-L., b. Dec. 30, 1854; m. 1887, Alice Cummings, daughter of Stephen Cummings; x. Mary-M., b. Dec. 28, 1859). III. Josiah. IV. Mary. V. Margaret. VI. Phebe. VII. Jeanette.

JOHN PRITCHARD or PRICHARD, was born in Wales, 1775 (son of Jesse Pritchard, who was born in 1750); emigrated to America with his father, 1785, settling at Frederick, Maryland, whence, in 1795, he removed to Uniontown, Fayette county, Penn., and from there to Cadiz, Ohio, in 1807; d. June 28, 1844; m. Feb. 7, 1798, Sarah Beeson Bromfield, b. Jan. 7, 1782; d. Sept. 15, 1877; daughter of Captain Benjamin (1745-1824) and Mrs. Mary White Bromfield (or Brounfield); had issue: 1. Mary, b. May 18, 1800; d. May 13, 1825; m. 1816, Daniel Kilgore, d. 1850 (had issue: i. Narcissa, m. Charles Paulson, of Pittsburg; ii. John-P., m. Mary, daughter of Rev. Alexander Wilson, of Cadiz and Philadelphia); 2. Jesse, b. July 3, 1802; d. 1835; m. 1825, Jane S. Lacey (had issue:

i. William-Lee, b. 1826; d. unmarried; ii. John, b. 1827; d. 1847; iii. Martha-Jane, b. Sept. 13, 1829; m. Daniel Spencer; iv. Sarah, b. July 29, 1831; m. William V. Keepers, of Uhrichsville, Ohio; v. Jesse, b. Dec. 17, 1830; removed to Gilpin county, Colo., in 1859, and thence to Leavenworth, Kan.; vi. Clara-J., b. December, 1834; m. Thomas J. Forbes, of Coshocton, Ohio); 3. Nancy, b. Oct. 27, 1804; d. Sept. 6, 1897; m. Chauncey Dewey (for issue, see Dewey Family); 4. Maria, b. April 3, 1807; m. William Lee (had issue: i. James; ii. Emma; iii. Albert; iv. William; v. Elizabeth, m. Samuel Hilles, of Barnesville, Ohio); 5. Benjamin, b. Nov. 3, 1809; m. Mary Deardorff (had issue: i. Sarah; ii. John); 6. Eliza, b. Feb. 4, 1812; m. William Houston, of Wheeling, West Va. (had issue: i. Sarah, d. unm.; ii. William, m. —— Mason); 7. Sarah, b. Aug. 11, 1814; d. 1820; 8. Isabella, b. Jan. 18, 1817; d. 1849; m. Samuel Douglass (had issue, both married, and living in Chicago: i. Sarah; ii. Ella); 9. Clarissa, b. Aug. 10, 1819; d. Dec. 18, 1837; 10. Sarah-Jane, b. Oct. 7, 1821; m. George Anderson, of St. Clairsville, Ohio (had issue: i. William, m. Alice Russell; ii. Clara, m. S. W. Dodds; iii. Margaret); 11. Rebecca, b. March 7, 1825; m. John Hamilton, of Cadiz (had issue: i. Sarah, m. Benjamin Funk; ii. Mary, m. Andrew Wilson; iii. Alice, m. Joseph Dalbey; iv. Eleanor, m. William Anderson; v. Isabella, m. H. V. Moore; vi. Elizabeth, m. Charles H. Pierson; vii. Ernest); 12. Mary, b. Sept. 29, 1827; d. Nov. 27, 1896; m. Basil Lee Williams Phillips, of Cadiz and Chicago (had issue: i. Elizabeth; ii. Adaline; iii. Virginia-Jane-Anderson; iv. Mary-Isabella, m. 1869, William Moseback, of Chicago; v. Clara-Anderson, m. H. G. Cass, of Chicago).

ANDREW RALSTON, b. in Adams county, Penn., 1753, of Scotch-Irish descent; his father, mother, sister, and brother were killed by Indians in Adams county, in 1761, one sister (who afterwards married and settled at Pittsburg) and himself escaping the massacre; served in the Revolutionary War; m. in Adams county, Sophia Waltermeyer, a native of that county; Andrew removed to Jefferson county, Ohio, in 1814, where he d. 1827; had issue, among others: 1. Lewis-W., b. in

Adams county, Nov. 30, 1806; settled in German township, Harrison county, about 1833, where he d. Sept. 6, 1884; m. (1st) 1828, Ann Darr, of Jefferson county; d. 1832; m. (2d) 1832, Eleanor Moorhead, daughter of William and Elizabeth Scott Moorhead (the former a native of Virginia, of Irish descent); (had issue by first wife: i. ———, d. in infancy; ii. ———, d. in infancy; iii. John-N., d. aged eighteen years; had issue by second wife: iv. Andrew, d. in infancy; v. Elizabeth, d. aged twenty-five years; vi. Lewis-B., b. Feb. 16, 1839; m. Jan. 8, 1861, Maria V. Sanders, daughter of Joseph and Elizabeth Oliver Sanders, both of whom settled in Ohio, 1830; the former a native of England, the latter of Scotland; vii. Ruth; viii. Sophia; ix. Mary-E., m. James Bosley, and settled in Springfield, Ohio).

WILLIAM RAMAGE, of Scottish birth or descent; settled on Wheeling Creek, Wheeling township, Belmont county, Ohio, before 1800; had issue:
I. William, settled in Moorefield township, Harrison county.
II. John, b. April 7, 1788; settled in Moorefield township; m. (1st) Esther Bell, d. 1815; m. (2d) Elizabeth Lafferty, b. about 1808; had issue by first wife: 1. William, b. Jan. 8, 1813; d. July 29, 1888; m. Rebecca Smith, b. in Belmont county, April 1, 1816, daughter of William and Rebecca Smith, who settled in Belmont county, in 1805, having come from Allegheny county, Penn. (had issue: i. Thomas-L.; ii. Esther-A., b. July 24, 1837; m. Nov. 3, 1853, Harrison Kirkpatrick, b. in Athens township, Harrison county, Oct. 27, 1822; settled in Moorefield township; iii. John-C.; iv. William-S.; v. Sarah-R.; vi. Mary-M., m. ——— Jackson, and settled at Jackson, Mich.; vii. James-O.; viii. Robert-B.; ix. Joseph-B.); had issue by second wife; 2. Samuel; 3. Louisa; 4. John.
III. James, d. March 11, 1849.
IV. Joseph, settled at St. Clairsville, Belmont county.
V. Samuel.
VI. Archibald-C., b. Oct. 12, 1808; settled in Smith township, Belmont county; served as a member of the Ohio Legislature, and as a member of the State Board of Equalization.
VII. Elizabeth.
VIII. Jane.

IX. Mary.
X. Letitia.
XI. Margaret.
William and Rebecca Smith, parents of Rebecca Smith Ramage, had issue: 1. Sarah, m. ——— Ramage; 2. John; 3. Joseph; 4. James; 5. William; 6. Robert; 7. Steel; 8. Washington; 9. Smiley.

GEORGE RAMSEY, a native of Ireland, emigrated to America and settled in Washington county, Penn.; m. (1st) ———; m. (2d) ——— Leeper, d. aged ninety-nine years; had issue by first wife, six children, among whom:
I. John, b. in Washington county, 1781; removed with his family to Green township; served as a Lieutenant of Captain Allen Scroggs's Company of Col. John Andrews' Ohio Militia in the War of 1812, and died in that service, at Lower Sandusky, Ohio, 1812; m. 1800, Nancy McLaughlin (who m., 2d, 1818, James Lyons, a resident of Jefferson county, their daughter, Elizabeth, marrying ——— Gladman, of Franklin township, Harrison county); had issue: 1. Hugh; 2. George; 3. John, b. June 23, 1805; m. (1st) May 24, 1827, Rebecca McCurdy; d. Feb. 12, 1833, daughter of John McCurdy, of Cadiz; m. (2d) Jan. 7, 1839, Mary Barr, b. July 22, 1817; d. Nov. 11, 1889, daughter of John Barr, of Carroll county, Ohio (had issue by first wife: i. Ebenezer, settled in California; ii. Thomas-Vincent, m. Sarah Patrick, and settled at Mount Vernon, Ohio; iii. Samuel, b. July 13, 1832; d. Sept. 18, 1872; a Presbyterian minister; settled at Tarentum, Penn.; m. June 28, 1864, Nancy J. Randolph; had issue by second wife: iv. William-Marshall, m. Mary Elizabeth Howell; v. John-Barr, b. June 20, 1841; served in the Civil War; killed in battle at Perryville, Oct. 8, 1862; m. 1862, Anna Vermillion; vi. Nancy-Elizabeth, m. John Vermillion, and settled in Jefferson county; vii. Margaret-Rebecca, m. John Lease, and settled in Green township; viii. Mary-A.; ix. Jennie, m. Samuel F. Birney); 4. Mary; 5. Samuel; 6. Nancy, d. Nov. 22, 1889, in Colorado, m. ——— Maxwell; George Ramsey had issue by second wife: II. David, b. Jan. 6, 1792; d. July 31, 1852; m. Mary Ann ———, b. April, 1797; d. Aug. 17, 1875; had issue, among others: 1. Matthew-J.; 2. David; 3. William-L.; 4. Moses. III. Nancy. IV. William.

JAMES RAMSEY, b. in Ireland, about 1744; emigrated to America with his parents, and settled in York county, Penn., about 1756; settled in Washington county, 1802, where he d. 1837; served in the Revolutionary War; his wife, whom he m. in York county, was of Scotch-Irish descent; had issue, among others:

I. William, b. in York county, Penn.; removed with his parents to Washington county, in the same State, where he resided until 1837; thence removed to Nottingham township, Harrison county, Ohio, where he d. 1856, aged sixty-six years; served in the War of 1812; m. Mary Anderson, daughter of Robert Anderson, of Washington county, Penn.; had issue: 1. James; 2. Robert, d. in Iowa, 1889; 3. William, b. in Washington county, May 1, 1817; settled at Cadiz, in 1874; m. 1840, Mary Hines, a native of Harrison county, daughter of John and Rebecca Dickens Hines (had issue: i. John, b. 1843; served in the Civil War; killed at the battle of Spottsylvania Court House, 1864; ii. James, settled in Texas; iii. William-Robert, settled in Texas; iv. F.-Marion, settled in Texas; v. Anderson-Deacons, settled in Texas; vi. Jennie, m. David Oglevee; vii. Philene; viii. Mary, d. in infancy); 4. Thomas, settled in Coshocton county, Ohio; 5. John, b. Nov. 4, 1823; m. (1st) March 16, 1847, Sarah J. Hines, a native of Nottingham township, d. 1865; daughter of Isaac and Sarah Patterson Hines, m. (2d) 1865, Emily Ford, b. in Harrison county, 1825; d. about 1880; m. (3d) 1882, Angeline Hines, b. Oct. 31, 1831, daughter of Abraham and Hannah Carson Hines (had issue by first wife: i. Isaac-L.; ii. Mary-E.; iii. William-B., b. March 14, 1852; settled in Williamson county, Tenn.; iv. John-F., b. Dec. 20, 1853; settled in Cadiz township; v. James-P., b. Feb. 5, 1856; settled in Freeport township; vi. Harvey-C., b. April 19, 1859; vii. Robert-F., b. Oct. 6, 1861; viii. Martha-A., b. Nov. 25, 1863); 6. Samuel; 7. Margaret, m. B. S. Ford; 8. Mary, m. John Mahanna; 9. Jane.

John Hines, b. 1778; d. 1871: father of Mary Ramsey, m. 1807, Rebecca Dickens or Deacons, d. 1859; removed from Pennsylvania to Harrison county, settling in Cadiz: had issue, fourteen children, among whom: 1. Jeremiah; 2. David; 3. James, settled in Nottingham township; 4. Abram; 5. Mary, m. William Ramsey.

SAMUEL RAMSEY, see Family of Philip Fulton.

DAVID RANKIN, emigrated from the north of Ireland, and settled in Frederick county, Virginia, about 1738-50; d. near Winchester, Va., 1768; leaving a widow, Jennet, and children, David, William, Hugh, and Barbara; of these: William Rankin, b. about 1720; d. 1793; m. in Virginia, Abigail Tassia; removed to Mount Pleasant township, Washington county, Penn., 1774, and purchased 1,600 acres of land on Raccoon Creek; had issue:

I. David, m. and remained in Virginia.

II. William, m. and remained in Virginia.

III. Zachariah, d. 1785-86, from the bite of a mad wolf; m. Nancy ———; had issue: 1. ———, m. Jesse Woods.

IV. Matthew.

V. John, d. April, 1788; m. Rebecca ———; had issue: 1. James; 2. Mary.

VI. James, killed by the Indians while on a return trip from Kentucky to Pennsylvania.

VII. Thomas, b. in Virginia, 1760; d. May 12, 1832; removed to Moorefield township, Harrison county, about 1805; served in the Indian wars of the border; m. Nancy Foreman; had issue: 1. James, b. in Washington county, Dec. 22, 1784; settled in Athens township, Harrison county; served in the War of 1812; m. Dec. 15, 1809, Hester Early, b. near Chartiers Creek, Washington county, Penn., May 31, 1793; d. March 29, 1874 (had issue: i. Jane; ii. Thomas; iii. Margaret; iv. Nancy; v. Sarah; vi. William, b. in Athens township, March 12, 1822; d. Jan. 3, 1864; m. Nov. 27, 1856, Mary Dunlap, daughter of John Dunlap; vii. Matilda; viii. Israel, b. Nov. 20, 1830; m. Aug. 18, 1870, Sarah Dickerson; d. Aug. 29, 1886; daughter of Adam Dickerson); 2. William; 3. David; 4. Jane; 5. Nancy.

VIII. Mary.

IX. Abigail, m. William Campbell (?)

X. Jesse, d. in Pennsylvania.

XI. Samuel, b. in Winchester, Virginia, July 18, 1769; d. October, 1820; m. Jan. 7, 1796, Jane McConahey, b. Feb. 18, 1775; d. July 20, 1869: had issue: 1. William, b. Nov. 24, 1796; d. Jan. 13, 1884; m. Dec. 16, 1819, Nancy Lyle,

b. Jan. 22, 1801; d. 1870; daughter of John Lyle (had issue: i. Elizabeth, b. Jan. 21, 1821; d. Feb. 14, 1880; ii. Samuel, b. July 19, 1823; d. September, 1845; iii. John-L., b. Oct. 16, 1826; m. 1849, Elizabeth Campbell; iv. David, b. May 30, 1829; d. September, 1845; v. William, b. April 4, 1832; vi. Jane, b. March 24, 1834; vii. James, b. Sept. 2, 1836; m. (1st) 1864, Elizabeth F. Barnes: d. 1870; m. (2d) 1880, Margaret E. Forsythe, of Burgettstown, Penn.); 2. John, b. April 4, 1798; d. April, 1866; 3. David, b. Feb. 15, 1800; d. July 27, 1858; 4. Matthew, b. Feb. 15, 1802; d. June, 1880; 5. Matilda, b. March 22, 1804; d. February, 1875; 6. Samuel, b. June 3, 1806; d. May 27, 1834; 7. Abigail, b. October, 1808; d. Nov. 17, 1892; 8. James, b. March 24, 1811; d. July 27, 1887; 9. Stephen, b. Aug. 20, 1813; d. February, 1877; 10. Jane, b. Feb. 6, 1817.

JOHN REA, b. 1771-2; d. Feb. 12, 1855; son of Joseph and Isabella Rea, of Tully, Ireland; emigrated to America about 1790, and first settled in Washington county; organized the Presbyterian churches of Beech Spring, Crabapple, Nottingham, and Cadiz; m. 1793, Elizabeth Christy, of Washington county, Penn.; settled in Green township, Harrison county, Ohio, 1803; had issue, nine children, of whom: I. Joseph, b. in Hopewell township, Washington county, Penn., Sept. 20, 1796; d. April —, 1862; m. Sept. 22, 1818, near New Athens, Jane McConnell, b. 1800; d. 1859; daughter of John and Mary McConnell, the former an early settler in Harrison county; had issue: 1. Elizabeth, m. John Lafferty, and settled in Cadiz township; 2. Mary, m. Samuel Dunlap, and settled in Nottingham township; 3. John, settled in Kansas; 4. Andrew-Jackson, b. in Moorefield township, Nov. —, 1826; m. 1856, Mary Moore, daughter of John and Elsie Johnson Moore, who were of Scotch-Irish extraction, coming to Harrison county shortly after 1800; settled in Cadiz township shortly after his marriage (had issue: i. Martha-Elizabeth, m. George Holliday, of Moorefield township; ii. Elsie-J.; iii. Joseph, d. aged fourteen years; iv. Lenora; v. John-M.); 5. Martha; 6. William; 7. Joseph. II. William Purdy, b. 1810; d. 1846; m. Jane Hanna. III. John, m. Sarah Daniels; had issue: 1. Martha; 2.

May; 3. William-P. IV. Sarah, m. David Thompson. V. James.

JOHN REAVES, b. in Norfolk county, Va., 1740; had issue: I. John, settled in Harrison county, Ohio. II. Richard, settled in Harrison county, Ohio. III. James, b. in Virginia, Aug. 4, 1776; removed to Harrison county, about 1811, and subsequently settled in Freeport township, where he d. Jan. 3, 1851; m. in Virginia, 1801, Sarah Howell, b. Nov. 20, 1775; d. June 28, 1856; had issue: 1. John, b. Dec. 15, 1802; 2. Nancy, b. Oct. 10, 1804; 3. Lydia, b. Dec. 27, 1805; 4. Jesse, b. April 20, 1807; 5. Winifred, b. May 1, 1809; 6. Elizabeth, b. Nov. 30, 1810; 7. Hallowell, b. April 30, 1813; 8. Sarah, b. Aug. 17, 1815; 9. James, b. April 28, 1818; settled in Washington township; m. July 2, 1841, Susan Clark, of Freeport township (had issue: i. Matthew-C., b. 1842; m. Dec. 31, 1868, Mary E. Rogers, d. April 30, 1874, daughter of Thomas Rogers; ii. Joshua; iii. Harrison; iv. Martha-J.; v. James-F., m. Feb. 3, 1886, Anna Leinard, daughter of Alexander and Mary Leinard, of Washington township, Harrison county). IV. William, settled in Harrison county, Ohio. V. Thomas, settled in Harrison county, Ohio.

ARTHUR REED, b. 1791; d. May 12, 1859; a native of Pennsylvania; settled in Archer township, Harrison county, Ohio, 1810; had issue: 1. John, b. June 6, 1818; d. March 18, 1884; settled in Green township; m. March 3, 1846, Dorcas Orr, b. in Green township, June 4, 1812 (had issue: i. Robert-W., b. May 17, 1848; m. Elizabeth McClellan; daughter of William and Eve Rinehart McClellan; ii. Elizabeth-Ann, b. 1850; d. 1853); 2. James; 3. William; 4. Nancy; 5. Ellen; 6. Margaret; 7. Mary-Anne; 8. Catharine; 9. ———, m. Lemuel Hale, of Bloomfield; 10. ———, m. Alexander Dennis, and settled in Indiana.

ADAM RITCHEY, of Scotch-Irish descent, emigrated to America and settled in York county, Pennsylvania, before 1750; m. in Pennsylvania; had issue: John, Thomas, Isaac, William, David, Andrew; the first four named served in the Revolutionary War; Isaac and William died in that service.

Andrew Ritchey, above named, was b. 1758, in York county; removed about 1780 to Washington county, Penn., where he d. 1838; m. in York county, Ann Campbell; d. 1834; had issue:

I. David.

II. John, b. in York county, Dec. 8, 1776; removed with his parents to Washington county, Penn.; settled in Short Creek township, Harrison county, Ohio, 1807, where he d. March 24, 1852; m. Jan. 10, 1809, Mrs. Elizabeth Brown Patterson, b. in Pennsylvania, 1781; d. Nov. 11. 1859: had issue: 1. David, b. Aug. 26, 1810; removed to Mercer county, Ill., 1845, where he d. June 19, 1847; m. Feb. 11, 1840, Susan Dossy (had issue: i. Mary-Ann. b. Dec. 22, 1840; ii. John. b. Sept. 15. 1842; iii. George, b. July 28, 1844; iv. Elizabeth-Jane, b. Feb. 28. 1848): 2. Mary-Ann, b. Dec. 11, 1813; d. in Illinois, 1872; m. Jonah Nicholls (had issue, four children); 3. John-P., b. Jan. 7, 1816; 4. William, b. May 24, 1821; m. 1860, Jane Leach, of Green township, Harrison county, Ohio, daughter of James Leach, a pioneer in Harrison county, who d. 1860 (his wife d. 1856).

III. Andrew, b. Oct. 2. 1778; d. in Short Creek township, May 30, 1859, where he had settled in 1803; m. (1st) Nancy Trinnel, of York county, Penn., b. 1780; d. 1814; m. (2d) June, 1818, Margaret Boggs, of Belmont county, county, Ohio, b. June, 1794; d. Jan. 20, 1861; had issue by first wife, seven children, and by second wife, eleven children, among whom were: 1. Alexander; 2. Jane; 3. Griselda-Ann, m. Hugh B. Hawthorn; 4. Hannah, m. —— Bell; 5. Elizabeth; 6. Hester; 7. Abigail; 8. Catherine, m. —— Beatty; 9. Margaret.

IV. Charles, removed to Short Creek township, in 1805, where he resided until 1829, thence returned to Washington county, Penn.; settled in Logan county, Ohio, 1835, where he d. 1839; m. Jane McWilliams, of Belmont county, Ohio; had issue, fifteen children, most of whom settled in Logan county.

V. James.

VI. Hannah.

VII. Ann.

VIII. Catherine.

THOMAS RICHEY, a native of Ireland, b. 1769; d. in Cadiz township, Sept. 29, 1824, where he had settled in 1805; m. Mary Clifford, b. in Ireland, 1771; d. Aug. 12, 1823; emigrated to America, and first settled in New York City about 1795, removing thence to Harrison county; had issue:

I. Margaret, m. —— Milliken, of Allen county, Ohio.

II. Mary, m. James Haverfield, of Harrison county.

III. Jane, m. Joseph Watson, of Harrison county.

IV. Samuel.

V. John-M., b. in Cadiz township, Nov. 2, 1808; d. Jan. 30, 1897; m. 1834, Anne Gilmore, b. 1817; d. 1880; daughter of Robert and Elizabeth Collins Gilmore; settled at Cadiz, in 1877; had issue: 1. Mary, m. Samuel McFadden; 2. Ruth, m. Craig Gilmore. and settled in Illinois; 3. George; 4. Eliza-Jane, m. Samuel McFadden, and settled in Cadiz township; 5. Arabella, m. James McFadden. and settled in Cadiz township; 6. Thomas-J., b. July 5, 1845; served in the Civil War; m. 1868, Margaret McFadden, daughter of Samuel McFadden. of Cadiz township (who d. 1863); 7. Robert-Gilmore, m. Susan C. Dickerson, and settled in Missouri; 8. Samuel, settled in Cadiz township; 9. Martha, m. 1876, Charles Osburn, son of John Osburn, of Archer township.

VI. Sarah, m. (1st) Nimrod Wagers; m. (2d) John Weaver.

VII. Thomas, settled in Cadiz township.

VIII. Nancy, m. John Haverfield, and settled in Cadiz township.

IX. ——, d. in infancy.

X. ——, d. in infancy.

GEORGE RIFE, b. in Pennsylvania (?), 1801; d. in Cincinnati, 1873; m. in Harrison county, 1829, Sarah Croskey, b. 1811; d. 1870; daughter of John and Catherine Croskey; had issue: 1. John, b. 1830; m. 1853. Anna Smith, daughter of Joseph and Nancy Martin Smith, of Virginia; 2. George-W., b. 1833; m. Rebecca Cartwright; 3. Katharine, b. 1834; m. David Spencer; 4. Jackson, b. 1837; m. —— Hanna; 5. Mary-Jane, b. 1839; m. James Stone; 6. David, b. 1841; m. Emma ——; 7. Rachel, b. 1844; m. William Wallace; 8. Samuel, b. 1847.

WILLIAM ROGERS, b. in Maryland, Aug. 20, 1749; d. in Harrison county,

Dec. 27, 1830, where he settled 1809; of British descent, his parents having come to America early in the eighteenth century; settled in Jefferson county, in 1808, removing to Lee's Run, in Harrison county, a year later; m. Susanna Barrett, b. in Maryland, July 30, 1752; d. Dec. 27, 1830; had issue, eleven children, the youngest of whom: I. John, b. in Maryland, 1795; d. 1878, in Cadiz township; m. Sept. 28, 1815, Nancy Lemasters. b. near Hopedale: d. 1869; daughter of Isaac and Jane Lemasters, early settlers in Jefferson and Harrison counties; had issue: 1. William, b. in Cadiz township, Dec. 14, 1817; m. June 21, 1838, Maria Adams, d. July 24, 1881, a native of Harrison county, daughter of Thomas and Charity Blair Adams (had issue: i. James-Birney; settled at Cadiz; ii. John-Thomas, settled at Newark, Ohio; iii. Isabella-Jane. m. John Freeburn; iv. William-Pinckney; v. Albert-Lawson; vi. Nancy-Ellen, m. A. B. Cutshall, and settled in Stock township; vii. Bailey-Sumner, settled at Scio).

WILLIAM ROGERS, b. in Maryland, Nov. 30, 1798; son of Joseph Rogers, who settled in Cadiz township. Harrison county, Ohio, 1808; removed to Nottingham township, in 1856, where he d. April 28, 1863; m. Susan Carson, b. Aug. 14, 1803; d. May 25, 1844; had issue: 1. Snydonia, b. Nov. 5, 1823; d. March 12, 1855; 2. John-B., b. May 18, 1825; 3. Jesse-B., b. April 24, 1828; 4. Hannah, b. April 24, 1830; d. Feb. 4, 1871; 5. Nancy-C., b. Sept. 17, 1832; 6. William-F., b. Oct. 28, 1834; 7. Calvin, b. in Cadiz township, Jan. 19, 1837; settled in Nottingham township; m. Sept. 29, 1859, Mary E. Finical, b. in Cadiz township. Nov. 10, 1833, daughter of Isaac and Margaret Anderson Finical; 8. Barrett. b. March 29, 1839; 9. Susanna, b. July 8. 1842; d. March 4, 1847; 10. Lydia, b. May 22, 1844; d. June 9, 1844.

JAMES ROSS. b. in West Nottingham township. Chester county, Penn., 1797; d. in Nottingham township. Harrison county, Ohio, 1878; removed to Harrison county about 1827; m. (1st) Martha Phillips, daughter of William and Rachel Hamilton Phillips, d. 1836; m. (2d) Jemima Hines, d. July 5, 1882; had issue by first wife: 1. Rachel, m. Immer Knight; 2. Deborah, m. William Poulson; 3. Jane, m. Isaac Drummond;

4. William-P.; 5. Mary-E.; 6. Thomas-H.; 7, Martha, m. Thomas McMil'an; 8. Barbara, m. Beall Pumphrey; had issue by second wife: 9. Eliza, m. George Oglevee; 10. John-H.; 11. James-N.; 12. Rebecca, m. Anthony Blackburn; 13. Sarah, m. William Nash.

JOHN ROSS, b. in Ireland, Sept. 13, 1750; d. Sept. 8, 1833; emigrated to Pennsylvania, and thence removed to Harrison county, Ohio, about 1804, settling within four miles of Cadiz; m. in Pennsylvania, Charlotte Hatcher, d. in Morgan county, Ohio; had issue: I. Adam, b. in Pennsylvania; settled in Cadiz township; served in the War of 1812; d. in that service at Sandusky, Ohio; m. in Pennsylvania, Susannah Rowe, b. 1778; d. 1848; had issue: 1. John; 2. Adam; 3. George, twin brother to Adam; settled in Missouri; 4. Caleb; 5. Joseph; 6. Aaron, twin brother to Joseph, b. in Cadiz township, July 3, 1811; m. June 16, 1853, Nancy Harper, a native of Harrison county, daughter of Samuel and Cassandra Cox Harper, both of whom died in Cadiz township. II. William. III. John. IV. James. V. Hannah. VI. Eve. VII. Susannah, b. 1798; d. Aug. 31, 1889, m. Miles Tipton. VIII. Mary.

ROBERT ROBERTS, b. in Brooke county, West Virginia, 1790; d. in German township, Harrison county, Ohio, 1834, where he had settled in 1827; was one of five children, viz.: Samuel, Alexander, William, Robert, Mary; m. 1817. Ruth Atkinson, d. 1885, daughter of James Atkinson, a resident of German township; had issue: 1. William; 2. Thomas; 3. George; 4. Mary; 5. James-Ross, b. at Annapolis, Ohio, May 20, 1826; settled at Jewett; m. (1st) February, 1851, Dillie Ann Potts. d. 1856, daughter of Samuel and Elizabeth Potts, natives of Ohio; m. (2d) 1858, Margaret Ryder, daughter of George and Catherine Culp Ryder (had issue by first wife: i. Elizabeth, m. Jacob Miller; ii. Samuel, settled at Dennison. Ohio; iii. Richard, d. in infancy; had issue by second wife: iv. Catherine-Bell, m. Minden Hall, and settled at Crafton, Penn.: v. John, settled at Dennison; vi. Thomas; vii. McClellan; viii. William); 6. Ellen; 7. John; 8. Caroline.

ROBERT ROWLAND, a native of

Scotland or Wales, emigrated to America and settled in York county, Penn., about 1750, where he was twice married; had issue:

I. Matthew, settled near Mansfield, Ohio.

II. James, settled near Cincinnati, Ohio.

III. John, b. in York county, Penn., 1758; d. in Moorefield township, Harrison county, Ohio, April 20, 1855; served in the Revolutionary War; was an Indian scout for three years along the Muskingum and Ohio Rivers, from Steubenville, Ohio, to Louisville, Ky.; settled at Steubenville, where he remained until 1815, and then located in Moorefield township, Harrison county; m. Rachel Ingle, of Steubenville, daughter of William and Rachel Edington Ingle, early settlers in that place; had issue, among others: 1. James, b. Feb. 24, 1805; d. July 31, 1890; m. 1829, Elizabeth Leinard, b. April 17, 1808; d. March 4, 1884; daughter of Yost and Elizabeth Leinard (had issue: i. John, settled in Kansas; ii. Matthew, settled in Nottingham township, Harrison county; iii. Henry; iv. James; v. Leinard, b. in Monroe township, March 1, 1848; settled in Cadiz township; m. 1873, Margaret Mehollin, d. Dec. 13, 1890, daughter of John and Elizabeth Mehollin, of Cadiz township; vi. Sarah-Jane; vii. Ann-Christina, m. John Houser, and settled in Mercer county, Ill.; viii. Elizabeth, m. Eli Moore, and settled in Freeport township; ix. Rachel, m. John Mitchell, and settled in Knox county, Ill.; x. Mary; xi. Margaret, m. John F. Poulson, and settled at Allegheny, Penn.; xii. Nancy-Ellen); 2. Sarah; 3. William, b. May 19, 1796; d. Jan. 13, 1873; removed to Maryland; subsequently he returned to Ohio, settling in Nottingham township, Harrison county; m. Jane Fulton, b. Dec. 15, 1801; d. Nov. 17, 1881; daughter of Philip Fulton (had issue: i. John, settled in Freeport; ii. Levi; iii. Philip, b. May 25, 1825, in Nottingham township; m. (1st) August, 1847, Piety Ann Ford, d. 1865, daughter of Lewis and Ann Ford; m. (2d) Julia Hart, daughter of Benjamin and Myrtilla Hart, of Harrison county; iv. James, settled in Freeport; v. Sarah; vi. William, settled in Freeport; vii. Hannah; viii. Rachel; ix. Mary, m. Elihu Petty; x. Alexander); 4. Mary; 5. Rachel; 6.

Levi; 7. Elizabeth; 8. Cyrus; 9. Rebecca; 10. John.

CHARLES SAMPSON, b. at Claughter, county Tyrone, Ireland; had issue, among others, John Sampson, who emigrated to America and first settled in York county, Penn.; removed to Stock township, Harrison county, Ohio, about 1827, where he d. April 28, 1841; m. in Ireland, Sarah Gibson; had issue, among others: 1. Francis, b. in county Tyrone, Ireland, 1804; d. March 15, 1870; m. in New York, Aug. 30, 1827, Margaret Evans, a native of Wales, b. 1801; d. Nov. 9, 1884; daughter of Christmas Evans (had issue, among others: i. John-G., b. July 4, 1828; settled at Wichita, Kan.; served in the Civil War; m. Feb. 14, 1850, Elizabeth Birney; ii. Sarah-Ann, d. in infancy; iii. William-E., b. March 20, 1833; settled in Stock township; m. Oct. 25, 1866, Susan M. Welch, daughter of William Welch, of Archer township; iv. Charles-W., b. March 12, 1836; served in the Civil War; m. May 21. 1867, Rachel A. Poulson, daughter of Jehu and Elizabeth Cox Poulson, who came to Ohio from Maryland about 1802; v. Archibald-J., b. June 21, 1839; served as an officer in the Civil War; as United States Consul to Paso del Norte, Mexico; attorney for the State Board of Education of Missouri, etc.; m. 1866, Kate Turner, d. Dec. 15. 1886, daughter of Allen C. Turner, of Cadiz; vi. Francis-A.. b. Feb. 6, 1842; m. July 1, 1869, Mrs. Harriet Lacey, a native of England; removed to Sedalia, Mo.).

ADAM SAWVEL, of German descent; came from Pennsylvania and settled in Rumley township, Harrison county, Ohio, 1815; served in the Revolutionary War; had issue:

I. Mary.

II. Christina.

III. Michael.

IV. Jacob, b. in York county. Penn., 1780; resided in Adams county, Penn.. where he remained until 1827; thence located in Rumley township; removed to Van Buren county, Iowa, in 1850, where his wife d. 1853; thence removed to Hillsboro, Texas, 1857, where he died; m. Margaret Epley; had issue: 1. Michael, settled in Arkansas; 2. John; 3. Jacob, d. in infancy; 4. Jonathan. b. in Adams county, Penn., Dec. 17, 1826; settled in Rumley township; m. (1st)

Jan. 16, 1851, Lydia A. Arbaugh, d. in Iowa, 1863, daughter of John and Rosanna Wentz Arbaugh; m. (2d) 1863, Sarah Shambaugh, daughter of Philip and Catherine Arbaugh Shambaugh; 5. Emanuel, settled in Iowa; 6. Jeremiah; 7. Johanna, settled in Iowa; 8. Rebecca, m. Joseph Martin, and settled in Vinton county, Ohio; 9. Amy, m. Isaac Kimmel, and settled in Darke county, Ohio; 10. Elizabeth, m. Adam Arbaugh, and settled in Iowa; 11. Lydia, m. —— Dillin, and settled in Iowa; 12. Sarah-Ann, m. —— Marrow, and settled in Iowa; 13. Mary-A., m. —— Reniker, and settled in Iowa.

THOMAS SCARBOROUGH, see Family of Peter Martin.

ABRAHAM SCOTT, b. 1677, son of Hugh Scott, who emigrated from the North of Ireland, and settled in Chester county, Penn., probably before 1700; had issue, among others: 1. Anne, b. October, 1699; d. 1792; m. about 1720, Arthur Patterson, b. about 1700; d. about 1763 (had issue: William, Rebecca, Samuel, Arthur, Ellen, James, Catherine, Elizabeth, and Jane); 2. Samuel, b. about 1705; 3. Rebecca, b. Dec. 17, 1707; m. 1757, James Agnew (had issue: Samuel, Martha, James, David, Margaret, Rebecca, Sarah, Abraham, Anne); 4. Alexander, b. 1716-17; 5. Grace; 6. Hugh, b. 1726; m. 1754, Jennet Agnew, daughter of James Agnew by a former marriage (had issue: Rebecca, Abraham, James, Hugh, John, Elizabeth, Sarah, Margaret, and Josiah); 7. Josiah.

Josiah Scott, last named, son of Abraham Scott (1st), was born in Chester county, Penn., 1735, removed to Washington county, where he d. Feb. 20, 1819; m. (1st) 1760, Violet Foster; m. (2d) Jane ——; had issue by first wife, eight children, of whom:

I. Alexander, m. Rachel McDowell, daughter of John and Agnes Bradford McDowell; had issue, among others: 1. Josiah, settled at Bucyrus, Ohio.

II. Abraham, m. Rebecca McDowell, sister to Rachel McDowell; had issue, among others: 1. Josiah, settled near Cadiz, Ohio (had issue, among others: i. Lawson, settled at Oak Park, a suburb of Chicago, Ill.; ii. J.-Edward, a physician, settled at San Bernardino, Cal.); 2. William, a minister, settled in Guernsey county, Ohio; 3. James, a minister, settled at Mt. Vernon, Ohio; 4. Josiah, settled in Columbiana county, Ohio; 5. Mary, m. William Cotton, of Beaver county, Penn.; 6. Elizabeth, m. Robert Stevenson, of Beaver county, Penn.

Josiah Scott (1st) had issue by second wife:

IX. Robert, m. 1804, Elizabeth Munell; settled in Carroll county, Ohio, 1827, where he d. 1830; had issue, among others: 1. Robert-G., b. in Washington county, Sept. 18, 1813; m. April, 1835, Elizabeth Steeves, b. in New Brunswick, Canada, 1814, daughter of Christian and Olive Lutz Steeves, who removed to Scio, Ohio, in 1829 (had issue: i. Isabelle, m. Jesse Campbell, of Carroll county; ii. Eliza, m. Henry Spence, of Jefferson; iii. Margaret; iv. Josiah-R., d. while in the army, at Jackson, Tenn.; v. Dorinda, m. James McGeary; vi. James; vii. Mary-Jane, m. H. H. Meiser; viii. Robert-C.; ix. Olive-A.; x. Martha; xi. William-W., settled at Jefferson).

X. Hugh, d. in Washington county, Penn.

XI. Samuel.

XII. John, d. in Washington county, Penn.

JAMES SCOTT, a native of Sowerby Bridge, Yorkshire, England; son of Timothy Scott, who died in England; emigrated to America and settled at York (now Toronto), Canada, about 1816, thence removed to New York; located in Cadiz, Harrison county, Ohio, 1819, where he died; m. (1st) —— Howarth, d. in England; m. (2d) Harriet Arnold; had issue by first wife: 1. John-W., b. in Yorkshire, England, September, 1811; d. in Cadiz, Oct. 8, 1886; m. 1839, Jane Pittis, daughter of Robert Pittis, who emigrated with his family from the Isle of Wight and settled at Deersville, Harrison county, Ohio (had issue: i. James, d. young; ii. Albert, d. young; iii. Julia, m. Dr. George W. Woodburne, and settled at Uhrichsville, Ohio; iv. Cyrus-M., served as an Indian scout in the Indian Territory; settled at Arkansas City, Kan.; m. Margaret Gardner; v. Robert-P., settled at Baltimore; vi. Lanphear; vii. Charles-S.; viii. Thomas-A., m. Susan Pittis, daughter of George Pitt's, of Scio; ix. Mary, d. young); 2. William; 3. Eliza; had issue by second

110   OHIO VALLEY GENEALOGIES

wife: 4. Daniel; 5. James, settled at Akron, Ohio; 6. Thomas, settled in Texas (had issue, among others: 1. Emma, m. Charles P. Dewey; ii. Edward); 7. Mary, m. —— McMasters, and settled at Mount Pleasant, Ohio.

WILLIAM SCOTT, a native of county Antrim, Ireland; had issue: 1. Thomas, b. in Ireland, 1793; emigrated to America and in 1822 settled in Harrison county, Ohio; d. in Mooreneld township, Jan. 16, 1875; m. Sarah Hogg, b. 1802; d. 1875 (had issue: i. Jane; ii. ——, d. in infancy; iii. Susan; iv. William, b. March 7, 1833; settled in Mooreneld township; m. April 9, 1859, Ann Eliza Sloan, daughter of John Sloan, one of the earliest settlers in Moorefield township; v. Eleanor; vi. Mary; vii. ——, d. in infancy; viii. James; ix. John; x. Martha; xi. Sarah; xii. Robert-W., twin brother to Sarah; b. Dec. 28, 1846; m. May 17, 1877, Mary A. Wallace, b. Feb. 23, 1849, daughter of Nathaniel and Julia Fulton Wallace [the former of whom d. March 25, 1855, and his widow m. William Pickering, of Moorefield township]); 2. John; 3. William; 4. Mary; 5. Eleanor.

WILLIAM SCOTT, a native of Ireland; emigrated to America and settled near Pigeon Creek, Somerset township, Washington county, Penn., where he died; m. in Ireland, Rebecca ——; had issue:

I. Joseph.

II. Thomas.

III. Alexander, b. in Ireland, 1775; d. in Tuscarawas county, Nov. 2, 1853; m. in Washington county, 1813, Gertrude Kerr, b. 1790; d. April 5, 1868; daughter of Samuel and Rhoda Byshire Kerr (the former an early settler in Washington county); had issue: 1. William-H., b. Jan. 15, 1814, on Pigeon Creek, Washington county, Penn.; settled at Scio, Harrison county, Ohio, 1840; m. (1st) 1842, Jane Whittaker, b. 1818; d. 1866; daughter of James and Arabell Whittaker; m. (2d) Dec. 10, 1868, Mrs. Sarah J. Kerr Elder, b. in Washington county, Penn., May 24, 1827, widow of John Elder, Jr., and daughter of Aaron and Margaret Nevin Kerr (the latter a daughter of John Nevin, a native of Ireland, who settled in Beaver county, Penn.) (had issue by first wife: i. Alexander, m. Margaret A. Calhoon; ii. James, b. Sept. 30, 1844;

settled in North township; m. May 25, 1875, Gelina M. Elder, a native of Carroll county, daughter of John Elder, Jr., and Sarah J. Kerr [second wife of William H. Scott]; iii. Maria; iv. Christian; v. Thomas-W., twin brother to Christian; vi. William; vii. Mary-Arabell; viii. Caroline-G., m. Philip C. Spiker of Tippecanoe); 2. Samuel, settled at Uhrichsville; 3. Robert, d. in Uhrichsville; 4. Albert, settled near New Cumberland, Tuscarawas county; 5. Lewis-L., settled at Waynesburg, Stark county, Ohio; 6. Eliza, m. Joseph Meek, of Washington, Iowa; 7. Maria, m. Rev. Moses M. Bartholomew, of Goshen, Ind.; 8. Sarah, m. John Ralston, of Spencer, Owen county, Ind.; 9. Caroline, m. Dr. John C. McGregor, and settled at Brazil, Clay county, Ind.; 10. Margaret, m. Samuel G. Smith, of Uhrichsville.

Aaron Kerr, father of Sarah J. Scott, was a native of Washington county, Penn.; settled in Carroll county, Ohio, 1831, where he died Sept. 28, 1856; m. Margaret Nevin, daughter of John Nevin, a native of Ireland, who settled in Beaver county, Penn.; had issue: 1. Samuel Lewis, a physician, settled at El Paso, Ill.; 2. John-Jackson, m. Cornelia E. Hutchinson, and settled at Wintersett, Iowa; 3. Sarah-Jane, m. (1st) in Carroll county, July 10, 1857, John Elder, Jr., b. in Washington county, Penn., 1799; d. in Carroll county, Ohio, 1866; m. (2d) Dec. 10, 1868, William H. Scott (had issue by first husband: i. Gelina-M., m. James Scott; ii. John-S., settled in Holmes county; iii. Flora; iv. Lissa; v. Clara-S.); 4. Joseph-Alexander, m. Carrie E. Grizzell, and settled at Salem, Ohio; 5. Margaret-Ann, d. 1869; m. Uriah Coulson, an officer in the Civil War; 6. Aaron-Wylie, d. in Dallas, Tex.; 7. George-Nevin, served in the Civil War; d. at Cottonwood Falls, Kan., Nov. 14, 1890; 8. Robert-Hervey, m. Alice Miller, and settled in Jefferson county; 9. James-McMillan, served in the Civil War; removed to Washington, Iowa, where he m. Mary Young, daughter of Judge —— Young; afterward settled at Cottonwood Falls, Kan.

John Elder, b. in New York, about 1750; d. Dec. 16, 1840; his parents, who were natives of Ireland, emigrated to America and landed on the date of his birth; removed to near Buffalo, Washington county, Penn.; m. Elizabeth Mc-Kinney, who d.aged seventy-five years; had issue: 1. Samuel, b. Jan. 24, 1791; d. Nov. 13, 1826; 2. Mary, b. Feb. 12, 1793; d. Aug. 6, 1877; 3. Jane, b. Oct. 13, 1794; d. Jan. 6, 1830; 4. Sarah, b. May 28, 1797; m. March 4, 1831, Samuel McEldeny (had issue, among others: i. Margaret-A., m. —— Smith, and settled near Carrollton); 5. Thomas, b. June 23, 1799; d. July 30, 1831; 6. James, b. Oct. 4, 1803; d. Oct. 12, 1829; 7. David, b. Oct. 23, 1805; d. Sept. 2, 1831; 8. John, b. April 4, 1807; d. in Carroll county, 1866; m. July 10, 1857, Jane Kerr.

PETER SEWELL, of German descent; b. in Delaware, 1796; removed to Maryland, and thence to Harrison county, Ohio, in 1828, where he d. 1885; m. 1826, Susan Wiley, of Scotch-Irish descent, b. in Virginia, 1801; d. 1883 (daughter of John Wiley, who served in the War of 1812 and died at Alexandria, Va., from effects of a wound received in that service); had issue: 1. Rebecca; 2. Mary-Ann; 3. Theodore; 4. John-William; 5. Thomas-M., b. in Belmont county, Oct. 29, 1342; settled at New Athens, Ohio; served in the Civil War; m. 1870, Eliza J. Hughes, daughter of Edward and Sarah Hughes, of New Athens; 6. Josephus.

GEORGE SHAMBAUGH, b. in Pennsylvania about 1745; d. in Perry county, that State, 1827, son of George Shambaugh, a native of Germany, who emigrated to Pennsylvania; had issue:

I. George, b. in Perry county, Penn., 1787; removed to Rumley township, Harrison county, Ohio, 1817, where he d. Sept. 4, 1867; served in the War of 1812; m. in Pennsylvania, Mrs. Elizabeth Brown Wirt, a widow, b. 1777; d. about 1863; daughter of Michael Brown, of German descent; had issue: 1. Philip; 2. Michael, b. in Perry county, June 18, 1811; d. March 20, 1863; settled in Rumley township; m. May 31, 1832, Hettie Hazlett, b. April 16, 1816; d. Oct. 22, 1884 (had issue: i. James, b. March 5. 1833; settled near New Rumley; ii. Elizabeth, b. Aug. 1, 1834; d. in Iowa, March, 1864, m. Abraham Fetroe; iii. Mary-A., b. July 27, 1836; m. John W. Finnicum, of Rumley township; iv. Simon-B., b. Sept. 7, 1838; d. Oct. 14, 1873; v. Adam-H., b. Sept. 11, 1841; m. Mary Jane Scott, daughter of Samuel Scott, of Rumley township; vi. Char-lotte, b. June 21, 1842; d. January, 1879; m. May, 1873, Peter Overholt, d. February, 1877; vii. Maria, b. Aug. 22, 1844; m. Aug. 3, 1871, Harvey L. Thompson, and settled in Archer township; viii. Jane, b. Nov. 28, 1846; d. Oct. 30, 1867; ix. John, b. Oct. 13, 1848; m. Elizabeth Gutshall, daughter of Jacob Gutshall, and settled near Des Moines, Iowa; x. Philip, b. Feb. 18, 1851; m. March 15, 1881, Eliza Loretta Scott, of New Rumley, daughter of John A. and Eliza Bivington Scott; 3. George; 4. Margaret, m. Samuel Hazlett.

II. Jacob, served in the Revolutionary War.

III. John.

IV. Philip.

V. Mary.

VI. Barbara.

VII. Catherine.

WILLIAM SHARON, of Scotch-Irish descent, removed from Westmoreland county, Penn., to Wells township, Jefferson county, Ohio, about 1802; d. 1809; m. Mrs. Sarah Whitaker; had issue: 1. James, b. 1790; m. about 1815, Martha Eaton (had issue, two sons and two daughters); 2. William, b. 1793; d. April 24, 1875; m. about 1815, Susan Kirk (had issue: i. John, a physician, b. about 1816; d. Sept. 2, 1860; settled at Carrollton, Ill.; ii. Mary-Ann, b. about 1818; m. 1863, Dr. Jacob Hammond, and settled in Steubenville; iii. Sarah, b. 1820; removed to California; iv. William, b. Jan. 9, 1821; d. Nov. 13, 1885; removed to California; represented Nevada in the United States Senate, 1875-81; v. Lewis, b. 1822; m. 1855, Sarah McKim; vi. Susan, b. 1825; m. Isaac M. Davis; vii. Smiley, b. Feb. 14, 1827; m. 1848, Sarah Ann Hurford); 3. Smiley, b. June, 1795; d. Oct. 16, 1876; m. June, 1827, Martha Kithcart (had issue, five sons and three daughters); 4. John, b. September, 1798; d. Oct. 23, 1870; m. February, 1832, Helen Hall (had issue, three sons and six daughters).

GEORGE SHARP, d. in Hopewell township, June, 1812, leaving a wife, Rachel, and children: 1. Joseph (possibly the son-in-law of John Sharp); 2. John; 3. Thomas; 4. Mary.

Joseph and Thomas Sharp, of Washington county, probably the sons of George, or son and son-in-law of John, took up two sections of land in Wheeling township, Belmont county, Ohio, in 1806, just south of Athens and Short Creek townships, Harrison county; of these:

1. Thomas, b. 1768; d. Dec. 29, 1825; m. Jane ———, b. Feb. 1, 1766; d. April 24, 1859; had issue, among others: 1. George, b. July 9, 1795; d. June 25, 1877; m. Nancy ———, b. April 21, 1807; d. Dec. 13, 1877; 2. John; 3. Margaret; 4. Rachel; 5. Jane, b. 1812; d. June 6, 1844; m. 1834, David Welling; 6. Saran, b. Feb. 3, 1813; d. Sept. 4, 1831; 7. Joseph, b. Aug. 23, 1815; d. May 13, 1833.

II. Joseph, d. near Cadiz, and buried in the Old Cemetery; but dates illegible.

Besides the above, the following Sharp families appear on the early records of Harrison county:

Thomas Sharp, m. 1828, Margaret Stine.

William Sharp, b. 1809; d. May 18, 1859; buried at Unity; probably the same who m. 1836, Elizabeth Goriet.

Caroline Sharp, b. Jan. 23, 1814; d. Oct. 20, 1886; buried at Unity.

Caroline T. Sharp, b. July 10, 1838; d. Dec. 24, 1881.

James Sharp, b. 1832; d. 1838.

George Sharp, of Hopewell township, first above named, who died in 1812, was an elder in North Buffalo United Presbyterian Church.

William Sharp, probably closely connected with Thomas or Joseph Sharp; removed from Hopewell (?) township, Washington county, to Wheeling township, Belmont county, Ohio, and d. near Union town, 1835; m. in Washington county, Mary McFadden, daughter of John (?) and Mary McFadden; had issue, among others: 1. John, b. in Harrison or Belmont county, 1807; d. at Millersburg, Holmes county, Ohio, 1893, where he had settled in 1834; m. 1832, Catharine Thompson, b. 1814; d. 1900; daughter of David Thompson, of Cadiz township (had issue: i. William-Thompson, a physician, b. Dec. 16, 1833; d. 1899; served in the Civil War; m. Oct. 12, 1859, Elizabeth Carnahan; ii. David, m. Lydia Armstrong; settled in Holmes county; iii. John; settled at Millersburg, Holmes county; iv. James, a United Presbyterian minister, m. Agnes Ballantine; settled at Sidney, Ohio; v. George, m. Annette Donnan; settled at Millersburg; vi. Samuel, a physician, m. Cordelia Maxwell; set-

tled in Oregon; vii. Martha, m. John T. Maxwell, of Millersburg; viii. Mary, d. young; ix. Margaret; x. Joseph, m. Margaret Maxwell; settled in Holmes county); 2. Nancy, b. 1810; d. Oct. 10, 1875; m. 1829, John Cunningham, son of David and Mary McLaughlin Cunningham.

JOHN SHARP, d. in Hopewell township, Washington county, Penn., 1797; m. Agnes ———; had issue: 1. Mary, m. ———; 2. Agnes, m. ——— Girvan; 3. John; 4. Margaret; 5. Ramsey; 6. Thomas; besides these children, John Sharp mentions in his will two sons-in-law, Joseph Sharp and Andrew Garret, probably the husbands of his two daughters, Margaret and Janet. He also mentions as one of his executors, John McFadden.

JOSEPH SHERIFF, b. (probably) in the North of Ireland, 1787; emigrated to America with his parents, and settled in Mercer county, Penn., where he d. 1872; m. at Steubenville, Ohio, Nancy Fulton, b. 1797; d. 1841; daughter of ——— and Nancy Liggett Fulton; had issue: 1. Sarah, m. William Weimer; 2. Joseph, m. Nancy Shipler; 3. Martha, m. Alexander Thompson; 4. William, m. Anna Glenn; 5. Ellen, m. John McElheney; 6. Adam-N., b. July 6, 1832; d. 1880; m. 1856, Mary Vickery; 7. Margaret, m. Allen Turner; 8. Thomas, m. Jane Boyd; 9. John, m. ——— Hosick; 10. Mary, m. William Fowler.

William Vickery, father of Mary Vickery Sheriff, was born in England, 1791; d. at Steubenville, Ohio, 1856; emigrated to America and first settled in Beaver county, Penn., thence removed, 1839, to Steubenville, Ohio; m. in England, Mary Collings, daughter of ——— and Mary Wellington Collings; had issue: 1. Johanna, m. William Johnston; 2. Mary, b. 1831; d. 1896; m. Adam N. Sheriff; 3. Ellen, m. John McMurray.

JOHN SHOTWELL, came from England, Scotland, or New England, to New Jersey, and settled on the road between Scotch Plains and Plainfield; m. (1st) ——— Smith, daughter of Shubal Smith; m. (2d) Mary Webster; had issue: John-Smith, Jacob, William, Isaiah, James, Hugh, Mary, m. James Stevens, Sarah, and Martha. Of these: Hugh Shotwell, b. near Plainfield, N. J., March 19, 1764; d. at Freeport,

Ohio, March 17, 1854; removed before 1790 to Franklin township, Fayette county, Penn., thence, about 1808, to Harrison county, Ohio, settling in Washington township about 1828; m. in Sussex county, New Jersey, Feb. 23, 1783, Rosetta Arrison, b. 1764; d. 1836; daughter of John Arrison (who lived at Wyoming, Pa., and was driven thence by the Indians during the Revolutionary War, settling in New Jersey); had issue: I. John, b. 1784; d. 1869; m. (1st) Sarah Shanklin; m. (2d) Hannah Myers. II. Esther, b. 1785; d. 1870; m. (1st) Timothy Smith; m. (2d) Major George Clark Seton. III. Susanna, b. 1789; d. 1874; m. Charles Wintermute. IV. Charlotte, b. 1790; d. 1827; m. Ephraim Sears. V. Nancy, b. 1796; d. 1861; m. (1st) Peter Vandolah; m. (2d) Jacob Ebert. VI. William, b. in Fayette county, Penn., 1798; settled in Cadiz township, about 1837; m. 1819, at Wilbraham, Hampden county, Mass., Rhoda Beebe, b. June 19, 1792; d. March, 1876; daughter of Stuart and Huldah Beebe (see Family of Stewart Beebe); had issue: 1. Stuart-Beebe, b. Nov. 22, 1819; d. Dec. 3, 1890; m. 1851, Nancy Gaston, daughter of James and Elizabeth Kilgore Gaston, of Columbiana county, Ohio (had issue: i. Mary, b. 1853; d. in infancy; ii. Walter-Gaston; a judge; b. Dec. 27, 1856; m. Dec. 24, 1884, Belle McIlvaine, daughter of George W. and Caroline Rinehart McIlvaine; iii. Stuart-Beebe, b. 1867; m. Caroline McIlvaine, sister of Belle McIlvaine; settled at St. Paul, Minn.; iv. Martha; v. William-James, d. in infancy; 2. John, b. 1821; d. young; 3. Samuel, b. 1823; d. young; 4. William, b. 1825; d. Dec. 1, 1849; 5. Theodore, b. March 20, 1828; d. Jan. 28, 1899; m. (1st) Sarah J. Lucas, of Steubenville; m. (2d) Anna G. Seton Beckwith; settled at Minneapolis; 6. Walter-Beebe, b. 1831; d. May 21, 1847; 7. Rhoda-Loretta, b. July 27, 1834; d. August, 1888; m. Smiley Sharon. VII. Joseph, b. 1801; d. 1883; m. Mary Arrison. VIII. Arrison, b. 1812; d. 1893; m. Mary Dickerson.

James Gaston, father of Nancy Gaston Shotwell, was the son of Hugh and grandson of Joseph Gaston, who d. in Mount Bethel township, Northampton county, Penn, 1775; Hugh was b. Jan. 18, 1764; d. June 24, 1839; m. March 14, 1789, Grace Gaston, b. Nov. 25, 1764;

d. March 14, 1838. Grace Gaston, wife of Hugh, was the daughter of Robert Gaston, of Somerset county, N. J., b. Jan. 28, 1732; d. near Warrior's Run Presbyterian Church, Northumberland county, Penn., Sept. 2, 1793; served as a colonel in the Revolutionary War, and as a member of the Committee of Safety for Morris county, N. J.; m. May 15, 1762, Rosanna Cooper, b. March 23, 1742; d. Jan. 14, 1817. Robert Gaston, father of Grace Gaston, was the son of Joseph Gaston, of Bernard township, Somerset county, N. J., who d. 1777 (see Gaston Family).

JAMES SIMERAL, b. 1792; d. Sept. 21, 1849; m. Mary Ann Vincent, b. June 11, 1790; d. April 16, 1866; daughter of Robert Vincent; had issue: 1. Jane, b. Nov. 16, 1815; 2. Martha, b. Jan. 3, 1817; m. 1838, William Boggs (had issue: i. Vincent-Simeral; ii. William-Edwin; d. 1878; m. Adaline Friend, of Wheeling; iii. Oliver-Stevenson, d. 1882; iv. Albert-Whitten; v. Emmet-Addison; vi. Anna-Mary); 3. Matilda, b. Dec. 25, 1818; m. George S. Atkinson (see Atkinson Family); 4. Robert-Vincent, b. July 26, 1822; d. April 15, 1852; m. Sarah Ann Hogg, daughter of John and Miriam Hogg, of Mount Pleasant, Jefferson county (had issue: i. Mary-Ann, m. —— Jenkins; ii. George-H., m. Margaret Kidd, of Bloomington, Ill.; iii. James-V.; iv. Ann-Elizabeth); 5. Amanda, b. July 10, 1826; m. 1857, Rev. William M. Grimes.

The name, Simeral, is a corruption. It was originally Somerville, and was so written many times during the eighteenth century by the ancestors of families now bearing the name, Simeral. The Harrison county Simerals are probably descended from John Simeral, who removed from Adams county and settled in Hempfield (now South Huntingdon) township, Westmoreland county, Penn., before 1772, with his brother, Thomas Simeral (who died there in 1772) and sister, Mary Kincaid (wife of Robert Kincaid). John Simeral established a ferry across the Youghiogheny River at the present town of West Newton (originally called Simeral's Ferry, and later, Robbstown). He died there after 1794, leaving children: Joseph, John, Alexander, Mary, and Elizabeth. Margaret Simeral died in Westmoreland county, 1779, leaving

8

children, Isaac and Martha, and perhaps more, as George Simeral's name appears as a witness to her will. James Simeral died there in 1781; and William Simeral, in 1796, leaving as next of kin, Sarah Simeral, who was appointed administratrix of his estate.

JAMES SIMPSON, b. in Ireland, April 30, 1750; d. Sept. 20, 1819; settled in Washington county, Penn., near the close of the last century; m. in America, Margaret Conner, b. in Ireland, Oct. 25, 1755; d. March 25, 1815; had issue: I. John. II. Margaret. III. William. IV. Elizabeth. V. James, b. in Washington county, Penn., July 14, 1791; d. in Green township, Harrison county, Dec. 8, 1871; first settled in Belmont county, about 1816, removing to Harrison county in 1820; m. in Washington county, 1816, Violet Scott, d. June 30, 1855; daughter of Rev. Abram Scott, a Presbyterian minister, had issue: 1. Margaret-Rebecca, b. Dec. 25, 1818; d. July 26, 1843; 2. Abram-Scott, b. in Belmont county, Jan. 3, 1821; d. Nov. 3, 1884; m. March 26, 1857, Celia Davis, daughter of John Davis, of German township; 3. John-McDowell, b. Oct. 4, 1822; d. April 16, 1825; 4. William, b. April 30, 1825; settled in Green township; 6. Josiah-Marshall, b. Sept. 15, 1828; d. May 30, 1830; 7. Sarah-Mariah, b. Dec. 29, 1833. VI. Mary. VII. Robert. VIII. Sarah.

THOMAS SIMPSON, a native of the North of Ireland, of Scottish descent, emigrated from county Londonderry to Baltimore, Md., in 1793, and thence removed to Jefferson county after 1800; had issue: 1. Andrew, settled at Chillicothe, Ohio; 2. John, a native of county Tyrone, Ireland, emigrated to America, and settled in Washington county, Penn., where he m. Margaret (or Mary) McElroy; removed to Harrison county, Ohio, about 1800, and settled in Stock township, where he d. 1836; had issue, among others: 1. John, b. 1814; d. 1877; m. 1839, Margaret Law, b. in county Tyrone, Ireland, 1820, daughter of John and Bessie Linn Law, who settled in Harrison county, 1830 (had issue: i. Mary-Ann, b. 1841; m. Joseph C. Patterson; ii. Martha, b. 1842, m. Robert Birney; iii. Margaret, b. 1844, m. Francis Welch; iv. Matthew-W., b. Aug. 20, 1846; settled in Wash-

ington township; served in the Civil War; m. Sept. 16, 1869, Rebecca Birney, daughter of John Birney of Tippecanoe, Ohio; v. James, b. 1850; vi. Henry, b. 1851; vii. William, twin brother to Henry, b. 1851; viii. Ella, b. 1857; ix. Homer, b. 1860; x. Frank-H., b. 1860; m. Dec. 7, 1883, Phœbe Taylor, b. 1865, daughter of Samuel Taylor, of Tuscarawas county (of English descent), who m. Melissa Laken, and removed to Stock township), 2. William, settled at Watertown, Erie county, Penn., before 1813; 3. Matthew, b. June, 1776; d. in Allegheny, Penn., 1874; emigrated to America, 1793, and settled at Cadiz; served in the Ohio Legislature; 4. James, d. at Pittsburg, June, 1815; emigrated to America, 1793, and settled at Cadiz; m. June 10, 1806, Sarah Tingley, b. in New Jersey, May 23, 1781; daughter of Jeremiah Tingley, who served in the Revolution, and about 1790 removed from South Amboy, N. J., to Winchester, Va., thence to Warren township, Jefferson county, Ohio, about 1801 (had issue: i. Matthew, b. at Cadiz, June 20, 1811; d. at Philadelphia, June 18, 1884; bishop in the Methodist Episcopal Church, m. Ellen H. Verner); 5. Mary, m. John Eagleson, and settled in Harrison county.

WILLIAM SKELLEY, a native of Ireland, emigrated to America and settled in the Ligonier Valley, Westmoreland county, Penn., about 1792; m. in Ireland, —— Ferguson; both died at the place of their first settlement; had issue: 1. John, settled in Green township, Harrison county; 2. William; 3. Robert, b. in Ireland, 1788; d. 1868; removed to Stark county, Ohio, in 1820, and thence to Green township, Harrison county, December, 1842; served in the War of 1812; m. in Pennsylvania (1st), 1816, Elizabeth Creighton; b. in Pennsylvania, about 1796; d. in Stark county, Ohio, 1838; daughter of Patrick and Elizabeth Creighton, who were both born in Ireland; m. (2d) 1845, Hannah Miller (had issue by first wife: i. Sarah; ii. Elizabeth; iii. John; iv. Elinor; v. Elizabeth; vi. Jane; vii. Robert; viii. William, b. in Stark county, Aug. 6, 1831; removed to Green township; served as an officer in the Civil War; m. in Hopedale, 1862, Mary Frances Moore, a native of Harrison county, daughter of James and Ellen

Moore; ix. James, settled at Milford, Kosciusko county, Indiana).

JOSEPH SKINNER, b. in France, June 14, 1766; emigrated to America and first settled near the Natural Bridge in Rockbridge county, Virginia; afterward removed to Morristown, Belmont county, Ohio, where he d. April 18, 1837; his wife was b. in Scotland, Dec. 21, 1770; d. Jan. 5, 1811; had issue: I. William. II. Philip. III. Madison. IV. John. V. Joseph. VI. Samuel, b. in Virginia, Jan. 26, 1794; d. in Moorefield township, Harrison county, June 2, 1860, where he had located in 1820; m. July 22, 1817, Catharine Clements, b. Aug. 14, 1796; d. April 3, 1885; daughter of Abraham Clements, of Guernsey county, Ohio; had issue: 1. Malinda-Martin, b. 1818; d. Sept. 5, 1864; 2. Carleton-Adolphus, b. in Moorefield township, Aug. 18, 1829; m. July 3, 1856, Lucy A. Thompson, b. Jan. 8, 1826, daughter of Robert and Elizabeth Hague Thompson, residents of Moorefield (the former of Scotch-Irish descent; the latter of English). VII. Charles. VIII. Nancy, m. —— Hull. IX. Lucy, m. —— Willis.

WILLIAM SLEMMONS, settled in Canton township, Washington county, Penn., about 1786, then well advanced in years, probably removing from Hamiltonban township, York (now Adams) county; died after 1800, leaving two sons, Thomas and William, of whom: I. Thomas, b. 1748-49; d. April 9, 1826; m. Elizabeth ——, b. 1754-55; d. April 17, 1835; had issue: 1. Samuel; 2. William; 3. Thomas-B., m. Jane Vasbinder, daughter of William and Mary Buchanan Vasbinder, of West Middletown, Hopewell township, Washington county (who had removed from Carlisle, Penn.); 4. John, m. Margaret Vasbinder; 5. James; 6. Susanna; 7. Eliza; 8. Jane; 9. Margaret, m. John Vasbinder; 10. Mary. II. William (probably the son of William and brother of Thomas above), b. 1761; d. Jan. 27, 1827; m. (1st) ——; m. (2d) Jane Osburn, b. 1775-76; d. July 4, 1851; had issue: 1. William-R. (?), b. 1780; d. Dec. 6, 1844; m. Nancy —— (had issue: i. John-D., b. 1807; d. 1821; ii. Henrietta); 2. Margaret, b. 1783-84; d. Feb. 2, 1873; m. Jacob Vasbinder; 3. Joseph-J., b. 1786; d. Dec. 4, 1868; m. Susanna ——, b. 1801; d.

Oct. 29, 1862; 4. Basil-Lee, m. S. —— (had issue, among others: i. William, b. 1829; d. 1848; ii. Obediah); 5. Thomas; 6. Samuel, b. 1808-09; d. July 26, 1867; m. (1st) 1829, Susanna Osburn, b. 1810; d. Oct. 22, 1851; m. (2d) Eliza Hearn, b. Feb. 22, 1829; d. Feb. 25, 1879; daughter of Launcelot and Barbara Sutherland Urquhart Hearn; 7. Matthew-G., m. 1842, Ann ——, b. 1818-19; d. March 26, 1857 (had issue, among others: i. William, b. 1845; d. 1846); 8. Alexander; 9. Jane, m. —— Amspoker; 10. Susanna, m. 1829, John Lyle; 11. Martha, b. Sept. 7, 1812; d. June 15, 1845; m. 1833, James Welsh, son of Samuel and Catherine Coulter Welsh, of Archer township.

MATTHEW M. SLOAN, see Family of William Grimes.

DANIEL SMITH, b. in Maryland, 1774; d. in Stock township, Harrison county, Ohio, July 14, 1856; removed to Huntingdon county, Penn., before 1803, and thence to Jefferson county in 1818, and to Stark township about 1821; m. Elizabeth Perrigo; had issue: I. William-P., b. in Huntingdon county, Sept. 20, 1803; d. May 15, 1890; m. Aug. 31, 1826, Margaret Parker, d. April 24, 1870, daughter of Richard Parker, an early settler in Stock township (had issue: i. James-P., b. June 23, 1827; m. (1st) Sept. 30, 1847, Anna Cramblet, d. June 21, 1876, daughter of John Cramblet, of Stock township; m. (2d) Oct. 13, 1877, Nancy C. Rogers, of Nottingham township; ii. Harriet, m. David Hines; iii. Lina, m. George W. Spiker; iv. Richard-P., b. July 20, 1832; m. Nov. 2, 1853, Mary Jane Miller, daughter of Samuel G. Miller; v. Daniel; vi. Margaret, m. John Miller; vii. David, d. in the army, 1861; viii. Hannah, m. Joseph E. Johnson; ix. Simeon, twin brother to Hannah, b. Jan. 2, 1841, m. Jan. 30, 1870, Rebecca Johnston, daughter of Samuel R. and Rebecca Barnhill Johnston).

JOHN SMITH, a native of Ireland; emigrated to America, and, about 1818, settled in Nottingham township, Harrison county, Ohio, where he died; his widow died in Deersville, aged ninety years; had issue: 1. Thomas, b. in Ireland, May 6, 1809; settled in North township; d. Feb. 23, 1881; m. 1838, in Ireland, Mary Hopkins, b. in Ireland, Aug. 27, 1813; d. in North township,

June 5, 1882, sister of Dr. Abram Hopkins, d. 1882, who settled in Canada (had issue: i. Joseph-J., settled in Cleveland, Ohio; ii. Robert-H., d. in Pittsburgh, Dec. 12, 1885; iii. Edward-A., d. 1861; iv. Theodore-W., b. March 17, 1846; settled in North township; m. Dec. 8, 1870, Malila English, a native of North township, daughter of James and Ann McCarroll English; v. Alice-J., d. in Leesville; vi. Sarah-E., m. M. Friesbaugh); 2. Robert; 3. William; 4. John; 5. Sarah, m. F. T. Simonton, of Deersville.

WILLIAM SMITH, see Family of William Ramage.

DAVID SMYLIE, a native of Ireland, emigrated to America and first settled in Washington county, Penn., before 1794; removed to Westmoreland county, Penn., and in 1815 located at Cadiz, Harrison county, Ohio, where he died Sept. 13, 1843; m. in Ireland, Sarah Jane Coon, d. 1843; had issue, among others: 1. William, b. in Washington county, Penn., 1794; settled in Archer township, Harrison county, 1825, where he remained until 1855, and then located in Washington county, Iowa, dying there February, 1858; m. 1820, Rachel Borland, d. March, 1875, daughter of James Borland, of Butler county, Penn. (had issue: i. David; ii. James; iii. Margaret; iv. John, b. Nov. 9, 1826; m. May 1, 1849, Julia A. Cox, daughter of George and Sarah Titus Cox; v. Samuel; vi. Robert; vii. Matthew; viii. Hugh; ix. Thomas; x. Sarah-Jane; xi. William; xii. Joseph; xiii. Rachel; xiv. David).

George Cox, father of Julia A. Smylie, was b. 1784; d. Sept. 12, 1849; son of Richard Cox, of Dutch descent, who came from New Jersey to Steubenville, Ohio, before 1800, and later settled in Archer township; m. 1808, Sarah Titus, b. 1786; d. 1877, daughter of Jonathan Titus and wife, who were natives of Wales, and settled near Cadiz, before 1812; had issue: 1. Mary; 2. Hiram; 3. Rachel, b. in Steubenville; 4. Jeremiah; 5. George; 6. Jonathan; 7. Sarah; 8. Obediah; 9. John; 10. Julia-A., m. John Smylie; 11. Martin.

GARRETT SNEDEKER, settled in Washington county, Penn., before 1789; removed to Harrison county, Ohio, about 1800; had issue:

I. John, b. in Washington county, 1789; settled in German township, 1816,

where he died the same year; m. in German township, Elizabeth Cutshall, b. in Pennsylvania; d. Sept. 19, 1875; daughter of Nicholas Cutshall, who settled in German township, 1800; had issue: 1. Rebecca, m. Jacob Dunmire, and settled in Jasper county, Iowa; 2. Samuel, b. in Wayne township, Jefferson county, Feb. 9, 1812; settled in German township; m. Oct. 30, 1849, Mary J. Glasener, daughter of Garrett and Ann Maholm Glasener, natives of Pennsylvania, who settled at Cadiz, 1800; 3. Garrett, d. in infancy; 4. Elizabeth. II. Jacob. III. Elizabeth. IV. Mary.

MARTIN SNYDER, a native of Germany, b. 1728; d. Nov. 7, 1810; emigrated to America and first settled in Adams county, Penn., before 1775, where he married Catherine Amon, b. in Pennsylvania, 1759; d. Aug. 29, 1821; settled in Green township, Harrison county, Ohio, about 1802; had issue:

I. Martin, b. in Adams county, Penn., 1775; d. in Green township, April 12, 1819; m. 1803, Ruth Tipton, b. near Baltimore, 1779; d. Feb. 5, 1850; daughter of Samuel and Nancy Tipton (the former, after the death of his wife, located in Jefferson county, Ohio, about 1802); had issue: 1. Catherine; 2. Martin, b. 1805; d. 1882; 3. Mary, b. in Green township, Sept. 7, 1808; m. July 13, 1837, Walter Jamison (his second wife), b. Feb. 24, 1801; d. July 1, 1883; son of John and Ann Craig Jamison, who settled in Cadiz township, about 1802 (had issue: i. Martin-S., settled in Cadiz; ii. Jane-A., m. George W. Glover; iii. Ruth-Ellen, d. in infancy; iv. William-Walter, b. 1849; d. 1879—); 4. Amon; 5. Jacob, b. July 5, 1814; m. June 24, 1847, Elizabeth Bradford, daughter of Thomas Bradford, of Green township (had issue: i. Martin, b. March 7, 1848; m. (1st) Mary J. Carson, d. August, 1857; m. (2d) Nancy Jane McGuire; ii. Mary-Catherine, m. Leander Bigger, of Cadiz; iii. Sarah; iv. Caroline; v. Isabella, m. Finley Mattern); 6. Nancy; 7. Zachariah; 8. Samuel. II. Adam. III. Henry. IV. John. V. Catherine, b. in Ireland, 1794; d. Feb. 5, 1869; m. 1820, Dr. Moses Kennedy, b. Dec. 24, 1797; d. April 7, 1857; son of Michael and Margaret Thompson Kennedy, of the North of Ireland; had issue: 1. Margaret, b. 1821; d. 1871;

m. 1837, Allen G. Turner (had issue, among others: i. Moses-Kennedy, m. Eliza J. Craig, daughter of Johnson and Martha Thompson Craig; settled at Columbus, Neb.); 2. Elizabeth-Ann, b. 1822; d. young; 3. Michael-Butler, m. Lucinda Crossan; 4. Isabella, b. 1837; m. 1847, Ephraim Clark (see Family of Roger Clark); 5. Martin-Snyder, b. 1829; m. Martha McKee; 6. Caroline-M., b. 1832; 7. Martha-A., b. 1834; m. John McConnell; 8. Benjamin-F., b. 1836; m. Mary Jane Harrison. VI. Mary. VII. Eve. VIII. Elizabeth. IX. Magdalene, m. —— Pumphrey.

CHRISTIAN SPIKER, of Dutch descent, emigrated from Pennsylvania, and settled in Stock township, before 1806; d. December, 1820; m. Diana ——; had issue:
I. Christian, or Christopher, b. in Stock township, Harrison county, Ohio, 1806; d. 1879; m. Aerie Carnes, b. 1804; d. March 1870; had issue: 1. William, b. 1826; settled at Deersville; m. 1845, Mary Cottrell, daughter of Adam Cottrell, a native of Scotland (d. 1842; his wife d. 1886) (had issue, among others: i. George-D., b. Dec. 26, 1846; settled at Scio, Harrison county; m. 1871, Elizabeth Gibson, daughter of Edward and Catherine Gibson (both of whom died in Harrison county); 2. George-W.; 3. Mary-J., m. Cornelius Vickers; 4. John-W., b. July 31, 1833; m. 1859, Nancy Crawford, daughter of Josiah Crawford, of Stock township; 5. Henry-C.; 6. Henry; 7. Elizabeth, m. David Christy; 8. Christiana, m. William Hines; 9. Catherine, m. Samuel Hines; 10. Sarah-Ann.
II. John.
III. Joseph.

THOMAS SPROULL, b. in Ireland, 1799, son of Robert Sproull; emigrated to America, and, about 1819, settled in Short Creek township, Harrison county, Ohio; removed in 1823 to Moorefield township, where he d. April 19, 1872; m. (1st) in Ireland, Mary Hastings; d. about 1822; m. (2d) Elizabeth Caldwell; had issue by first wife: 1. William, settled in Coshocton county, Ohio; had issue by second wife: 2. Andrew; 3. Robert; 4. John, b. Sept. 23, 1842; m. Amanda White, b. July 26, 1854, daughter of Joseph and Sarah Lee White, of Nottingham township; 5. Hugh; 6. Thomas.

RALPH SPURRIER, see Family of John Heberling.

JACOB STAHL, b. in Maryland, Aug. 13, 1784; d. 1845; settled in Rumley township, Harrison county, Ohio, in 1816; had issue: 1. William, b. in Charles county, Md., 1810; d. 1876; m.in Rumley township, Susanna Canaga, b. 1811; d. 1872 (had issue: i. Sarah, m. Abram Busby; ii. Maria, m. James Shambaugh; iii. Elizabeth, m. A. L. Ridenaur; iv. James, b. Oct. 6, 1845; m. Oct. 11, 1866, Sarah Jane Braden, b. Feb. 2, 1844, daughter of Gettys and Rachel Cox Braden); 2. Elizabeth, m. George Simmons; 3. John, b. in Frederick, Md., June 12, 1810; d. Aug. 27, 1881; m. March 18, 1832, Mary Ann Condo, b. in Penn., Feb. 28, 1813; d. Feb. 9, 1896; daughter of Jacob and Mary Ann Shuss Condo (had issue: i. Jacob, b. 1833; d. 1872; m. (1st) Catherine Knauf; m. (2d) Elizabeth Kimmel; ii. Margaret, b. July, 1835; m. Thomas Lucas; iii. Catherine, b. 1837; m. Arnold Wheeler; iv. Mary-Ann, b. 1839; m. David Hazlitt; v. Susan, b. 1841; d. young; vi. Samuel, b. 1846; d. in infancy; vii. Samantha-Jane, b. Jan. 20, 1854; m. Albert Houck); 4. Margaret, m. Peter Manbeck; 5. Catherine, m. Abraham Gotshall, and settled in Meigs county, Ohio; 6. Mary, m. Daniel Hilbert, and settled in Defiance county, Ohio; 7. Matilda, d. young; 8. Susanna, m. Abraham Kimmel; 9. James, m. Elizabeth Shuss; 10. Lydia, m. Jeremiah Condo.
Gettys Braden, d. April 13, 1851, in Crawford county, Ohio, father of Sarah Jane Braden Stahl, was a son of Thomas and Jane Braden, of Gettysburg, Penn., m. May 2, 1842, Rachel Cox, d. at Baxter Springs, Cherokee county, Kan., Feb. 7, 1883, daughter of George and Sarah Cox; had issue: 1. Sarah-Jane; 2. Rachel-Ann, b. 1846; d. 1867; 3. George-Thomas, settled at Caney, Kan.; 4. William-Wilson; settled at Conneaut, Ohio.

JAMES STEEL, a native of Virginia; had issue:
I. John.
II. Basil-E., b. in Berkeley county, West Va.; removed to Pennsylvania, and thence, about 1815, to Washington township, Harrison county, Ohio; d. 1857; m. in Pennsylvania, Rachel Spaulding, d. 1874; had issue: 1. John;

2. Sarah; 3. Mary; 4. Matilda-Jane; 5. Nancy; 6. Andrew; 7. Basil; 8. William; 9. Daniel; 10. David, b. Oct. 31, 1822; m. (1st) April 10, 1845, Elizabeth Vermillion, of Guernsey county, Ohio; d. Dec. 17, 1885; m. (2d) Feb. 11, 1890, Mrs. Comfort Lindsey, of Flushing (had issue by first wife: i. John-B.; ii. Andrew-J.; iii. Joseph-M.; iv. Franklin; v. William; vi. Henry; vii. Spaulding; viii. Amanda; ix. Matilda; x. Olive).

SILAS STEPHEN, settled in Short Creek township, Harrison county, Ohio, about 1808 or 1810; had issue among others: 1. Jonathan, b. June 5, 1799; d. 1880; m. Feb. 24, 1825, Elizabeth Salomons, b. Jan. 22, 1808 (had issue, among others: i.Zachariah, served in the Civil War, and died in that service; ii. Silas, b. Dec. 23, 1841; served in the Civil War; m. May 7, 1889. Sarah R. Barcroft, daughter of Joseph and Elizabeth Hunter Barcroft (the former b. in Jefferson county, 1814; d. in Hopedale, Nov. 6, 1886; the latter, a native of Westmoreland county, Penn., who came with her parents to Ohio in 1835).

ARCHIBALD STEWART, a native of Ireland; emigrated to Pennsylvania with his parents, and about 1816 removed to Harrison county, Ohio, settling near Cadiz, where he d. March 18, 1854; m. in Pennsylvania, 1805, Margaret Donaldson; d. Nov. 13, 1849; had issue: 1. James; 2. Samuel, b. June 25, 1809; settled in Washington township; m. June 2, 1840, Maria Auld, daughter of William and Mary McAdoo Auld (had issue: i. Mary, b. April 6, 1841; ii. Archibald, b. Jan. 10, 1843; iii. William-Alexander, b. Aug. 16, 1845; iv. Margaret, b. Sept. 10, 1847; v. James-M., b. Jan. 25, 1850; vi. Samuel-D.; vii. Thomas-M., b. Nov. 3, 1855); 3. Mary; 4. Isabelle; 5. Margaret.

Samuel Auld, grandfather of Maria Auld, was a native of Ireland; emigrated to Pennsylvania and thence removed to Nottingham township, Harrison county; had issue: 1. John; 2. Samuel; 3. Mary; 4. James; 5. William, 6. Eliza; 7. Diana; 8. Robert; 9. Stewart; 10. Grace; 11. William, d. Jan. 11, 1880; m. (1st) Mary McAdoo; d. 1820; m. (2d) Elizabeth Todd (had issue by first wife: i. Maria, m. Samuel Stewart; had issue by second wife: ii. James; iii. George-T.; iv. Alexander-T.).

JACOB STONER, b. near Hagerstown, Md., Dec. 25, 1815; son of Jacob and Mary Stoner, the former of whom died in Maryland in 1817; settled in Colerain township, Belmont county, Ohio, 1818, thence removed to Deersville, Harrison county, some years afterward, and later located in Monroe township; m. April 26, 1838, Honor Sneider, b. in Washington county, Penn., June 25, 1820, daughter of David and Christina Sneider, of Monroe township; had issue: 1. Mary-E., m. Urias B. Hite, and settled at Dennison, Ohio; 2. Sarah, m. Michael Lynch, and settled at Dennison, Ohio; 3. William, settled in Monroe township; served in the Civil War; 4. David, b. Sept. 23, 1845; served in the Civil War; m. (1st) March 14, 1867, Mary Fowler; d. March 31, 1874; daughter of John E. Fowler; m. (2d) Sept. 26, 1879, Susan Winrod, b. in Belmont county, Ohio; 5. Jacob-S., settled in Franklin township; 6. James-M., settled at Tippecanoe, Ohio; 7. Ella-C., m. James M. Evans, and settled at Auburn, Sangamon county, Ill.; 8. George-W., served in the Civil War; d. March 30, 1865, at Camp Chase.

JOHN STRINGER, b. in Chester county, Penn., 1776; removed to Jefferson county, Ohio, about 1800; settled near York, Ohio, 1811, where he d. July 10, 1845; his wife, whom he had married in Pennsylvania, d. May 12, 1850; had issue: 1. William, b. in Jefferson county. Aug. 19. 1803; d. Aug. 16, 1859; m. (1st) March 19, 1829, Jane Johnston; d. June 5, 1838; daughter of Richard Johnston, a resident of Harrison county, Ohio; m. (2d) 1839, Isabella Ferguson; d. Oct. 15, 1888, daughter of Henry Ferguson (had issue by first wife: i. Jane; ii. John-M., b. March 4, 1832; settled in Green township, where he d. May 4, 1889; m. Sept. 5, 1861, Susanna Buchanan, b. Oct. 9, 1841, daughter of John Buchanan, a pioneer in Harrison county; iii. Johnston; iv. Ann-E.; had issue by second wife: v. Henry; vi. Thomas-J.; vii. Joseph-E.; viii. Frederick-M.; ix. Sarah; x. Maria); 2. James; 3. John; 4. Sarah; 5. Elizabeth; 6. Mary; 7. Rebecca.

JAMES TAGGART, a native of Pennsylvania, m. Mary Ferguson; had issue:
I. John. b. in Washington county, Penn., 1778; d. June 4, 1843; removed to

Green township, Harrison county, Ohio, 1803, where he died; m. in Pennsylvania, Margaret Miller, b. March 12, 1779; d. Aug. 31, 1861; had issue: 1. James, b. July 22, 1806; d. Oct. 15, 1890; m. March 12, 1835, Anne Craig, d. Feb. 24, 1887, daughter of John Craig, an early settler in Ohio (had issue: i. Margaret, b. April 23, 1836; m. Dr. J. B. Crawford, and settled at Gillespie, Ill.; ii. John, b. May 28, 1839; d. Dec. 31, 1842; iii. Milton-J., b. July 19, 1842; served in the Civil War; m. Oct. 25, 1887, Anna Patten, of Sidney, Shelby county, Ohio, daughter of H. T. Patten; iv. Elizabeth-A., b. March 10, 1845; m. J. B. Mansfield, and settled in Jefferson county; v. James-A., b. Jan. 8, 1848; d. May 7, 1849; vi. Mary-R., b. May 27, 1850; vii. Luella-K., b. Oct. 26, 1856; m. W. H. Eagleson, and settled in Green township); 2. Margaret; 3. Mary; 4. John; 5. George; 6. Jane; 7. David; 8. Alexander. II. James. III. Samuel. IV. Robert. V. Jane. VI. Elizabeth.

ISAAC THOMAS, see account of Abraham Branson.

AARON THOMPSON, see account of Alexander Green.

DAVID THOMPSON, a native of county Tyrone, Ireland, b. 1772; d. 1868; son of Joseph Thompson, who emigrated to America and settled near Chambersburg, Penn., in 1792 (Joseph Thompson d. about 1819); David m. in Pennsylvania, Martha Gift, of German parentage, b. 1778; d. 1843; settled about one mile north of Cadiz, Harrison county, Ohio, in 1814; had issue: 1. Joseph; 2. Elizabeth, m. William McFadden, and settled in Iowa; 3. Mary, m. Joseph McFadden, and settled in Cadiz township; 4. David; 5. John, d. in Washington county, Iowa; 6. Katherine, m. John Sharp, of Holmes county, Ohio; 7. Martha, m. Adam Dunlap; 8. Rachel, m. S. Atkinson, and settled in Holmes county, Ohio; 9. James, b. March 3, 1818; m. 1848, Margaret Croskey, daughter of William and Mary Crabb Croskey, of Harrison county; removed to Cadiz, 1889 (had issue: i. Mary-Emma, d. aged sixteen years; ii. Martha-Elizabeth, m. A. W. McDonald, of Pittsburg, Penn.; iii. Anna-Caroline, m. William H. Arnold, of Cadiz; iv. David); 10. Sophia, m. John Hitchcock.

GABRIEL THOMPSON, b. in Harford county, Md.; d. at Jewett, Ohio, February, 1879; m. in Carroll county, 1830, Elizabeth Allen, d. in Carroll county, Aug. 26, 1866; daughter of Joseph and Sarah Allen, of Otsego county, N. Y.; had issue: 1. Gilbert, m. 1854, Elizabeth A. Carr; 2. H——-W., m. 1865, Catherine Kirby; 3. Lydia-A., m. 1848, Henry Pittenger; 4. Antoinette, m. 1848, Samuel Pittenger; 5. Bathsheba, m. 1860, Henry Mook; 6. Harvey-L., b. in Perry township, Carroll county, June 7, 1842; settled in Archer township, Harrison county, 1878; m. Aug. 3, 1871, at New Rumley, Maria Shambaugh, b. Aug. 22, 1844; daughter of Michael (b. in Penn., 1811; d. 1863) and Hetta Hazlett (b. in Penn., 1816; d. 1884) Shambaugh; 7. Sarah-A., m. 1873, Josiah Long; 8. Joseph-W., d. May, 1882.

THOMAS THOMPSON, b. in Pennsylvania, 1780; d. Jan. 18, 1875; removed to Harrison county, Ohio, 1816 (his father, who was twice married—Eleanor Lindsey, of Scotch descent, having been his first wife—was a native of Ireland who had settled in Half Moon Valley, Centre county, Penn.); m. May 4, 1803, Catherine Weston, b. 1785; d. May 29, 1860, of German descent, daughter of Thomas Weston, whose family were pioneers in Pennsylvania; had issue: 1. Nancy; 2. John, b. in Half Moon Valley, Penn., Aug. 8, 1808; removed to Green township, Harrison county, about 1831, where he settled; m. (1st) Elizabeth Baker, d. 1851; m. (2d) Sept. 27, 1859, Hannah Lewis, daughter of Joseph Lewis (had issue by first wife: i. Thomas; ii. Margaret; iii. John-B.; iv. Mary; v. Rezin; vi. Joseph-M.; vii. Sarah-C.; viii. Nancy-E.; ix. Elijah); 3. Sarah; 4. Thomas; 5. Mary; 6. Catherine; 7. Elijah; 8. Eleanor; 9. Joseph; 10. Rachel-Jane.

WILLIAM THOMPSON, of Scotch-Irish descent, a native of Franklin county, Penn.; removed from Chambersburg to Westmoreland county, Penn., about 1780, where he died; served in the Revolutionary War; had issue, among others: I. Samuel, b. Nov. 6, 1781; d. June 6, 1866; settled in Harrison county, 1813; m. in Pennsylvania, 1810, Elizabeth Stewart, b. Dec. 14, 1785; d. Aug. 29, 1873; daughter of John Stewart, of Scotch descent, who had settled in Butler county, Penn.; had issue: 1. Samuel, b. Sept. 18, 1822; m. Sept. 18, 1851, Sarah Jane Moorhead, daughter of Judge Moorhead, of Archer township; settled in Green township; 2. Jane, m. H. Stewart Black; settled in Green township; 3. Eliza, m. ―― Gray, and settled in Delaware county, Ohio; 4. Ellen, m. ―― Moorhead, and settled in Delaware county, Ohio; 5. Martha, b. Dec. 26, 1810; d. July 16, 1890; m. 1834, Johnson Craig, b. Dec. 3, 1803; d. July 14, 1888; 6. Maria, b. Jan. 13, 1813; d. Aug. 25, 1875; m. Jonathan Gray, b. 1807, d. July 14, 1873; 7. Isabel, m. ―― Rea; 8. Margaret, b. July 11, 1820; m. Samuel Cochran.

CHARLES TIMMONS, b. 1751; d. 1820; removed from Martinsburg, West Va., to Cadiz, Ohio, about 1812; m., probably in West Virginia, Mary Magdalene Forney, b. 1775; d. 1850; daughter of Abraham (1740-1824) and Susanna (1752-1842) Forney, all of German descent; had issue: 1. Abraham, b. Aug. 11, 1794; m. Martha Dent; 2. Eli, b. Aug. 18, 1796; 3. William, b. June 15, 1798; 4. Charles, b. Sept. 28, 1800; d. 1801; 5. Catherine, b. Oct. 27, 1802; 6. Frederick, b. July 15, 1805; m. Eliza Lacey; 7. Emanuel, b. May 9, 1808; 8. Benjamin, b. at Martinsburg, Nov. 17, 1810; d. June 3, 1898; m. at Mount Pleasant, Ohio, 1854, Mary Ann Meek, daughter of Joseph (1798-1833) and Rachel Cuppy (1784-1843) Meek; 9. Samuel, b. 1813; 10. Forney, b. March 3, 1817; d. 1886; m. at Cadiz, 1839, Elizabeth Stinson Lacey, b. June 8, 1818; d. 1898; daughter of ―― and Mary Clifton Lacey (had issue: i. Caroline, b. 1840; m. 1864, Charles N. Allen; ii. Milton-J., b. 1841; served in the Civil War; m. Josephine B. McLean; settled at Peabody, Kan.; iii. Benjamin-F., b. 1844; served in the Civil War; m. Frances Jones; settled at Peabody, Kan.; iv. Robert-Lacey, b. January, 1850; m. 1879, Isabel Amanda Howard, daughter of John M. and Elizabeth Edna Howard, of Barnesville, Ohio).

WILLIAM TINGLEY, b. in New Jersey, 1787; d. at Cadiz, Ohio, 1863; removed to West Virginia, and thence, about 1806, to Cadiz; m. Rachel Paulson, b. in Maryland, 1789; d. 1876; daughter of James and Rachel Durbin Paulson, of Harrison county (the former d. 1816); had issue: 1. Amanda,

b. 1816; d. 1888; m. 1836, Sylvanus Wood, b. 1805; d. 1845; son of James and Elizabeth Steel Wood, from Washington county, N. Y. (had issue: i. Elizabeth, m. Andrew Henderson Carnahan; ii. Tingley-Sylvanus, m. Leonora Chestnut, and settled at Leadville, Colo.); 2. Joseph, b. 1822; 3. Jeremiah, b. 1826; 4. Temperance, b. 1830. William Tingley's father (Jeremiah Tingley) and grandfather (Joseph Tingley), both natives of New Jersey, both served in the Revolutionary War.

AQUILA TIPTON, removed from Jefferson county, and settled in Stock township, Harrison county, about 1800, where he died October, 1826; had issue, among others: 1. Aquila, b. June 1, 1800; d. May 30, 1875; m. Nancy Waller, b. in Maryland, Dec. 26, 1802; d. May 4, 1871; daughter of George Waller, a native of Maryland (had issue: i. Benjamin, b. Jan. 5, 1823; ii. Mary-J., b. Aug. 22, 1824; settled in Missouri; iii. Sarah-A., b. Aug. 24, 1826; iv. Ruth, b. Jan. 15, 1829; m. ―― Hines; settled in Uhrichsville, Ohio; v. Rachel, b. Aug. 10, 1830, m. ―― Abrams, and settled in Oregon; vi. Charlotte-H., b. Aug. 4, 1832; vii. Jared, b. Sept. 4, 1834; viii. Ephraim, b. May 4, 1836; ix. Aquila, b. May 24, 1838; settled in Nottingham township; m. April 28, 1861, Maria Scott, b. July 25, 1840, daughter of Charles and Margaret Dodds Scott [the former a native of Jefferson county, Ohio; the latter a native of Ireland]; x. Martha, b. 1840; xi. Nancy, b. Aug. 31, 1841; xii. George-W., b. Sept. 7, 1844; settled in Archer township; xiii. Thomas-B., b. Sept. 15, 1856; settled in Illinois); 2. Rebecca, m. ―― Waller; 3. Charity, m. ―― Gugan; 4. Nancy; 5. Keziah; 6. Ketura, m. ―― Cox; 7. William; 8. Shadrach; 9. Samuel; 10. John.

DAVID TOWNSEND, d. near Harrisville, 1874, where he had settled in 1812, having removed from Bucks county, Penn., with his father, Joseph Townsend (d. about 1815); m. in Ohio, Catherine Cherry, d. 1872; had issue, among others: I. Joseph, b. June 2, 1818; m. 1842, Albina Strodes, a native of Harrisville, d. 1874; had issue: 1. David-C., b. March 13, 1846; m. 1870, Adeline Morris.

ROBERT TRIMBLE, see Family of John Law.

JOHN TRUSHEL, b. 1802; d. 1884; son of Solomon Trushel, an old settler in Harrison county, Ohio; m. Frances Little, b. 1796; d. 1876; had issue: 1. Solomon; 2. Eli, settled in Tuscarawas county, Ohio; 3. Peter, settled in North township; 4. David, settled in Carroll county; 5. William; 6. Valentine, b. Oct. 17, 1846; settled in North township; m. 1875, Rebecca Stearns, daughter of William and Susan Stearns, of Carroll county, Ohio; 7. Abraham; 8. Joshua; 9. Mahala; 10. Elizabeth, m. James Morgan, of Carroll county; 11. Susanne; 12. Mary, m. Thomas Rea, of Monroe township; 13. Sarah.

ROBERT VINCENT, d. 1841; emigrated from the North of Ireland, and about 1801, settled in Green township, Harrison county, Ohio; had issue, among others: 1. Thomas-C., m. 1820, Jane Macurdy, daughter of John Macurdy (had issue: i. Agnes-T., m. John Beall—see Beall Family; ii. Jane-C., m. James Deary; iii. Thomas-M., m. Laura Lancaster; iv. Albert; v. Mary, m. Thomas Craig; vi. Sarah; vii. Oliver); 2. Jane, m. William Chambers.

THOMAS VINCENT, a physician, b. 1754; d. Aug. 31, 1841; settled in Green township before 1827; m. Jane ———, b. 1783; d. Oct. 11, 1858; had issue: 1. Joseph; 2. Thomas-W.; 3. Robert; 4. James; 5. Amanda; 6. Sarah; 7. Martha, m. 1827, Thomas Milligan; 8. Jane, m. 1834, Isaac Holmes.

JACOB VOORHEES, a native of New Jersey, b. 1767; d. July 4, 1876; son of Jacob Voorhees (of German descent, the family having first settled in America about 1670); removed to Wellsburg, Va., thence to Jefferson county, Ohio, with his father, before 1803; settled in North township, Harrison county, Ohio, 1833, where he died; m. in Fayette county, Penn., Elizabeth Gaskell, b. 1795; d. Jan. 16, 1876; daughter of Budd and Hannah G. Gaskell (the former served in the Revolutionary War, and d. in Crawford county, Penn.); had issue: 1. Samuel-Sickles; 2. Andrew-Linn; 3. Charles-F., settled at Millersburg, Ohio; 4. John-Alexander, b. Oct. 20, 1823, in Jefferson county; settled in North township; m. 1864, Ann Doyle, b. in Ireland, 1842; d. July 2, 1890; daughter of Patrick and Honora Hickey Doyle (the latter d. in Ireland, 1848; the former settled in America, 1853); 5.

Crawford-B., settled at Scio; 6. Louise, m. Benjamin Simms, and settled in Missouri; 7. George-W., b. 1830; d. in Coshocton county, Ohio, Nov. 11, 1890; 8. Jacob-Ogden, settled at Uhrichsville; 9. Richard-Marion, settled in Coshocton, Ohio.

WILLIAM WADDINGTON, see Family of John Harrison.

JOSEPH WALKER, b. in county Derry, Ireland, 1757; emigrated to America and settled in New York City, 1813; a short time later removed to Greensburg, Penn., and in 1822 to near Laceysville, Stock township, Harrison county, Ohio, where he d. 1842; m. in Ireland, Constancia Stewart, b. 1755; d. 1846; had issue: 1. John; 2. James; 3. George; 4. William, b. in Ireland, 1806; settled in Stark township, where he d. April 27, 1886; m. June 10, 1834, Jane McKinney, b. in Washington county, Penn., July 14, 1802; d. July 5, 1878; daughter of George and Mary McKinney (had issue: i. Joseph, b. June 24, 1836; m. Feb. 12, 1863, Agnes Gibson, b. Jan. 4, 1843, daughter of James B. and Lillian Maxwell Gibson, natives of Pennsylvania; ii. Mary, m. ——— Anderson, and settled in Auglaize county, Ohio); 5. Mary; 6. Elizabeth.

JOHN WALLACE, a native of York county, Penn., b. 1760; d. May 1, 1832; removed to Washington county, Penn., about 1804, and a year later to Putney township, Belmont county, Ohio; settled in Moorefield township, Harrison county, 1822; m. Margaret Anderson, b. in York county, Penn., 1767; d. March 25, 1848; had issue: 1. William, d. 1842; m. Mary W. ——— (had issue: i. John; ii. Nathaniel-S.; iii. William-A.; iv. Samuel-M.; v. Wilson-E.; vi. Sarah-Ann; vii. Eleanor-S.; viii. Margaret-J.); 2. Allen, b. in York county, Penn., April 15, 1793; settled in Moorefield township, where he d. Feb. 21, 1880; m. in Belmont county, Mary Brown (had issue: i. John; ii. Andrew; iii. William; iv. Mary; v. James; vi. Elijah-R., b. March 16, 1828; m. Jan. 23, 1868, Elizabeth Brokaw, b. March 25, 1842, daughter of Abraham and Mary Guthrie Brokaw, natives of Ohio; vii. Anderson, settled at Wooster, Ohio; viii. Samuel, settled at Wooster, Ohio); 3. Nancy; 4. Jane.

THOMAS WALLACE, of Scotch-Irish descent; resided in York county, Penn., about 1775; had issue, among others: I. John, b. in York county, Penn., May 8, 1774; removed to Warren township, Jefferson county, Ohio, 1796, where he remained until 1804, thence located in Green township, Harrison county, Ohio, where he d. June 4, 1863; m. in York county, Oct. 6, 1795, Elizabeth McCleary, b. Sept. 23, 1776; d. Feb. 19, 1855; daughter of Abel McCleary, a resident of York county; had issue: 1. William, b. Oct. 3, 1796; 2. Isaac, b. Oct. 9, 1798; 3. Thomas, b. Sept. 20, 1800; 4. Robert, b. Oct. 26, 1802; 5. Rebecca, b. June 6, 1804; 6. Margaret, b. July 16, 1806; 7. John, b. May 5, 1809; 8. Nathaniel-Anderson, b. July 16, 1811; d. Dec. 28, 1892; m. (1st) March 4, 1834, Jane Watson; d. Feb. 18, 1868, daughter of Robert Watson, of Athens township, Harrison county; m. (2d) Sept. 2, 1869, Sarah Goodrich; d. Oct. 9, 1873, daughter of George Goodrich, formerly a resident of Carroll county, Ohio; m. (3d) June 24, 1875, Elizabeth Marsh, daughter of Oliver Marsh, a resident of Pennsylvania; 9. Abraham, b. Aug. 24, 1813; 10. Elizabeth, b. March 22, 1821.

JOSHUA P. WATSON, of Scotch-Welsh descent, b. near West Liberty, West Va., March 21, 1802; son of Aaron and Nancy Watson, who settled in West Virginia about 1800; removed, about 1831, to New Athens, Harrison county, Ohio; settled in Harrisville, Harrison county, 1835, where he d. July 27, 1882; m. (1st) in West Virginia, 1823, Martha Humes, b. May 29. 1804; d. Feb. 27, 1836; m. (2d) Sarah M. McMillan, a native of Harrisville, d. Aug. 8, 1844; m. (3d) Louise M. Rimby, had issue by first wife: 1. Samuel-H., settled at Vinton, Iowa; 2. Martha-Ann, m. —— Collins, and settled at Vacaville, Cal.; 3. Louis-W., b. March 2, 1827; d. May 25, 1861; m. March 16, 1848, Julia Carver, b. Nov. 14, 1830, daughter of Thomas and Tomson Gray Carver, the former b. in Bucks county, Penn., 1788; d. Oct. 13, 1855, having come there from Downingtown, Penn., 1815; the latter b. 1797; d. Feb. 4, 1843; daughter of Thomas Gray, who settled in Harrisville, 1803 (had issue: i. William, b. June 29, 1848; d. in infancy; ii. Albert, b. July 30, 1849; d. in infancy;

iii. Thomas-Wesley, b. Sept. 21, 1850; settled in Harrisville; m. Nov. 22, 1876, Nancy J. King, b. Aug. 28, 1848, daughter of Charles Edward and Hannah Mary Hanna King, of Mount Pleasant, Ohio (the former b. near Baltimore, Md., 1808; d. March 27, 1857; the latter a native of Loudoun county, Virginia, b. Sept. 17, 1815; d. Jan. 8, 1872); iv. Florence, b. July 11, 1853; d. Oct. 10, 1873; v. Mary-Narcissa, b. March 25, 1856; m. Aug. 30, 1875, J. W. Adams, and settled in Short Creek township); 4. ——; 5. ——; 6. ——; 7. ——; 8. ——; 9. ——; had issue by second wife: 10. James-M., settled at Vinton, Iowa; 11. ——; 12. ——; had issue by third wife: 13. ——. m. Dr. R. D. Wilkin; settled in Atlantic, Iowa; 14. Charles-N.; 15. George-W.; 16. Frank, settled at Chicago; 17. Harvey, settled at Chicago.

WILLIAM WATSON, emigrated from Scotland and settled at Baltimore; removed to Pennsylvania about 1790; had issue: I. Robert, b. in Scotland or in Baltimore, March 3, 1786; removed to Athens township, Harrison county, Ohio, 1831, where he d. Nov. 19, 1872; m. in Washington county, Penn., Oct. 25, 1810, Rachel Wilson, d. May 18, 1866, daughter of Robert Wilson; had issue: 1. James, b. March 2, 1812; d. Aug. 15, 1815; 2. John-W., b. in Washington county, Feb. 7, 1814; d. July 22, 1859; m. (1st) Julia Barricklow; m. (2d) March 16, 1848, Rebecca Dunlap, daughter of John Dunlap, of Athens township (had issue by first wife: i. Rachel; had issue by second wife: ii. Robert, b. May 7, 1849; d. Aug. 28. 1849; iii. Adam-D., b. March 24, 1850; iv. Nancy-A., b. March 28, 1853); 3. Jane, b. May 1. 1815; d. Feb. 9, 1868. m. N. Anderson Wallace; 4. Alexander, b. July 3, 1817; d. Nov. 7, 1817; 5. Rachel, b. Jan. 30, 1819; d. March 30, 1839; m. John Barricklow; 6. Smith-R., b. Oct. 12, 1821; d. April 30, 1877; served as a member of the Ohio Legislature, 1864; m. Dec. 9, 1847, Susan J. McDowell. daughter of Samuel McDowell, of Athens township; 7. Nancy-G., b. Jan. 30, 1823; m. Joshua Dunlap.

WILLIAM WATTERS, a native of Maryland, of Scotch descent, settled in Harrison county, Ohio, before 1813, where he died; had issue, among others: 1. Nathan, b. in Harrison county, 1813; d. April 29, 1887; m. Catherine Foutz, b. in North township, Harrison county, 1813; d. April 28, 1874; daughter of Michael Foutz, a pioneer of Harrison county (had issue: i. John; ii. Elizabeth; iii. Jonathan; iv. Elijah; v. William, b. Sept. 12, 1848; settled in North township; m. March 23, 1882, Mrs. Sarah A. Clemens, widow of Jephtha Clemens (who d. in Youngstown, Ohio), daughter of George W. and Sophia Simmonds, of Monroe township; vi. Isaiah, settled in Tuscarawas county, Ohio).

JACOB WEBB, a native of Maryland, b. 1773; removed to Brownsville, Penn., before 1800, where he m. Hannah Kirk, b. 1775; d. 1858; daughter of Adam Kirk, a native of Pennsylvania; settled in Athens township, Harrison county, Ohio, 1809, where he d. 1833; had issue: 1. Sarah; 2. Esther, m. Joseph Huff, and settled in Athens township; 3. Edith, m. John Major, and settled in Athens township; 4. Hannah, m. Cyrus Holt; 5. John, b. Feb. 5, 1806; settled in Athens township; m. Nov. 11, 1830, Martha Holmes, b. in Short Creek township, Jan. 8, 1811, daughter of Col. Joseph Holmes (had issue: i. Joseph, b. 1833; ii. Jacob, b. Nov. 8, 1833; m. 1860, Sarah Dickerson, daughter of John Dickerson, of Athens township; settled in Athens township); 6. Mary, m. Robert Eanos, and settled near Columbus, Ohio; 7. Jacob, d. in western Illinois; 8. Ann, m. John Perrego, and settled in Athens township; 9. Ezekiel, m. Mary Corbin (had issue: i. John, settled in Athens township; ii. Rebecca, m. Joseph Figley, and settled in Indiana); 10. Joseph; 11. Robert, settled in Illinois; 12. Phœbe, d. aged seven years.

JOHN WEBSTER, removed from Maryland to Rumley township, Harrison county, Ohio, before 1824; d. before 1824; m. Mary ——, b. April 30, 1775; d. March 1, 1848; had issue, six children, of whom: I. John, b. March 20, 1811; d. Oct. 28, 1876; m. (1st) 1832, Margaret Buchanan, d. 1841, a resident of Rumley township; m. (2d) 1847, Ann Patton, daughter of Joseph Patton, of Rumley township; had issue by first wife: 1. Maria; 2. David, b. Oct. 3, 1836; settled in Archer township; m. (1st) 1870, Susanna Devore, d. Feb. 20, 1875; m. (2d) April 15, 1884, Rosella Work, daughter of Alexander Work, of Ger-

man township; 3. Sarah; had issue by second wife: 4. John; 5. Joseph; 6. Mary-M.; 7. Catherine-Jane; 8. Matthew; 9. Florence; 10. Robert; 11. Mansfield; 12. Cora; 13. Ira-B.

JOHN WELLING, d. about 1821; m. Mima ——; had issue: 1. William, m. Dorcas ——, b. Aug. 15, 1773; d. April 24, 1848; 2. John; 3. David, b. Feb. 1, 1779; d. June 19, 1864; settled in Athens township before 1817; m. (1st) Margaret ——; m. (2d) Nancy Elizabeth Black, of Guernsey county, b. 1823; d. Feb. 18, 1873 (had issue by first wife, six children; had issue by second wife: vii. Margaret-Jane, m. Finley Butler; viii. William-W.; ix. Nancy-Jane; x. Martha-A., m. Joseph White; xi. George-W., b. June 15, 1855; xii. Harriet-C.; xiii. John); 4. Thomas; 5. Henry; 6. Nancy; 7. Mary; 8. Elizabeth. Other Welling families in Harrison county, are those of the following, most or all of them probably descended from John and Mima:

John Welling, m. 1821, Mary McCullough.

John Welling, b. 1814; d. 1887; m. Jane McFadden.

David Welling, m. 1834, Jane Sharp, b. 1812; d. 1844.

William Welling, m. 1830, Margaret Davis.

DANIEL WELCH, a native of Ireland, of Scottish descent; emigrated to America and probably first settled at Carlisle, in Cumberland county (as the name, Daniel Welch, appears on the Carlisle tax-list from 1767 until after 1776): had issue, among others:

I. Daniel, b. 1763; d. Sept. 7, 1819; settled in Cecil township, Washington county, Penn., as early as 1786 (probably accompanied by his father, for the names of two Daniel Welches appear on the tax-lists of that township for 1787 and 1788); m. Elizabeth Waits, b. 1770; d. March 29, 1844; daughter of John (d. before 1786) and Sarah (d. 1818) Waits; removed to Harrison county, Ohio, about 1801, and settled at Beech Spring, on the head waters of Short Creek, in Green township; established here a horse-mill, probably the first in Harrison county; organized Beech Spring Church; had issue: 1. John, served in Captain John Allen Scroggs' company of Colonel John Andrews' regiment of Ohio Militia in the

War of 1812; died in that service, unmarried; 2. Daniel, b. 1790; d. Aug. 9, 1868; m. (1st) Margaret Bayless, b. 1796; d. Sept. 9, 1833; m. (2d) 1834, Mary Gray, b. 1806; d. Feb. 5. 1848 (had issue, among others, by first wife: i. Elizabeth, d. aged fifteen years; had issue by second wife, among others: ii. E.-Gray, b. 1842; d. Nov. 30, 1877); 3. Rezin, b. in Cecil township, Washington county, Penn., April 27, 1795; d. at Cadiz, Nov. 24, 1881; where he had settled in 1833; m. (1st) at Steubenville, 1818, Eliza Bayless, b. 1801; d. Aug. 6, 1842; daughter of Elias and Margaret Barclay Bayless, natives of Maryland; m. (2d) 1846, Maria Bayless, b. Sept. 12, 1807; d. Aug. 19, 1886; sister to his Eliza Bayless (had issue by first wife: i. Maria-B., b. 1822; d. Aug. 10, 1891; m. Walter Butler Beebe, of Cadiz; ii. Rachel-Anne, m. William R. Allison, and settled at Steubenville; iii. Caroline, m. Thomas C. Rowles, and settled at Topeka, Kan.; iv. David-Barclay, b. at Smithfield, Ohio, Nov. 23, 1830; m. 1857, Martha Collins Lyons, daughter of Robert and Ann Bowland Lyons, of Cadiz; v. Eliza, m. H. Parks MacAdam, and settled at New York Mills, N. Y.); 4. Benjamin; 5. Pressley; 6. William, m. 1835, Adaline Phillips, daughter of Thomas and Elizabeth Williams Phillips, of Cadiz; removed to Mount Pleasant, Iowa, where he died, and his widow removed thence to Osceola, Neb. (had issue, eight children, four of whom died in infancy, of the others: i. William; ii. Thomas; iii. Daniel-P., b. 1839; d. May 6, 1864; served in the Civil War, and died in that service; iv. John-Ross, m. Anna Sherwood; settled near Osceola, Neb.); 7. Jacob, m. Charlotte Pumphrey; 8. Cyrus; 9. Samuel, m. Martha Moore, b. 1815; d. April 13, 1836; 10. Mary, m. 1829, Dr. Jacob Voorhes; 11. Rhoda, m. 1828, John Mansfield.

Elizabeth Waits Welch, wife of Daniel Welch, was the daughter of John Waits, whose name appears on the taxlist of Springhill township. Fayette (then Bedford, and later, Westmoreland) county, Penn., in 1772, the first year after the organization of Bedford county, and in 1783; he settled in Cecil township, Washington county, on the head waters of Chartiers Creek in the spring of 1785; and died before April 5, 1786, at which date his land was pat-

ented to his widow, "in trust, for the use of his heirs;" he m. Mrs. Sarah Blair, d. 1818, a widow (who had three grown sons by her first husband living in Cecil township in 1788—Joseph, Samuel, and William—who later removed to Kentucky); had issue: 1. Elizabeth, m. Daniel Welch, and removed to Ohio; 2. Richard; 3. Reuben; 4. Mary, m. ——— Phillips; 5. Sarah; 6. Jacob.

JOHN WELSH, b. in Ireland, 1782-83; d. Dec. 30, 1871; removed to Westmoreland county, Penn., about 1797, and thence to Archer township, Harrison county, Ohio, before 1822, where he remained until 1860, and then settled in Stock township; m. Jane McClellan. b. in Pennsylvania, 1793; d. Feb. 17, 1872; had issue: 1. Mary; 2. Elizabeth; 3. Ann; 4. Samuel; 5. John-K.; 6. Jane; 7. Matthew; 8. James-M., b. Oct. 11, 1832; settled in Stock township; 9. David; 10. William-A., b. April 5, 1835; settled in Washington township; m. April 7, 1859, Margaret McFadden, daughter of Robert McFadden.

SAMUEL WELSH (or Welch), b. in Ireland, 1772; d. March 30, 1850; emigrated to America and settled in Westmoreland county, Penn.; removed before 1814 to Archer township, Harrison county, Ohio; m. (1st) Catherine Coulter, d. 1842; m. (2d) 1846, Mrs. William Keepers, of Stock township; had issue by first wife: 1. John, b. Nov. 20, 1808; settled at Cadiz; d. Nov. 10, 1881; m. 1833, Margaret Gilmore (had issue: i. Samuel, settled in Missouri; ii. Jason, settled in Iowa; iii. Sarah-Jane, m. John Adams, and settled in Archer township; iv. Amanda, m. Samuel F. Ross, a Methodist Episcopal minister, and settled at New Philadelphia); 2. James, b. July 9, 1815; settled at Deersville; m. (1st) March 28, 1833, Martha Slemmons, b. Sept. 7, 1812; d. June 15, 1845, daughter of William and Jane Osburn Slemmons; m. (2d) Nov. 17, 1860, Mrs. Louisa Cope, b. June 18, 1826, daughter of Barrett and Nancy Carson Rogers (had issue by first wife: i. Catherine, settled in Nottingham township; ii. Samuel-S., settled in Franklin township; iii. William-C., settled in Kansas; iv. Martha-J., m. ——— Johnson; settled in Nottingham township; v. John-M., a physician, b. Dec. 19, 1842;

settled in Deersville; m. Aug. 28, 1862, Martha Moore, b. in Nottingham township, Oct. 12, 1841, daughter of Samuel and Margaret Given Moore, natives of Ireland; vi. James-Cameron; had issue by second wife: vii. Flora-J., m. ――― Wagers, of Deersville; viii. Emmet-A., a physician; ix. Bingham, d. in infancy); 3. William, b. in Archer township, Sept. 18, 1818; m. (1st) Oct. 22, 1840, Agnes Fisher, b. 1820; d. Feb. 14, 1845; daughter of George Fisher, of Rumley township; m. (2d) Sept. 18, 1845, Emily Jane Nixon, of Archer township; d. Feb. 28, 1887 (had issue by first wife: i. Susan, m. William Sampson, and settled in Stock township; had issue by second wife: ii. James-W., b. July 1, 1847; m. May 25, 1869, Kate M. Conaway, daughter of Aaron Conaway; iii. Rebecca-Jane, m. A. J. Palmer and settled in Stock township; iv. John-N., settled in North township; v. A.-C., a Methodist Episcopal minister; settled in Youngstown, Ohio); 4. Mary, b. 1811; d. Dec. 15, 1844; m. 1833, George Fisher, b. 1792; d. 1872 (had issue, among others: i. Elizabeth; ii. Samuel, d. in infancy; iii. Jacob, d. in infancy); 5. Eleanor, m. 1839, Joseph Dunbar; 6. Nancy, m. 1840, Matthew Johnson.

Francis Gilmore, father of Margaret Welsh, was a native of Ireland; emigrated to America and settled in Archer township, Harrison county, Ohio, before 1815; m. Sarah McBride, a native of Ireland; d. March 30, 1840; had issue, eight children, of whom: 1. William; 2. Margaret, m. John Welsh; 3. John, settled in Oskaloosa, Iowa; 4. Thomas, settled in Iowa; 5. Samuel, settled in Iowa.

JAMES WEST, b. in Kirkcaldy, Fifeshire, Scotland, June 11, 1791; d. in Fox township, Carroll county, Ohio, 1851, where he had located in 1828; son of John West; emigrated to America, and first settled in Maryland, 1815; removed to Wood county, West Virginia, in 1817, and thence, in 1825, to Summit county, Ohio, whence he came to Carroll county; m. in Wood county, W. Va., 1825, Isabella Douglass, b. Sept. 15, 1802, in Akeld, Northumberland, England, daughter of John and Susan Howey Douglass, natives of Scotland (the latter a daughter of Andrew and Margaret Mitchison Howey; and the former a son of Anna Davidson Doug-

las); had issue: 1. Susanna, m. Robert Philpot, of Humboldt, Neb.; 2. John-Douglass, a physician, b. in Carroll county, Ohio; settled at Hopedale, Green township, Harrison county, Nov., 1866; m. (1st) 1853, Martha Jane Merrick, b. June 9, 1832; d. April 12, 1884; daughter of Israel J. Merrick, a native of Maryland (b. 1802; d. 1881), and Sarah Arbuckle (b. 1812); m. (2d) November, 1886, Mrs. Josephine M. Mansfield, widow of Thomas Mansfield, and daughter of Isaac Holmes, an early settler in Green township; 3. Katherine, m. John Hunter, of Delroy, Carroll county; 4. Margaret-Ann, m. John Bebout, of Mechanicstown; 5. Isabella, m. William A. Frater, of Douglas county, Oregon; 6. James-D., settled at East Liverpool, Ohio; 7. Mary-Elizabeth, m. (1st) John Smalley; m. (2d) William Kerr; settled near New Lisbon, Ohio; 8. ―――, d. in infancy; 9. ―――, d. in infancy.

JONATHAN WEST, a native of Pennsylvania, of Scotch-Irish descent, settled in Cadiz township, Harrison county, Ohio, 1811; m. Comfort Arnold, daughter of Benjamin and Comfort Arnold, of Fayette county, Pennsylvania; had issue: 1. Amos, b. in Pennsylvania; settled in Franklin township, Harrison county; m. 1832, Margaret Baker, daughter of Otto Baker, of Archer township (had issue: i. Mary; ii. Samuel; iii. Wilson-S., b. Aug. 7, 1842; m. 1868, Susannah Renshaw; iv. Sarah; v. Naomi, m. John Renshaw); 2. Rezin, b. April 19, 1812; m. Dec. 10, 1835, Nancy Arthurs, daughter of Gavin Arthurs, of Harrison county (had issue: i. Jonathan; ii. Comfort; iii. Rachel; iv. Amos, m. Melissa Copeland; v. Japheth, m. (1st) Lucinda Yant, of Tuscarawas county, Ohio; d. Sept. 21, 1883; m. (2d) Martha J. Baker; vi. Sarah-E.; vii. William-G., m. April 15, 1881, Rebecca Wright, daughter of Sylvanus Wright; viii. James-M., m. Elizabeth Rinehart, of Franklin township; ix. Esther); 3. Samuel; 4. Jonathan; 5. Mary; 6. Esther; 7. Actia; 8. James; 9. Elizabeth; 10. Comfort; 11. Sarah.

Gavin Arthurs, father of Nancy Arthurs West, was a native of Ireland; settled in Harrison county, where he d. Feb. 1, 1876; m. Rachel Hall, of Maryland; d. 1845; had issue: 1. Robert; 2. William; 3. James; 4. Eliza; 5. Mary-

J.; 6. Amelia; 7. Nancy, m. Rezin West; 8. Sarah; 9. Louisa.

JOHN WEYANDT, of German descent, removed probably from Pennsylvania or Maryland to Monroe township, Harrison county, before 1817; d. 1848; m. Motlena ———; had issue: 1. Daniel; 2. Jacob; 3. Abraham, b. 1821; d. 1899; m. (1st) Roxanna Warner; m. (2d) Margaret Gamble (had issue: i. Amadilla, m. E. M. Long; ii. Eleanor, m. M. Rohan; iii. Martha-Ann, m. William B. Penn; iv. Webster, m. Ruth Myers; v. Olive, m. L. D. Price; vi. Melinda, m. Oscar Price); 4. Mary, m. 1837, Henry B. Heller; 5. Christina, m. ——— Warner.

JOHN WHAN, b. in Chester county, Penn., Sept. 25, 1776; removed to Harrison county, Ohio, 1815; m. Aug. 21, 1804, Margaret Boggs, b. Nov. 17, 1779; had issue: 1. William, b. July 7, 1805; d. March 18, 1833; 2. Sarah, b. Jan. 7, 1807; d. in New Athens, Dec. 9, 1875; m. George McCullough, b. 1803; d. April 3, 1845 (had issue: i. Margaret, m. S. K. Kane, of Darlington, Penn.; d. in Mississippi; ii. Martha, m. James Stewart; d. in Pittsburg, Penn.; iii. John, b. 1834; d. 1855; iv. Robert, settled in Milwaukee, Wis.; v. William, b. 1840; settled in New Athens); 3. Hannah, b. Oct. 16, 1808; 4. Mary, b. Dec. 1, 1810; d. Aug. 6, 1851; 5. Ellen, b. May 13, 1813; m. Michael Morgan, and settled in Short Creek township; 6. James, b. Jan. 9, 1816; d. Sept. 19, 1856; 7. John, b. May 10, 1821; d. July 19, 1849.

EZRA WHARTON, removed· from Bucks county, Penn., to Harrison county, Ohio, about 1820, and settled in Short Creek township; had issue, among others: I. Joel, settled in Washington township, before 1833, where he d. 1863; m. about 1822, Abigail Bundy, d. 1874; had issue: 1. Martha; 2. Bethia; 3. Josiah; 4. Rachel; 5. Tabitha-A.; 6. Matilda; 7. Ezra, b. June 21, 1833; m. Feb. 22, 1859, Martha Myers, of Franklin township, daughter of Samuel and Mary Connell Myers (had issue: i. Olive, m. William Laizure; ii. Samuel-M.; iii. David-B.; iv. Oscar-E.; v. Arthur-B.); 8. Abigail; 9. Susannah. II. Anna. III. Hannah. IV. Daniel. V. Lynton. VI. Amos. VII. James. VIII. Silas. IX. Levi.

Michael Myers, a native of Pennsylvania, grandfather of Martha Myers Wharton, settled near Tippecanoe, Harrison county, Ohio, before 1830; m. in Pennsylvania, Martha Huffman; had issue: 1. George; 2. John; 3. Michael; 4. Samuel; 5. Philip; 6. David; 7. Berlin; 8. Eliza; 9. Catherine; 10. Rachel; 11. James. Samuel Myers was b. 1802; d. in Franklin township, June 3, 1879; m. 1820, Mary Connell (had issue: i. Jemima; ii. David; iii. Martha, m. Ezra Wharton; iv. Jonathan; v. Wesley; vi. George; vii. Catherine; viii. Sarah-J.; ix. Amanda; x. Sansom; xi. Mary-J.; xii. Samuel-S.; xiii. John).

JOSEPH WHITE, of Scotch descent; settled in Frederick county, Md., before 1775, where he d. about 1818; served in the Revolutionary War; m. Mary Fulton, cf Scotch-Irish descent; b. 1756-1766; d. in Franklin township, Harrison county, Ohio, Feb. 20, 1856; had issue: 1. Catherine; 2. William; 3. Joseph, b. in Frederick, Md., Sept. 12, 1798; removed with his mother to Harrison county in 1819, and first located in Nottingham township; later settled in Franklin township, where he d. Sept. 29, 1877; m. April 12, 1828, Hannah Rogers, d. May 17, 1866, daughter of Joseph and Pamela Rogers, early settlers in Harrison county, who came from Maryland (had issue: i. Jackson-R.; ii. William-P.; iii. Pamela [or Pamalah]; iv. Joseph-T.; v. Benjamin-F.; vi. Warren-R.; vii. Mary-Ann; viii. Joshua-P., b. Nov. 15, 1840; served in the Civil War [as did also three of his brothers]; m. Sept. 29. 1870, Agnes C. Glandon, daughter of William and Mary Glandon, early pioneers in Harrison county; ix. Charles-W.; x. Hannah-E.); 4. Charles.

WILLIAM WILEY, b. in Washington county, Penn., 1776; d. in Short Creek township, Harrison county, Ohio, 1853, where he had settled about 1804; son of Thomas and Rebecca Lytle Wiley, natives of Lancaster county, Penn.; m. in Pennsylvania, 1804, Elizabeth Vance; had issue: 1. Joseph; 2. Thomas, m. Mary Tendeley; 3. Anna, m. Hugh Martin; 4. John; 5. David, m. Laura J. Stanley; 6. James, m. Harriet Wight; 7. William, b. in Short Creek township; m. Nov. 3, 1864, Olive M. Stanley, daughter cf Noah Stanley (b. in Trumbu'l county, Ohio, where he d. 1873), and Sarah Bowman Stanley (b. in Columbiana county, Ohio); 8. Rebecca;

9. Mary-Jane, m. N. W. Shannon; 10. Elizabeth; 11. Clarissa, m. Joseph Jamison; 12. Wilson, m. Eliza Mc-Gowan; 13. Priscilla.

ROBERT WILKIN, settled in Pennsylvania, 1770; removed to near the present site of Cadiz, Harrison county, Ohio, about 1802, and a few years later settled at Londonderry, Guernsey county; m. in Pennsylvania, Mary Hyde; had issue: I. Elizabeth. II. Nancy. III. Jane. IV. Rebecca. V. Mary. VI. Samuel. VII. Thomas. IX. Archibald, b. in Pennsylvania; settled in Washington township, Harrison county, before 1818, where he d. 1870; m. Hannah Davidson, d. 1856, daughter of Samuel Davidson, of Washington township; had issue: 1. Samuel, b. in Washington township, May 23, 1818; m. (1st) April 18, 1843, Margaret Foraker, of Guernsey county; d. Oct. 22, 1864; m. (2d) Aug. 6, 1866, Jeanette McCormick, of Guernsey county (had issue by first wife: i. Ellis; ii. Mary-Ann; iii. Archibald; iv. Hannah; v. Samuel; vi. Margaret-S.); 2. Mary-Ann; 3. Jane; 4. Angelina. X. William. XI. James. XII. Robert.

CHARLES WILLISON, settled in Moorefield township, Harrison county, Ohio, before 1818; had issue: 1. Amos; 2. Jeremiah, b. in Moorefield township, where he d. 1850; m. 1847, Rebecca Figley (had issue: i. Rachel-A.; ii. John-M., b. July 3, 1850; m. Jan. 8. 1879, Julia McCullough, daughter of William and Julia Laizure McCullough); 3. Elijah; 4. Abijah; 5. Charles; 6. Rosilla; 7. Annie; 8. Rusha; 9. Rachel.

JOHN WILSON, a native of Washington county, Penn.; removed to Short Creek township, Harrison county, Ohio, 1806; and in May, 1834, settled in Rumley township; m. in Pennsylvania, Esther Fisher; had issue: 1. William-H., b. Sept. 22, 1803; d. in Rumley township, August, 1887; m. Margaret A. McComb, d. March, 1884 (had issue: i. Eliza-J., m. C. N. Coulter, and settled in Michigan; ii. John-A.; iii. Hadassah, m. James V. Thompson, and settled in Richland county, Ohio; iv. R.-M.; v. W.-L., b. Oct. 29, 1841; m. August, 1880, M. A. Mehaffey, of near Mount Hope, Washington county, Penn.; vi. Mary-E.; vii. James-R., settled at Arkansas City, Ark.; viii. David-Mc.; ix. T.-H., m. S. G. Phillips, and settled at Arkansas City, Ark.); 2. James; 3. Hugh; 4. John; 5. Samuel; 6. David; 7. Esther; 8. Margaret; 9. Elizabeth, d. in infancy.

GEORGE WORK, a native of Ireland; emigrated to America, and, before 1800, settled in Hopewell township, Washington county, Penn., where he d. 1820; m. in Ireland, Martha Dunlap; had issue, among others: 1. Alexander, b. in Ireland, 1781; settled in Pennsylvania with his parents; removed to German township, Harrison county, Ohio, 1818, where he d. May, 1851; m. in Pennsylvania. April 10, 1809. Jane Taggart, a native of Washington county; d. April, 1851 (had issue: i. George; ii. James; iii. John; iv. Mary-K., m. John Hervey Black; v. Samuel; vi. Anderson-D.; vii. Jane; viii. Margaret; ix. Alexander).

THOMAS WORLEY, b. in Pennsylvania; removed to Harrison county, and settled in Athens township, about 1802, where he d. May, 1859; m. Mary Walker, daughter of Gabriel Walker; had issue: 1. Thomas; 2. Daniel, b. 1792; d. 1887; m. 1849, Mary Goodwin, b. 1827; daughter of Jesse and Anne Michner Goodwin, of Short Creek township (had issue: i. William, m. Eliza Morrison; ii. Jesse, m. Ella Skouten; iii. Emory, m. Mary Morrison; iv. Martha, m. Samuel Parks; v. Emma; vi. John-Brough, m. Auta Groves; vii. Alice, m. Edwin Aukerman; viii. Lafayette. m. Ella McManus); 3. David, m. 1836, Mary Jane Luke; 4. James, b. May, 1782; d. April 7, 1857; m. Susanna ———, b. 1766; d. Feb. 4, 1839; 5. Susanna, m. 1822, Samuel Martin; 6. Julianna, m. 1827, Smith Bonham; 7. Margaret, m. 1840, Ichabod Ross; 8. Elizabeth, m. ——— Yarnell; 9. Mary (?). m. Jacob Figley.

Other Worley families of Harrison county:

Wesley J. Worley, m. 1823, Jane Virtue, b. Jan. 13, 1804; d. March 18, 1857.

Daniel Worley, m. 1834, Sarah Peregoy.

Josiah Worley, m. 1836, Mary Ann Minor.

Michael Worley, m. 1828, Eve Ann Markley.

Mary Goodwin Worley (b. 1827) is the daughter of Jesse Goodwin, b. in Pennsylvania. Oct. 11, 1784; d. in Harrison county, Ohio, Oct. 2, 1856; m. (1st) Anne Michner, b. 1789; d. Feb. 27, 1843; m. (2d) Ruth McMillan; had issue by first wife: 1. Lydia, b. 1810; 2. Hannah, b. 1812; 3. Lewis, b. 1813; 4. Wilson, b. 1816; 5. Elisha, b. 1818; 6. Tace, b. 1820; 7. Alice, b. 1821; 8. Anne, b. 1824; 9. Kinsey, b. 1826; 10. Mary, b. Nov. 27, 1827; m. Daniel Worley; 11. Abi, b. May 22, 1829; m. Jackson Shields; 12. Martha, b. 1830; 13. Jesse, b. 1834.

Anne Michner Goodwin was the daughter of Baruch and Jane Wilson Michner, who were married in Pennsylvania, and removed to Harrison county; had issue: 1. Anne; 2. John; 3. Hannah; 4. Sarah; 5. Alice; 6. Jane.

MATTHEW WORSTELL, b. in Bucks county, Penn.; a descendant of James Worstell, who emigrated before 1700; removed to Philadelphia, before 1804, and in 1805 settled near Steubenville, Ohio; m. Rachel Price; had issue: 1. Ceneath; 2. Hiram, b. in Philadelphia, Sept. 7, 1804; settled in Franklin township, Harrison county, Ohio, where he d. in January, 1884; m. near Steubenville, Ann Pittis, d. 1873, daughter of John Pittis, of Deersville (had issue: i. John; ii. Mary; iii. Thomas; iv. Robert; v. Edward; vi. Elizabeth; vii. Jane; viii. William; ix. Julia; x. Henry-P., b. in Tuscarawas county, May 18, 1836; settled in Franklin township; m. Jan. 5, 1860, Eleanor Scott, daughter of Charles Scott, of Harrison county); 3. Martha; 4. Smith; 5. Matthew; 6. Sarah; 7. John; 8. Rachel; 9. William; 10. James.

LOT WORTMAN, b. in New Jersey, about 1779; d. 1839; probably a descendant of John Wortman, who emigrated from Holland to America in 1750, and settled in Bedminster township, Somerset county, N. J.; m. in Westmoreland county, Penn., Margaret Metzlar, d. 1860; removed to Muskingum county, Ohio, about 1808; had issue, twelve children, of whom: 1. Jesse-David, b. in Muskingum county, 1824;

d. Dec. 28, 1898; m. 1860, Jane P. Jamison, daughter of Barkley and Margaret Jamison; 2. Jonathan-Washington, settled in Zanesville; 3. John, settled in Kansas.

AARON YARNALL, son of Thomas Yarnall, b. in Washington county, Penn., about 1783; settled in Nottingham township, Harrison county, Ohio, 1811, where he died 1851; m. Mary A. Bell, of Washington county; d. 1857; had issue: 1. Ziba; 2. William; 3. Aaron; 4. Eli; 5. Colver; 6. John, b. Feb. 27, 1827; m. (1st) April 24, 1850, "Nackkey" Rogers, d. 1861; m. (2d) 1863, Mrs. Elizabeth Ross, b. June 28, 1833, widow of Thomas Ross, and daughter of Alexander and Sarah Ramsey Fulton, of Nottingham township (had issue by first wife: i. Henry-H., settled in Tuscarawas county, Ohio; ii. Sylvester-F., settled at Oberlin, Kan.; iii. Jasper; had issue by second wife: iv. Mary-R.; v. Ida-B.); 7. Nelson; 8. Lydia; 9. Mary-A.

MICHAEL YOST, a native of Virginia, b. Nov. 3, 1766; d. Feb. 2, 1849, of German descent, as was also his wife; the fathers of both having served in the Revolutionary War; removed to Short Creek township, Harrison county, Ohio, 1806; m. Rachel Keckley, b. in Virginia, 1780; d. Feb. 19, 1849; had issue, among others: 1. Elias, b. near Winchester, Frederick county, Va., Dec. 2, 1805; settled in Short Creek township; m. (1st) Dec. 30, 1834, Kezia Kithcart, b. in Pennsylvania, April 25, 1812; d. 1878; daughter of Joseph Kithcart (d. in Pennsylvania; his wife settled in Harrison county, 1824); m. (2d) March 7, 1880, Ann Macklin, b. in county Armagh, Ireland, Dec. 2, 1842, daughter of Samuel and Ann Benson Macklin (both of whom died in Scotland, the former in 1847; the latter in 1858) (had issue by first wife, eleven children).